American Women Speak

American Women Speak

An Encyclopedia and Document Collection of Women's Oratory

Volume 2: I–Z

Mary Ellen Snodgrass

ABC-CLIO™

An Imprint of ABC-CLIO, LLC
Santa Barbara, California • Denver, Colorado

Library of Congress Cataloging-in-Publication Data

Names: Snodgrass, Mary Ellen, author.
Title: American women speak : an encyclopedia and document collection of women's oratory / Mary Ellen Snodgrass.
Other titles: Encyclopedia and document collection of women's oratory | Women's oratory
Description: Santa Barbara, California : ABC-CLIO, 2017. Contents: Volume 1. A - H — Volume 2. I - Z. | Includes bibliographical references and index.
Identifiers: LCCN 2016012283| ISBN 9781440837845 (hardback set) | ISBN 9781440847424 (print (vol. 1)) | ISBN 9781440847431 (print (vol. 2)) | ISBN 9781440837852 (e-book)
Subjects: LCSH: Speeches, addresses, etc., American—Women authors—Encyclopedias. | Women—United States—History—Sources—Encyclopedias.
Classification: LCC PS663.W65 S56 2016 | DDC 815.008/09287—dc23
LC record available at https://lccn.loc.gov/2016012283

ISBN: 978-1-4408-3784-5 (set)
EISBN: 978-1-4408-3785-2
ISBN: 978-1-4408-4742-4 (vol. 1)
ISBN: 978-1-4408-4743-1 (vol. 2)

21 20 19 18 17 1 2 3 4 5

This book is also available as an eBook.

ABC-CLIO
An Imprint of ABC-CLIO, LLC

ABC-CLIO, LLC
130 Cremona Drive, P.O. Box 1911
Santa Barbara, California 93116-1911
www.abc-clio.com

This book is printed on acid-free paper ∞

Manufactured in the United States of America

for historian Alice George

We've been taught that silence would save us,
but it won't.
Audre Lorde

Contents

Alphabetical List of Entries

Volume 1: A–H

Volume 2: I–Z

Guide to Related Topics

Abolitionist
Paulina W. Davis
Anna Dickinson
Abby Kelley Foster
Matilda Joslyn Gage
Frances Ellen Watkins Harper
Isabella Beecher Hooker
Julia Ward Howe
Mary Ashton Livermore
Lucretia Mott
Harriet Jane Robinson
Ernestine L. Rose
Elizabeth Cady Stanton
Sojourner Truth
Angelina Grimké Weld

Actor
Jane Alexander
Maya Angelou
Mary Calderone
Helen Gahagan Douglas
Jane Fonda
Betty Furness
Madeleine L'Engle
Clare Boothe Luce
Carry Nation
Leslie Marmon Silko
Barbra Streisand

Administrator
Madeleine Albright
Blanche Ames Ames
Susan B. Anthony
Clara Barton
Mary McLeod Bethune
Anna Julia Cooper
Jeanne Diebolt
Lavinia Dock
Mary Baker Eddy
Julia Ward Howe
Barbara Coombs Lee
Mary Ashton Livermore
Aimee Semple McPherson
Sue Suter
Urvashi Vaid
Lillian Wald
Sarah Winnemucca

Agricultural Laborer
Fannie Lou Hamer
Golda Meir
Mary Reynolds
Sojourner Truth

Anarchist
Dorothy Day
Voltairine de Cleyre

Andrea Dworkin
Emma Goldman

Antiquarian
Esther Forbes

Archivist
Mary Ritter Beard

Artist
Blanche Ames Ames
Judy Chicago
Shulamith Firestone
Mary Fisher
Charlotte Perkins Gilman
Anne Koedt

Astronaut
Eileen Collins
Sally Ride

Astrophysicist
Margaret J. Geller
Sally Ride

Athlete
Bonnie Kestner

Attorney
Bella Abzug
Charlene Barshefsky
Carol Bellamy
Sophonisba P. Breckinridge
Hillary Rodham Clinton
Crystal Eastman
Marian Wright Edelman
Geraldine Ferraro
Kathryn Fuller
Martha Wright Griffiths
Anita Hill
Patricia Ireland
Barbara Jordan
Julia Lathrop
Barbara Coombs Lee
Patsy T. Mink
Michelle Obama
Samantha Power
Urvashi Vaid
Sarah Weddington

Barber
Margaret Chase Smith

Biologist
Ginette Hemley

Cashier
Rose Schneiderman

Choreographer
Meredith Monk

City Councilwoman
Patsy T. Mink

Civil Service Worker
Rachel Carson
Anna Dickinson
Alice Leopold
Golda Meir

Clerk
Mary Calderone
Jamaica Kincaid
Madeleine L'Engle
Alice Leopold

Audre Lorde
Wilma Mankiller
Margaret Chase Smith

Conservationist
Rachel Carson
Ginette Hemlet
Lady Bird Johnson
Alice Walker

Consultant
Aileen Hernandez
Naomi Wolf

Cook
Golda Meir
Mary Reynolds
Sojourner Truth

Counselor
Sojourner Truth

Critic
Andrea Dworkin
Elizabeth Janeway
Toni Morrison
Naomi Wolf

Designer
Jane Alexander
Iman
Jeannette Rankin

Diarist
Alice Stone Blackwell
Lillie Devereux Blake
Julia Ward Howe
Lady Bird Johnson
Harriet Jane Robinson
Ida B. Wells

Domestic
Jamaica Kincaid
Tillie Olsen
Mary Reynolds
Sojourner Truth

Dramatist
Maya Angelou

Ecofeminist
Barbara Kingsolver
Starhawk

Economist
Emily Greene Balch
Juanita Kreps
Winona LaDuke

Editor
Toni Morrison

Engineer
Blanche Ames Ames
Lillian Moller Gilbreth

Environmentalist
Winona LaDuke

Ethicist
Barbara Coombs Lee

Factory Worker
Bella Abzug
Hillary Rodham Clinton

Mother Ann Lee
Audre Lorde
Tillie Olsen
Harriet Jane Robinson

Fashion Model
Iman

File Clerk
Susan Brownmiller

Film Director
Maya Angelou
Meredith Monk
Barbra Streisand

Film Producer
Barbra Streisand

Financier
Victoria Woodhull

Fitness Expert
Jane Fonda

Flight Attendant
Patricia Ireland

Fund-Raiser
Jane Addams
Blanche Ames Ames
Clara Barton
Catherine Esther Beecher
Mary McLeod Bethune
Alice Stone Blackwell
Antoinette Brown Blackwell
Pearl S. Buck
Voltairine de Cleyre
Crystal Eastman
Elizabeth Gurley Flynn
Jane Fonda
Abby Kelley Foster
Betty Furness
Matilda Joslyn Gage
Emma Goldman
Tipper Gore
Fannie Lou Hamer
Oveta Culp Hobby
Helen Keller
Golda Meir
Margaret Sanger
Lillian Wald

Gardener
Jamaica Kincaid

Government Appointee
Bella Abzug
Jane Addams
Madeleine Albright
Jane Alexander
Charlene Barshefsky
Carol Bellamy
Mary McLeod Bethune
Harriot Eaton Stanton Blatch
Crystal Eastman
Joycelyn Elders
Dianne Feinstein
Mary Fisher
Kathryn Fuller
Betty Furness
Tipper Gore
Florence Jaffray Harriman
Aileen Hernandez
Oveta Culp Hobby
Jane M. Hoey

Health Worker

Historian

Home Economist

Humanitarian

Humorist

Innkeeper
Carry Nation

Integrationist
Mary Church Terrell
Lillian D. Wald
Alice Walker

Inventor
Blanche Ames Ames
Lillian Perkins Gilman
Alice Leopold
Ernestine L. Rose

Janitor
Rose Schneiderman

Journalist
Isabel Allende
Maya Angelou
Caroline Bird
Alice Stone Blackwell
Susan Brownmiller
Hope Cooke
Dorothy Day
Crystal Eastman
Barbara Ehrenreich
Susan Faludi
Elizabeth Gurley Flynn
Esther Forbes
Betty Friedan
Betty Furness
Matilda Joslyn Gage
Charlotte Perkins Gilman
Katharine Graham
Oveta Culp Hobby
Zora Neale Hurston
Winona LaDuke
Katha Pollitt
Samantha Power
Anna Quindlen
Margaret Sanger
Margaret Chase Smith
Dorothy Thompson
Ida B. Wells

Judge
Martha Wright Griffiths

Laundress
Freedwoman Holmes
Mother Ann Lee
Tillie Olsen
Rose Schneiderman

Librarian
Kathryn Fuller
Madeline L'Engle
Audre Lorde

Librettist
Toni Morrison

Lobbyist
Blanche Ames Ames
Susan B. Anthony
Alice Stone Blackwell
Antoinette Brown Blackwell
Lillie Devereux Blake
Sarah Brady
Carrie Chapman Catt
Dorothy Day
Marian Wright Edelman
Joycelyn Elders
Mary Fisher
Jane Fonda

Betty Friedan
Elizabeth Glaser
Tipper Gore
Martha Wright Griffiths
Ginette Hemley
Oveta Culp Hobby
Isabella Beecher Hooker
Dolores Huerta
Patricia Ireland
Elizabeth Janeway
Julia Lathrop
Kate Michelman
Ai-jen Poo
Jeannette Rankin
Rose Schneiderman
Anna Howard Shaw
Elizabeth Cady Stanton
Sue Suter
Sarah Weddington
Molly Yard

Mathematician
Sophonisba P. Breckinridge
Anna Julia Cooper

Mayor
Dianne Feinstein

Media Mogul
Lady Bird Johnson

Midwife
Jane Addams
Emma Goldman
Anne Hutchinson

Military Leader
Oveta Culp Hobby

Model
Jane Fonda
Betty Furness

Moralist
Tipper Gore
Isabella Beecher Hooker
Mother Ann Lee
Anne Graham Lotz
Aimee Semple McPherson
Carry Nation
Anna Howard Shaw

Museum Director
Elizabeth Glaser

Musician/Composer
Julia Ward Howe
Meredith Monk
Harriet Jane Robinson
Barbra Streisand

Pacifist
Jane Addams
Paula Gunn Allen
Alice Stone Blackwell
Harriot Eaton Stanton Blatch
Dorothy Day
Lavinia Dock
Crystal Eastman
Jeanne Wakatsuki Houston
Julia Ward Howe
Helen Keller
Barbara Kingsolver
Ursula Le Guin
Aimee Semple McPherson
Queen Noor
Jeannette Rankin

Starhawk
Mary Church Terrell
Lillian D. Wald
Alice Walker

Pamphleteer
Jane Addams
Kathie Amatniek
Blanche Ames Ames
Emily Greene Balch
Mary Ritter Beard
Alice Stone Blackwell
Pearl S. Buck
Mary Calderone
Rachel Carson
Crystal Eastman
Mary Baker Eddy
Shulamith Firestone
Elizabeth Gurley Flynn
Florence Jaffray Harriman
Isabella Beecher Hooker
Patricia Ireland
Anne Koedt
Elizabeth Koontz
Julia Lathrop
Alice Leopold
Lucretia Mott
Margaret Sanger
Rose Schneiderman
Gloria Steinem
Lucy Stone
Dorothy Thompson
Victoria Woodhull

Peace Corps Volunteer
Carol Bellamy

Philanthropist
Isabel Allende
Blanche Ames Ames
Alice Stone Blackwell
Sophonisba P. Breckinridge
Pearl S. Buck
Rosalynn Carter
Paulina W. Davis
Anna Dickinson
Helen Gahagan Douglas
Kathryn Fuller
Katharine Graham
Dolores Huerta
Iman
Elizabeth Janeway
Lady Bird Johnson
Barbara Kingsolver
Clare Boothe Luce
Queen Noor
Eleanor Roosevelt
Ernestine L. Rose
Janet Southby
Barbra Streisand
Amy Tan

Philosopher
Antoinette Brown Blackwell
Angela Davis
Clarissa Pinkola Estés
Shulamith Firestone
Betty Friedan
Emma Goldman
Starhawk

Photographer
Tipper Gore
Jamaica Kincaid

Pianist
Meredith Monk

Pilot
Eileen Collins
Patricia Schroeder

Poet
Paula Gunn Allen
Maya Angelou
Shulamith Firestone
Frances Ellen Watkins Harper
Julia Ward Howe
Erica Jong
Denise Levertov
Audre Lorde
Toni Morrison
Adrienne Rich
Leslie Marmon Silko
Alice Walker

Political Cartoonist
Blanche Ames Ames

Politician
Bella Abzug
Madeleine Albright
Carol Bellamy
Harriot Eaton Stanton Blatch
Hillary Rodham Clinton
Rosa DeLauro
Helen Gahagan Douglas
Anna Eshoo
Dianne Feinstein
Geraldine Ferraro
Elizabeth Gurley Flynn
Fannie Lou Hamer
Alexis Herman
Oveta Culp Hobby
Barbara Jordan
Nancy Keenan
Winona LaDuke
Alice Leopold
Clare Boothe Luce
Wilma Mankiller
Golda Meir
Patsy T. Mink
Ann Richards
Patricia Schroeder
Sue Suter
Molly Yard

Prime Minister
Golda Meir

Prison Warden
Jane M. Hoey

Prisoner
Dorothy Day
Lavinia Dock
Emma Goldman
Mother Jones
Mother Ann Lee
Margaret Sanger

Prophet
Paulina W. Davis
Fannie Lou Hamer
Sojourner Truth

Prostitute
Andrea Dworkin

Psychologist
Clarissa Pinkola Estés
Lillian Moller Gilbreth
Sue Suter
Judith Wallerstein

Publicist
Caroline Bird
Ann Richards

Publisher
Paulina W. Davis
Dorothy Day

Olympia Snowe
Sarah Weddington

State Lieutenant Governor
Martha Wright Griffiths

State Senator
Olympia Snowe

State Superintendent of Schools
Nancy Keenan

State Treasurer
Ann Richards

Statistician
Jane Addams
Blanche Ames Ames
Sophonisba P. Breckinridge
Jane M. Hoey
Florence Kelley
Juanita Kreps
Mary Ashton Livermore
Lillian D. Wald

Storyteller
Paula Gunn Allen
Clarissa Pinkola Estés
Zora Neale Hurston
Leslie Marmon Silko

Street Car Conductor
Maya Angelou

Suffragist
Blanche Ames Ames
Susan B. Anthony
Clara Barton
Alice Stone Blackwell
Antoinette Brown Blackwell
Lillie Devereux Blake
Harriot Eaton Stanton Blatch
Carrie Chapman Catt
Paulina W. Davis
Anna Dickinson
Lavinia Dock
Crystal Eastman
Matilda Joslyn Gage
Florence Jaffray Harriman
Adelle Hazlett
Isabella Beecher Hooker
Julia Ward Howe
Lucretia Mott
Jeannette Rankin
Harriet Jane Robinson
Elizabeth Cady Stanton
Lucy Stone
Mary Church Terrell
Dorothy Thompson
Lillian D. Wald
Sarah Winnemucca
Victoria Woodhull

Swim Coach
Bonnie Kestner

Teacher
Jane Addams
Madeleine Albright
Isabel Allende
Kathie Amatniek
Maya Angelou
Emily Greene Balch
Catharine Esther Beecher
Mary McLeod Bethune
Caroline Bird
Antoinette Brown Blackwell
Sarah Brady
Sophonisba P. Breckinridge

Susan Brownmiller
Pearl S. Buck
Rachel Carson
Judy Chicago
Shirley Chisholm
Hillary Rodham Clinton
Eileen Collins
Hope Cooke
Anna Julia Cooper
Angela Davis
Voltairine de Cleyre
Andrew Dworkin
Mary Baker Eddy
Barbara Ehrenreich
Joycelyn Elders
Susan Faludi
Geraldine Ferraro
Elizabeth Gurley Flynn
Abby Kelley Foster
Margaret J. Geller
Nancy Gertner
Lillian Moller Gilbreth
Elizabeth Glaser
Aileen Hernandez
Anita Hill
Dolores Huerta
Irene Hunt
Zora Neale Hurston
Molly Ivins
Elizabeth Janeway
Barbara Jordan
Nancy Keenan
Bonnie Kestner
Bathsheba Kingsley
Elizabeth Koontz
Juanita Kreps
Barbara Coombs Lee
Ursula Le Guin
Madeleine L'Engle
Denise Levertov
Mary Ashton Livermore
Audre Lorde
Wilma Mankiller
Golda Meir
Kate Michelman
Meredith Monk
Toni Morrison
Lucretia Mott
Tillie Olsen
Katha Pollitt
Samantha Power
Jeannette Rankin
Adrienne Rich
Ann Richards
Sally Ride
Eleanor Roosevelt
Ernestine L. Rose
Deborah Sampson
Margaret Sanger
Patricia Schroeder
Donna Shalala
Anna Howard Shaw
Margaret Chase Smith
Janet Southby
Starhawk
Lucy Stone
Paula Treckel
Lillian D. Wald
Alice Walker
Sarah Weddington
Angelina Grimké Weld
Ida B. Wells

Television Commentator

Caroline Bird
Betty Furness

Temperance Crusader

Susan B. Anthony
Paulina W. Davis
Frances Ellen Watkins Harper

Mary Ashton Livermore
Aimee Semple McPherson
Carry Nation
Anna Howard Shaw
Elizabeth Cady Stanton

Textbook Author
Mary Ritter Beard
Lavinia Dock
Oveta Culp Hobby

Theologian
Antoinette Brown Blackwell
Mary Baker Eddy
Anne Hutchinson
Bathsheba Kingsley
Mother Ann Lee
Anne Graham Lotz
Aimee Semple McPherson
Lucretia Mott
Anna Howard Shaw
Sojourner Truth

Tour Guide
Hope Cooke

Trade Unionist
Harriot Eaton Stanton Blatch
Dorothy Day
Voltairine de Cleyre
Lavinia Dock
Helen Gahagan Douglas
Crystal Eastman
Elizabeth Gurley Flynn
Emma Goldman
Fannie Lou Hamer
Aileen Hernandez
Dolores Huerta
Mother Jones
Helen Keller
Florence Kelley
Ai-jen Poo
Eleanor Roosevelt
Rose Schneiderman
Lillian D. Wald

Translator
Isabel Allende
Alice Stone Blackwell
Anna Julia Cooper
Voltairine de Cleyre
Emma Goldman
Iman
Florence Kelley
Madeleine L'Engle
Denise Levertov
Adrienne Rich
Eleanor Roosevelt
Mary Church Terrell
Sarah Winnemucca

Tribal Chief
Wilma Mankiller

U.N. Ambassador
Madeleine Albright
Geraldine Ferraro
Mary Fisher
Samantha Power
Eleanor Roosevelt

U.S. Congresswoman
Bella Abzug
Shirley Chisholm
Rosa L. DeLauro
Helen Gahagan Douglas

Anna Eshoo
Geraldine Ferraro
Martha Wright Griffiths
Barbara Jordan
Clare Boothe Luce
Patsy T. Mink
Jeannette Rankin
Patricia Schroeder
Margaret Chase Smith
Olympia Snowe

U.S. Federal Judge
Nancy Gertner

U.S. First Lady
Rosalynn Carter
Hillary Rodham Clinton
Lady Bird Johnson
Michelle Obama
Eleanor Roosevelt

U.S. Rehabilitation Services Director
Sue Suter

U.S. Second Lady
Tipper Gore

U.S. Secretary of Health and Human Services
Donna Shalala

U.S. Secretary of Labor
Alexis Herman

U.S. Secretary of State
Madeleine Albright
Hillary Rodham Clinton

U.S. Senator
Hillary Rodham Clinton
Dianne Feinstein
Margaret Chase Smith
Olympia Snowe

U.S. Surgeon General
Joycelyn Elders

University President
Donna Shalala

Waitress
Susan Brownmiller
Shulamith Firestone
Tillie Olsen
Deborah Sampson

Witness
Susan Brownmiller
Lucinda Davis
Jeanne Diebolt
Andrea Dworkin
Marian Wright Edelman
Florence Jaffray Harriman
Anita Hill
Freedwoman Holmes
Anne Hutchinson
Mary Reynolds
Ernestine L. Rose
Sojourner Truth

Writer
Bella Abzug
Jane Addams
Paula Gunn Allen
Isabel Allende
Kathy Amatniek

Maya Angelou
Emily Greene Balch
Caroline Bird
Alice Stone Blackwell
Lillie Devereux Blake
Harriot Eaton Stanton Blatch
Sarah Brady
Susan Brownmiller
Pearl S. Buck
Rachel Carson
Hillary Rodham Clinton
Anna Julia Cooper
Angela Davis
Paulina W. Davis
Dorothy Day
Anna Dickinson
Lavinia Dock
Andrea Dworkin
Barbara Ehrenreich
Clarissa Pinkola Estés
Susan Faludi
Geraldine Ferraro
Mary Fisher
Esther Forbes
Betty Friedan
Kathryn Fuller
Matilda Joslyn Gage
Nancy Gertner
Charlotte Perkins Gilman
Tipper Gore
Fannie Lou Hamer
Frances Ellen Watkins Harper
Florence Jaffray Harriman
Ginette Hemley
Aileen Hernandez
Jane M. Hoey
Isabella Beecher Hooker
Jeanne Wakatsuki Houston
Irene Hunt
Zora Neale Hurston
Elizabeth Janeway
Erica Jong
Jamaica Kincaid
Barbara Kingsolver
Anne Koedt
Winona LaDuke
Ursula Le Guin
Madeleine L'Engle
Clare Boothe Luce
Wilma Mankiller
Kate Michelman
Toni Morrison
Queen Noor
Michelle Obama
Tillie Olsen
Ai-jen Poo
Samantha Power
Anna Quindlen
Sally Ride
Harriet Jane Robinson
Eleanor Roosevelt
Donna Shalala
Leslie Marmon Silko
Janet Southby
Starhawk
Elizabeth Cady Stanton
Amy Tan
Mary Church Terrell
Paula Treckel
Alice Walker
Judith Wallerstein
Naomi Wolf

I

IMAN (1955–)

A Somali American philanthropist and exemplar of grace and beauty, Iman Mohamed Abdulmajid nurtures fund-raising campaigns for African agencies that empower women and improve health and literacy for children. Born the second of five children in Mogadishu, Somalia, on July 25, 1955, to gynecologist Marian and Mohamed Abdulmajid, an Ethiopian diplomat to Saudi Arabia, she and sisters Idil and Nadia and brothers Elias and Feisal grew up in a conservative household. Iman fasted at Ramadan, made a pilgrimage to Mecca, and had no experience walking in high heels or applying hair color or makeup.

Iman's father envisioned her future as a politician. Her grandfather insisted that the parents drop plans to name her Zahara and proposed instead "Iman," the masculine Arabic term for "faith in Allah." She spent three years in her grandparents' care and, at age five, entered boarding school.

In an Italian colony, Iman learned to converse in Somali and Italian as well as Arabic, French, and English. Because of the assassination of Somali president Abdirashid Ali Shermarke on October 15, 1969, Mohamed retrieved his children from his embassy in Saudi Arabia, fled by van, and crossed on foot into Kenya. Iman completed high school in Egypt.

Iman worked as a translator and entered a brief marriage with a Kenyan youth but longed to leave Africa for greater opportunities in Europe or America. She served two years in the Somali military and enrolled in political science at Nairobi University in Kenya. In March 1975, she came to the attention of fashion photographer Peter Beard, who traded her poses for $8,000 to pay her tuition. He sold photos of her to the Wilhelmina Modeling Agency in New York and helped her elude Islamic laws that required a husband's permission to apply for a passport. She fled with a single suitcase and signed a three-year contract with Wilhelmina. The news displeased her parents.

Beard popularized Iman's looks at age 20 among fashion houses that had previously rejected African features. To introduce her to demanding New Yorkers, he orchestrated lies in a news blitz about a poor nomadic tribeswoman who herded cattle. Quickly, she replaced rumors and fabrications with poses and interviews that elevated her to the top of a sophisticated fashion world under the single name. She revived Tia Maria with a posed ad, the beginning of phenomenal earnings that reached two million dollars per year.

Iman the Supermodel

In 1975, Iman's appearance—coppery brown complexion, deep mahogany eyes, and a remarkable posture highlighting a long neck and slender frame—startled clothing fanciers and upended traditional definitions of female grace and elegance. For makeup artists who had no experience with black skin, she mixed her personal foundation and applied her own colorants. Within the year, she headquartered in London and began a photo shoot for *Vogue*.

Iman's dignity and serene looks inspired designers Ralph Lauren, Gianni Versace, Calvin Klein, Halston, Issey Miyake, Guy LaRoche, Kenzo, Givenchy, and Donna Karan. Yves St. Laurent designed a couture line around her elongated torso and dubbed it African Queen. Over a 14-year career in modeling high fashion, she posed for Richard Avedon, Francesco Scavullo, Irving Penn, Helmut Newton, and Annie Liebovitz. Iman's achievement as the world's top fashion model supplanted dominance by the wholesome, blue-eyed blonde girl-next-door and replaced stereotypes with visions of diversity.

Still employed by *Vogue* in 1977, Iman married Spencer Haywood, a professional basketball player for the Los Angeles Lakers. They moved to Los Angeles, where she bore daughter Zulekha Haywood. By 1979, Iman had debuted in the British film *The Human Factor* and clashed with Spencer over a nude photo spread in *Playboy*.

Due to Haywood's cocaine addiction, abuse, as well as fathering a child by a mistress, Iman fought him for over six years for custody of Zulekha and retrieved her daughter from Detroit. Iman played a small part in the 1985 classic movie *Out of Africa* (1985) as the mistress of a white Englishman. She followed with roles in *Miami Vice*, *The Cosby Show*, *In the Heat of the Night*, and the films *Love at First Sight*, *Star Trek VI: The Undiscovered Country*, and *No Way Out*.

A car accident sidelined Iman in 1983 for reconstructive surgery and the healing of a dislocated shoulder, glass cuts to the face, and fractured cheek and ear bones, clavicle, and three ribs. After posing for a 1985 Pirelli calendar, she began runway work in 1986 for Valentino and continued in 1991 for Thierry Mugler. She also posed for a Revlon ad in 1987 that netted a multimillion-dollar contract, the highest for any model.

In her mid-thirties, Iman earned up to $100,000 per day. She lived the dream of the jet setter and squandered cash on flights aboard the Concorde. Despite wealth, she felt discontent with a self-limiting career, which could be brutal to middle-aged women. She divorced Haywood and retired in 1989. She met English rock singer David Bowie a year later in 1990, and the two wed at St. James Episcopal Church in Florence, Italy, on April 24, 1992. The ceremony featured a black-on-white color scheme that symbolized a bicultural union.

In 1992, Iman traveled to Baidoa with a BBC crew to film the documentary *Somalia Diary*, which pictured children's corpses in city streets. Her commentary informed news reporters of the crisis in Somalia, Djibouti, Kenya, and Ethiopia caused by drought, famine, piracy, and war. The on-camera appeal explained the complex politics of north and south and netted security, medicines, shelter, and food. In 1999, she and Bowie played characters on the computer game *Omikron*. On August 15, she bore Alexandria Zahra "Alexi" Jones and published a memoir, *I Am Iman* (2001).

Iman the Entrepreneur

In the early 2000s, Iman began a professional speaking career that revealed her identification with refugees and her outrage at the mass rape of Congolese women, the focus of Raise Hope for Congo. In Ottawa, she co-hosted *The Fashion Show* for the Bravo television network in 2005 and commented for Internet sites on modeling and beauty standards. In addition to appearing on covers for *Elle*, *Town & Country*, *Newsweek*, *Essence*, *Ebony*, *West End*, *Photo*, *Cosmopolitan*, and *Vanity Fair*, she published *The Beauty of Color* (2005). She directed her celebrity toward philanthropy for Action against Hunger, Enough Project, and Children's Defense Fund. To end diamond miners' sufferings, she terminated a contract with DeBeers. For Save the Children, she saluted the strength of families at feeding centers throughout the Horn of Africa. An advocate for Sister Somalia, she deplored the terrorism of Al-Shabaab and forced marriages that jeopardized brides.

As spokeswoman for Keep a Child Alive, Iman addressed the need for pediatric antiretroviral medicines and paid tribute to African women who nursed young victims of HIV/AIDS. With an urgent tone, she spoke at charity venues for the protection and empowerment of a whole generation of Congolese women and children. Without blaming any faction, she stated facts and statistics from tent cities and feeding stations and found hope in the response of the international community to hunger in Africa.

Still attuned to the demands of fashion, fragrance, and skincare, Iman sketched for the Home Shopping Network the embroidered caftans that paired with turbans and head wraps to fulfill everyday and festive needs in Eastern Africa. In 2010, she launched IMAN Cosmetics, a multiracial line favoring black, Chicana, Asian,

Native American, Mediterranean, and Middle Eastern skin tones with 16 foundation hues. Her product suited the complexions of women in Africa, Brazil, the West Indies, France, England, and North America. Her accessories for IMAN Global Chic included ethnic bags and jewelry. For her housewares collection, she won a Fashion Icon Lifetime Achievement Award from the Council of Fashion Designers.

In 2012, Iman appeared on the *Wendy Williams Show* to discuss marital relationships, specifically her 20-year marriage. She favored a boundary between professional life and the personal side. In the fall of 2013, she directed remarks to the need of Somali children for literacy, especially for girls. She lauded reading as an opportunity to raise the horizons for females and for their children and invested her fame and income in humanitarian outreach.

Reference

Iman, David Bowie, and Peter Hill Beard. *I Am Iman*. New York: Universe, 2001.

IRELAND, PATRICIA (1945–)

Women's advocate Patricia Ireland embraces the most controversial, least popular civil rights issues. A native of Oak Park, Illinois, she was born on October 19, 1945, and grew up in Valparaiso, Indiana. Because of her pregnancy at age 16, she left DePauw University and sought an abortion in Japan. She studied German at the University of Tennessee, graduating in 1966. She married artist James Humble before abandoning graduate school, moving to Miami, and taking a job as a stewardess for Pan-American Airlines.

To defend the rights of flight attendants and other women, Ireland attended Florida State University College of Law. The public's low opinion of stewardesses and devaluation of stereotypical female work enhanced her decision to become a women's advocate. She obtained an LLD in 1975 from the University of Miami School of Law. For 12 years, she specialized in commerce and corporate litigation and offered free counsel for women's rights cases in Dade County. She volunteered as counselor for the National Organization for Women (NOW) and defended homosexuals, African American women, and the poor.

In the 1980s, Ireland headed the NOW by-laws committee and spoke on affirmative action. She backed boycotts of numerous companies and pressed a racketeering case against the Pro-Life Action League for threatening violence to women entering abortion facilities. While running for executive vice president of NOW, she collaborated with the United Feminist Action Campaign team. In 1989, she coordinated a global Stand Up for Women crusade, defending client access to health clinics and combating other barriers to reproductive choices.

After replacing Molly Yard as president of NOW, Ireland held the post from 1991 to 2001 and addressed national conferences. Her speaking agenda involved numerous television appearances, even opposing Supreme Court nominee Clarence Thomas, whom employee Anita Hill charged with on-the-job sexual harassment. Ireland campaigned against anti-abortion protestors and stood up for pro-gay initiatives, even declaring her own bisexual lifestyle in an interview with *The Advocate*. She spearheaded NOW's Global Feminist Program and World March of Women and led the 1992 March for Women's Lives, a pro-choice rally on the Washington Mall of 500,000 advocates. She led another demonstration in 1993 for gay, lesbian, and bisexual rights.

Ireland spoke at length nationwide in the late 1990s. Her talks addressed issues such as women's body image, sports, spousal abuse, medicine, Meals on Wheels, and Take Back the Night. In April 2003, she began six months' employment as chief executive officer of the Young Women's Christian Association and activist for racial justice and female empowerment. In the 2000s, she returned to a private law practice and continued debating conservatives on women's issues. She led pro-choice initiatives and defended a NOW campaign listing groups that oppose women's access to contraception, abortifacients, and surgical or vacuum abortion.

See Also: Hill, Anita; Obama, Michelle; Yard, Molly.

Reference

Myers, JoAnne. *The A to Z of the Lesbian Liberation Movement: Still the Rage*. Lanham, MD: Scarecrow Press, 2003.

THE HOLY WAR AGAINST WOMEN BY PATRICIA IRELAND FREEDOM FROM RELIGION FOUNDATION, ANN ARBOR, MICHIGAN OCTOBER 6, 1990

Attorney and women's advocate Patricia Ireland, former president of NOW, aggressively combated the encroachment of antiwoman fundamentalism, led by Pat Robertson, founder of the Christian Coalition. By comparing coercive dogma in America with restraints on freedoms in Algeria, Mexico, Poland, even Renaissance Italy, she stressed the nature of religious oppression on unenlightened adherents. Her alert to coming feminist battles for gender equality anticipated

Catholic denunciation of morning-after pills, the Affordable Care Act, and the abortifacient RU-486 as well as same-sex marriage, stem cell research, and euthanasia, the issues still in contention in the 21st century.

. . . It's clear to me that those of us in the women's rights movement share a great deal with those involved in the Freedom from Religion Foundation and the freethinking movement in the country. We have only to look at the hierarchy of most churches to know that organized religions are predominantly male and are using the religious dogma to keep women in their place—our place. Of course, we have quite a disagreement about what our place might be. Remember, with all the locker-room sports writers controversy going on now, that many of the sports figures historically have used religion as an excuse to keep women out of positions of authority. I think back to Bob Nepper and the umpire woman. He said his religious view did not include any woman having any authority over any man, so he would not accept her as an umpire. In fact, she has had a very hard time staying as an umpire in the national baseball arena.

The Supreme Court is another common enemy that we share. Remember in this last session they heard a case on separation of church and state where they allowed religious clubs to meet on school property. It was certainly a step backward for all of us, although I may say there may be some slight silver lining in that cloud, given that the women's rights movement has always had trouble getting into the public high schools. We feel now it would be very difficult for them to allow religious groups as extracurricular activities and deny the "feminist church" the opportunity to reach the same audience! We will be using that decision to go into the high schools, organizing this next young generation of feminists, women and men, to at least have an opportunity to hear another point of view.

Congress is considering what is called the Act for Better Child Care. From our beginning as NOW in 1966 we've felt very strongly about child care and in particular would like to see it not as a poverty program, because that's very likely to be cut, but as a universal entitlement in the same way that public education is a universal entitlement. That is, early childhood development and the care of our children should be something that all of us have the opportunity to take advantage of. The bill that's currently before Congress, called the Act for Better Child Care, we have renamed, "The Act for a Bigger Catholic Church." ABC is another place where we are going head-to-head with the Catholic bishops.

Most childcare in this country right now is provided in churches, often by the churches, but certainly in church facilities. The Catholic bishops have knocked out a provision that would have precluded them from taking my tax dollars and your tax dollars and using them to discriminate based on gender or religion. They've also succeeded in getting vouchering into one version of the bill, to give people vouchers and allow them to take vouchers to a religious childcare facility. They would be allowed to both take federal funds, take vouchers, and use them for sectarian religious instruction. We're having a major fight on that.

Operation Rescue is a strong symbol, a very good way for us to analyze not just what's happening in this country but around the world, in terms of the rise of religious fundamentalism. Whether we're talking about Catholic or Protestant or Islamic fundamentalism, it is the same force that sanctions or uses the cover of religious beliefs to sanction the use of force to impose a religious view on all of us, whether we share that view or not. In particular, it's often imposed in ways that restrict women.

We've seen in Algeria, for instance, and in the Persian Gulf, the use of force and threats of force to put women back behind the veil. In Algeria women had made some measure of progress. The new religious fundamentalist government was just elected there this spring. During the period of the election and subsequently, young women who are at the University in Algeria have been beaten by gangs of thugs who are there to enforce the religious requirement that these women wear a full veil. In the United States we're seeing the use of force and threats of force against us on the abortion issue. First we see the attempted use of the force of the power of government, that is, attempts to force a particular religious view on the rest of us through law.

I do not relish the idea of spending the rest of my life in hand-to-hand combat going state by state, state legislature by state legislature, trying to preserve reproductive freedom in this country, but that's where we are right now. We're facing a very well-funded enemy. You all, I'm sure, recall that the Catholic Church has a $5 million contract with Hill and Knowlton to sell the Catholic hierarchy's point of view. I'm very careful to speak of the Catholic *hierarchy's* point of view because it is not the point of view of all the Catholics in the country. Catholics use birth control and use abortion in higher proportions than other religions. Why? Because contraception's supposed to be a sin. So you have an abortion instead. A Catholic woman told me she'd been sterilized. When I asked if that wasn't opposed to her religion's point of view, she said, yes, but it was only one sin. She could go to confession and be absolved of that sin, whereas if she used birth control, she had to do it all the time! We have some very powerful enemies, and they're trying to use PR to project an image that will allow them to enact their religious views into law. . . . I'm very anxious that we recognize not only the imagery but also the terminology that has been used here, and that we not use it ourselves. When we're talking about "parental consent," we give the argument away. What we're really talking about is limiting young women's right to abortion. What we're really talking about is trying to mandate communication in a family. It's either there or it's not there. It cannot be created by law. When we're talking about "informed consent," what we're usually talking about is dictating the communication between the patient, a woman, and her doctor, dictating that that doctor has to present her with antiabortion propaganda. When we're talking about "waiting periods," again what we're really talking about is mandatory delays, any type of roadblock that can be put in the way of legal abortion. We also have direct force at the clinics. Although these people are trying to wear the mantle of Martin Luther King and the civil rights movement of the sixties, we are not fooled. These are not people who support women's rights or civil rights. They are not nonviolent. We have seen clinic invasions where people are injured. The antiabortionists sent a pregnant woman sprawling in the sidewalk in Atlanta during their clinic blockades.

If these people were in the civil rights movement in the sixties operating the way Operation Rescue is acting, the sit-in at the Woolworth's in Greensboro would not have been a peaceful sit-in. It would have been people bursting through the doors knocking customers down as they went, going up to the lunch counter, grabbing somebody by the collar, throwing them off of the stool, reaching over and pulling the wiring out of the equipment, going home that night and calling the staff and the owners, threatening them and their children. The real equivalent to Randy Terry's Operation Rescue is Joe Schiedler. Pick your favorite antiabortion bully. The real counterpart are those infamous men who stood in the doorways, blocking blacks from exercising their right to vote, blocking in the same way that these bullies are in the doorways blocking women who are exercising their constitutional right to choose abortion.

Everything that happens in this country has an impact on women around the world. The Mexico City policy, which I'm sure you're familiar with, was announced by the U.S. under Reagan. Now Bush has adopted the same policy denying public funding to any group that so much as mentions the word abortion. Countries that are so desperately poor and so desperate to control their own fertility accept this restriction because the U.S. provides 40% of the family planning funds worldwide. They are not only not referring abortion to women but are going so far for fear of losing family planning funding that they have turned away and refused to treat women coming to them suffering the effects of illegal, botched abortion.

As a result of our Mexico City policy and other policies, we are now seeing as conservatively estimated by the World Health Organization 200,000 women dying around the world every year from illegal, botched abortions. That is one woman every three minutes. It's a public health epidemic in many countries, where scarce resources, hospital beds that are very limited, blood supplies, critical medicines, physicians' and health care workers' time, are being used to treat the thousands and thousands of women who are dying, and the hundreds of thousands more who are being maimed.

We're certainly concerned to see around the world the rise of the Vatican's influence. All of us, I think, cheered the symbolism of seeing the Berlin Wall come down. We were taken aback by the speed of events, which was very thrilling. At the same time, the results have been very bad for women. Remember in Poland that Lech Walesa and Solidarity are tight with the Pope. That is a place where the Vatican has tremendous influence. What was the first thing that Solidarity came in with? A proposal to limit access to birth control and abortion. They tried to get it through the Parliament and the Polish women demonstrated in large numbers, and forced Solidarity to drop that provision in the first elections. Solidarity simply enacted regulations that were not voted on by anybody but Solidarity and the administration. Abortions can only be performed if they have permission from *four* doctors, including one psychiatrist. The Catholic Church is providing the list of approved psychiatrists! There is a major fight on our hands worldwide. . . .

Eventually the Catholic Church and the rightwing religious Protestants will have to give, in the same way the Church had to acknowledge that Copernicus was right and indeed the sun does not rotate around the earth and the earth is not indeed the center of the universe. In the meantime, a lot of suffering and persecution takes place.

I'm pleased to say that one of the other things that's happening is that people are fighting back, and fighting back in a big way. I want to remind you that *Roe v. Wade* did not happen in 1973 because we had seven good justices on the Supreme Court. It happened because we had a mobilized, energized, organized movement for women's rights in this country, that had impacted the politics and the judicial branch of this country. . . .

We have to create the same kind of worldwide movement against the religious fundamentalism that's on the rise, against the oppression of women. . . . We're going to join hands, we're going to fight together as long as it takes until we truly have equality and justice for all.

Source: Ireland, Patricia. "The Holy War Against Women." Freedom from Religion Foundation, Ann Arbor, Michigan, October 6, 1990. Reprinted with permission from Patricia Ireland.

IVINS, MOLLY (1944–2007)

A populist columnist and witty television commentator, Mary Tyler "Molly" Ivins made a vital career of egalitarian muckraking. Born on August 30, 1944, in Monterey, California, to well-heeled conservative parents—typical Southern mother Margot Milne and Republican attorney Jim Ivins, a gas and oil executive for Tenneco—she grew up tall and gangly in Houston, Texas, with siblings Andy and Sara Ivins. Out of idealism, Molly protested racism during black-white face-offs in east Texas, but she felt left out of the more dramatic civil rights conflicts that set off riots in Mississippi and Alabama.

At age 18, Ivins wrote for the yearbook and newspaper while completing 12th grade at St. John's School, an elite college preparatory academy. In 1962, she finished a semester at Scripps College in Claremont, California. The death of a boyfriend, Henry "Hank" Holland Jr., a Yale student, in a motorcycle accident left her uninterested in other suitors.

Writing the News

With a history major from Smith College, a 1964 summer internship at the *Houston Chronicle*, and a graduate degree in journalism from Columbia University, Ivins parlayed her skills for a year at the Institute of Political Science in Paris. For the *Minneapolis Tribune* in the late 1960s, she became the first female to cover the police beat. As coeditor and political savant earning poverty-level wages for an independent journal, the *Texas Observer*, in 1970, she concentrated on fairness and accuracy on public issues and full disclosure of the workings of the Texas legislature.

A lover of humor, Ivins developed a tone similar to the irreverence of sports announcers for baseball and football. She submitted editorials to the *Washington Post* and the *New York Times*. For the latter paper, she worked from 1976 to 1982 in New York City and Albany, then as Rocky Mountain bureau chief until she offended a humorless urban editor. During her tenure in the West, in 1980, she joined a whitewater rafting group that included Donna Shalala. After the death of Elvis Presley, Ivins's coverage of the obituary and funeral followed the stiff *New York Times* tone and style rather than her own rollicking instincts.

Disgruntled by the authoritarian editors in New York, in 1982, Ivins acknowledged the need of citizens for an outlet for frustrations. Through jocular anecdotes exposing corporate felonies and the brawn of big money, she produced a Pulitzer Prize–winning column for the Austin bureau of the *Dallas Times Herald* and zany reportage for *Morning Edition*. Her backing of humanitarian and liberal causes included Amnesty International and the American Civil Liberties Union as well as public presentations on free speech. In 1985, she supported Emily's List, an organization that amassed capital for feminist candidates.

Assailing the Powerful

The election of President George H. W. Bush in 1989, and his diminution of affirmative action, provided Ivins with the ideal platform for drollery. While writing for the *Fort Worth Star-Telegram*, she extracted quips and observations from her columns and compiled them into a political humor series beginning with *Molly Ivins Can't Say That, Can She?* (1991) and *Nothin' But Good Times Ahead* (1995). For a *Mother Jones* fund-raiser in 1992, she declared herself a First Amendment feminist and urged the audience to support the alternative press, which enlarged the forum for momentous discussions.

A rousing, crowd-pleasing oration, "Progressives: Have Fun While Ye May," which Ivins presented on November 23, 1995, to the Alliance for Democracy in Hunt, Texas, saluted the Million Man March for boosting the black male vote by 52 percent. With a willingness to have fun at the expense of too many earnest candidates, she concluded with a strand of humor that reverberated in her speeches. Less laughable, in 1996, she debated three male Republicans on the difficult decision faced by women to choose late-term abortion over bearing a doomed child, ruining the mother's health, or possibly ending her life.

In 1997, Ivins taught journalism for one quarter at the University of California at Berkeley. She enjoyed the high level of student intelligence and idealism and predicted that reporting for the media would rein in youthful high-mindedness. Pacific Coast liberalism and eccentricity fueled more mocking essays for *Mother Jones*, *The Nation*, *Harper's Esquire*, National Public Radio, and *The Progressive*, for whom she wrote for two decades.

During the Clinton administration, Ivins aimed audacious blasts at the idiocies of politics in *You Got to Dance with Them What Brung You: Politics in the Clinton Years* (1998). On C-SPAN, she addressed the interlinking issues of lobbying and the corruption of legislation. She added jabs at political correctness and stated a preference for folksy insults and vigorous language rather than prissy, spruced up rhetoric. Her views on good governance extolled Texas governor Ann Richards for vetoing a state push to legitimize concealed weapons and accepted U.S. Secretary of State Robert McNamara's apology for the Vietnam War debacle. As an antidote to postwar cynicism, she hailed honest self-doubt.

Simultaneous with a diagnosis of breast cancer and nine months of chemotherapy, Ivins developed a darker tone in three critiques: *Shrub: The Short But Happy Political Life of George W. Bush* (2000), *The Betrayal of America: How the Supreme Court Undermined the Constitution and Chose Our President* (2001), and *Bushwhacked: Life in George W. Bush's America* (2003). At a pinnacle in her career, in 2001, her syndicated column in 400 newspapers freed her of editorial control. Unleashed at last, she denounced the controversial election of George Bush in 2000 by the courts and the political exploitation of the 9/11 calamity. Astute observations won her a William Allen White Award, the Smith Medal from her alma mater, and election to the National Academy of Arts and Sciences.

Lacking trust in the Bush administration, Ivins predicted the discovery of no weapons of mass destruction in Iraq and a quagmire in the Middle East by 2003. For the next three years, she salted columns with the assertion that John Kerry's "got no Elvis" and the verbal gaffes of George W. Bush, whose name she shortened to Dubya and W. as a way to distinguish him from the first President Bush. Through the foolery of "charisma transplants," "Republican lite," and "testosterone poisoning," she prodded recalcitrant Democrats to replace rightwing cronyism and incipient fascism with some people-centered legislation (Ivins 2003). More honors to her writing included the 2003 Eugene V. Debs Award, Pringle Prize for Washington Journalism, and an Ivan Allen Prize for Progress and Service.

Contemporary with Ivins's publication of *Who Let the Dogs In? Incredible Political Animals I have Known*, in April 13, 2004, she entertained students at Tulane University with jokes about indictments of members of Bush's staff and comparisons of the president to Louisiana governor Earl "Kingfish" Long. With more gravitas, she expressed excitement over the impact of the Internet in deciding elections. She applauded the electronic forum for involving more citizens but warned that no gatekeeper monitors accuracy.

After quoting lines from the Declaration of Independence, Ivins spurred college students to take part in the democratic process. The question and answer session revealed her disappointment in a weak press owned by massive syndicates, such as Knight-Ridder, and her disdain for secret government machinations legalized by the Patriot Act. In reply to concerns about wealthy candidates, she promoted public campaign financing over corporate donations.

At a return trip to Berkeley in October 2004, over UCTV, Ivins entertained students with political gaffes and her approval of more indictments. She chaffed liberal pomposity and red state self-righteousness and conformity. At the heart of her speech lay concern that too many citizens disengaged from the democratic process and took no stand against the ill-considered war in Iraq.

Still slamming the president, in 2005, Ivins told readers that the government's failure to rescue victims of Hurricane Katrina proved that, in real time, Bush's faulty policies hurt the vulnerable. She addressed the Progressive Forum in Houston on April 17, 2006, with a sly dig at Bush as evidence that Texas exports its mistakes and a straightforward warning that government spying and patriotic bullying of dissenters threatened freedom. In a final assessment of early 21st-century politics, *Bill of Wrongs: The Executive Branch's Assault on America's Fundamental Rights* (2007), she took a graver tone in alerting readers to presidential overreaching that diminished the Bill of Rights.

Following a mastectomy and chemotherapy, Ivins continued writing in the last weeks of hospice care. She died of breast cancer in Austin, Texas, on January 31, 2007. Sister playwrights Allison and Margaret Engel captured the author's sassy style with the one-woman play *Red Hot Patriot: The Kick-Ass Wit of Molly Ivins* (2010), performed by actor Kathleen Turner.

See Also: Richards, Ann; Shalala, Donna.

Reference

Ivins, Molly. "Who Can Beat President Doofus?" *The Progressive*, July 31, 2003.

J

JANEWAY, ELIZABETH (1913–2005)

A critic, historian, and social analyst of modern trends, Elizabeth Ames Hall Janeway assessed trends in American feminism and cultural habits. A native New Yorker from Brooklyn, she was born on October 7, 1913, to philanthropist Jeannette Filley Searle and naval architect and engineer Charles Henry Hall of the Milton Boat Works in Rye, New York, and editor of *Yachting* magazine. In the late 1920s, Janeway attended Shore Road Academy in Bay Ridge, New York.

Because of a decline in family fortunes during the Great Depression, Janeway left Swarthmore College in Pennsylvania in 1931 after completing her freshman year. To earn money for her family, for the next year, she created bargain basement advertising slogans for Abraham & Straus department store and processed orders for the Book-of-the-Month Club. She finished a BA degree in history at Barnard College in 1935. To improve basic composition skills, she repeated creative writing classes.

Janeway married Jewish economist and columnist Eliot Janeway in 1938 and established a marital partnership that acknowledged women's need for autonomy and monetary independence. The couple settled in a Manhattan townhouse to rear their sons, Michael Charles and William Hall Janeway. Husband and wife maintained offices on separate floors and supported each other's writing and speaking projects, including her 1944 appearance opposite Clifton Fadiman on the radio program *Information Please*.

Writer and Critic

After publishing in a campus literary magazine and winning the 1935 Intercollegiate Short Story Contest in *Story* magazine, Janeway launched a career in fiction. She submitted short works to *Harper's* and issued two best-selling character novels, *The Walsh Girls* (1943) and *Daisy Kenyon* (1945). Her talent for encapsulating intimate power struggles in dialogue earned her the sobriquet "the modern Jane Austen."

While living in Redding, Connecticut, in the late 1940s, Janeway shifted her focus from fictional and semi-autobiographical works to well-researched social histories. In a well-worded tribute, she lauded the efforts of Eleanor Roosevelt for global human rights in the article "The First Lady of the U.N." (1950) and judged the 1955 National Book Awards (NBA). Janeway's book *The Third Choice* (1960) won an NBA third place award, outranking fiction by William Faulkner, Saul Bellow, John Hersey, and Shirley Jackson.

Janeway began building a reputation for lectures and writing by contributing essays to the *Harvard Guide*, editing literature texts for Houghton Mifflin and McGraw-Hill, and serving on the boards of the McDowell artists' colony in Peterborough, New Hampshire, and the American Center for Poets, Essayists and Novelists. Her literary reviews in the *New York Times*, *Christian Science Monitor*, *Chicago Tribune*, *Atlantic Monthly*, *Harper's*, and *Ms.* promoted authors Isaac Babel, Jean Stafford, and Rebecca West. Janeway's book musings introduced readers to the feminism of Pearl Buck's novels and survivalism in James Vance Marshall's *Walkabout*. She made objective assessments of the sexual themes and situations of Vladimir Nabokov's *Lolita* and Erica Jong's *Fear of Flying*. In 1968 at Monmouth College in New Jersey, Janeway participated in a lecture series that included speakers Mike Wallace, John Kenneth Galbraith, Vincent Price, and Ann Landers.

In the late sixties, Janeway allied with feminists Betty Friedan, Kate Millett, and Gloria Steinem in the fight for pay equity for women and the Equal Rights Amendment (ERA). Janeway focused on women's reproductive rights and revealed having undergone an abortion. To aid pregnant students at Barnard, she donated to the Women's Center Emergency Medical and Legal Loan Fund.

Janeway advised the legal and education boards of the National Organization for Women and served on the Federation of State Humanities Councils. In Harriman, New York, at the 1971 Arden House Conference on Women's Challenge to Management, she spoke on "Family Life in Transition." In May 1972 at a debate of the female condition sponsored by the *American Scholar*, she advocated economic opportunity as a confidence builder in women's lives.

Social Historian

In addition to judging the 1971 Pulitzer Prize in collaboration with novelist Philip Roth, Janeway held an office in International PEN. On April 17, 1972, for the Sperry & Hutchinson Foundation lecture series at Alverno College in Milwaukee, Wisconsin, she introduced emerging social and educational patterns in "Social Myths and Sex Roles—Implications for Communication and Education." The following day, she led audience discussion of "The Social History of Women's Rights," a reprise of people and events from the suffrage era through second wave feminism.

In the same year, Janeway joined a feminist panel discussion in New York City at the 92nd Street Y with poet Carolyn Kizer, novelist Nora Ephron, and critic Helen Vendler on the topic of "Women Writers: Has Anything Changed?" Janeway declared women's literature a different category from men's works because female writing demanded its own place in the arts and produced a unique survey of universal themes and topics. She noted in "Reflections on the History of Women" (1973) the fragmentation and gaps indicating that women's existence over millennia had depended on male demands and control. She charged her generation of women with losing track of their accomplishments by misjudging the significance of women's history.

The orator focused her speaking engagements on young audiences at colleges and universities. During a feminist lecture series in Fargo, North Dakota, entitled "A Declaration of Interdependence" in 1975 and 1976, she joined orator Betty Friedan in petitioning support from women of the Great Lakes and plains area for the ERA. To advance libertarian ideals, Janeway taught young feminists at the New York Womanschool, an adult education center taught by and for women. For a 1976 *Women and Leadership* series at Loyola University in Chicago, she delivered "Higher Education: A Two-Sex System."

With *Powers of the Weak* (1980), Janeway influenced national thinking on tactics of the underdog to inform and cow the ruling class. She warned that women had lost ground because of the ebbing of affirmative action programs and the return of a male-dominated society in which women labored at the lowest levels of the workforce. As an antidote, she hoped that the ERA would earn enough votes to change the U.S. Constitution.

Janeway turned her attention to all society in *Cross Sections: From a Decade of Change* (1982) and *Improper Behavior: When and How Misconduct Can Be Healthy for Society* (1987), a perusal of aberrant actions and civil disobedience as necessary agents of reform. On November 8, 1982, she queried students at the University of California at Santa Barbara on the rhetorical question "Are Women's Rights Human Rights?" At the Women's Research Conference at the University of South Dakota on April 12, 1984, she delivered the keynote address "Woman's Place." Twelve years after her husband's death, she died of stroke at a Rye, New York, retirement home on January 15, 2005.

See Also: Buck, Pearl; Friedan, Betty; Roosevelt, Eleanor; Steinem, Gloria.

Reference

Bernstein, Adam. "Elizabeth Janeway Dies; Feminist Author." *Washington Post*, January 13, 2005, B5.

WOMEN AND THE HOME (EXCERPT)
BY ELIZABETH JANEWAY
UNIVERSITY OF WISCONSIN AT MILWAUKEE
APRIL 19, 1972

A critic, historian, and social analyst of social and gender myths, Elizabeth Janeway examined shifts in family earnings and decision making. In her speech on the second half of the 20th century, she emphasized that family power structures have traditionally denied workingwomen any assistance with home duties.

. . . Women now are not at home. There are over 43 percent of American women who have jobs. And if you take the age range of women whose children are school age, 53 percent of these women have jobs. So you're not being descriptively accurate when you say that women's place is in the home. What are you doing? You're being prescriptive. You're telling women that their place is in the home. Why are you doing that? . . .

Our old myths, our old stereotypes of thinking divide the world up into two parts, man's world, the world of action and events. They say, "Women, stay away from here. Don't come out. It's not good for you. If you come out here, you will get competitive and harsh and hard. You really want to be tender and warm and gentle and nurturing. Stay home and raise your children. And, in this interior place, woman's place, you will have great power. We will give you the power over everything that happens in this emotional interior place. You let us run things out here." That is, at any rate, what we conceive the traditional role to be.

We're wrong because the traditional role was not that. Women have always throughout history been involved with the outer world. They have always done work of economic value. It's just that in the past they were able to do it at home. When they were able to do it, that is, where they lived. Now, women who have to work, very few of them can make a living at home, such a tiny minimum that it's not worth thinking about statistically. If you have to make money because, for instance, you're widowed or divorced, you've got to go away from your home and get a job someplace.

But the old myth is saying, "This is wrong, you know. You are breaking the rules. You belong there with your children." And the result of this is that women don't get any help with raising their children when, economically speaking, they can't be with them. The idea really is that society doesn't have to worry about them. It's their fault in some fashion and we can ignore the whole thing and maybe it will go away and women will go back home.

But they can't go back home. The six million women who are heads of families and have to work, the 16 million other women whose wages or salaries or income in any case keep their families above the poverty line so that they get by, these women, they need to work and they need community support. But it's much easier for society to pretend that nothing really has to be done and that the women have to cope with the question of childcare all by themselves than to sit down and change its ideas about things and, for instance, set up really good childcare centers where children will not simply be dumped, but enriched, have experience that extends their enjoyment of life.

The point about myths is that they tend to preserve the way things used to be even though things have changed. We're used to them. We're accustomed to think that way.

Source: From the Archives Department, University of Wisconsin-Milwaukee Libraries.

JOHNSON, CLAUDIA "LADY BIRD" (1912–2007)

A beloved first lady and conservationist, Claudia Alta Taylor "Lady Bird" Johnson used her position as the president's wife to crusade for a cleaner, more verdant America. A native of Karnack, Texas, she was born in an historic plantation house on December 22, 1912, to Mary Minnie Lee Pattillo of Billingly, Alabama, and agrarian investor "Cap'n" Thomas Jefferson Taylor II, the owner of a general store. Lady Bird was baptized Methodist and received her lasting nickname from a nurse, Alice Tittle, who declared her pretty as a ladybird.

Silent communion with pine glades, the bayous of Caddo Lake, and Texas wildflowers instilled in Johnson a love of natural beauty. She completed journalism courses in 1928–1929 at the University of Alabama, and then enrolled at St. Mary's Episcopal College for Women in Dallas for her sophomore year. While she earned a BA degree in history and journalism from the University of Texas in 1933 and 1934, she read the canon of Southern novelist William Faulkner.

Introduction to Washington

Johnson met congressional aide Lyndon Baines Johnson (LBJ) of Stonewall, Texas, whom she married three months later at St. Mark's Episcopal Church in San Antonio on November 17, 1934. From money inherited from Mary Taylor, in 1937, she invested $10,000 in LBJ's first congressional campaign. Her father doubled her investment with $20,000 of his own. During LBJ's eight months of U.S. Navy service in the Pacific in 1941 and 1942, she managed his office and gave tours to visiting constituents.

Johnson supported the presidency of Franklin D. Roosevelt and accompanied Eleanor Roosevelt on a tour of impoverished dwellings in Washington, D.C. In 1943, Johnson bought KTBC-radio in Austin with the remaining $17,500 of her inheritance. Her media investments increased in 1952 with an expenditure of $41,000 for KTBC-TV, a CBS affiliate, the beginning of the Johnson fortune. Her shrewd purchases of ranches, a bank, and land made her the first millionaire first lady. The couple's partnership involved her in the issues and decisions of the Senate after LBJ's 1955 heart attack and recovery at Bethesda Naval Hospital.

Before the 1960 presidential election, in which LBJ won the vice presidency, Johnson took coursework in public speaking. She insisted on racially integrated audiences and delivered campaign speeches for nine weeks, covering 35,000 miles. Racist sneers and spitting marred her public appearances and interrupted her addresses but did not ruffle her composure. Robert Kennedy credited her with carrying the state of Texas for the ticket and shoring up the Southern Democratic bloc.

During LBJ's term as vice president, Johnson addressed citizens in 33 nations and received the 1958 Togetherness Award, followed in 1961 by the B'nai B'rith Humanitarian citation and an honorarium from Business and Professional Women. More public appearances in 1962 won her a Theta Sigma Phi honor and a Washington Heart Association Distinguished Achievement Award. For promotion of worthy causes, she achieved the 1963 American Women in Radio & Television and a humanitarian award from Volunteers of America.

A First Lady's Agenda

Following the assassination of President John F. Kennedy on November 22, 1963, Johnson entered the White House as the nation's 36th first lady and a lifetime advocate of the capital city, which she described in a daily diary. She initiated urban beautification with the Society for a More Beautiful National Capital and promoted sustainable wildflower and native flora along highways. With a personal staff, she opened rural clinics and community colleges, supported adult literacy campaigns, and launched school lunch programs and National Head Start.

During LBJ's 1964 reelection campaign, his wife toured the country by train and plane. With television spokeswoman Betty Furness, Johnson crusaded for civil rights, child development, and VISTA. She spoke at the rate of nine addresses per day, including her talks to Women Doers luncheons, her acceptance speech of an award from the University of Texas, and a keynote address at the April 20, 1964, YMCA National Convention. In 1965, she boarded the "Lady Bird Special" and delivered whistle-stop speeches in eight states.

At the May 24–25, 1965, White House Conference on Natural Beauty, Johnson delivered the welcome address, "Beauty for America." With the hospitality indigenous in genteel Southerners, she involved all citizens in a communal effort to clean and restore cities and the countryside as an antidote to ugliness and depression. She won the 1966 George Foster Peabody Award for a television appearance, "A Visit to Washington with Mrs. Lyndon B. Johnson on Behalf of a More Beautiful America."

During the social upheaval and rioting of 1967 and 1968, Johnson concealed her despair while supporting the president in a trying term of office. She continued making platform appearances and accepted the 1968 Eleanor Roosevelt Golden Candlestick Award from the Women's National Press Club. In 1969, she advised the National Park Service on national parks and historic monuments, buildings, and sites. On leaving the White House in 1970, she composed *A White House Diary*, a memoir of activism and protests of racism, poverty, and the Vietnam War. In 1971, she accepted appointment to the University of Texas Board of Regents.

In widowhood after the former president's death on January 22, 1973, Johnson promoted preservation of the Austin riverfront. She served as a board member of *National Geographic* magazine and the National Park Service and accepted numerous honors and awards from the Department of the Interior, *Ladies' Home Journal*, and the American Legion. Because of her boost to state and national ecology, in January 1977, Gerald R. Ford presented her the Presidential Medal of Freedom.

After her 1982 donation of 60 acres along the Colorado River and raising $10 million to fund the National Wildflower Research Center in Austin as part of the University of Texas sheltering of native plants, in 1988, Johnson received the Congressional Gold Medal from President Ronald Reagan. While directing LBJ, Inc., she assumed primary responsibility at LBJ Library functions and conducted interviews with journalists and historians.

Johnson's activism earned the 1990 Gold Seal for Distinguished Service and Achievement from the National Council of State Garden Clubs and the 1990 Lone Star Lifestyle Visionary Award from the JCPenney Company. After a second stroke in 2002, she earned love and thanks from the Garden Clubs of America and the American Red Cross. She died at home in West Lake Hills, Texas, on July 11, 2007.

Reference

Holley, Joe. "Champion of Conservation, Loyal Force behind LBJ." *Washington Post*, July 12, 2007.

BEAUTY FOR AMERICA
BY LADY BIRD JOHNSON
WHITE HOUSE CONFERENCE ON NATURAL BEAUTY
WHITE HOUSE, WASHINGTON, D.C.
MAY 24, 1965

A genteel organizer of esthetic reform, Lady Bird Johnson of Karnack, Texas, promoted her husband's initiatives for civil rights, literacy, and urban renewal. Passage of the 1965 Highway Beautification Act resulted from her coordination of a nationwide drive to clean and restore cities, shores, and scenic byways. By rallying support for wildflowers, citizen antilitter campaigns, and the National Park Service, she systematically buoyed public pride in landscaping along interstate and primary highways. Among her efforts were industrial and commercial zoning and bans on roadside billboards and junkyards. In ensuing decades, proponents added cutting of obstructive vegetation and promotion of tourism.

Welcome to the White House Conference on Natural Beauty. We are grateful that you have taken two days of your busy lives to come here and discuss ways to restore and increase the beauty of our land.

In the catalogue of ills which afflicts mankind, ugliness and the decay of our cities and countryside are high on America's agenda.

It seems to me that one of the most pressing challenges for the individual is the depression and the tension resulting from existence in a world which is increasingly less pleasing to the eye. Our peace of mind, our emotions, our spirit even our souls are conditioned by what our eyes see.

Ugliness is bitterness. We are all here to try and change that. This conference is a step towards the solution and I think a great one.

Our immediate problem is: How can one best fight ugliness in a nation such as ours where there is great freedom of action or inaction for every individual and every interest where there is virtually no artistic control and where all action must originate with the single citizen or group of citizens?

That is the immediate problem and challenge. Most of the great cities and great works of beauty of the past were built by autocratic societies. The Caesars built Rome. Paris represents the will of the Kings of France and the Empire. Vienna is the handiwork of the Hapsburgs, and Florence of the Medici.

Can a great democratic society generate the concerted drive to plan, and having planned, to execute great projects of beauty?

I not only hope so, I am certain that it can.

All our national history proves that a committed citizenry is a mighty force when it bends itself to a determined effort. There is a growing feeling in this land today that ugliness has been allowed too long, that it is time to say "Enough," and to act.

During these two days you will discuss and originate plans and projects both great and small. Great must be the scope of the major projects to redesign our urban areas, renew and brighten the gateways to our cities, cleanse, set in order and dignify our riverfronts and our ports. Small, but equally important perhaps most important is the single citizen who plants a tree or tends his own front yard. There are 190 million of him. He is everybody.

Perhaps the most important part of this conference will be to help educate our people that the beauty of their land depends upon their own initiative and their will.

I have heard said many times that among our greatest ills is the deep sense of frustration which the individual feels when he faces the complex and large problems of our century. Ugliness is not that sort of problem. Its vast scope will call for much coordination on the highest levels. But this is the blessing of it—it is one problem which every man and women and child can attack and contribute to defeating. Natural beauty may be a national concern and there is much that government can and should do, but it is the individual who not only benefits, but who must protect a heritage of beauty for future generations.

There are no autocrats in our land to decree beauty, only a national will. Through your work, I firmly believe this national will can be given energy and force and produce a more beautiful America.

Source: Johnson, Lady Bird. "Beauty for America." *Proceedings of the White House Conference on Natural Beauty, May 24–25, 1965.* Washington, DC: U.S. Government Printing Office, 1965, 17–18.

JONES, MARY "MOTHER" (1830–1930)

An Irish mother figure and rowdy organizer of workers, Mary Frances Harris "Mother" Jones mobilized the poor and unemployed with pragmatic advice on combating the cruelties of capitalism. A Cork native born to Ellen Cotter Harris on May 1, 1830, Jones was reared during the clash between British peacekeepers and Irish libertarians that sent her grandfather to the gibbet. Her father, railway and canal builder Richard Harris, incited the anger of antilabor forces.

The Harrises and their children—Mary, Richard, William, Catherine, and Ellen—immigrated in 1838 to Toronto, where Jones learned debate and worked toward a degree in education. In 1860, she taught in Monroe, Michigan, at the St. Mary convent school. At a teaching position in Memphis, Tennessee, she met and, on December 18, 1860, married a union advocate, iron molder George E. Jones. During a yellow fever epidemic of October 1867, Mary nursed the sick, but lost George and their preschoolers Catherine, Elizabeth, Terence, and Mary to contagion.

With George's union pension, Jones made a new life in Chicago as a seamstress. At the loss of her shop during the cataclysmic fire of October 8, 1871, she retreated to the basement of Old St. Mary's Church to share space with other traumatized residents. Because members of the Knights of Labor treated her like a daughter, she became an itinerant lecturer for unionism in machine shops, canals and railways, lumber and mining camps, coal docks, telegraph offices, weaving and sewing shops, cigar-rolling parlors, and streetcars.

Action and Oratory

The tone of Jones's addresses varied from inside jokes and gentle drollery to swear words and fiery exhortations. Her reasoning appealed to worker aims—offer fair labor in exchange for safe workplaces, reasonable pay, and eight-hour days. During the Long Strike of 1875 in Reading, Pennsylvania, she spewed hostility toward mine owners and glorified striker solidarity against railroad mogul Franklin Benjamin Gowen, who lowered miner income by 20 percent. At a Pittsburgh labor revolt in July 1877, she launched a phalanx of wives to bolster rail strikers against the Baltimore & Ohio Railroad and, in 1890, co-formed the United Mine Workers (UMW).

Dubbed "Mother Jones" at age 60, she addressed tense, sometimes lethal situations, including protests of child fiber and textile workers in the South, a volley of antilabor bullets in Las Vegas, New Mexico, and the march of the unemployed in Jacob Coxey's army from Oklahoma to the U.S. Capitol on April 30, 1894. During a summer strike in West Virginia in 1897, she delivered "The Lives of the Coal Miners." At the Erie mines in Arnot, Pennsylvania, in November 1899, she mustered women to bang dishpans and sing patriotic songs while marching 15 miles. Her tactics succeeded in securing fresh produce for sale from area farms and in forcing management to raise hourly pay, winning her the name the "Miners' Angel."

A situation in Scranton, Pennsylvania, on February 18, 1901, required Jones's defense of silk workers. Before an audience, she humiliated the company for unsanitary conditions, underage crews, and low pay rates. At the 1901 UMW convention in Indianapolis, she delivered a personal statement, "My Epitaph," a graceful utterance to "fellow toilers" that the *Reading Times* described as forceful and convincing ("Mother" 1901, 1).

An acid-tongued agitator, Jones reached a height of oratory in 1902, when she shamed investors in Manayunk and Port Richmond, Pennsylvania, by setting up free food distribution to nourish underpaid Italian and Polish millworkers. By June 20, 1902, when she delivered "Lay Down Your Picks and Shovels and Quit Work!" in Clarksburg, West Virginia, she had acquired the descriptor "America's most dangerous woman." On July 19, she won the loyalty of miners with "Be True to the Principles of Our Forefathers"; on July 23, she informed Cincinnati's labor council, "Women Are Fighters." The next day, she rebuked a federal judge in Parkersburg, West Virginia, for siding with the Fairmont Coal Company against labor.

In March 1903, Jones testified to a Toledo audience on the efficacy of "Agitation, the Greatest Factor for Progress," a truism about confrontational labor tactics. For 22 days the next July, she paraded scrawny, underage, and stunted carpet and textile workers from Kensington, Pennsylvania, across New Jersey and New York to the music of a brass band. At Coney Island on July 28, she appealed to social consciousness with "The Wail of the Children."

As Jones aged, her addresses took on the air of jovial, grandmotherly advice. At Louisville, Colorado, on November 21, 1903, she emphasized the "we" in "We Must Stand Together." On August 7, 1904, she presented to the New York City Central Federated Union "A Tribute to Italian Miners," a salute to immigrant employees. After the April 18, 1905, entreaty "Appeal to Copper Miners to Organize," she made headway in Red Jacket, Michigan, against the Calumet and Hecla Mining Company. By June, she and socialist backer William Dudley "Big Bill" Haywood formed the Industrial Workers of the World, to which she presented a founding address in Chicago on July 7, 1905.

Jones crusaded against big money by supporting copper miners in Bisbee, Arizona, ale bottlers in Milwaukee, Wisconsin, and peasants robbed of their homes during the Mexican Revolution, the focus of the 1909 speeches "Plea on Behalf of Mexican Revolutionaries Imprisoned in the United States" and "The Tyranny of Mexico." To expose persecution of humble Mexicans, on June 14, 1910, she testified before the U.S. Congress. She provoked an all-night sing-along by incarcerated women and children in Butte, Montana, and advised miners with "Don't Give the Master Class Any Weapon to Strike You With" (1911).

Jones faced a sophisticated audience in May 1913 when she mounted a Carnegie Hall dais to state "I Want to Give the Nation a More Highly Developed Citizenship." As conditions for miners worsened in 1912, she delivered "Barbarous West Virginia" five times between August 1 and September 21. After she proclaimed "Rise Up and Strike!" and "You Are Less Free Than the Negroes Were before the Civil War!" in the autumn of 1913, her stamina faltered from pneumonia during her winter jailing in Charleston, West Virginia, on the charge of inciting a riot. With "Labor's Memorial Day" on May 30, 1914, Jones aroused sympathy in Seattle, Washington, for the 32 men, women, and children slain by the Colorado militia's machine gunners at the Ludlow Massacre. She pressed on to Vancouver's Labor Temple 11 days later to assert an historic redefinition, "Not an Industrial War, But a Civil War," a call for defeat of plutocrats. She continued hacking at the roots of oligarchy with "You Can't Fool My Boys, Mr. Rockefeller," an oration to New York City's Cooper Union on January 28, 1915. A year later, she sparked humor on the UMW agenda with "Thank God I Have Lived to Be a Grandmother in Agitation!" (1916).

Still crusading from state to state, on October 23, 1919, to steel strikers in Gary, Indiana, Jones claimed "I'm a Bolshevist from the Bottom of My Feet to the Top of My Head." She moved on to Kanawha County, West Virginia, to mediate for 15 prisoners chained in a labor camp. The terror tactics employed on August 1, 1921, at the Matewan, West Virginia, clash forced her to cut human loss by negotiating for miners with Governor Ephraim Franklin Morgan.

Jones uplifted farm laborers in Chicago on July 3, 1923, with "My Old Eyes Can See the Coming of Another Day," a prophecy of improvement in laboring class prosperity. By her last year, she resorted to radio harangues as a means of unionizing labor. She declared, "Power Lies in the Hands of Labor to Retain American Liberty" (1930), a credo she had followed from early widowhood. She died on November 30, 1930, in Silver Spring, Maryland.

References

Green, James. *The Devil Is Here in These Hills: West Virginia's Coal Miners and Their Battle for Freedom.* New York: Grove Press, 2015.

"'Mother' Jones Speaks." *Reading* (Pennsylvania) *Times*, March 18, 1901, 1.

A SUMMARY
BY MARY "MOTHER" JONES
MOUNT CARBON, WEST VIRGINIA
NOVEMBER 21, 1903

A sharp-tongued speaker during the mining wars of the early 1900s, Mother Jones of Cork, Ireland, incited the laboring class to end child employment and to demand fair wages, a shorter workday, and safe conditions. In incendiary situations at strikes and protests where hired guards assaulted organizers, she hurled swear words, salty humor, and patriotic slogans to boost worker morale. Although the 1902–1903 miners' strikes failed, at Mount Carbon in the Kanawha River Valley, she led 7,000 miners for one year in unionizing to secure improved conditions and the reduction of a 14-hour workday to 9 hours.

Every miner in the West Virginia coalfields must dig twenty tons at the very lowest estimate to pay the various company assessments before he has anything for food and clothing and powder. He receives a wage that will average anywhere from $1.60 to $1.80 per day.

Out of this comes house rent of not less than $5 a month; water, $1 per month, squibs, 25 cents per month; 2 gallons oil per month at 50 cents per gallon, and which can be bought anywhere in open market for 25 cents per gallon; powder, of which he uses between three and four kegs per month in order to mine enough coal to pay him $1.60 per day, at $2.25 per keg, costing operators 98 cents delivered at mouth of mine; 60 cents per month for blacksmith; $1 per month for company doctor, no difference whether he ever has occasion for his services or not, and 19 cents per month for the hospital at Paint Creek.

All he has left he is at liberty to spend for food and clothing at the "Pluck-me," the miner's vernacular for the company store. It is truly well named. The prices charged for everything are exorbitant in the extreme. Flour of quality that can be bought in any city or railroad town or village in the land for $4.50 per barrel these people pay for at the rate of $6.75 per barrel.

"But then we bring the capital into the country and give these people work," an operator tried to argue with Mother Jones, "and it is nothing more than fair that they should patronize the company store. If it wasn't for us and our capital they would starve to death." To which befuddled logician Mother Jones replied, "Fool, go and work as these men do and learn the truth before you speak to me!"

Source: "The Workingman's Heroine." *The Tammany Times* 17, no. 15 (August 12, 1901): 10.

JONG, ERICA (1942–)

Feminist poet and author Erica Mann Jong became a pop culture icon for defining women's desire for sexual fulfillment. A New Yorker born on March 26, 1942, to Eda Mirsky and Seymour Mann, she grew up in a privileged bohemian household open to guilt-free nudity and experimental sex. Her father supported her aims to be a poet and literary academic, paying for quality education for his three daughters.

At Barnard College, Jong majored in composition and English and Italian literature and primarily read male poets. Out of enjoyment of satire from the 1770s, she completed a graduate degree from Columbia in 18th-century English literature. In 1966, she wed psychiatrist Allan Jong.

In pursuit of her dream career, in 1971, Jong issued an award-winning collection of verse, *Fruits and Vegetables.* She saw herself in old age like Colette, the amply published French novelist. Her notoriety as a poet initiated demand for platform readings, workshops, and speeches.

Publication of *The Man Who Murdered Poets* and *Fear of Flying* brought Jong international fame. The latter, a semi-autobiographical novel, defied the double standard of the World War II generation that rated men's pleasure above that of women. The theme of sexual liberation, spur-of-the-moment eroticism, and ambiguity toward marriage defined a central concern of second wave feminism.

Jong received a deluge of invitations for interviews and speeches. In 1974, she completed an extensive book tour to college campuses. She produced more verse for *Loveroot* (1975), the novel *How to Save Your Own Life* (1977), the poetry compendium *At the Edge of the Body* (1979), a retro 18th-century novel, *Fanny: Being the True History of the Adventures of Fanny Hackabout-Jones* (1980), and more verse in *Witches* (1981). Later in the 1980s, she wrote new poems for *Ordinary Miracles* (1983) and the novel *Parachutes and Kisses* (1984) and *Serenissima,* retitled *Shylock's Daughter: A Novel of Love in Venice* (1987).

On June 22, 1995, Jong addressed the American Civil Liberties Union in New York on the effects of censorship on creativity. She declared suppression an outgrowth of social diversity and substantiated her speech with a reprise of literary landmarks by James Joyce, Kitty MacKinnon, and Andrea Dworkin.

In May 2008, Jong published an essay lauding the loyalty and tolerance of gay couples. She addressed an assembly at Union Theological Seminary on the placement of her mock memoir, *Fear of Flying*, in the feminist canon. The lecture commented on how readers from Belgrade to Tokyo and Hong Kong still identified with the character Isadora Wing and on the 35-year blessing and curse of having written a sexually controversial best-seller.

See Also: Dworkin, Andrea.

Reference

Bowman, David. "The 'Sex Woman.'" Salon, June 14, 2003. Accessed April 24, 2015. http://www.salon.com/2003/06/14/jong_2/.

FREE SPEECH
BY ERICA JONG
AMERICAN CIVIL LIBERTIES UNION
BIENNIAL CONFERENCE, NEW YORK
JUNE 22, 1995

Author Erica Jong knew firsthand the rabid demand for censorship. By reprising the history of 20th-century court cases, she built a case against suppression of literature based on conservative reactions to a diverse society. In the aftermath of the Communications Decency Act of 1996 and its overturn by the Supreme Court in 1997, First Amendment rights extended to the Internet until passage of the Children's Internet Protection Act of 2000, which allowed schools and libraries to filter age-inappropriate sites.

You know, I want to speak to you today about the creative imagination and censorship and why censorship is such a dire threat to creative people. But first I want to define some terms. I think that one of the reasons that we are embroiled in this tremendous argument about censorship and where we are vis-a-vis censorship, the so-called Communications Decency Act that is being floated in the Congress of the United States, is because we live in a time when we have a very diverse population.

And interesting enough, calls for censorship always increase when the population is extremely diverse and different standards prevail. This is almost a given: when you have an elitist or traditional society in which everybody agrees about who gets access to stuff, you don't have calls for censorship. They only occur in a society in which there are many different groups struggling for a place and trying to figure out whose word goes.

So it's very interesting. It's almost a product of the diversity of our society that we have these new calls for censorship. And I think, although it seems very depressing some days to open the paper and see so many of the things that we've fought for going down the drain, it's in a way a symbol of how much we have reached people, that there should be a worry about pornography on the internet, too free an expression of ideas and so on. So maybe there is a little bit of hope here.

Forty years ago Margaret Mead, who wrote beautifully about so many things that were not in her anthropological purview, supposedly said that censorship would always increase in a pluralistic democracy as each group warred with the other, trying to figure out who had the right to be on top and who had the right to say what other people could speak about.

I think we live in a time where the freedom to publish sexually oriented material is increasingly coming under attack. Large publishing conglomerates increasingly control all means of communication and the forces of cultural reaction are becoming extremely well organized. The brief cultural glasnost that we enjoyed in the sixties is already beginning to seem quaint. And when you think about this century and you think that it's the century that started with *The Wasteland*, with Prufrock, with *Ulysses*, and with great fights to liberate literature, which came to fruition just about 1962 when the Supreme Court liberated *Tropic of Cancer*.

And then, in the sixties, a time that we all remember, probably well, there was a moment when literature all over the world was changed by the release of *Tropic of Cancer*. Suddenly authors didn't have to shut the bedroom door when they wrote about sexuality. Suddenly, the tremendous force and passion of sexuality inspired the whole culture and created a kind of exuberance that went to other areas as well.

But that period of time was extremely narrow. I would say 20 years, 25 years. And then there was a tremendous desire for censorship again. And we come to the end of the century, and we seem to be back in 1895. It seems that we have made a complete circle.

And now the calls for censorship are coming not just from the right, but also from the left. They are coming distressingly from feminists, members of my own movement, who believe, some of them, like Andrea Dworkin and Catharine MacKinnon, that there is no danger in their joining forces with the forces of reaction. For example, Andrea Dworkin and Kitty MacKinnon joined the Meese Commission in 1986, which was very strange.

So there are feminists who are saying: We don't care about the First Amendment; the First Amendment is sentimental; the First Amendment is foolish; the First Amendment is romantic and Rousseauish. We don't need that, a higher good is protecting women and protecting women against rape and protecting women against being denigrated in print, in pictures, on the internet, and so on.

Well, let's look at that and what that has really accomplished in the last few years. Basically what it has accomplished, is it has given guys like Dole, like Gramm, a new vocabulary. And it's given people like Pat Robertson a new vocabulary. Instead of having to say now they are for censorship, because they want to keep all women barefoot and pregnant in Christ, they can now say: We are protecting women against denigration and abuse. And the reason that we want the Communications Decency Act is in order to protect women.

In other words, they have taken the vocabulary that Dworkin and MacKinnon have given them and they've used it to drape their old barefoot and pregnant ideas. So they've become very much harder to counter. All those same old farts, the alter knockers in the Congress who sat there when Anita Hill was being pilloried and tormented, and who didn't understand anything, who didn't get it, they are getting up and saying: We are protecting women against denigration and abuse.

So basically, what Dworkin and MacKinnon have done for the evangelical right, is that they've given them a new dialect that they can use to cloak their very, very ancient ideas. And that's even more terrifying, I think, than anything else that they've done and they seem not to understand that they've done this.

I'm not so interested in talking to you about why it's important to have free sexual expression in society, because I think probably many of us here agree with that. But I want to talk about why people are so interested in censoring expression when there are so many other problems in our society that need addressing.

I think that people become hysterical about expression when they feel out of control: They cannot stop rape. Children are raised in a way that they are not parented, they are not educated, they are not given values, there are too many of them, they are too poor, they are too ill, they are too hungry. Instead of addressing these problems in society, problems that come from overpopulation, problems that come from the breakdown of the family, problems that come from the severe inequity of financial access between races, between rich and poor, instead of addressing these questions, which are the real questions, it's easier to address expression and censorship. It's easier to get up and rave about how our society is being corrupted by pornographic images on the Internet. Much easier to talk about that than it is to talk about the fact that there is inequality economically and that because there is inequality economically, we have people who are not socialized to be part of our society, and we don't know what to do about that problem, so let's talk about censorship and expression.

It is absolutely a red herring. It is total bullshit. It is like arresting prostitutes instead of Johns.

Do you remember last year there was a mayor, I believe it was in Miami, who decided that she was going to have the names of the Johns who frequented prostitutes read on television and printed in the newspaper? And I thought, what a sensible idea. Rather than arresting these women whose financial lack of access has put them in this profession, which is the only way they can make money, instead, expose the guys who are using the prostitutes. Don't criminalize these poor women.

It never lasted very long. It spread to a couple of other cities, but basically it didn't last very long. And we have a perfectly analogous situation, for example, in the whole debate about pornography. If criminal acts are perpetrated when pornography is made, if a child is injured, if a woman is drugged and raped during the making of a pornographic film, why not arrest these guys for rape or for child molestation. We have plenty of laws on the books that protect against rape and child molestation.

But, no, that would mean that we were going to come down on organized crime, which basically profits from pornography, and that's too hard. Perhaps it's too hard because organized crime basically contributes to the PAC funds of the people in the Congress. Who knows why? Maybe it's too hard to do that. Better to jump on expression and say that free expression is causing these problems.

So look at the underside of the problem. Look at this great debate that we've been having about censorship, free expression, the Internet. It's not really about that. It's not really about whether it's good or bad to have *Tropic of Cancer* out there so people can read it. It is not really about any of the things that it claims to be about.

What it is really about is that people do not know how to stop the Mafia from selling pornography in which children are abused, or they don't want to do it because they profit in some way from it.

And so instead of going to the root of the problem, instead of exposing the Johns, basically it's much, much easier to beat up on a bunch of fuzzy minded liberals who want to make little distinctions about what is right and what is wrong, i.e. us.

And we play right into their tendency to smokescreen the real problems, because as members of the left we're more interested in fighting each other than in fighting our real enemies. We love to fight each other. We love to make subtle distinctions and argue with each other.

And I think that we better really look at what's going on in our culture and we better look at who profits from pornography. And we better look at the laws that we already have and which ones are enforced and which ones aren't. And we better stop letting them make it an issue of censorship versus free speech, because really it's not about that. It's about economics at the bottom. It's about the fact that women and children are the lowest priority in this society. It's about the fact that women and children's rights are cut first. It's about the fact that our teenage daughters can't walk on the streets without danger of being raped. It's about a total social breakdown and it has absolutely nothing to do with expression, that is a smokescreen.

And suddenly, after having these endless conversations on TV with all kinds of people from Phyllis Schafly to Claire Short—the shadow minister of labor in England who is calling for censorship of pornography because it's a wonderful way for her to get elected—it suddenly occurred to me that this is not the issue at all. And I would ask you, as my colleagues, to please address the basic issue.

Rather than arguing with the people who would censor about whether or not this is censorship. I would look at the root causes. I would look at the root causes of why people participate in pornography. I would look at the inequalities, the economic inequalities that underlie the system, and I would address those and not be jollied into this whole argument about censorship. Because the truth is that anybody's political agenda, if it is not your own, is obscene.

And basically censorship, once it gets on the books, is always used in that way, to politically harass the dissenter. The reason I remain a First Amendment fundamentalist is because I understand as a feminist, as a Jew, as a woman, as a woman who has been battered for expressing herself freely in all her books, I understand the First Amendment protects the minority, protects the dissenter, protects the woman, protects the witch.

Basically, I understand that unless you have a government of laws, rather than a government of people, you cannot protect dissent. And I understand, as a woman who probably would have been burned in the marketplace for witchcraft only about 200 years ago, that I need the First Amendment more than anybody does. And that even if I am repelled by child pornography or Bob Guccione's productions, that I have to protect those things, because essentially it's in my self-interest to do so.

Source: Jong, Erica. "Free Speech." American Civil Liberties Union Biennial Conference, New York, June 22, 1995. Reprinted with permission from Erica Jong.

JORDAN, BARBARA (1963–1996)

A Texas politician and civil rights leader, Barbara Charline Jordan achieved a number of firsts—notably, being the first black Texas state senator, the first Southern black U.S. Representative, and the first black woman to present a keynote speech at a Democratic presidential convention. Born in Houston, Texas, on February 21, 1936, to Arlyne Patten Jordan and Benjamin Meredith Jordan, she learned to think independently from her grandfather, Charles Jordan. With a rich, accentuated cadence and scholarly phrasing, she excelled at oratorical contests, poetry recitation, and debate at Texas Southern University.

The only female enrolled at Boston University School of Law, in 1959, Jordan earned an LLD and taught political science at Tuskegee Institute. On admission to the Texas bar in 1960, she specialized in probate and domestic relations. After her two failed runs for the Texas legislature, in 1967, a U.S. Supreme Court ban on discriminatory reapportionment secured her election as the state's first woman and first black senator.

A progressive in style and content, Jordan promoted formation of a Fair Employment Practices Commission, a community affairs agency, and a minimum wage and workers' compensation that covered Texas farmworkers. President Lyndon B. Johnson consulted with her on formulation of his 1967 civil rights plan. Following the assassination of Martin Luther King, Jr., on April 4, 1968, she addressed media publishers on "Who Speaks for the Negro?" In 1972, she earned the position of Senate president pro tempore, another first for black women.

On election to the U.S. Congress in 1972, Jordan began the first of three terms with a speech on the Democratic mandate to suppress overreaching of the executive branch by President Richard Nixon. In a televised presentation, she addressed the House Judiciary Committee during the 1974 discussion of presidential impeachment. In a 15-minute oration tinged with wry humor, she reviewed the crimes of the Watergate Scandal involving Nixon's administration. She declared them a betrayal of the highest office and a subversion of the Constitution. The terse, incisive speech concluded, "It is reason, and not passion, which must guide our deliberations, guide our debate, and guide our decision" (Jordan 1974, 113).

Jordan maintained a reputation for integrity and ethics and spoke to Howard University graduates on optimism and truth. She introduced a crime bill demanding enforcement of civil rights amendments and harangued the House of Representatives for continuing to allot funds to violators. In 1974, she toured Beijing and Shanghai, China, at the request of President Gerald Ford, a diplomatic venture promoting Sino-American relations.

In 1975, Jordan spoke to the Committee on the Judiciary about extending the Voting Rights Act of 1965. She proposed augmenting the original act by demanding bilingual ballots, supporting the proposal with facts and statistics concerning participation in elections by non-English-speaking citizens. She hammered white-dominated communities for abolishing school boards with minority membership, closing polling places to impede voting, gerrymandering, and annexing districts and at-large elections to dilute minority participation.

Jordan's aggressive stance on fairness continued in Houston at the May 27, 1976, National Conference on Magnet Schools, to which she stated "Simple Justice Requires an All Out Effort to Foster Integration and Quality Education," a speech stressing the concept of equality in the Declaration of Independence. On July 25, 1976, in New York City's Madison Square Garden, she became the first black woman to present a keynote speech at a Democratic presidential convention. Profoundly patriotic, her coherent affirmations to the party, delivered with steely dignity, carried the authority of a fundamentalist sermon and the pride of the signers of the Declaration of Independence.

Classic Oratory

In subsequent public service, Jordan spoke candidly on the issues. In September 24, 1976, she followed up her pursuit of fairness and a common destiny by delivering to the Congressional Black Caucus a keynote speech entitled "Marching on the Ballot Boxes." The text noted the lack of registration by seven million blacks, whose disengagement from the democratic process skewed congressional votes on jobs. In 1977, her Community Reinvestment Bill proposed extending financial services to poor and minority bank depositors.

On September 26, 1977, Jordan gave the focal commentary on civil rights enforcement at a Title VI Conference in Washington, D.C., and followed up in the House of Representatives on October 14 with a treatise from the National Association for the Advancement of Colored People. She crusaded for busing and the Equal Rights Amendment and against poverty and racial marginalization but did not attain President Jimmy Carter's nomination to attorney general.

Because of advancing multiple sclerosis, Jordan retired from Congress. In 1979, she joined the public affairs faculty of the University of Texas in Austin and presented three weekly seminars on election styles and political values. Her role as public educator involved frequent academic and governmental receptions and banquets. At the 1984 dinner of the Joint Center for Political Studies, she delivered "A Salute to Black Elected Officials." Her oratory revealed acquired wisdom on "Potomac fever" and the workings of bureaucracies.

In 1991, Jordan advised Texas governor Ann Richards and, in her wheelchair, returned to the 1992 Democratic convention to exhort the audience on "Change: From What to What?" She received a Presidential Medal of Freedom from President Bill Clinton. She obtained top secret security clearance to preside over the 1994 Commission on Immigration Reform.

In February 1995, Jordan summarized guidelines for naturalizing or deporting undocumented immigrants. On the subject of new citizens, she published in the *New York Times* "The Americanization Ideal" (1995), an outline of laws to protect the nation and economy from undesirable aliens and to ensure birthright citizenship to any child born in the United States. On receipt of the Thayer Award at West Point on October 5, 1995, she stressed service and selflessness and praised the corps' dedication to duty, honor, and country. Under treatment for leukemia, she remained a moral, spiritual force until her death from viral pneumonia on January 17, 1996.

References

Jordan, Barbara. *Debate on Articles of Impeachment Hearings of the Committee on the Judiciary House of Representatives.* 93rd Cong., 2d sess. Washington, DC: U.S. Government Printing Office, 1974, 110–113.

Marshall, Brenda DeVore, and Molly A. Mayhead, eds. *Telling Political Lives: The Rhetorical Autobiographies of Women Leaders in the United States.* Lanham, MD: Lexington Books, 2008.

STATEMENT ON THE ARTICLES OF IMPEACHMENT (EXCERPT) BY BARBARA JORDAN HOUSE JUDICIARY COMMITTEE U.S. HOUSE OF REPRESENTATIVES, WASHINGTON, D.C. JULY 25, 1974

U.S. Congresswoman Barbara Jordan of Houston, Texas, gave a televised statement on the nature of impeachment and on President Richard Nixon's eligibility for legal action through crimes committed during the Watergate scandal. By examining constitutional precedent line by line, she left no doubt that Congress was obligated to charge Nixon with "high crimes and misdemeanors." The speech established her integrity and fairness and elevated her to one of the most reasoned, respected members of Congress. As evidence and public opinion substantiated Nixon's guilt, on August 9, 1974, he resigned from office.

Today, I am an inquisitor, I believe hyperbole would not be fictional and would not overstate the solemnness that I feel right now. My faith in the Constitution is whole, it is complete, it is total. I am not going to sit here and be an idle spectator to the diminution, the subversion, the destruction of the Constitution. . . .

It is wrong, I suggest, it is a misreading of the Constitution for any member here to assert that for a member to vote for an article of impeachment means that that member must be convinced that the President should be removed from office. The Constitution doesn't say that. The powers relating to impeachment are an essential check in the hands of the body of the legislature against and upon the encroachments of the executive. The division between the two branches of the legislature, the House and the Senate, assigning to the one the right to accuse and to the other the right to judge, the framers of this Constitution were very astute. They did not make the accusers and the judges the same person.

We know the nature of impeachment. We've been talking about it awhile now. It is chiefly designed for the President and his high ministers to somehow be called into account. It is designed to "bridle" the executive if he engages in excesses. "It is designed as a method of national inquest into the conduct of public men." The framers confided in the Congress the power if need be, to remove the President in order to strike a delicate balance between a President swollen with power and grown tyrannical, and preservation of the independence of the executive. . . .

Common sense would be revolted if we engaged upon this process for petty reasons. Congress has a lot to do: appropriations, tax reform, health insurance, campaign finance reform, housing, environmental protection, energy sufficiency, mass transportation. Pettiness cannot be allowed to stand in the face of such overwhelming problems. So today we are not being petty. We are trying to be big, because the task we have before us is a big one. . . .

Beginning shortly after the Watergate break-in and continuing to the present time, the President has engaged in a series of public statements and actions designed to thwart the lawful investigation by government prosecutors. Moreover, the President has made public announcements and assertions bearing on the Watergate case, which the evidence will show he knew to be false. . . .

The Constitution charges the President with the task of taking care that the laws be faithfully executed, and yet the President has counseled his aides to commit perjury, willfully disregard the secrecy of grand jury proceedings, conceal surreptitious entry, attempt to compromise a federal judge, while publicly displaying his cooperation with the processes of criminal justice. "A President is impeachable if he attempts to subvert the Constitution."

If the impeachment provision in the Constitution of the United States will not reach the offenses charged here, then perhaps that 18th-century Constitution should be abandoned to a 20th-century paper shredder. Has the President committed offenses, and planned, and directed, and acquiesced in a course of conduct which the Constitution will not tolerate? That's the question. We know that. We know the question. We should now forthwith proceed to answer the question. It is reason and not passion which must guide our deliberations, guide our debate, and guide our decision.

Source: Jordan, Barbara. *Debate on Articles of Impeachment Hearings of the Committee on the Judiciary House of Representatives.* 93rd Cong., 2d sess. Washington, DC: U.S. Government Printing Office, 1974, 110–113.

K

KEENAN, NANCY (1952–)

A savvy, moral progressive, Nancy Keenan propelled the abortion debate into 21st century parlance for both urban and rural women by demanding privacy and access to health care. Born to an Irish Catholic household in Anaconda, Montana, on Valentine's Day, 1952, she was the daughter of Ann E. and Patrick John Keenan, a former state senator. While earning a degree in special education, Keenan worked at the Anaconda copper smelter.

In sympathy with pregnant coeds, Keenan gave them cash for travel to Mexico for abortions. She graduated from Montana State University in 1974. In Anaconda and Billings, she taught special needs classes. She won a seat in the state House of Representatives and advocated laws to serve veterans, trade unionists, Native Americans, students, and the elderly. In 1988, she began three four-year terms as state superintendent of public schools.

Keenan completed an MA in school administration in 1999 from the University of Montana. In May of that year, she campaigned unsuccessfully for the U.S. Congress on an agenda of women's rights, quality schools, unions, and gay rights. In 2003, she joined the staff of People for the American Way as director of education policy and, on March 18, chastised the George W. Bush administration for underfunding public schools. She exposed the use of national television programming to propagandize the Bush promotion of "No Child Left Behind."

In 2004, Keenan began chairing the National Abortion and Reproductive Rights Action League Pro-Choice America (NARAL). She applauded the March for Women's Life on the Washington Mall on April 25, 2004, and informed Americans of restrictions on women's privacy and reproductive choice imposed by state bills and federal courts. In March 2006, after South Dakota banned abortion, Keenan crusaded for a repeal of the legislation. She addressed the judiciary committee of the U.S. legislature on March 2, 2006, on "Scope and Myths of *Roe vs.*

Wade" and led a backlash in Sioux Falls against anti-choice politicians with Prevention First, a crusade against unplanned conceptions and tolerance for women's moral decisions. She achieved a place on the *Washingtonian Magazine*'s 2006 listing of the 100 most powerful females in Washington, D.C.

Because the United States logged a higher rate of unintended pregnancies than other industrialized nations, Keenan initiated ideas about reproductive rights, family planning, and medically accurate sex education in public schools. One-on-one, she lectured President Bush on women's need for accessible birth control. She became the face of pro-woman rhetoric. On frequent television and radio interviews she lobbied against punitive physician lectures and ultrasounds and for women's access to health clinics, contraceptives, and RU-486 emergency contraception. She popularized the elevation of tone during extreme arguments limiting women's rights.

Keenan celebrated gains in pro-choice advocates elected in 2008 to Congress and incorporated into the administration of President Barack Obama and the lower courts. At the University of Texas at Austin on January 17, 2008, she and members of Law Students for Reproductive Justice observed the 35th anniversary of the U.S. Supreme Court decision on *Roe v. Wade* by extolling Sarah Weddington, the attorney who secured the rights of Jane Roe in 1973. Keenan honored the Reverend Howard Moody and the Clergy Consultation Service that began abortion referrals in 1967 and declared herself weary of defending the feminist view against equally adamant anti-choice voices demonizing the safe termination of a pregnancy.

Keenan's speech regretted the erosion of reproductive rights through 550 restrictive laws whittling at the legal provision of female health care. Her speech questioned the morality of forcing maternity on girls and women who were impoverished, ashamed, or unready to produce babies. She linked female hesitance at parenting to life in a society that devalued the rights and needs of children for nutrition, safety, schooling, and the Children's Health Insurance Program.

Unlike contentious hardliners on both sides of the issues, Keenan allied with the "postmenopausal militia" in reeducating millennials and teens on the backstreet abortions of the early 1900s. She proposed respect for all women and a more realistic evaluation of the complex dilemmas of choice and the outcomes of abortion. In an address to the 2008 Democratic National Convention in Denver, Colorado, she favored birth control over the use of abortion as a contraceptive method.

After the assassination of Wichita physician George Tiller at the Reformation Lutheran Church on May 31, 2009, by Scott Roeder, a pro-life extremist, Keenan's compassionate oratory reviled the hate speech of Operation Rescue. As a panel member at a National Press Club event on June 23, 2009, she urged women to demand the privacy and security to make personal decisions and to engage law enforcement to shield workers at women's health clinics.

On February 2, 2010, Keenan rallied support for the 37th anniversary of *Roe v. Wade* with the speech, "Attitude Is Everything," the source of pro-choice lapel buttons. She thanked President Obama for being a pro-choice president and for repealing the global gag rule and reducing funds for abstinence-until-marriage programs, which she described as ineffective and medically inaccurate. The speech welcomed pro-woman Justice Sonia Sotomayor to the Supreme Court and rallied attendees to guarantee a better future for women. She repeated the speech on March 16 at the Power of Choice luncheon in San Francisco.

At enactment of the Obama health care package in March 2010 that insured an additional 30 million citizens, Keenan protested abstinence-only sex education policies and bans of federal funding for abortion. In 2011, she backed training for medical students in abortion procedures and denounced the crusade of House Speaker John Boehner for denying female soldiers access to abortion following rape. At the 2012 National Democratic Convention in Charlotte, North Carolina, she asked that citizens reserve judgment on women who choose to end a pregnancy out of respect for the variable affecting family size, finances, and ability to parent another child. In January 2013, she marked the 40th anniversary of *Roe* with comments on challenges to women's liberty by Mississippi "personhood" bills and Virginia law requiring ultrasounds. She also detailed the immorality of "heartbeat" bills in Ohio, coercion of clients at "crisis pregnancy" centers, and cruelty toward survivors of incest and rape.

After 13 years of residency in Washington, at age 61, Keenan moved to Bonner, Montana, on the Blackfoot River to join Hilltop Public Solutions and counsel Democratic candidates for public office. In Billings on April 25, 2014, she presented the keynote speech at the annual Harry S. Truman Dinner to Yellowstone County Democrats. She advocated electing more female candidates and holding Republicans accountable for divisive legislation that she said disempowered women, children, and the underclass, especially in Idaho and Wyoming. She accused opponents of hypocrisy in claiming to advocate freedom and privacy except on the issue of abortion.

In October 2014, Keenan collaborated with female politicians to shield 27 Montana health clinics from conservative restrictions on the Title X Public Service Act, which funds family planning. In the spring of 2015, the Montana Democratic Party named her executive director. She crusaded for expanded Medicaid that covered more members of the Crow Nation.

See Also: Michelman, Kate; Weddington, Sarah.

Reference

Payne, Erica. *Practical Progressive: How to Build a 21st Century Political Movement.* New York: PublicAffairs, 2008.

OPPOSITION TO SOUTH DAKOTA LEGAL BAN ON ABORTION (EXCERPT) BY NANCY KEENAN C-SPAN, WASHINGTON, D.C. AUGUST 18, 2008

A savvy, succinct progressive, Nancy Keenan opposed a ban on abortion in South Dakota that preceded an onslaught of legislative attempts to legalize killing abortion providers and the passage of a bill requiring a 72-hour wait and counseling discouraging abortion. In June 2011, a federal court overturned the undue burden of requiring humiliation of a pregnant woman at a prenatal help center. Nonetheless, on pain of life in prison, state law forced doctors to inform women of their relationship with the fetus and of the danger of suicide if they chose termination. Her speech propelled the abortion debate into 21st century parlance for both urban and rural women by demanding privacy and access to health care.

I come from Montana . . . There's one thing about the West that we know . . . We understand that people in places like South Dakota have to be real clear about who they listen to. Even though we're all here today, it is important that the people of South Dakota have this conversation.

It is unfortunate, quite honestly, that the same national activists who unsuccessfully attempted to ban abortion in South Dakota in 2006 are again working very, very hard to create a challenge to *Roe vs. Wade* that has implications for women's health and privacy in all 50 states. So let's not kid ourselves. The people behind the effort see South Dakota as the first step in a long-term campaign to mount a legal challenge to Roe.

As a story in today's *Wall Street Journal* reminded us, the people behind this ban see it as a direct challenge to *Roe* and that means that the presidential election is vitally important. Senator Barack Obama supports *Roe*. John McCain has called for *Roe's* reversal and has pledged to appoint justices to the Supreme Court who share his hostile views toward freedom and privacy.

So every American who values a woman's right to make personal, private decisions with her doctor has a stake in the outcome of this election in South Dakota. That's why we're working vigorously with NARAL's Pro-choice South Dakota and other state leaders gathered here today to say no again to government intrusion in personal, private decisions. My hope is this: that when South Dakotans have the conversation in their churches, across the backyard fence, around the dinner table about abortion care and the role of politicians and government in their personal, private decisions, they will again unequivocally say no to this ban.

Source: Keenan, Nancy. "Opposition to South Dakota Legal Ban on Abortion." C-SPAN, August 12, 2008. Available at: http://www.c-span.org/video/?280411-1/opposition-south-dakota-legal-ban-abortion.

KELLER, HELEN (1880–1968)

A revered activist and author, Helen Adams Keller overcame the barriers of deafness and blindness to become a pacifist orator. An Alabaman born with normal faculties in Tuscumbia on June 27, 1880, she was the third of the five children of Katherine "Kate" Adams and Arthur Henley Keller. A bout of scarlet fever and meningitis in late December 1881 robbed 19-month-old Helen of the senses of sight, sound, and smell.

In 1886, the family sought the advice of inventor Alexander Graham Bell, who directed them to experts in Boston at the Perkins Institution for the Blind. He determined that the child had superior intelligence. In-home instruction by Anne Mansfield Sullivan, the prize pupil of educator Michael Anagnos, began in March 1887. Through discipline and compassion, Sullivan enlightened Helen to 625 words imparted by a finger spelling code.

The teacher escorted Helen to New York in 1888 to interview with Anagnos at the Perkins Institution for the Deaf and, in May, to meet President Grover Cleveland at the White House. By age ten, Keller learned to speak by touching her teachers' lips, tongue, and throat and to read and write braille. For Anagnos, she composed a first short story, "The Frost King" (1891). In 1894, she compiled *Light in My Darkness* and, in October, sought advanced studies in New York City at the Wright-Humason School for the Deaf.

Humane Causes

In 1900, Keller entered the freshman class of Radcliffe College and aided the staff of the campus newspaper. Three years later, she wrote *The Story of My Life* (1903). With a diploma from Radcliffe and a new home in Wrentham shared with Sullivan, Keller promoted the Massachusetts Commission for the Blind and investigated the plight of the poor and unemployed in the lecture "Our Duties to the Blind" (1904).

At age 25, Keller became a socialist and joined the Industrial Workers of the World (IWW). She advocated women's rights at Harvard and began composing *The World I Live In* (1908). In Boston, she supported the Massachusetts Association for Promoting Interests of the Blind with the oration "Social Causes of Blindness" (1911). The *New York Call* published her 1912 essay "How I Became a Socialist," a radical alliance that surprised critics who preferred thinking of her as vulnerable.

With a solid background in publishing, Keller ventured into public oratory in February 1913 in Montclair, New Jersey, where blind children rushed to spell their names in her hand. After fostering female workers' rights in 1913 with "Why Men Need Woman Suffrage" and "New Vision for the Blind," she completed a lecture tour in 1914 to rally support for the handicapped and, in Toronto, to raise donations for the American Foundation for the Blind. In Sacramento, she honored striking California laborers with the address "Brutal Treatment of the Unemployed" (1914).

While living in Boston, Keller traveled to the 1915 San Francisco Exposition. Supporters formed Helen Keller International, a global effort to save the sight of the impoverished and disadvantaged in numerous African and Asian countries through medical treatment of cataracts, intestinal parasites, trachoma, river blindness, and diabetic retinopathy. In December 1915, she lectured delegates of a labor forum on "Menace of the Militarist Program," a warning similar in tone and direction to the antimilitarism of lecturer Emma Goldman.

An Agent of Peace

As a force for peace, in 1916, Keller delivered an antiviolence exhortation, "Strike Against War," to the Women's Peace Party at Carnegie Hall in New York and collected patriotic orations in the series *America First in Peace.* To the New York City Civic Club in 1918, Keller confronted conservatives with "What Is the IWW?"—a consortium that she identified with lumber camps, mills, mines, truck driving, and harvests. On December 31, 1920, she lifted spirits at the Rand School ball in New York City with a socialist salute, "Onward, Comrades!" Her anguish for famine in Siberia precipitated "Help Soviet Russia" (1921), which concluded with a prayer for courage and liberty.

Keller co-formed the American Civil Liberties Union and, in 1924, made a professional career of championing the blind. In 1925, Lion International in Cedar Point, Ohio, adopted her as spokeswoman for the visually impaired, particularly workers blinded in factory accidents. Her humanitarian addresses earned a meeting with President Calvin Coolidge. Keller balanced public appearances with the writing of *My Religion* (1927) and *Midstream: My Later Life at 49* (1929).

At Keller's promotion of braille with the World Council for the Blind, in 1932, the Royal Institute for the Blind in Great Britain standardized the alphabet for the visually impaired. She furthered her writing throughout the decade and, in 1933, submitted "Three Days to See" to *Atlantic Monthly.* While making 97 lectures in 39 cities of Japan in 1937, she acquired an Akita and introduced the dog breed in the United States as a guide for the sightless.

International fame from biographical movies increased Keller's range of charitable and altruistic works in 35 nations among the disabled. Traveling to Europe in 1945, she visited more hospital patients and victims of war. To 1,200 children in

Adelaide, Australia, in 1948, she reminded them of the value of struggle and perseverance, a concept she repeated in 1950 in Kentucky at the Lexington School for the Deaf and in 1951 to inmates of the Eye Hospital in Johannesburg, South Africa.

At the Sorbonne in Paris in 1953, Keller honored Louis Braille, the codifier of the touch alphabet. The next year at the National University of Mexico, she urged sacrifice on behalf of the handicapped who chose self-determination over charity. Her outreach to the Boston Jewish Club in 1952 reminded listeners that teachers of special needs students labored for low wages.

Keller greeted the blind at the University of Concepción, Chile, in 1953, and expressed Christian faith in a 1955 after-dinner address, "One of the Numberless Instruments in God's Hand." She honored her revered mentor with *Teacher—Anne Sullivan* (1955). A doctorate from Harvard in 1956 made Keller the first female honored by the university. She praised President Dwight D. Eisenhower in 1960 for using talking books to ease his rehabilitation from a heart attack.

After Keller suffered a debilitating stroke in 1961, she lived with housekeepers. From President Lyndon B. Johnson, she accepted the 1963 American Medal of Freedom. At home in Easton, northwest of Bridgeport, Connecticut, on June 1, 1968, she died in her sleep.

Reference

Berne, Emma Carlson, and Marie Hodge. *Helen Keller: Courage in Darkness*. New York: Sterling, 2009.

I WANT TO BE ADOPTED (EXCERPT) BY HELEN KELLER LIONS CLUBS INTERNATIONAL CONVENTION LIONS CONVENTION HALL, CEDAR POINT, OHIO JUNE 30, 1925

An advocate for the blind since 1924, Helen Keller of Tuscumbia, Alabama, nurtured charities for the handicapped and backed legislation protecting workers from factory accidents that endangered vision. As spokeswoman for the Lions Club initiative, she lectured on aid to the visually impaired and carried her message of hope to state legislatures and to efforts in Europe, Australia, Africa, and the Americas. Her backing of braille literature and volunteer readers and writers of letters preceded post–World War II visits to war veterans blinded in combat. She continued promoting aid to the blind for 37 years.

I suppose you have heard the legend that represents opportunity as a capricious lady who knocks at every door but once, and if the door isn't opened quickly, she passes on, never to return. And that is as it should be. Lovely, desirable ladies won't wait. You have to go out and grab 'em.

I am your opportunity. I am knocking at your door. I want to be adopted. The legend doesn't say what you are to do when several beautiful opportunities present themselves at the same door. I guess you have to choose the one you love best. I hope you will adopt me. I am the youngest here, and what I offer you is full of splendid opportunities for service.

The American Foundation for the Blind is only four years old. It grew out of the imperative needs of the blind, and was called into existence by the sightless themselves. It is national and international in scope and in importance. It represents the best and most enlightened thought on our subject that has been reached so far. Its object is to make the lives of the blind more worthwhile everywhere by increasing their economic value and giving them the joy of normal activity.

Try to imagine how you would feel if you were suddenly stricken blind today. Picture yourself stumbling and groping at noonday as in the night. Your work, your independence, gone. In that dark world, wouldn't you be glad if a friend took you by the hand and said, "Come with me and I will teach you how to do some of the things you used to do when you could see?" That is just the kind of friend the American Foundation is going to be to all the blind in this country if seeing people will give it the support it must have. . . .

The opportunity I bring to you, Lions, is this: To foster and sponsor the work of the American Foundation for the Blind. Will you not help me hasten the day when there shall be no preventable blindness; no little deaf, blind child untaught; no blind man or woman unaided? I appeal to you Lions, you who have your sight, your hearing, you who are strong and brave and kind. Will you not constitute yourselves Knights of the Blind in this crusade against darkness?

Source: Keller, Helen, "I Want to Be Adopted." June 30, 1925. Lions Clubs International. Accessed November 12, 2014. http://www.lionsclubs.org/EN/about-lions/mission-and-history/our-history/lions-history-hkspeech.php. With permission of media director Dana LaJoye. Reprinted by permission of the Lions Club International.

KELLEY, FLORENCE (1859–1932)

Labor investigator and advocate Florence Moltrop Kelley applied Quaker and Irish Protestant ideals to improving the lot of workers through state and federal government regulation. She was born in Philadelphia on September 12, 1859, the only surviving daughter of Caroline Bartram Bonsall and abolitionist William Darrah

Kelley. In girlhood, she absorbed the philanthropy of her great aunt, school administrator Sarah Pugh.

Kelley received home training by her father and read freely from his books. She followed him through glass factories and learned about the hard labors of children who had no opportunity to attend school. The scenarios fueled her lifetime dedication to correcting unjust labor laws.

Despite lengthy recuperation from diphtheria, in 1882, Kelley completed a degree from Cornell University. After rejection at the University of Pennsylvania and Oxford, in 1883, she toured Europe and enrolled in politics, law, and economics at the University of Zurich. In addition to promoting civil rights for women and blacks for the Intercollegiate Socialist Society, she translated Friedrich Engels's German polemical *The Condition of the Working Class in England* (1844), a classic economic treatise on the source of social ills.

In June 1884, Kelley married physician Lazare Wischnewetzky. After ending her Zurich studies in 1886, she began building public-speaking skills in May 1887 with an address to the New York Association of Collegiate Alumnae on "The Need of Theoretical Preparation for Philanthropic Work," which acknowledged the role of the caste system in furthering women's charitable volunteerism. On a more egalitarian level, at Chicago's All Souls Unitarian Church, her assertive grace impressed journalists reporting her denunciation of sweatshops. The address proposed consumer boycotts to discourage worker exploitation.

Facts and Goals

After divorcing her husband and moving to Chicago, Kelley opened an employment agency at Hull House, Jane Addams's settlement project in the Nineteenth Ward, and promoted women's education and a complaint system for directing garbage problems to the city council. As an agent of the Illinois State Bureau of Labor Statistics, Kelley tabulated and charted tenement occupancy by ethnicity and income. For the Illinois General Assembly, in 1892, she analyzed "The Sweating System of Chicago," a topic that permeated her oratory for three decades.

To enhance her knowledge, in 1893, Kelley entered Northwestern University School of Law and passed the bar the next year. Governor John Peter Altgeld appointed her the first Illinois state inspector of 66,000 factories. The post enabled her to research labor conditions for children under 13 and to further the success of Hull House.

Kelley's informative talk "The Relation of Women to Municipal Reform" (1894) linked female empowerment directly to their impact on urban improvements. While preparing a case profile of the 1894 smallpox epidemic, she protested lax quarantines, contagion in hospitals, and high infant mortality. To improve prosecution of sweatshop lawbreakers, in 1895, she initiated a career teaching law and literacy. She protested the overturning of state protective laws for women by attorney Levy Mayer, a challenger representing profiteers of the Illinois Manufacturers Association.

As the suffrage movement modernized, Kelley contributed to academic methods of collecting statistics for use in sociological debate and presentations at congressional hearings. Late in the 19th century, her initiatives jelled into a single crusade uniting labor and the economy with family welfare. Her solution to opposition appeared in the speeches "The Working Child" (1896), "The Object of the Labor Movement" (1898), and "Working Woman's Need of the Ballot," delivered to the 1898 assembly of the National American Woman Suffrage Association (NAWSA) in Washington, D.C.

Kelley and Child Welfare

Kelley moved in 1899 to the Henry Street settlement project begun in New York City by nurse Lillian Wald. Kelley fought sweatshop commerce by co-establishing the National Consumers League (NCL), which aimed to limit workday hours for women and children and to standardize a minimum wage. The NCL pioneered clothing labels and organized boycotts of substandard goods. Her activism involved addresses to unions, colleges, and women's clubs, particularly "Persuasion or Responsibility" (1900), an exposé of a decline in literacy among female workers.

In a series of lectures on Christian ethics, on November 16, 1904, Kelley queried members of the Park Avenue Methodist Episcopal Church on "What Shall We Do for Children Who Work for Us?" Her speech suggested a centralized agency superintending child welfare and offering such essentials as immunization and juvenile courts.

To a rabbinic symposium in Portland, Oregon, in July 1905, Kelley presented "The Child and Problems of Child Life," followed 10 days later in Philadelphia by "Child Labor and Women's Suffrage," a common strand of her oratory. To NAWSA in 1906, she shamed the U.S. government for allowing the child welfare standards to fall below those of England, Germany, France, Switzerland, Holland, and Scandinavia.

By producing data on the physical and emotional damage of long workdays, in 1907, Kelley pressed state legislators for a minimum wage and introduced the U.S. Supreme Court to sociological research. In 1907 and 1908, she informed NAWSA assemblies on the topics "Municipal Housekeeping" and "Laws for Women and Wage Earners," in which she referred to the family's disempowerment as a national cancer. She continued raising social consciousness at New York City's Church of the Ascension on January 23, 1910, with an entreaty entitled "Child Labor." At Kansas City, Missouri, on November 8, 1911, she specified $8 as a reasonable minimum wage for women.

In Cleveland at the 1912 National Conference of Charities and Correction, Kelley again endorsed the minimum wage and briefly condemned forced prison labor. As head of the National Child Labor Committee, in 1912, she co-initiated the U.S.

Children's Bureau, the only federal agency managed by women. On behalf of the National Association for the Advancement of Colored People, in 1913, she crusaded against disproportionate spending on white pupils in Southern schools. On April 26, 1913, she informed students and professors at Wellesley College on the sources and methods of her analysis of minimum wage issues.

Kelley's travels brought sociological concepts across the East to the Midwest. On May 14, 1916, she spoke to the First Congregational Church of Indianapolis on "The Social Conscience," an oration announcing the spread of the consumers' league to France, Germany, and Switzerland. In 1917, she crusaded for a 50 percent wage hike for overtime work. Her 1920 Thanksgiving message praised the results of minimum and overtime wages.

Following World War II, Kelley co-formed the Women's International League for Peace and Freedom, a movement for passive resistance to armed conflict. Her speech "The Women's Congress at Vienna" (1921) welcomed delegates from 28 countries and preceded her reports on factory laws and sweatshop suppression. Her labors for children yielded health and wellness advances federalized under the 1921 Maternity and Infancy Protection Act.

Kelley defended industrial and labor initiatives with statistics attesting to progress on behalf of child protection and worker health and education. She died in Germantown, Pennsylvania, on February 17, 1932. Her philosophy of woman and child safety influenced President Franklin D. Roosevelt's New Deal.

See Also: Addams, Jane; Anderson, Mary; Wald, Lillian.

Reference

Recchiuti, John Louis. *Civic Engagement: Social Science and Progressive-Era Reform in New York City*. Philadelphia: University of Pennsylvania Press, 2007.

WORKING WOMAN'S NEED OF THE BALLOT (EXCERPT) BY FLORENCE KELLEY NATIONAL AMERICAN WOMAN SUFFRAGE ASSOCIATION CHURCH OF OUR FATHER, WASHINGTON, D.C. FEBRUARY 15, 1898

One of the early demographers and statisticians of social reform, attorney and labor theorist Florence Kelley of Philadelphia, Illinois's first factory inspector, compiled details on female empowerment as an element of municipal and welfare reform. She applied her doctrine of female equality to New York City's Henry Street settlement and fought exploitive labor practices that turned women into unhealthy drudges working in confines and living hand to mouth.

. . . The lack of the ballot places the wage-earning woman upon a level of irresponsibility compared with her enfranchised fellow workingman. By impairing her standing in the community the general rating of her value as a human being, and consequently as a worker, is lowered. In order to be rated as good as a good man in the field of her earnings, she must show herself better than he. She must be more steady or more trustworthy or more skilled or more cheap in order to have the same chance of employment. Thus, while women are accused of lowering wages, might they not justly reply that it is only by conceding something from the pay which they would gladly claim, that they can hold their own in the market, so long as they labor under the disadvantage of disfranchisement?

Finally, the very fact that women now form about one-fifth of the employees in manufacture and commerce in this country has opened a vast field of industrial legislation directly affecting women as wage earners. The courts in some of the states, notably in Illinois, are taking the position that women cannot be treated as a class apart and legislated for by themselves, as has been done in the factory laws of England and on the continent of Europe, but must abide by that universal freedom of contract which characterizes labor in the United States. This renders the situation of the workingwoman absolutely anomalous. On the one hand, she is cut off from the protection awarded to her sisters abroad. On the other, she has no such power to defend her interests at the polls, as is the heritage of her brothers at home. This position is untenable, and there can be no pause in the agitation for full political power and responsibility until these are granted to all the women of the nation.

Source: Kelley, Florence. "Working Woman's Need of the Ballot." In *The History of Woman Suffrage.* Vol. IV. Indianapolis: Hollenbeck Press, 1902, 305–307.

KESTNER, BONNIE (1952–)

A master swimmer and pioneer of women's college athletics, Bonnie Kay Jackson Kestner coached swimming, developed a successful collegiate swimming program, and introduced concepts of female athleticism, health, and nutrition in the classroom. She was born in Phoenix, Arizona, on February 26, 1952, to Priscilla Rubens and Kermit Hatfield Jackson. She grew up on Long Island with three siblings—Wendy, Nan, and Bill Jackson—and, in her mid-teens, coached summer league teams.

Kestner's maternal grandmother taught her piano, but Bonnie preferred tennis and diving, which she learned at age 12 during a Florida vacation. In her junior high and high school years, she swam competitively and coached summer league teams. A strong athlete at Cold Spring Harbor High School in Long Island, she accepted Coach Frank Ranhofer's advice to apply to Yale University.

In 1970, the year after the university admitted women, Kestner entered Yale Divinity School. She wanted a competitive sports experience as well as preparation for Christian ministry. Coach Phil Moriarty invited her to be the first female to train with the men's swimming and diving teams, where she practiced bodybuilding by swimming laps.

Kestner sang in the Yale Glee Club, played tennis, and, for one semester, excelled on Yale's women's junior varsity tennis team. She coached the Yale Swim Club in her senior year and won the Connecticut Amateur Athletic Union Championship title in the 100-yard butterfly, scoring at the New England and Eastern Intercollegiate Championships and representing Yale at two Association for Intercollegiate Athletics for Women National Championships. For her leadership abilities, in 1973, she captained the university's first women's varsity swim team. In March 1974, she pushed the women's diving and swimming team to varsity level. For the International Swimming Hall of Fame, she posed at the Moriarty backstroke starting block.

Building a Career

Kestner's senior research on the history of swimming at Yale yielded a paper on the training techniques of master coach Robert Kiphuth, publisher of *Swimming World Magazine* and recipient of the Presidential Medal of Freedom. For two years, she coached Yale's swimmers while completing a BA. She converted to Christianity and pursued a master's degree in philosophy and religion from Yale in 1974 and 1977.

Because of newfound faith, Kestner envisioned further study in counseling or social work. She saw teaching and coaching as a context for ministry and felt called to explore spirituality through sports. In 1977, she received more advice from Moriarty, who was aiding Sweet Briar College in the building of a pool, a six-lane, 25-meter competitive pool and natatorium. Thinking Sweet Briar would benefit from hiring a female swim coach and aquatics director, he encouraged her to apply for the position.

Kestner joined the Sweet Briar faculty as teacher of nutrition and health counseling in the fall of 1977 and introduced the first swim team to five hard months of training. By February 1978, she ended team practices at a lake, introduced pool training, and finished the year undefeated with the strongest performance in long-distance events and diving. Her first collegiate team surprised many by winning the small college swimming and diving championship. In a summary for the alumnae magazine, she referred to her introduction to teaching as a "Cinderella year" (Jackson 1978, 5).

In the dedication of two books of verse, *Toweling Off* and *Tides Out*, Moriarty honored Kestner for setting standards of athleticism and camaraderie. From entry-level coach, she advanced to aquatics director. She chaired the athletic and physical education department and served as head coach from 1977 to 1987. With the aid of Coach Jason Gallaher, she founded the Vixen diving and swimming program. The Vixens won the 1978 Virginia small college swim championship.

In 1979, Kestner wed World War II veteran and civil engineer Charles Culver "Chuck" Kestner, the campus building director and designer of the Sweet Briar pool. She became the stepmother of Charles's children, Charles Wiley and Kristen Kestner, and made their home in Amherst, Virginia. She continued directing aquatics and physical education and coaching swimming during her first pregnancy.

Kestner promoted swimming as relaxation and exercise for toning muscles and building cardiac strength and respiratory endurance. The aquatic offerings of the 10-member staff of two professors, five assistant professors, and three instructors included beginning diving, beginning and intermediate swimming, synchronized swimming, adapted aquatics for the handicapped, swim-for-fitness, swimnastics and water games, sub-varsity and varsity swimming and diving, advanced lifesaving, and water safety instruction. In addition, her department offered fitness, running, weight training, ski conditioning, lacrosse, tennis, two levels of ballet, folk dance, and beginning, intermediate, and advanced dance.

During Kestner's service to the National Collegiate Athletic Association (NCAA) Swimming and Diving Committee, the Sweet Briar team won the 1980 regional competition. To upgrade her skills, she attended the American Swimming Coaches Association Mini School and the September 1980 World Coaches Clinic in Chicago. Her students thrived during 1983, 1984, and 1986 by capturing the Old Dominion Athletic Conference (ODAC) swim championship, which included a swimmer of the year trophy and three coach of the year titles. Three Sweet Briar swimmers achieved Division III national finals and All-America recognition. Two others received Honorable Mention All-America.

To benefit the team on projects and training trips, in 1984, parents of a Sweet Briar swim team member established the Bonnie Jackson Kestner Swimming and Diving Fund to be disbursed at the coach's discretion. After subsequent postgraduate training, in 1985, she earned a master of education degree in physical education at the University of Virginia, where she participated on the varsity swim team and sang in the chorus. Simultaneously, she became the first woman to chair the ODAC Conference.

In addition to teaching and sports, Kestner studied organ in Lynchburg for nine years. After Charles Kestner's retirement, for the Virginia Masters Swim in 1997, she extended her swimming career by joining other women in their upper forties in the 100- and 200-meter backstroke and 800-meter freestyle. She won the 200-meter butterfly and the 400-meter individual medley.

Words of Wisdom

In recognition of women's sports, at Yale's Pioneers and Competitors awards ceremony on April 10, 1999, Kestner addressed the audience on "Parenting and the Future Athlete." Using her children Kristen and Wiley as examples, she lectured parents on the necessity of committing to their children's activities, whatever they chose. She proposed that adults model fairness and sportsmanship and maintain upbeat, realistic attitudes toward childhood performances.

More honoraria followed Kestner's teaching career with a 2002 coach of the year for improving athletes through consistent training and building self-esteem. Her performance at the Virginia Master Swim in 2002 included the 100-meter butterfly, the 200-meter backstroke and the 200-meter individual medley, and the 500-meter freestyle. Involvement in adult competition guided her planning for vigorous activity after retirement from the Sweet Briar staff.

In looking back at her pupils, Kestner took pride in the 2003 success of a varsity swimmer as valedictorian, the first Sweet Briar NCAA postgraduate scholar, and a Presidential Medalist. Because of Kestner's stress on learning, in June 2003, the team achieved a 3.11 grade point average. Their high achievement earned an Academic All-American ranking from the College Swimming Coaches Association of America.

To avoid the caustic damage of chlorine on skin, hair, and thyroid, in 2010, Kestner began swimming regularly in Boathouse Lake. To mentor students, she set an example of a natural and holistic lifestyle by researching alternative medicine and advising on holistic wellness. She promoted a healthful lifestyle with classes on sleep, sobriety, exercise and fitness, organic diet, and environmental science. She predicted that Sweet Briar would eventually build a holistic wellness center.

At a ceremony at the Prothro Natatorium in early November 2013, Kestner retired as assistant professor from 37 years of instruction in physical education and water sports. In addition to a gift T-shirt autographed by swim team members, she treasured a final win over Ferrum College and a team member's breaking of the 400-meter freestyle record at Sweet Briar. Student planners of the event honored her nutritional program by replacing cheese and cookies with carrots, fruit, nuts, whole grain crackers, olive tapenade, and hummus. At the Spring 2014 Varsity Sports Awards Ceremony, the department presented her a canvas depicting her first and last Sweet Briar teams and the inscription "Bonnie Kestner, Coach, Colleague, Professor, Mentor, 1977–2014."

Reference

Jackson, Bonnie. "We Don't Mess Around." *Sweet Briar Alumnae Magazine* (1978): 4–5.

KINCAID, JAMAICA (1949–)

A spokeswoman for eastern Caribbean anticolonialism, feminist author and teacher Jamaica Kincaid incorporates the greater picture of human oppression. She was born of Afro-Carib-Scots heritage on May 25, 1949, and grew up in St. John, Antigua, under the birth name Elaine Cynthia Potter Richardson. She epitomized the cultural struggle of black West Indians like her father, illiterate taxi-driver and chauffeur Roderick Nathaniel Potter, and her mother, Annie Victoria Richardson Drew.

Ignored by her father, Kincaid lived the need and impotence common to black islanders. She came of age under the care of her mother and stepfather, David Drew, and a maternal grandmother who practiced obeah. Lacking water, sewage, and electricity, Kincaid learned to haul water from a community spigot, and roasted fish, meat, breadfruit, and christophine (chayote) over a coal pot.

A prodigy at a Moravian preschool, Kincaid flourished at history and botany. In 1955, she won a scholarship to the Princess Margaret School. At the Antiguan Girls School, she studied a syllabus extolling the British Empire and ignoring Caribbean bondage and colonialism. After school, she apprenticed with a seamstress and, on Thursdays, read the *London Times* at the city library.

Kincaid studied table setting in Brownie Scout meetings and shoplifted her favorite books. She clashed with her mother over reading sessions under the house rather than completing her chores. Kincaid raged at beatings from her mother for neglecting home and tending brothers Devon "Sugar," Joseph, and Dalma and protested the forced withdrawal from school in 1964. In retaliation, her mother set the home library aflame.

At 16, Kincaid accepted au pair work for the Mason family in Scarsdale, New York, an affluent white community, and sent none of her wages to her parents. Free of control, she drank and indulged in sex, marijuana, and drugs. In January 1966, she completed a GED and took night courses in White Plains at Westchester Community College while earning tuition with odd jobs filing, modeling, and singing with a backup group. While living in New York in 1974, she wrote 85 essays on rock music and art for a *New Yorker* column, "Talk of the Town," and submitted articles to *Harper's*, *Ms.*, *Village Voice*, *Glamour*, *Mademoiselle*, *Paris Review*, and *Rolling Stone*.

While Antiguans slid further into poverty and squalor during the departure of the British, in January 1977, Kincaid personalized a column on the island's servile class. She collected vignettes for an anthology, *At the Bottom of the River*, the first publication in which she revealed her Caribbean roots. In 1979, she wed Jewish composer Allen Shawn, father of their two children, Annie and Harold. In 1983, she began writing a classic coming of age novel, *Annie John* (1985), and serialized it in the *New Yorker*. The novel won a *Booklist* best young adult book of 1985, an Anisfield-Wolf Book Award, a Stanford University model of culture, and a Lila Wallace-Reader's Digest commendation.

Kincaid and her husband moved to Vermont to accept teaching posts at Bennington College. In disgust at Antiguans' fawning over British royalty, she issued *A Small Place* (1988), a postcolonial harangue detailing racial exploitation of West Indians. She began writing *Lucy* (1991), a feminist novella, and, following travel to Paris and London, composed "Seeing England for the First Time." After converting to Judaism, she reflected on African travel in "Out of Kenya" for the *New York Times*.

From 1993 to 1995, Kincaid made more public presentations and readings and expanded her range with *The Autobiography of My Mother* (1996), which won a Lannan Literary Award for insights into mother hunger and mother-daughter antipathies. After her brother's death from AIDs, she published *My Brother* in 1997, which condemned her bisexual sibling Devon for indulging in intimacy after his infection.

With *Mr. Potter* (1999), Kincaid returned to the kinship crucible to reflect on serial womanizers. For Temple Beth El, she endorsed a capital campaign and boosted the collection by 180 percent by delivering speeches on Jewish womanhood. At the University of Minnesota in 2001, she discussed an unsettling statelessness that haunted her. In 2002, she extended her Asian botanical studies with a hike of the Himalayas in Nepal and surprised audiences by addressing the issue of transplantation of native food plants, flowers, and trees to the gardens of imperialists.

In 2002, Kincaid divorced her husband and used her Bennington base to extend lectures and gardening articles for *Architectural Digest*. Her honors increased with a 2004 membership in the American Academy of Arts and Letters. On February 11, 2008, at the University of North Carolina at Wilmington, she delivered the speech "Coming of Age in a Small Place," which incriminated the British for enslaving Antiguans. Two weeks later, she spoke at Northwestern University on creative writing. In February 2015, she lectured at Indiana University on "Reading and Growing Up under Colonial Rule," a retrospect on her girlhood. To the May 2015 graduating class at Brandeis, she advised, "Don't Be afraid to Wonder Who You Are."

Reference

Bouson, J. Brooks. *Jamaica Kincaid: Writing Memory, Writing Back to the Mother*. Albany: State University of New York Press, 2005.

KINGSLEY, BATHSHEBA (?–1748)

A flamboyant evangelist in an era of radical revivalism in the Connecticut Valley, Bathsheba Kingsley incurred the remonstrance of the Puritan hierarchy, which attempted to silence her preaching. Scant information about her family indicates that she lived on 265 acres, which her husband, Hains Kingsley, purchased in 1732 on Little River Road at Westfield in south central Massachusetts. He outlived her by two years and took as his second wife a widow, Susanna Kendall Remington.

During the colonial "Great Awakening" of 1740, on receipt of salvation from damnation, Kingsley and other Congregationalist women rejoiced, prayed aloud, convulsed, and swooned with religious fervor. In a spiritual passion, in October 1741, she claimed to have received a divine revelation through what she described as cyclical impulses, impressions, imaginings, and visions. She repented and committed herself to God. As one of a dozen colonial "sisters in Christ," she accepted a spiritual duty to spread Congregationalist precepts to others to rescue them from hellfire.

A Self-Appointed Messenger

In her capacity as God's agent, Kingsley circumvented male control. Mirroring the open-air revivals held by preacher George Whitefield in 1740, she became a circuit rider visiting Massachusetts settlements on her husband's or their neighbor's horse. In town squares, she preached spontaneous sermons to onlookers. In one-on-one meetings, she singled out the wicked for their sins. She charged colonists to learn the whole truth about Christian salvation and not to rely on pulpit ministers to guide them on a moral path.

In a period of public hysteria and fear of the devil, Kingsley's offenses violated a gendered colonial order. She defied male familial control by protesting her husband's verbal and physical assaults. With unwarranted authority, she wished him a quick journey to hell. In a reversal of socioreligious protocol, she ordered ministers to remain silent while she disclosed God's intuitive message to her, a visitation claimed the previous century by Boston evangelist Anne Hutchinson.

Because of Kingsley's gender and her lack of theological training and official ordination, the religious community censured her for taking a horse on the Sabbath. On a wifely level, critics charged her with galloping on a juggernaut crusade without her husband's permission. She confessed to spontaneous enthusiasm for preaching, an experience that transcended gender in the style of Deborah, Anna, Phebe, and other scriptural examples.

Sixteen months later on February 15, 1743, Kingsley's husband requested that the church council intervene in the bizarre behavior of his wayward wife. Her

Harvard-educated pastor, 27-year-old John Ballantine, convened an ecclesiastical committee at the Kingsley home to chide and punish Bathsheba for continuing her revival orations. During a council session ending on February 17, she confounded the men with claims of her communion with the Almighty and her receipt of divine prophecy. She declared herself the appropriate evangelist to further the Christian ministry to the Massachusetts Bay Colony by revealing a higher truth than that expounded by pulpit preachers.

Silencing the Exhorter

A New Light theologian on a visit from Northampton, Massachusetts, Jonathan Edwards, the moderate author of *Thoughts on the Revival in New England* (1741), affirmed that God spoke to attendees through revivals, but he considered Kingsley delusional for claiming spiritual authority. He implied that females were unworthy of a true divine ecstasy because of innate vapidity of body and mind. In response to Kingsley's criticism of the clergy, he denounced her prediction that doom awaited failed ministers. He supported the primacy of the ordained clergy in a theocracy by declaring common citizens unfit for judging their pastors.

Edwards rebuked Kingsley as a brawler, a shameless, immodest woman devoid of the "goodwife's" virtues of subservience and humility. The church council verified her husband's right to discipline her, but members exhorted him to rely on kindness and forbearance and to forego striking his wife. The consortium suggested that he allow his wife to spread Christian fervor informally to others. Instead of scolding neighbors, she should visit the homes of fellow colonists in Westfield and surrounding towns to discuss Christian faith and behavior with wisdom and humility.

Edwards fostered Kingsley's scriptural studies and teachings to women's groups but denied her right to speak to assemblies composed of male and female attendees. Because she freed herself of the housewife's conventional duties and adopted an evangelical career, Edwards labeled her a tool of Satan. He stopped short of excommunicating her from the church and, by way of rehabilitation, ordered her to respect female proprieties by staying home and ceasing criticism of her husband.

In later reflection on the Kingsley case, Edwards feared for the nuclear family if housewives roamed the streets shrieking and "hallooing." He and other male ministers generalized that public impropriety could subvert the Great Awakening and mushroom into wantonness and prostitution. Nonetheless, Kingsley continued circuit riding, even after the church barred her from Holy Communion. She died on October 30, 1748.

See Also: Hutchinson, Anne.

Reference

Keller, Rosemary Skinner, and Marie Cantlon, eds. *Encyclopedia of Women and Religion in North America.* Bloomington: Indiana University Press, 2006.

KINGSOLVER, BARBARA (1955–)

A defender of peace and First Amendment rights, ecofeminist Barbara Kingsolver wields fiction, verse, and polemics as antidotes to war and pollution. Born on April 8, 1955, in Annapolis, Maryland, to naturalist Virginia Lee "Ginny" Henry and naval physician Wendell R. Kingsolver, she and siblings Robert and Ann came of age during free observation of the outdoors in Carlisle, Kentucky. From early childhood, she loved hearing books read aloud and blossomed at storytelling.

In the tobacco-growing part of Appalachia, Kingsolver developed a moral consciousness and worked out personal ethics in her diary. In 1962, she lived the life of the outsider in Léopoldville, Congo, while her parents served a public health mission. Overseas duty resumed in 1967, when she lived near a convent hospital in St. Lucia and learned the rudiments of obeah. Her evolving teen conscience challenged the Vietnam War and blamed the Reagan administration for fostering Nicaragua's political chaos.

In 1969, Kingsolver enrolled at Nicholas County High School and cultivated a love of fiction while cataloging library books. Reading affirmed her observations about Appalachia's haves and have-nots. On entry to summer school at the University of Kentucky in Lexington, she filled in educational gaps and began her hippie phase. On a music scholarship in 1973, she joined the BFA program at DePauw University to study keyboard composition and theory and internalized debate on feminism and abortion rights by reading the polemics of Gloria Steinem and Betty Friedan.

At a pivotal point in Kingsolver's understanding, she suffered rape in 1974 and sank into depression. Considerable rethinking turned her away from the arts to a BS in zoology and a minor in English and to personal analysis of international politics. She graduated magna cum laude and Phi Beta Kappa. From 1977 to 1979, she traveled Athens, Paris, and Beaurieux, France, on pickup jobs as a domestic, copy editor, archeologist, lab researcher, and radiation technician.

On a jaunt from Carlisle, Kentucky, to Tucson, Arizona, in 1979, Kingsolver embraced the biota of the Sonora Desert. At the University of Arizona, she earned an MS in animal behavior by researching a thesis on termites while secretly penning verse in the margins of her science notebooks. She enrolled in a PhD program but withdrew to assist in a physiology project. For five years, she wrote technical reports for the Arid Lands Institute.

Writing as a Career

Kingsolver began submitting articles and stories to magazines and issued a travel piece in *Architectural Digest* and *New York Times Magazine* and scientific essays in *Economic Botany* and *Biomass*. Winning short fiction in the Phoenix *New Times* initiated her professional career. Her résumé contained entries from *Cosmopolitan*, *Denver Post*, *Lexington Herald-Leader*, *Los Angeles Times Magazine*, *Mademoiselle*, *McCall's*, *The Nation*, *Natural History*, *Redbook*, and *Smithsonian*. She began composing advocacy pieces on human rights violations in Central America and nuclear infractions at the Palo Verde Nuclear Plant.

In 1985, Kingsolver wed Joseph "Joe" Hoffmann, a college chemistry teacher and expert on birdsong. At their Tucson farm, she planted vegetables, flowers, and fruit and raised rare Bourbon Red turkeys. While daughter Camille played with Tohono O'odham and Yaqui children, Barbara hiked and joined a Southwestern version of the Underground Railroad, which funneled escapees north from intimidation and torture in Chile, El Salvador, and Guatemala.

While awaiting the birth of her first child, Camille Hoffmann, Kingsolver covered a labor strike in Kentucky for the *Progressive* and earned commendation from the Arizona Press Club. By night, she held her typewriter on her knees and completed "Rose-Johnny" (1987), a story of an androgynous outsider for the *Virginia Quarterly*. Her first novel, *The Bean Trees* (1988), won the Enoch Pratt Library Youth-to-Youth Books Award, an American Library Association Notable Book, and a New York Times Notable Book.

In November 1988, Kingsolver returned to muckraking journalism to report on a 1983 miners' strike at the Phelps Dodge Copper Corporation. The text focused on the courage of Latinas and female Indians during collective bargaining. The coverage earned a commendation from the U.N. National Council of Women of the United States.

In 1990, Kingsolver cloaked her distaste for the Reagan administration in *Animal Dreams*, a Southwestern novel featuring Latinas who fight pollution from a copper mine. The work achieved an Edward Abbey Award for Ecofiction, American Library Association Notable Book and Best Book for Young Adults, Pen/USA West Fiction Award, Arizona Library Association Book of the Year, and *New York Times* Notable Book. By reading missionary journals, political handbooks, the Kikongo-French dictionary, and popular magazines from the mid-20th century, she began researching *The Poisonwood Bible*, a complex political allegory examining postcolonial turmoil in the former Belgian Congo. During the writing, in 1991, she protested U.S. involvement in the Persian Gulf War for the sake of the oil industry. Throughout U.S. bombing of Baghdad, she toured Hiroshima, Japan, and exiled herself to the Canary Islands at Tenerife, where residents welcomed Camille.

In the midst of a book tour and marital separation, Kingsolver had to secure royalty rights to her works. She delivered an address on writing techniques at the June 1993 American Booksellers Convention in Miami, where she promoted literacy and free libraries. To research more impressions for her African novel, she spent June 1993 in Benin and completed *Pigs in Heaven* (1993), which the *Los Angeles Times*, National Cowboy Hall of Fame, Mountains and Plains Booksellers, and Western Heritage Museum in Oklahoma City honored.

Kingsolver enlarged her connection with the reading public by scheduling creative writing seminars and teaching at Emory & Henry College. When she delivered a commencement address, "As Little Advice as Possible," to the class of 1994 at DePauw, she reflected on her own naïveté at age 22. She began a relationship with avian environmentalist Steven L. Hopp and married him in 1994. The couple and Camille drove from Tucson to Kentucky each summer to enjoy a mountain respite.

Kingsolver's nature love permeated *High Tide in Tucson: Essays from Now and Never* (1995), another award winner. The birth of Lily Hopp in July 1996 preceded Kingsolver's 1997 Tucson appearance to underwrite the rescue of traditional crops for Native Seeds/SEARCH. At the issuance of *The Poisonwood Bible* (1998), the historical fiction achieved the National Book Prize of South Africa and citations from the *Los Angeles Times*, *New York Times*, *Village Voice*, American Booksellers, and the Oprah Book Club.

In 1999, Kingsolver increased her platform oratory at the North Cascades Institute, University of Arizona, and the Journalists Workshop. She lashed out at the post-Columbine world for glorifying guns as solutions to problems and urged families to strip their homes of representations of killing on television, movies, video games, CDs, books, and toys. With *Prodigal Summer* (2000), she agreed to multiple interviews and readings at bookstores. Her work won a Pulitzer Prize nomination, an American Science and Nature Writing citation, a Kentucky Governor's Award in the Arts, and a 2000 National Humanities Medal for nurturing a peace-loving, humane world.

Celebrity and Philanthropist

Honoraria provided Kingsolver with funds for philanthropy to support Environmental Defense, Habitat for Humanity, Heifer International, and Physicians for Social Responsibility as well as California's San Dieguito River Project, Michigan's Huron River Watershed Council, the Washington State Environmental Learning Center, and community reading and literacy programs. In a pacifist crusade, in 2001, she attacked the Bush administration in print for fighting Arabs for oil and continued writing op-ed pieces against vengeful global conflicts. She compiled *Small Wonder* (2002), a collection of essays that opened with a request for a smaller human footprint on Earth. The book received the annual Nautilus Award for supporting social change.

With ads in the *Arizona Republic*, in March 2002, Kingsolver opposed drilling in the Arctic National Wildlife Refuge. She condemned the post-Taliban war in Afghanistan and, in 2003, joined Not in Our Name, a pacifist push against pro-war Middle East policies. Her name attached to efforts by the Women's International League for Peace and Freedom and Earth Day Award. Her book *Animal, Vegetable, Miracle: A Year of Food Life* (2007) mused on extreme idealism underlying self-sustaining communes and on locavore diets free from chemical preservatives and artificial colorants. For the historical novel *The Lacuna* (2009), she won the Orange Prize for her reprise of the McCarthy persecution of suspected Communists.

In May 2008, Kingsolver delivered the graduation address "How to Be Hopeful" to seniors at Duke University. She informed the audience that each generation produced its own truths, for example, the death of a carbon-based economy and internal combustion engines. In 2015, *Time* magazine featured *The Bean Trees* and *Pigs in Heaven* among books that enriched readers. At Sea Isle City, New Jersey, in September 2015, she addressed library patrons on the dangers of climate change.

See Also: Friedan, Betty; Steinem, Gloria.

Reference

Austenfeld, Thomas. *Critical Insights: Barbara Kingsolver.* Pasadena, CA: Salem, 2010.

KOEDT, ANNE (1941–)

Artist, set designer, and writer Anne Koedt initiated feminist philosophy on coitus and orgasmic sex as essentials of women's liberation from patriarchal exploitation. The daughter of architect Bobs Koedt and Inger Peschcke-Koedt, World War II resistance fighters against Nazi invaders, she was born in 1941 near Copenhagen, Denmark. Her father, a photographer, made fake passports for Jews in danger of deportation and smuggled them from hiding places in the family basement by boat to Sweden.

A decade later, when the family immigrated to Palo Alto, California, Koedt developed a radical, socialist agenda and joined the leftist campus group Students for a Democratic Society. Her father, who suffered from depression and seizures, committed suicide. With visionaries Shulamith Firestone, Kate Millett, Ellen Willis, Kathie Amatniek, and Robin Morgan, in 1967, Koedt co-formed New York Radical Women and wrote some of its first monographs. She composed "Women in the Radical Movement" (1969), an address on February 17, 1968, to a radical conference at the Free University in New York. Koedt joined Firestone in the "Stanton-Anthony Brigade," a tribute to 19th-century suffragist leaders. The group marched with a coffin swathed in a banner proclaiming "The Death of Traditional Womanhood" and identified with females from history.

In her soft-spoken style, on March 24, 1968, Koedt invigorated an abortion repeal protest group supporting the Hempstead, Long Island, Parents' Aid Society, which delivered birth control by van. She explained how personal problems generated a political stand-off and declared a colonial truism—that "one cannot achieve equality for some members of one's group while the rest are not free" (Koedt 1968, 28). The broad-based analysis revisited the American, Russian, and Black revolutions in Marxist terms and challenged women to demand not just economic change, but a complete shift in social attitudes toward females.

After study of two seminal works—*Sexual Behavior in the Human Female* (1953), Alfred Kinsey's research into human sexuality, and of *Human Sexual Response* (1966), a treatise by William Masters and Virginia E. Johnson—Koedt concluded that clumsy heterosexual mating oppressed women by concealing that clitoral stimulation could result from female-to-female coupling. In June 1968, she published in the journal-anthology *Notes from the First Year* the classic essay "The Myth of the Vaginal Orgasm," an exposé of sexist misinformation about vaginal sensitivity.

To introduce women to the enjoyment of sex, Koedt called for new guidelines on perceptions of female anatomy through exploration and discovery and on women's role in coitus. By repudiating Sigmund Freud's psychoanalytic theories of frigidity and clitoral orgasm, she exposed the validation of men's sexuality as the norm and women's as dependent or secondary. Her text directed women to stop feeling guilty for failure to enjoy marital intimacy and to take responsibility for their own sexual satisfaction.

Defiant Feminism

After joining Firestone and 150 others at a Thanksgiving planning session at the Lake Villa YWCA camp outside Chicago, Koedt directed a sex workshop and helped to outline the "anti-inauguration" of Richard Nixon for January 20, 1969. The freethinkers organized subsequent protest groups, beginning in the spring of 1969 with the New York Radical Feminists. Members advocated a return to matriarchy and, in September 1969, defied male tyranny by picketing New York's Marriage License Bureau.

In December 1969, Koedt influenced second wave liberationists with the manifesto "Politics of the Ego," a coauthored diatribe against arbitrary sex roles, but she chose discourse over violence. At the March 18, 1970, sit-in of 100 feminists at the editorial offices of *Ladies' Home Journal*, she objected to threats of her cohorts toward the editor for publishing articles and advertisements that reduced women's worth to physical beauty and housework. She served as an editor of *Notes from the Second Year* (1970) and issued the interview "Loving Another Woman" (1971) and the essay "Lesbianism and Feminism" (1971), which she distributed in pamphlet form. In 1973, she contributed theoretical essays to *Radical Feminism*, a treatise seeking the elimination of sex roles.

Through women's consciousness-raising sessions, Koedt and activist Ti-Grace Atkinson fostered female self-empowerment by combating the guilt and insecurity inflicted by Freudian psychoanalysis. Koedt encouraged the free exchange of individual sexual experiences and loving relationships with male or female. Among her suggestions for redirection of the self, she proposed an examination of children's toys for evidence of sex role stereotyping and the brainwashing of little girls to accept men's ideals of the perfect woman.

Koedt formed a four-decade relationship with children's author Ellen Deborah Levine and married her longtime mate in the fall of 2011. In their remaining months together, Koedt nursed Levine during her decline from lung cancer. Levine died on May 31, 2012.

References

Koedt, Anne. "On Abortion." In *Notes from the First Year* (June 1968): 28–29.

Koedt, Anne. "The Myth of the Vaginal Orgasm." In *Notes from the Second Year*, 37–41. New York: New York Radical Feminists 1970.

KOONTZ, ELIZABETH (1919–1989)

A spirited educator, reformer, and organizer, Elizabeth Duncan "Libby" Koontz led the National Education Association (NEA) as its first black president. A North Carolinian, she was born on June 3, 1919, in Salisbury to teacher Lena Bell Jordan and principal Samuel Edward Duncan. Because of her drive for reading and writing, she assisted in grading adult papers, an introduction to classroom evaluation.

At age 19, Koontz completed a bachelor's degree in elementary education and English from Livingstone College. With a graduate degree from Atlanta University, in 1941, she continued coursework in special education at the University of Indiana, North Carolina College at Durham, and Columbia University. In 1947, she married math teacher and basketball coach Harry Lee Koontz. A decade later, she chose special education as her focus and, in 1959, chaired the North Carolina Teachers Association of Classroom Teachers. In the early 1960s, she advised U.S. president Lyndon B. Johnson on education for disadvantaged children.

In 1965, Koontz received President Johnson's appointment to the National Council on the Education of the Disadvantaged. Her work preceded a 1966 report on language skills and curriculum for primary students and the problem of quality control of learning in poor counties. As president of the NEA in 1967, she led over one million U.S. educators and addressed as many as five conferences and seminars per day.

In Dallas, Texas, Koontz's inaugural address declared the docility of rural faculties a thing of the past and urged urban teachers not to think of themselves as tools of the school board. To encourage more black educators to defy the racism of conservative school boards, she coined the logo "A Time for Educational Statesmanship." Her savvy leadership earned her an appearance on the cover of *Jet* magazine on August 1, 1968.

In 1969, Koontz resigned from the NEA to become the highest-ranking black female in the Nixon administration. On April 14, 1969, she delivered the address "Household Employment: The Quiet Revolution," a commentary on domestic work. She researched discriminatory state statutes for Nixon's *Fifty States Project* and advised George Pratt Shultz, the U.S. Secretary of Labor, on teacher empowerment and employment standards. With a speech on industrial sexism on August 16, 1970, she led the labor department's drive for pay equity, opportunity, and higher employment standards. She persisted in investigating possibilities for women in Anaheim, California, in November 1970 with the speech "New Horizons: Household Employment and the Home-Related Arts." She explored the subject further in the 1970 essays "Women and Jobs in a Changing World," "Women as a Minority Group," "The Negro Woman and Work," and "Automation and Women Workers."

Although President Nixon chose not to reappoint Koontz to a federal office in 1973, she continued to crusade for women's rights and decision-making capacities through membership in the National Council of Negro Women. During the tenure of Governor James B. Hunt, she assisted the North Carolina Department of Human Resources in 1973 on a two-year program to improve child nutrition. In 1975, she began a seven-year task as assistant superintendent of North Carolina schools, for which she reviewed teacher education. In 1977, she received the North Carolina Award for Public Service as well as election to chair the North Carolina International Women's Year. Three years after her husband's death, she died of a heart attack on January 7, 1989.

Reference

Koontz, Elizabeth Duncan. "Complete Integration Must Be the Goal." *Ebony* 25, no. 10 (August 1970): 138–141.

TOWARD A FULL SHARE IN ABUNDANCE BY ELIZABETH DUNCAN KOONTZ U.S. SENATE, WASHINGTON, D.C. MAY 5, 1970

An advocate for older women and widows, as leader of the Women's Bureau, Elizabeth Koontz challenged gender inequities in pay and opportunity. She stressed the disadvantage of stay-at-home moms in the job market and their need for guidance in locating work. In her next position on the U.N. Commission on the Status of Women, she developed her concepts of abundance by suggesting child-rearing leave and benefits and loss of seniority for women who leave their jobs to give birth. Into the second decade of the 21st century, however, the focus of the U.N. commissioners turned to intervening in violence against women and the care of women with HIV/AIDS.

As director of the Women's Bureau of the Department of Labor, I am pleased to have the opportunity to appear before this important Senate Special Committee on Aging. In the Women's Bureau we receive numerous letters every year from middle-aged and older women seeking help to enter or reenter the labor force. Many are in dire economic circumstances—some recently widowed, others finding the monthly social security payment totally inadequate to meet bare necessities at a time of spiraling costs for food, shelter, transportation, and medical care. Many unfortunately, have already been victimized by fraudulent advertisements inviting them to earn money by addressing envelopes at home. They do not know where to turn to supplement their meager incomes.

We have read with great interest the working papers prepared for this committee. We note, however, that the data presented is largely related to males only. For that reason, we especially welcome the opportunity afforded by your invitation to supplement the record with respect to women.

We will also avail ourselves of your offer to submit more extensive information within the month, before the record is closed. This statement will, therefore, be briefer than the scope of the problem warrants and will be purely factual.

One reason the concerns of this committee are especially important for women is that the life expectancy of women is increasing more than that of men. The life expectancy of men in 1920 was 53.6 years and for women, 54.6 years—only one year difference. However, by 1967, whereas the life expectancy of men had increased by 13 years, that of women had increased by 20 years, a difference of 7 years.

Another important difference between men and women in relation to their relative capacity to attain "a full share of abundance" is the earnings gap in our economy between men and women workers. The median earnings of full-time, year-round women workers in 1968 were $4,457 compared with $7,664 for men. Women earned only 58 percent as much as men. This earnings gap is, in fact, widening. Back in 1955, women earned 64 percent as much as men.

This disparity between the earnings of women and men results in lower social security benefits for women. When this fact is combined with a longer post-retirement life for women, we understand why so many women face a long period of life with economic resources inadequate, in many cases, to provide a livelihood above the poverty level.

In 1967 the average retired male worker received $92.50 per month in social security benefits, but for women workers the average allotment was only $71.90. More than half of all retirees with benefit payments of less than $70 per month in 1967 were women. The average retirement benefit for women workers was 76 percent of the average for men.

I want to call attention also to the special problems of widows in our society. I have already indicated the greater longevity of women, which inevitably means a steadily increasing number of widows. Of course, not all widows are superannuated, although we do have approximately 2,800 Civil War widows receiving veterans' pensions, and as we know, there are no Civil War veterans.

However, the number of widows aged 55–64 in March 1969 was almost 2 million (1,994,000). There were over 6 million (6,078,000) aged 65 and over—altogether just over 8 million (8,072,900) women aged 55 and over, who were widows in 1969. If you add to that figure the number of older single women, plus women who are divorced or separated, the total of what we call "women on their own" who are aged 55 or older comes to 10.5 million (10,501,000) persons—no insignificant number.

The average benefit payment in 1967 under social security for widows labeled "aged" was $75.20. It is no wonder that the Women's Bureau receives so many requests for help in finding jobs, requests from mature women who "can no longer hold body and soul together," as several correspondents have put it.

The Women's Bureau noted with great interest the conclusions of your task force report concerning needed changes in the social security system. We are not in a position at this time to comment on these recommendations. However, I would like to call your attention to the report of the Task Force on Social Insurance and Taxes adopted by the Citizens' Advisory Council on the Status of Women, a council appointed by the President. I submit it for the record.

Unlike men, many of the women aged 45 and over who are seeking to improve their economic status by securing a job have little or no recent work experience. They need training and retraining for today's labor market. They also need special projects designed to utilize their special skills in community service occupations at regular part-time or full-time work.

The Labor Department, through its operation mainstream, manpower development and training programs, and other such projects has been striving to provide job training and employment opportunities for all our people. The number of women aged 45 and over who are benefitting from these programs is, however, small. In response to the expressed need of middle-aged and older women seeking to return to the labor force without adequate "know-how," the Women's Bureau published a pamphlet, "Jobfinding Techniques for Mature Women," in February 1970. In 1969 we prepared a publication entitled "How You Can Help Reduce Barriers to the Employment of Mature Women." The response to both these publications has exceeded expectations. Copies are presented herewith for the committee's use, but are not being presented as a part of the official record.

We trust the above data will be helpful to the committee in its overall study of "Economics of Aging: Toward a Full Share in Abundance."

Source: Koontz, Elizabeth Duncan. "Toward a Full Share in Abundance." *Hearings before the Special Committee on Aging.* 91st Cong., 2d sess. Washington, DC: U.S. Government Printing Office, 1970, 1803–1806.

KREPS, JUANITA (1921–2010)

U.S. cabinet member Clara Juanita Morris Kreps became the first female Secretary of Commerce and the first economic and labor demographics scholar to serve in the position. Born in Lynch, Kentucky, on January 11, 1921, she was the sixth child of Larcenia Blair and coal mining superintendent Elmer M. Morris. After her parents divorced in 1925, for the next eight years, she lived in poverty with her mother.

In the Great Depression, Kreps attended a Presbyterian boarding school. During World War II, she earned a BA from a work-study program in economics at Berea College and Phi Beta Kappa membership for excellence. On scholarship, she continued coursework in economics at Duke University and wrote a dissertation on war era wage stabilization.

In 1943, Kreps joined the staff of the National War Labor Board. After marrying University of North Carolina at Chapel Hill economics and banking professor Clifton Holland Kreps Jr., in August 1944, she completed a doctorate in 1948. In this same period, she reared son Clifton III and daughters Laura Anne and Sarah.

Teaching and Speaking

Kreps taught labor statistics at Denison University, Hofstra College, and Queens College in New York City and compiled texts on economic principles, automation, taxation, and the national debt. Before the emergence of second wave feminism, she determined in 1962 that female citizens deserved both training and meaningful work. Her earliest speeches bore intriguing titles—"Economic Implications of Shortened

World Life" to a consortium on gerontology in Copenhagen in August 1963 and "Women, Wise and Otherwise" at Western Reserve University in October 1966.

At the 1971 White House Conference on Aging, Kreps recommended an end to mandatory retirement. The dean of Duke's Woman's College for three years, in 1972, she became the first female James B. Duke chair of economics and the first female director of the New York Stock Exchange. She published *Lifetime Allocation of Work and Leisure: Essays in the Economy of Aging* (1971) and *Sex in the Marketplace: American Women at Work* (1971), which warned that, as female employment quadrupled, female employees tended to rise no higher than typists, grade school teachers, and saleswomen.

In ensuing months, Kreps sought reasons for the absence of female progress. On February 23, 1972, she addressed a U.S. congressional hearing on "Unemployment and Underemployment of Women Workers." In 1974, she advanced to vice president emerita of Duke University. In Harriman, New York, she scheduled for October 30–November 2, 1975, a conference on "Women and the American Economy." She explored the need for preschool education and affirmative action, expressed in her treatise *Women and the American Economy* (1976).

National Influence

While advising the corporate boards of AT&T, Chrysler, Citicorp, GTE, JCPenney, Kodak, R.J. Reynolds, and Western Electric, in 1976, Kreps accepted President Jimmy Carter's appointment as Secretary of Commerce. The demanding cabinet post involved documenting patents and logos, organizing the census, standardizing weights and measures, and charting seas and the weather. In addition, she oversaw $6 billion in public works projects and compiled statistics on national productivity and services.

During her nomination hearing, Kreps informed legislators on the immediate need for more U.S. jobs. To buoy the nation's economy in a period of unemployment and inflation, in 1977, she negotiated commerce, exports, and global trade and technology expansion in Africa, Asia, and Europe, particularly with Japan and the Soviet Union. In addition to advocating affirmative action, privacy laws, and environmental responsibility, on May 11, 1979, she reached an accord with China to pursue business and banking with the United States.

Although Kreps resigned her federal post in November 1979 to attend her husband during his deep depression, she made frequent scholarly addresses on retirement and aging. In 1980, her oratorical topics included "Farewell to Superwoman" to the Pan-Hellenic Council and, at the College of William & Mary in Williamsburg, Virginia, "Women's Work: For Love or Money?" In 1983, she served the Democratic Caucus and began a six-year term as director of the Council on Foreign Relations.

In May 1993, President Bill Clinton named Kreps to the Commission on the Future of Worker-Management Relations. In widowhood in 2000, she received the Distinguished Women of North Carolina Award but curtailed future platform speeches. After a lengthy struggle with Alzheimer's disease, she died in Durham on July 5, 2010.

Reference

McFadden, Robert D. "Juanita M. Kreps, Commerce Secretary, Dies at 89." *New York Times*, July 7, 2010.

THE COST OF GOVERNMENT REGULATION (EXCERPT) BY JUANITA KREPS U.S. CONGRESS, WASHINGTON, D.C. APRIL 11, 1978

U.S. cabinet member Juanita Kreps became the first female and the first economic and labor demographics scholar to serve as Secretary of Commerce. In 1978, at the passage of significant pollution control laws, she summarized the necessity for government regulations, particularly those from the Occupational Safety and Health Administration. Her overview alerted legislators to the need for clarity.

. . . It is a primary function of government to regulate activities in the public interest. The question before us, and I am sure before this committee, is not whether regulation should occur, but how and when it should be used and how we can improve the system of regulation, how we can limit it and still accomplish the goals we have set forth.

Most of all, it is a question of how we assess the costs and benefits of regulations and how we make the public clearly aware of the tradeoffs we make.

Regulations crucially affect our efforts to curb inflation, to promote domestic economic growth, and to increase exports. While Congress and the executive branch have devoted significant effort to coordinating macroeconomic policies, we have treated piecemeal or ignored regulatory measures that may have as much influence on the marketplace.

Over the long term, the implications of regulations for business survival, investment, location, and technological change, while difficult to measure, merit the level of attention we have given to other policies affecting the economy.

By any measure, regulations have burgeoned, particularly during the last decade. The numbers and pervasiveness of these regulations tend to stifle business, frustrate the general public, and undermine the government's credibility. For these reasons regulatory reform has become a focus of debate and public interest. Thus far, attention has focused on individual regulations and regulatory programs, with protests being leveled at compliance costs, red tape, imposed delays, frequent inconsistencies, and burdensome paperwork.

Government officials do not deny the substance of these concerns. Nor have we been idle. The administration has taken a number of actions. Regulatory agencies have been requested to rewrite regulations. The Occupational Safety and Health Administration, for example, has proposed elimination of 1,100 of its 5,500 job safety standards. The administration has supported legislation to reform regulation that stifles competition in the airline industry. And, as you noted, on March 23 the President issued an executive order requiring agencies which formulate regulations to write them clearly and simply; to reduce paperwork in regulatory compliance; to provide more public information by publishing lists of the regulations that they propose; and to reveal the processes by which they issue regulations. This will produce more public information and participation, greater accountability, and clearer regulations.

It now seems appropriate to begin developing an analytical framework that will provide an overview of the regulatory system as a whole and give us a better understanding of the overall costs and benefits of regulations. I use the phrase "regulatory system" because I believe we have to reach beyond the problems of individual regulations to consider the totality of regulations that affect our economy and our citizens. . . .

We recognize that a primary function of Government is the regulation of the public interest. The question is not whether regulation should occur, but how and when it should be used; how we can improve the system of regulation; and whether we are fully aware costs and benefits involved. Our work should increase public sensitivity to the pros and cons of regulation and lead to an improved program. It should help to heighten our understanding of regulation as used to achieve necessary public goals. It should provide a basis for Congress, the Executive, and the regulatory to evaluate present regulatory actions and to assess any new ones that are proposed. The process should be salutary.

Source: Kreps, Juanita. "The Cost of Government Regulation." *Hearings before the Subcommittee on Economic Growth and Stabilization of the Joint Economic Committee Congress of the United States.* 95th Cong., 2d sess. Washington, DC: U.S. Government Printing Office, 1978, 3–7.

L

LADUKE, WINONA (1959–)

A Native American environmentalist and journalist, Winona LaDuke fosters Ojibwa reverence for Mother Earth and the reclamation of traditional lands. Born to the Bear Clan on August 18, 1959, in Los Angeles, she is the daughter of artist and printmaker Betty Bernstein, a Vietnam War protester and dissident at the 1960 Poor People's March on Washington, and Ojibwa activist and actor Vincent E. Sun Bear LaDuke, a tribesman of the White Earth Reservation in northwestern Minnesota. Reared in Ashland, Oregon, in 1964, she resided with her divorced mother, an outspoken New Yorker who taught painting and sketching at Southern Oregon University. Betty's second husband, entomologist Peter Westigard, added half-brother Jason to the household and taught the children a solid work ethic. In girlhood, she rode horseback with Vincent and developed a mystic kinship with living things and earth cycles.

LaDuke absorbed her father's tribal politics and developed polemics as a member of a high school debate team. At age 18 in September 1977, she became the youngest speaker to address the U.N. by offering expert testimony on the exploitation of native lands to the Non-Governmental Organization Conference on Discrimination against Indigenous Peoples of the Western Hemisphere in Geneva, Switzerland. In February 1979, she identified anti-Indian violations at the Commission on Human Rights in Geneva. For the *Black Hills/Paha Sapa Report*, she compiled the article "A History of Uranium Mining" (1979), in which she characterized the haphazard placement of lethal lead, polonium, thorium, and radium ores near Navajo lands, where hunters killed and ate polluted animals.

At the 1981 Non-Governmental Organization Conference on the Indigenous People and Their Land, LaDuke continued voicing viewpoints in Geneva on despoliation among First Peoples. At Harvard, she joined the campus Indian Student Organization and completed a degree in indigenous economic development in 1982. She served the White Earth Reservation high school as principal. While surveying Ojibwa economics as part of course requirements at Antioch University, she earned a graduate degree in community economics and a second MA in urban development from the Massachusetts Institute of Technology. In 1984, she addressed the University of Colorado at Boulder during International Women's Week.

Upholding Tradition

From scholarship and native humor, LaDuke evolved a platform presence that nurtured collegiality and cooperation to halt expenditure of Indian money at off-reservation utilities and stores. She co-formed the Indigenous Women's Network in 1985 and, as an agent of Women of All Red Nations, disclosed efforts to force sterilization on Indian women, adoption of native children outside tribes, and the nuclear radiation exposure that caused stillbirths, birth defects, and deaths to native infants. In 1988, she wed activist Randy Kapashesit, a Cree from northern Ontario, and raised daughter Waseyabin and son Ajuawak before divorcing. By founding the White Earth Land Recovery Project, at age 30, she entered lawsuits to retrieve 810,000 acres expropriated from traditional Ojibwa territory.

By promoting natural crafting and harvesting methods on reservation lands, LaDuke won the 1989 international Reebok human rights award. She invested the $20,000 honorarium in repurchasing 1,400 acres sold to non-Indian farmers and vacationers and reinstating forests and wild rice stands, which generated $42 million in yearly income. She championed cultural justice at such assemblies as the August 1990 International Conference of Indigenous Women in Norway. By nurturing native commerce, she increased the marketing of parched wild rice and hominy, buffalo sausage, fry bread ingredients, and chokecherry, strawberry, and raspberry jam. Her efforts led to the purchase of buffalo herds, a native language vocabulary and songs program, and farming short-stalk corn and sugar bushes for a localized diet. Concerning Indian co-ops operating sustainable energy through wind harvesting, she applauded the investment in the KILI turbine as a source of jobs in installing and monitoring equipment.

Simultaneous with joining the directors of Greenpeace, in 1991, LaDuke squabbled with white environmentalists over such nativist concerns as the annual hunt of gray whales by the Washington state Makah. She organized Honor the Earth, an agency promoting renewable energy, suppression of dams and nuclear waste, and honor to sacred landmarks. In riposte to a 500th anniversary of the Columbian voyages, she sanctioned the June 1991 First Peoples gathering in Winnipeg, Manitoba, and compiled research in the 1992 report "Native North America: The

Political Economy of Radioactive Colonialism," a white paper on the use of Indian lands as radioactive tailing dumps.

After divorcing Randy, LaDuke accompanied the Indigo Girls singing duo on a 1993 three-city tour, "Ban the Dam Jam." While sharing the stage, she prodded Quebec audiences on the disastrous James Bay dam project in Quebec, which leached mercury from soil into waters supplying fish to subsistence diets. She risked arrest in September 1994 by backing native civil disobedience in Clayoquot Sound, British Columbia. In protest of a General Telephone directory producer that clear-cut timber from ancient forests for paper, she chained herself to factory gates and incurred a four-hour jailing.

A Composite Philosophy

LaDuke's assertive oratory energized support for native communities and the cultural arts and wisdom and won a nomination to *Time* magazine's 1994 listing of the 50 top future leaders. Her speech "Somebody Else's Wealth" decried polluters from General Motors who fouled the St. Lawrence Seaway near the Akwesasne Mohawk Reservation with PCBs. In 1995, she boosted a tour schedule to 21 venues and rallied music lovers to stop wild buffalo slaughter in national parks of the Dakotas and nuclear waste dumps in Nevada. In August 1995, she led delegates to Beijing for the U.N. World Conference on Women and presented native views on living in harmony with nature in the opening plenary lecture "The Indigenous Women's Network: Our Future, Our Responsibility." The text protested the disenfranchisement of native tribes as opposed to capitalism by oil, mining, and communications corporations, the companies most likely to exploit Earth's waters and atmosphere with chemical poisons and atomic toxins.

In 1996, LaDuke revived native interest in national elections by campaigning for the vice presidency in partnership with Ralph Nader and the Green Party, source of a community service commendation, an Ann Bancroft Fellowship for Women's Leadership, and the Thomas Merton Award for Peace and Social Justice. In reference to the 1996 welfare reform bill, she called legislators antiwoman. The grassroots green federation advocated Winona "No Nukes" for her stands on racial and gender equity as well as proposals for the closure of the Fort Benning School of the Americas. On the subject of ecology, a First World issue, she documented native philosophy in the children's book *In the Sugarbush* (1997) and the historical treatise *All Our Relations: Native Struggles for Land and Life* (1999).

For LaDuke's directing expertise on business, finance, and investment toward ending poverty, *Ms.* magazine extolled her as Woman of the Year 1998. Her novel *Last Standing Woman* (1999) traced empowerment of Ojibwa women through seven generations that defied racism and sexism. In 2000, she bore a son, Gwekaanimad, sired by second husband Kevin Gasco, an Odawa tribesman she met at a Michigan powwow. While backing the Obama administration, she accused the United States of being war-obsessed in the oil-rich Middle East but not in defense of the peoples of East Timor, Rwanda, and Tibet.

In opposition to environmental racism, LaDuke delivered the speech "Native American Poverty," which linked the stolen assets of native tribes with white wealth such as that of the Frederick Weyerhaeuser lumber fortune. On spiritual issues, she compiled an overview of ancestral tenets in *Recovering the Sacred: The Power of Naming and Claiming* (2005), which she tinged with ancestral storytelling. She lectured in 2010 at Missouri State University on the religious fundamentals of a green economy and delivered to the spring convocation at United Theological Seminary the speech "Thinking beyond Empire" (2011), which questioned the naming of such landmarks as Pike's Peak and Kit Carson National Forest after despicable human beings. She incorporated into the diatribe against capitalism the militarization and exploitation of the Hawaiian Islands. In a television interview, she regretted the use of native names for Black Hawk and Apache LongBow helicopters, Tomahawk missiles, and the code term "Geronimo" for the assault on Osama bin Laden.

At Johns Hopkins Bloomberg School of Public Health in 2012, LaDuke spoke on the value of squash, corn, Hawaiian poi, and agro-biodiversity in "Food Sovereignty, Biopiracy, and the Future." She opened the We Are PowerShift conference in Ottawa with the address "We Have to Fight" (2012), which traced a predatory society to Columbian conquest. She proposed that demonstrators appear on site at nuclear power waste dumps, oil platforms, and dams to put real faces on protest for isolated peoples. In Washington, D.C., in 2014, she joined the Indigo Girls in protesting the Keystone XL Pipeline. In January 2016, she promoted a native agrarian custom of turning fish scraps into fertilizer.

Reference

Silverstone, Michael. *Winona LaDuke: Restoring Land and Culture in North America.* New York: Feminist Press at CUNY, 2001.

LATHROP, JULIA (1858–1932)

Humanitarian and welfare reformer Julia Clifford Lathrop set a women's history record as the first female head of a U.S. government agency. The daughter of suffragist Sarah Adeline Potter of Medina, New York, and attorney William Taggart Lathrop, a founder of the Republican Party, she was born on June 29, 1858, in Rockford, Illinois. From Rockford Female Seminary, she continued her studies at Vassar College in civic and institutional organization, statistics, and sociology.

At age 22, Lathrop returned to her father's Rockford law practice in 1880 to read law and pass the bar exam. To improve life for Chicago's slum dwellers, in 1890, she joined social worker Jane Addams and the staff at Hull House and performed necessary field investigations into the needs of immigrant families in the slums. For assistance with wellness programs, she contacted women's clubs and lobbied the U.S. legislature to enact child protective laws.

Field Explorations

As Governor John Peter Atgeld's appointee to the Illinois State Board of Charities in 1892, Lathrop modeled women's advancement in civil service as an inspector of tenements, soup kitchens, homeless shelters, orphanages, almshouses, infirmaries, contagion wards, and asylums. In addition to advancing the employment of female physicians in state hospitals, on May 18–25, 1898, at the Illinois Conference on Charities in New York City, she proposed the world's first juvenile court system, which Cook County implemented in 1899.

In 1908, Lathrop co-founded the Immigrant's Protective League, a subject of her articles for the *Chicago Evening Post*, *Survey*, and *American Journal of Sociology*. Her report to the board of public charities, "A Visit to Stirling Asylum," summarized an on-site survey of a nurse training system in the 700-bed facility at Larbert, Scotland. She lauded the use of nurse escorts rather than police officers as a means of identifying the patient as ill rather than criminal. The conclusion lauded systems dependent on expert care rather than penal control.

A Feminist First

At the suggestion of Jane Addams, on April 17, 1912, President William Howard Taft selected Lathrop to head the new Children's Bureau, a directorship that won her the nickname "America's First Official Mother." Intent on lowering America's high mortality rates, she staffed the "baby bureau" office with expert statisticians. Canvassers went door to door to register births and collect data on juvenile crime, child labor, illegitimate births, innate handicaps, infant and maternal deaths, and mothers' pensions. Under her direction, the bureau crusaded for control of preventable killers of infants—poor sanitation and polluted drinking water.

To improve survival rates, Lathrop connected directly with citizens and shamed U.S. politicians with the high death rate of mother and child. She familiarized the public with the new federal agency by making speeches on specific issues. Her fieldwork reported on February 1, 1913, the loss of 300,000 babies the previous year, primarily because of inadequate prenatal care, birth injuries, and unsanitary home conditions for birthing and infant care.

In the second stage of Lathrop's studies, she compared tallies with official records of the Vital Statistics Office. In April 1913, she addressed the Chicago City Club on "Infant Welfare, a National Problem" and the Woman's City Club of Chicago, the National Conference of American Lecturers, and the New York Chautauqua on "The Children's Bureau," a popular topic among voters. Citing her "First Annual Report of the Chief, Children's Bureau, to the Secretary of Labor for the Fiscal Year Ended June 30, 1913," she enlightened politicians of discrepancies in population figures. To correct faulty record keeping, she proposed laws requiring doctors, nurses, and midwives to certify births and deaths, a beginning of official census figures nationwide.

For nine years, Lathrop formulated policy to improve child survival rates, declare all babies legitimate, and provide education for pregnant women on prenatal diet, rest, and exercise. She and other Hull House workers ensured that home advice reached laboring-class immigrant mothers on the care of undersized, malnourished, and disabled children and battled folklore that circulated among grandmothers and older women. Federal informational pamphlets "Prenatal Care" (1913) and "Infant Care" (1914) became the most popular publications of the U.S. Printing Office. During Lathrop's tenure, on September 1, 1916, Congress passed the Keating-Owen Child Labor Act banning interstate sale of merchandise made by underage workers.

Based on her knowledge of maternity insurance in England, France, Austria, and Germany, in 1917, Lathrop supported a minimum wage and federal health benefits for mother and child as means of reducing poverty and malnutrition. Under expert direction, some eight million American mothers began weighing and measuring infants and recording size and number of feedings on growth charts. To substantiate the agency's patriotic efforts during World War I, in November 1917, she published in the *North American Review* "The Children's Bureau in Wartime."

On April 6, 1918, Lathrop began rallying 11 million volunteers to promote the children's year with the logo "Save 100,000 Babies. Get a Square Deal for Children." By June 1918, the Children's Bureau directed state investigators to inspect 700 factories and mines for substandard sanitation and working conditions. Her staff elevated child happiness by keeping children in school and at play rather than on the job.

Under President Woodrow Wilson, in 1918, Lathrop represented the nation at a global conference on social work and assisted Czechoslovakia in establishing a juvenile bureau. She informed the House Military Affairs Committee of the need for commissioning nurses for war duty and alerted the media to a shortage of food and labor that increased demand for underage workers for farms, docks, and factories. In addition to issuing a series of departmental monographs and writing articles for the *American Child*, she addressed the Second White House Conference on Children and Youth. With orator Carrie Chapman Catt, Lathrop toured the West in 1919 and advocated votes for women as a means of assuring child welfare.

In 1920, Lathrop inspected postwar conditions in Austria, Poland, Hungary, and Yugoslavia. In speeches, she thanked the Americans, English, Swiss, Swedes, Norwegians, and Dutch for alleviating baby and juvenile distress through supplementary food distribution and treatment of tuberculosis. As a result of her promotion of family health with "Our Nation's Obligation to Its Children" at the 1921 National Conference on Social Work, the Sheppard-Towner Maternity and Infancy Act established prenatal care and baby health clinics.

Under Lathrop's proposals, federal and state agencies funded cadres of itinerant public health nurses to educate mothers on washing, tending, and feeding babies. In growing urban areas, midwifery classes and a visiting nurse program monitored problem pregnancies and hosted child wellness clinics that eventually become permanent community resources for families. By 1921, infant mortality declined nationwide by 24 percent. Subsequent demographics from the 1920s proved the strategy effective in boosting the viability of newborns and the health of birth mothers.

Because of poor health from goiter, at age 64, Julia Lathrop retired from civil service and headed the Illinois League of Women Voters. She continued lobbying for federal research into mental illness. In 1925, she aided the League of Nations as the U.S. delegate to the Child Welfare Committee in Geneva, Switzerland, and suggested the hiring of policewomen in Berlin to investigate domestic abuse. In 1930, she delivered a plea for social workers in the speech "What the Indian Service Needs." Following goiter surgery, she died in a Rockford, Illinois, hospital on April 15, 1932.

See Also: Addams, Jane; Catt, Carrie Chapman.

Reference

Tichi, Cecelia. *Civic Passions: Seven Who Launched Progressive America (and What They Teach Us)*. Chapel Hill: University of North Carolina Press, 2009.

TO SAVE 100,000 BABIES (EXCERPT)
BY JULIA LATHROP
SPEECH REPORTED IN THE *SAN FRANCISCO CALL*
OCTOBER 5, 1912

Sociologist Julia Lathrop of Rockford, Illinois, head of the Children's Bureau, directed American attention toward juvenile crime, child labor, illegitimate births, child handicaps, and infant and maternal deaths. By scheduling speeches on the causes of 300,000 infant deaths in 1912, she proposed policies to raise newborn survival rates and combat birth defects and malnutrition. As a means of limiting the poverty that stunted baby growth and well-being, she championed a minimum wage and federal health benefits for mother and child, the forerunners of the 1935 federal Aid to Families with Dependent Children assistance program.

This bureau was first urged by women who have lived long in settlements and who know as well as any person in this country certain aspects of the dumb misery which they desired this bureau to make articulate and intelligible. The bureau needs the sternest statistical accuracy at base, because its appeal to the noblest human passion of pity must never be founded upon anything but truth, because it must guard against the easy charge of sentimentality and must be able to present all its statements dispassionately with scientific candor and faithfulness. . . .

One of the most important inquiries will be into infant mortality. The great English statistician, Dr. Arthur Newsholme, has said: "Infant mortality is the most sensitive index we possess of social welfare. If babies were wellborn and well cared for, their mortality would be negligible. The infant death rate measures the intelligence, health, and right living of the fathers and mothers; the standards of morals and sanitation of communities and governments; the efficiency of physicians, nurses, health officers, and educators."

It is a conservative estimate that 200,000 babies die in the United States every year. Dr. Cressy Wilbur, chief statistician of the census bureau, says that the lives of half could be saved by the application of methods within the reach of every community. Professor Dietrich, a great German authority, says: "It was formerly believed that the rate of mortality among children who had not reached the first anniversary of their birth was a wise dispensation of nature intended to prevent children with weak constitutions from becoming too plentiful."

Today we know that a great infant mortality is a national disaster on the one hand because numerous economic values are created without purpose and prematurely destroyed, and on the other hand because the causes of the high rate of infant mortality affect the powers of resistance of the other infants and weaken the strength of the nation in its next generation. Can you conceive a more satisfying purpose than to save the 100,000 babies who are now lost plainly by neglect?

Source: Lathrop, Julia C. "To Save 100,000 Babies." *San Francisco Call* 112, no. 128 (October 6, 1912): 35.

LE GUIN, URSULA (1929–)

Proto-feminist author Ursula Kroeber Le Guin prefigured the field of women's futurism. Born in Berkeley, California, on October 21, 1929, she grew up in an eclectic environment vitalized by brilliant parents, psychologist Theodora Kracaw "Krakie" Kroeber and pioneering German American cultural anthropologist Alfred Louis Kroeber, the director of the University of California Museum of Anthropology. She chose writing as a career at age five and began dramatizing social ideals in invented fantasies in 1938.

Le Guin sought her father's help with submitting poems and stories to little magazines and *Astounding Science Fiction*. In 1951, she began the first of five novels by characterizing a series of strivers in the arts and academia. She created an imaginary setting, Orsinia, an Eastern European country reflecting a version of her first name, meaning bearlike. She graduated from Radcliffe with a degree in medieval and Renaissance French and Italian literature.

In 1964, Le Guin developed a first mythic novel, *Rocannon's World*, on the theme of time bending. The fairy tale quality anticipated imaginative extremes of the Earthsea trilogy and Hainish alternate worlds, a cycle comprising eight parts written over a 34-year period. While absorbing second wave feminist classics in the 1960s, she developed the Orsinian series of short stories. In this same period, she plotted a magical universe of small islands in a vast sea in the Earthsea trilogy—*A Wizard of Earthsea* (1968), winner of the Horn Book and Lewis Carroll Shelf awards; *The Tombs of Atuan* (1971), a Newbery Silver Medal winner; and *The Farthest Shore* (1972), recipient of a National Book Award for Children's Literature.

At the height of the Vietnam War, Le Guin's brutal sequences in *The Word for World Is Forest* (1972) achieved a Hugo award. *The Dispossessed* (1974) won numerous awards for its premises about physics, pacifism, and political chaos. In 1976, she published short works in *The Little Magazine* and *The Magazine of Fantasy & Science Fiction* and anthologized 11 stories in *Orsinian Tales*, which received a National Book award nomination. With *The Eye of the Heron* (1978), she broke free of the macho hero to investigate the female consciousness.

At Mills College in Oakland, Le Guin delivered to May graduates "A Left-Handed Commencement Address" (1983) on the subjects of feminism and social responsibility. She achieved a Kafka Prize, a major feminist award from the University of Rochester, for the utopian novel *Always Coming Home* (1985). In 1989, Le Guin's story "Unlocking the Air" predicted the collapse of the European Communist power structure, a prophecy that won a Pulitzer Prize nomination for her anthology *Unlocking the Air and Other Stories*. She rounded the speculative trilogy with *Tehanu: The Last Book of Earthsea* (1990), which attained both the Locus and Nebula citations for its representation of reconciliation and peace.

Mounting interest in women's futurism yielded scholarly analysis of Le Guin's work and demand for her lectures. Academia began to dissect her fantasies into parable, myth, fable, and mystic scenarios that scrutinize assumptions about reality. Children's literature enthusiasts praised her *Annals of the Western Shore* trilogy, composed of *Gifts* (2004), a study of birth talents; *Voices* (2006), based on literary silencing; and *Powers* (2007), the wanderer's tale of a persecuted clairvoyant. At the National Book Foundation Medal awards ceremony on November 19, 2014, she championed fantasy and science fiction and predicted that visionaries would bolster nations in hard times to come. To profiteers who turned books into commodities, she defied them to subsume the writer's art.

References

Le Guin, Ursula K. "Bryn Mawr Commencement Address (1986)." Serendip Studio. Accessed March 20, 2015. http://serendip.brynmawr.edu/sci_cult/leguin/.

Wray, John. "Ursula Le Guin, the Art of Fiction." *Paris Review* 206 (Fall 2013): 48–78.

A LEFT-HANDED COMMENCEMENT ADDRESS BY URSULA LE GUIN MILLS COLLEGE, OAKLAND, CALIFORNIA MAY 22, 1983

Proto-feminist author Ursula Kroeber Le Guin prefigured the field of women's futurism by referencing the obstacles to female education and the macho mindset of war and dominance. Her vision of the female domain urged women to avoid adopting male attitudes and to thrive in a milieu of peace and contentment.

I want to thank the Mills College Class of '83 for offering me a rare chance: to speak aloud in public in the language of women.

I know there are men graduating, and I don't mean to exclude them, far from it. There is a Greek tragedy where the Greek says to the foreigner, "If you don't understand Greek, please signify by nodding." Anyhow, commencements are usually operated under the unspoken agreement that everybody graduating is either male or ought to be. That's why we are all wearing these twelfth-century dresses that look so great on men and make women look either like a mushroom or a pregnant stork. Intellectual tradition is male. Public speaking is done in the public tongue, the national or tribal language; and the language of our tribe is the men's language. Of course women learn it. We're not dumb. If you can tell Margaret Thatcher from Ronald Reagan, or Indira Gandhi from General Somoza, by anything they say, tell me how. This is a man's world, so it talks a man's language. The words are all words of power. You've come a long way, baby, but no way is long enough. You can't even get there by selling yourself out: because there is theirs, not yours.

Maybe we've had enough words of power and talk about the battle of life. Maybe we need some words of weakness. Instead of saying now that I hope you will all go forth from this ivory tower of college into the Real World and forge a triumphant career or at least help your husband to keep our country strong and be a success in everything—instead of talking about power, what if I talked like a woman right here in public? It won't sound right. It's going to sound terrible. What if I said what I hope for you is first, if—only if—you want kids, I hope you have them. Not hordes of them. A couple, enough. I hope they're beautiful. I hope you and they have enough to eat, and a place to be warm and clean in, and friends, and work you like doing. Well, is that what you went to college for? Is that all? What about success?

Success is somebody else's failure. Success is the American Dream we can keep dreaming because most people in most places, including thirty million of ourselves, live wide awake in the terrible reality of poverty. No, I do not wish you success. I don't even want to talk about it. I want to talk about failure.

Because you are human beings you are going to meet failure. You are going to meet disappointment, injustice, betrayal, and irreparable loss. You will find you're weak where you thought yourself strong. You'll work for possessions and then find they possess you. You will find yourself—as I know you already have—in dark places, alone, and afraid.

What I hope for you, for all my sisters and daughters, brothers and sons, is that you will be able to live there, in the dark place. To live in the place that our rationalizing culture of success denies, calling it a place of exile, uninhabitable, foreign.

Well, we're already foreigners. Women as women are largely excluded from, alien to, the self-declared male norms of this society, where human beings are called Man, the only respectable god is male, the only direction is up. So that's their country; let's explore our own. I'm not talking about sex; that's a whole other universe, where every man and woman is on their own. I'm talking about society, the so-called man's world of institutionalized competition, aggression, violence, authority, and power. If we want to live as women, some separatism is forced upon us: Mills College is a wise embodiment of that separatism. The war games world wasn't made by us or for us; we can't even breathe the air there without masks. And if you put the mask on you'll have a hard time getting it off. So how about going on doing things our own way, as to some extent you did here at Mills? Not for men and the male power hierarchy—that's their game. Not against men, either—that's still playing by their rules. But with any men who are with us: that's our game. Why should a free woman with a college education either fight Machoman or serve him? Why should she live her life on his terms?

Machoman is afraid of our terms, which are not all rational, positive, competitive, etc. And so he has taught us to despise and deny them. In our society, women have lived, and have been despised for living, the whole side of life that includes and takes responsibility for helplessness, weakness, and illness, for the irrational and the irreparable, for all that is obscure, passive, uncontrolled, animal, unclean—the valley of the shadow, the deep, the depths of life. All that the Warrior denies and refuses is left to us and the men who share it with us and therefore, like us, can't play doctor, only nurse, can't be warriors, only civilians, can't be chiefs, only indians. Well so that is our country. The night side of our country. If there is a day side to it, high sierras, prairies of bright grass, we only know pioneers' tales about it, we haven't got there yet. We're never going to get there by imitating Machoman. We are only going to get there by going our own way, by living there, by living through the night in our own country.

So what I hope for you is that you live there not as prisoners, ashamed of being women, consenting captives of a psychopathic social system, but as natives. That you will be at home there, keep house there, be your own mistress, with a room of your own. That you will do your work there, whatever you're good at, art or science or tech or running a company or sweeping under the beds, and when they tell you that it's second-class work because a woman is doing it, I hope you tell them to go to hell and while they're going to give you equal pay for equal time. I hope you live without the need to dominate, and without the need to be dominated. I hope you are never victims, but I hope you have no power over other people. And when you fail, and are defeated, and in pain, and in the dark, then I hope you will remember that darkness is your country, where you live, where no wars are fought and no wars are won, but where the future is. Our roots are in the dark; the earth is our country. Why did we look up for blessing—instead of around, and down? What hope we have lies there. Not in the sky full of orbiting spy-eyes and weaponry, but in the earth we have looked down upon. Not from above, but from below. Not in the light that blinds, but in the dark that nourishes, where human beings grow human souls.

Source: Le Guin, Ursula K. "A Left-Handed Commencement Address (Mills College, 1983)." Available at: http://www.ursulakleguin.com/LeftHandMillsCollege.html.

LEE, BARBARA COOMBS (1947–)

A proponent of patient control of health care, attorney and nurse-ethicist Barbara J. Coombs Lee advocates for patients in end-of-life situations. She was born in Evanston, Illinois, on June 20, 1947, to Marie Rose Kolarik, and Frank Edward Schmid. With a literature degree from Vassar in 1969, nursing credentials from Cornell in 1970, and specialized training in hospice nursing from the University of Washington, she entered the health care professions.

Lee spent a quarter century as a physician's assistant in cardiology and family medicine at Oregon Health Sciences University. Her background included clinical nursing in rest homes, public health in Harlem, operating rooms, coronary and intensive care units, and partnering with ambulance crews in Seattle. To free the dying to chart their own lives, choose a serene setting, and ensure peace of mind about letting go, she completed a law degree at Lewis and Clark School of Law.

As an adviser to the Oregon Senate Healthcare and Bioethics Committee in Portland, in 1991, Lee supported a state law empowering individuals to make personal decisions about end-of-life aid. Central to the bill, she insisted that psychiatrists choose a means of measuring depression to determine whether candidates had the judgment to make an informed choice about taking barbiturates to die on their own terms. She co-drafted the Oregon Death with Dignity Act of 1994 and crusaded for public and judicial acceptance of rational decisions rather than hasty or botched suicide attempts. Her version of the law included a 15-day waiting period before the prescription of self-administered lethal drugs, a compromise with conservatives who rejected immediate action to end patient misery.

Lee encountered end-of-life quandaries in Multnomah, Oregon, where her widowed mother Marie struggled with Parkinson's disease, and in 1998, chose to stop taking liquids or nourishment. The choice to kill herself with an overdose of morphine imposed anger and hardship on Lee. Before the U.S. House of Representatives on April 29, 1996, she informed policy makers on the need for merciful aid to competent citizens dehumanized by imminent death and relentless pain. She advised legislators in Washington State, where voters approved a law on November 5, 2008, that would not prosecute a physician assisting the terminally ill in opting for immediate death. Throughout 2009, she spoke directly to interested citizens on end-of-life topics that affected their parents and themselves. With volunteers trained in medicine or social work, she offered clear explanations of state versions of living wills. Her orations clarified the legality of various forms of euthanasia and the effects of cessation of food, water, chemotherapy, and oxygen.

Disability rights activists protested Lee's oration to a senior center in Colorado in October 2014, claiming end-of-life aid devalued the vulnerable, and criticized for-profit institutions as using the strategy as a cost-cutting measure. Counter opinions motivated her to address Chicagoans at the Cultural Center on December 15, 2014, about the advocacy of Brittany Maynard, a 29-year-old bride and victim of a fast-growing brain tumor the previous January who used her experience with terminal illness as a model of reason in ending her life. For humanitarian activism, Lee's honors cover the range of her professions—an American Jurisprudence Award for mastering research in medical law, a National Health Policy Fellowship from the Boehringer Ingelheim Foundation, and a National Health Lawyers Association scholarship.

Reference

Lee, Barbara Coombs. "Review of Book about the Death-with-Dignity Movement." September 5, 2012. Accessed April 27, 2015. http://zoefitzgeraldcarter.com/blog/tag/barbara-coombs-lee/.

ASSISTED SUICIDE BY BARBARA COOMBS LEE SUBCOMMITTEE ON THE CONSTITUTION OF THE COMMITTEE ON THE JUDICIARY U.S. HOUSE OF REPRESENTATIVES, WASHINGTON, D.C. APRIL 29, 1996

An opponent to the medicalization of death, nurse-ethicist Barbara Coombs Lee of Evanston, Illinois, crusades for a merciful end to suffering in patients dehumanized by imminent death and relentless pain. Her speeches clarify the difference between criminal homicide and voluntary suicide. She stresses the significance of living wills and patient choice of euthanasia or the cessation of food, water, chemotherapy, and respiratory support. Her influence in North America and Europe coincides with the rise in hospice care in residences, nursing home, veterans' facilities, hospitals, and prisons.

My name is Barbara Coombs Lee. By training I am a nurse, physician assistant, and attorney at law. I appear today in my role as a Chief Petitioner of Oregon's Death with Dignity Act, which was passed by citizen's initiative in November 1994. The act creates a safe harbor in Oregon's assisted suicide laws for an attending physician to provide a prescription for lethal medication, upon repeated voluntary and informed requests from a competent, adult, terminally ill patient. The patient may then obtain the means for a humane and dignified death at the time of his or her own choosing.

The act imposes numerous safeguards, such as repeated written and oral requests, second medical opinions, waiting periods, and consultation regarding comfort care, hospice and pain control. It also provides for documentation by the attending physician and oversight by the State Health Division. Upon constitutional challenge, the act was found by a federal district court judge to fail the equal protection rational basis test, and the state is currently appealing that ruling at the Ninth Circuit.

The movement for Oregon's Death with Dignity Act began with Oregon families that had struggled through prolonged and painful deaths and resolved to change the law. Elvin Sinnard's wife Sarah suffered with a terminal heart condition that brought excruciating pain with any activity, including reading and talking. She reached her decision in consultation with her family and minister, stockpiled medication, and learned how to apply a plastic bag. Heartened by her empowerment, she continued to live for a number of months, but gradually her suffering became too great to bear. When the day of her decision arrived, she carefully constructed an alibi for her husband and instructed him to go where he would be seen, not to return for a stated number of hours. When he returned she indeed was "at peace," but his grief was intensified at his inability to be with her when she died. In spite of Sarah's precautions, Elvin was still subjected to a criminal investigation. The house was searched and articles confiscated, including Sarah's farewell letters to her family. Elvin vowed, "This isn't right," and formed an organization called Oregon Right to Die, which met in his basement.

Patty Rosen's daughter Jody was dying of bone cancer. All the narcotics doctors could provide didn't dull her pain and Jody pleaded with her mother, a nurse, to help her die. The day Patty finally agreed was a happy one for Jody, but complying with her request was not easy because of the drug tolerance that had developed over the previous weeks. Patty eventually succeeded and lay next to her daughter as she died in her bed.

The problem is that medical science has conquered the gentle and peaceful deaths and left the humiliating and agonizing to run their relentless downhill course. The suffering of these individuals is not trivial, and it is not addressed by anything medical science has to offer. Faced with this dilemma, the problem for many is that the law turns loving families into criminals. It separates loved ones at the end when it is most important to be close. It encourages patients to choose violent and premature deaths while they still have the strength to act. And it forces some to suffer through a slow and agonizing death that contradicts the very meaning and fabric of their lives.

In Oregon the Death with Dignity Act received wide support across genders, ages, and political philosophies. The state Democratic Party, American Civil Liberties Union, and local National Organization for Women supported the act as a compassionate response to the dilemma many find themselves in at the end of their lives. But our most vocal support and largest contributions came from people who describe themselves as politically very conservative. They resent a government that interferes in an intensely personal, private decision, and restricts their individual liberty. Many who would oppose a woman's abortion option on the grounds that there is another life to be considered, see no such moral issue in assisted death for terminally ill adults.

During our campaign we argued that physicians already assist their patients with death in hidden and unstated ways. The initiative would merely bring covert, surreptitious activity into the open and add safeguards. Recent scientific evidence confirms this belief. In February the *New England Journal of Medicine* published a survey of Oregon physicians taken in early 1995, in which 21 percent said they had been asked for a prescription for a lethal dose of medication within the preceding year. Seven percent stated they had written such a prescription prior to passage of the act, and most of these stated their patients had taken the medication. A survey of Washington State physicians published in the *Journal of the American Medical Association* last month revealed that 26 percent of physicians have been asked at least once for a lethal prescription or euthanasia. 147 physicians provided 207 case descriptions of patients who made requests. The physician provided lethal prescriptions to 38 (24 percent) of those requesting them and 21 patients (55 percent) took the medication and died. 15 patients (39 percent) did not use their prescriptions.

Physicians who respond to such requests do so without guidelines, without consultation with their peers, and without referral for second opinion. Improvement in these professional practices is one of the chief salutary effects of decriminalization. With open discussion of symptoms and options comes improvement in care. Since passage of the Death with Dignity Act, palliative care has received greatly increased attention in Oregon's medical community and referrals to hospice have increased 20 percent. Dying individuals and their families are relieved of their burden of secrecy, isolation, and fear of prosecution.

Incredibly, some would contend that covert, illegal assistance is preferable to decriminalization. As a citizen and attorney I believe in an ordered society, and I could not accept a stated policy to wink at the law. When we know that certain rare and desperate cases call for a compassionate response in the form of assisted death our democratic heritage demands that the law be consistent with that knowledge. Perhaps this is uniquely American, but it is how we govern with integrity to retain the consent of the governed.

I believe that one reason people like Sarah or Jody or Francois Mitterand choose a hastened death is because they believe the circumstances of their deaths are very important to the meaning, the story, even the sanctity of their lives. There is something about facing death with courage and grace with senses intact that serves their most cherished values and spiritual needs. And I believe, quoting philosopher and legal scholar Ronald Dworkin, that "Making someone die in a way others approve, but he believes a horrifying contradiction of this life, is a devastating, odious form of tyranny."

Source: Lee, Barbara Coombs. "Death with Dignity." *Hearing before the Subcommittee on the Constitution of the Committee on the Judiciary.* 104th Cong., 2d sess. Washington, DC: U.S. Government Printing Office, 1996, 163–166.

LEE, MOTHER ANN (1736–1784)

An innovative religious ascetic and millennialist, Ann Lee founded the Shakers, an American Christian sect. Born to Quaker blacksmith and tailor John Lees and a pious mother, Ann Beswick Lees, in Manchester, England, on February 29, 1736, she faulted materialism and greed for misleading humankind. At age 22, she joined the congregation of 12 led by Quaker tailor James Wardley. He relied on inspiration from his wife, Jane, a mystic who experienced visitations by angelic voices and celestial lights. The Wardleys' followers adopted the name the United Society of Believers in Christ's Second Appearing. From scorners, they earned the name "Shaking Quakers" for the tremors that seized the flesh when God's power rid the body of sin and lust.

Despite Lee's loathing of sexuality, on January 5, 1762, she obeyed her father's command that she wed Abraham Standerin (also Standley or Stanley), an illiterate apprentice blacksmith. After an Anglican church wedding, the couple moved into her father's house, but Lee maintained her maiden name. Four childbirths and the deaths of three babes in infancy and daughter Elizabeth in 1766 heightened Lee's distaste for marital coitus.

Religious Emotionalism

Because of urgent divine revelations, Lee felt compelled to broadcast her anticipation of the imminent return of Jesus in female form. She delivered sermons from memory, leaving no written evidence of her oratory. By preaching in the streets, twitching, dancing, speaking in tongues, prophesying, and shouting, Shakers relayed her exhortations to nonbelievers.

Because of a period of intolerance of minority faiths, authorities dragged Lee and her father from his home and confined them to Bailey prison on the Irwell River. She worsened suspicions of her gender beliefs by demanding female equality with men. In an asylum following extreme weight loss and nervous collapse in 1770, she saw herself as an incarnation of Jesus and answered to the name "Ann the Word." During a lengthy jail sentence, she experienced a revelation of God's gender duality and of Adam and Eve as the founders of original sin.

In 1771, the Quakers elevated Lee to their church leader. Congregants began calling her "Mother Ann," a true expounder of God's word and a miracle worker capable of healing the sick. Her notoriety increased along with the sect's bold lawlessness. On July 14, 1772, a constable incarcerated Ann, her father, and three Shakers. The jailing preceded another roundup of zealots on October 3 at the home of Shaker John Townley and another arrest and two-day confinement on May 30 and 31, 1773.

An American Experiment

Lee emigrated from Liverpool to America on May 19, 1774, with eight disciples. Her lack of education fostered a distrust of written theology, testimonials, and credos and faith in dynamic verbal witness. Despite poverty, by carriage and sleigh, she continued a mission to awaken others to the imminent return of Christ.

In September 1776, Lee's patron, John Hocknell, funded Niskayuna commune on swampland 100 miles north on the Hudson River at Watervliet, New York. The men cut logs for a two-floor cabin, which housed three women on the ground floor and six men in the attic. The spread of Shakerism spawned eight communes. The original commune financed its efforts on farming, herb gardening, blacksmithing, weaving, and woodcrafts.

Unique to Lee's evolution as a spiritual revolutionary was her declaration that she embodied Christ in female form. Expressed before hearers, her public confessions and adages roused mobs in Petersham and Shirley, Massachusetts. Notoriety ended her isolation at Niskayuna, where, in the winter of 1780, converts flocked for consolation and hope, overrunning the commune's facilities.

Lee's piety took the form of aphorisms. In grief and declining strength from mob beatings, she lapsed into a trance and died on September 8, 1784. By welcoming the poor and homeless, her sect accepted the leadership of elders Lucy Wright and Joseph Meacham, who erected the first Shaker church at Harvard.

The congregation grew to 6,000 believers, who reared orphans communally in Lebanon, New York. During the rise of revivalism in 1805, Shakers infiltrated communities as far west as Ohio, Indiana, and Kentucky. To preserve her tenets and anecdotes about industry and faith, Rufus Bishop and Seth Youngs Wells published *Testimonies of the Life, Character, Revelations and Doctrines of Mother Ann Lee, and the Elders with Her* (1816).

Reference

Haskett, William J. *Shakerism Unmasked, or the History of the Shakers.* Pittsfield, MA: self-published, 1828.

SAYINGS OF MOTHER ANN LEE
BY MOTHER ANN LEE
1758–1784

A humble Christian millennialist from Manchester, England, Mother Ann Lee began delivering aphorisms in Shaker meetings from 1758. Her commentaries on celibacy, gender equality, and public repentance continued in 1774, when she began a 10-year ministry in New York at the Niskayuna commune. Her insightful tenets survived in her believers' journals, providing a philosophical basis for Shakerism.

It does not appear that Ann Lee made any attempts to settle her followers in colonies or communities, or that she interrupted the family life, except that she insisted on celibacy. But she seems to have gathered her followers in congregations, because she from the first required, as a sign of true repentance and a condition of admission, that "oral confession of all the sins of the past life, to God, in the presence of an elder brother," which is still one of the most rigorous rules of the order.

She is reported to have said: "When I confessed my sins, I labored to remember the time when and the place where I committed them. And when I had confessed them [to Jane and James Wardley, in Manchester], I cried to God to know if my confession was accepted; and by crying to God continually I traveled out of my loss." Also she said: "The first step of obedience that any of you can take is to confess your sins to God before his witnesses." "To those who came to confess to her she said: 'If you confess your sins, you must confess them to God; we are but his witnesses.' To such as asked her forgiveness, she used to say: 'I can freely forgive you, and I pray God to forgive you. It is God that forgives you; I am but your fellow-servant.'"

Ann Lee died at Watervliet, New York, on the 8th of September, 1784, in the forty-ninth year of her age. In the "Summary View of the Millennial Church," as well as in some other works published by the Shakers, there are recorded details of her life and conversation, from which one gets the idea that she was a woman of practical sense, sincerely pious, and humble-minded. She was "rather below the common stature of woman, thickset but straight, and otherwise well-proportioned and regular in form and feature. Her complexion was light and fair, and her eyes were blue, but keen and penetrating; her countenance mild and expressive, but grave and solemn. Her manners were plain, simple, and easy. She possessed a certain dignity of appearance that inspired confidence and commanded respect. By many of the world who saw her without prejudice she was called beautiful; and to her faithful children she appeared to possess a degree of dignified beauty and heavenly love which they had never before discovered among mortals." She never learned to read or write. Aside from her strictly religious teachings, she appears to have inculcated upon her followers the practical virtues of honesty, industry, frugality, charity, and temperance. "Put your hands to work and give your hearts to God." "You ought never to speak to your children in a passion; for if you do, you will put devils into them." "Do all your work as though you had a thousand years to live; and as you would if you knew you must die to-morrow." "You can never enter the kingdom of God with hardness against any one, for God is love, and if you love God you will love one another." "Be diligent with your hands, for godliness does not lead to idleness." "You ought not to cross your children unnecessarily, for it makes them ill-natured." To a woman: "You ought to dress yourself in modest apparel, such as becomes the people of God, and teach your family to do likewise. You ought to be industrious and prudent, and not live a sumptuous and gluttonous life, but labor for a meek and quiet spirit, and see that your family is kept decent and regular in all their goings forth, that others may see your example of faith and good works, and acknowledge the work of God in your family." To some farmers who had gathered at Ashfield, in Massachusetts, in the winter, to listen to her instructions: "It is now spring of the year, and you have all had the privilege of being taught the way of God; and now you may all go home and be faithful with your hands. Every faithful man will go forth and put up his fences in season, and will plow his ground in season, and put his crops into the ground in season; and such a man may with confidence look for a blessing." These are some of the sayings reported of her.

Source: Nordhoff, Charles. *The Communistic Societies of the United States*. New York: Harper & Brothers, 1875, 128–130.

L'ENGLE, MADELEINE (1918–2007)

A Christian author of some 60 works, Madeleine L'Engle Camp wrote young adult fiction that connected imagination, spirituality, and science through candid humanistic themes. A native Manhattanite, she was born on November 29, 1918, the only child of pianist Madeleine Hall Barnett and World War I veteran and foreign correspondent Charles Wadsworth Camp, subsequent music and theater critic for the *New York Sun*. She grew up under the influence of arty houseguests and an English nanny from Liverpool.

By 1923, L'Engle began producing and illustrating narratives with watercolors and reading *Chatterbox*, a weekly children's magazine her grandfather sent from England. While studying among elite girls at Brearley at age eight, she preferred novels of good and evil. She began objectifying events in a diary and playing the piano and won a poetry contest in fifth grade.

L'Engle's years in private schools were troubled by shyness and withdrawal from bullies, but she credited solitude and isolation with strengthening her character. Because of awkward movements from a congenitally malformed knee, some of her teachers thought her stupid. During a vacation in Brittany, she learned the art of French cookery.

Because of her father's respiratory illness and the financial privations of the Great Depression, at age 12, L'Engle sailed to Europe with her parents. They resided at an 11th-century chateau in Chamonix. She vacationed with her grandfather in

Provence, where she read his stack of *Punch* magazines. Her parents abruptly enrolled her in Châtelard, an international boarding academy in Montreux, Switzerland. Among mostly British students, she escaped isolation and despair by reading the works of Louisa May Alcott.

To be near her ailing grandmother, Caroline L'Engle Barnett, at age 15, L'Engle settled with her family at a beach cottage in Jacksonville, Florida. Within months of her father's death from pneumonia and alcoholism, she finished high school at Ashley Hall, an elite female boarding academy in Charleston, South Carolina, where she played a breeches role in *Twelfth Night* and exercised leadership as the class president. She wrote dialogues during summer courses at Bartram School for Girls and, in 1941, earned an English degree with honors at Smith, where she coedited the *Smith College Monthly* with Betty Friedan.

After L'Engle moved to Greenwich Village and established membership in an Episcopalian parish, she served actor Eva Le Gallienne as private secretary and planned to write stage productions. To aid the war effort, she sold U.S. war bonds on Broadway during intermissions and played a role in *Uncle Harry*. While on tour acting in Anton Chekov's *The Cherry Orchard* in the winter of 1942, she met her future husband, actor Hugh Hale Franklin. Under her literary name, she translated French literature, published a short narrative in *Mademoiselle*, and had Franklin read aloud the manuscript of *The Small Rain* (1945), a story she had begun at Smith.

Following marriage in Chicago on January 26, 1946, L'Engle settled with Franklin at Crosswicks, a farm in Goshen, Connecticut. At a residence that was once the first trading post on an Indian trail, she enjoyed a green apple orchard, antique stone walls, a brook, and Dog Pond. The couple operated a successful general store and post office while rearing their children, Josephine and Bion Franklin, and Maria Franklin, an adopted daughter. L'Engle directed the choir of the Goshen Congregational Church and wrote *Ilsa* (1946) and *And Both Were Young* (1949).

Writing a Masterwork

During a difficult time getting published in 1958, the family took a 10-week coast-to-coast camping trip. The following year, the family settled in New York City, where Franklin took a role in the series *All My Children*. At their apartment on West End Avenue, L'Engle composed the beginning of a time quintet.

After a dismaying number of rejections, the author won a Newbery Medal for her Cold War era masterwork, *A Wrinkle in Time* (1962), a tale of time travel and female daring that she tested on her children. Her acceptance address, "The Expanding Universe," delivered in August 1963, ennobled the bibliophile's calling to unleash the imagination of the younger generation. The text identified children's stories and legends as a universal language that stirs fresh life in the mind. The controversial religious allegory met with frequent accusations of occultism and banning for blending spirituality with Einsteinian physics, quantum mechanics, feminism, fantasy, and myth.

An Episcopalian laywoman and proponent of Christian universalism, L'Engle taught three classes per day at St. Hilda's and St. Hugh's, a coeducational Anglican day school. In 1965, as writer in residence at the Cathedral of St. John the Divine, she volunteered at the library and directed a Christmas pageant. She received the 1965 Sequoyah Book Award from the Oklahoma Library Association, composed the oration "The Difference between Man and Beast" for the Authors Guild in the summer of 1967, and earned an Austrian State Prize for *The Moon by Night* (1969). While the family summered at Crosswicks, she replied to letters from fans and composed the autobiographical *A Wind in the Door* (1973), the extension of a pamphlet, "Intergalactic P.S. 3" (1970).

In the summer of 1972, L'Engle served Ohio State University at Columbus as writer in residence. Of the responsibility for caring for a dying mother, she wrote *The Summer of the Great-Grandmother* (1974). Honors for L'Engle's framework novels included a University of Southern Mississippi medal for the Kairos trio, concluding with musings on Celtic lore, and relativity theory in *A Swiftly Tilting Planet* (1978), winner of a National Book Award. She earned consecutive National Religious Book commendations for *The Weather of the Heart* (1979) and *Ladder of Angels* (1980).

At a height of productivity in a stone tower at the Goshen farm, L'Engle acquired a fan base among teachers and science fiction experts. After issuing a glimpse of death in *A Ring of Endless Light* (1980), she received the California Young Reader Medal, Colorado Children's Book Award, Dorothy Canfield Fisher Children's Book Award, a Newbery Honor Book designation, and a Smith College service award. Following publication of *A Severed Wasp* (1982), in November 1983, she delivered the talk "Dare to Be Creative" at the Library of Congress.

L'Engle's speech "Do I Dare Disturb the Universe," a 1983 address to the Chicago Sunday Evening Club, preceded subsequent invitations from the group in 1988, 1990, and 1991. On success with *A House Like a Lotus* (1984), she accepted a Smith College Sophia citation for distinguished writing and an honorary degree from Berkeley Divinity School in 1984. On receipt of a 1985 Regina Medal from the Catholic Library Association, she delivered a formal thank-you and advanced to presidency of the Authors Guild.

Achievements and Honors

In widowhood after her husband's death from cancer on September 26, 1986, L'Engle published *Many Waters* (1986), winner of an American Library Association award for young adult literature, and spoke to groups in New York, Maine,

Texas, Michigan, Illinois, Indiana, South Carolina, and Alaska. She ventured into autobiography with *Two-Part Invention: The Story of a Marriage* (1988) and achieved a 1990 Kerlan Award from Children's Literature Research at the University of Minnesota. After she recuperated from a car accident, in 1992, she toured Antarctica. For *Victoria* magazine, she served as 1995 writer-in-residence and issued *A Live Coal in the Sea* (1996).

With daughter Maria, L'Engle collaborated on the books *Mothers and Daughters* (1997) and *Mothers and Sons* (1999). A year after a 1997 life achievement award from the World Fantasy Convention, she received a Margaret A. Edwards Award from the American Library Association. At the annual conference in Washington, D.C., on June 27, 1998, she presented "Reading for Children," which defined the ineluctability of truth. The theme exonerated science fiction as well as fairy tale, fantasy, and parable of harming children. She lauded literature for exalting the human spirit and praised librarians for bearing light in a dark world.

Because of osteoporosis, L'Engle retired from travel and teaching but continued writing *A Full House: An Austin Family Christmas* (1999). At age 81, she grieved the death of her son from alcoholism; in 2001, she suffered a stroke. Her more spiritual works—*Bright Evening Star: Mystery of the Incarnation* (2001), *WinterSong: Christmas Readings* (2003), and the posthumous *The Joys of Love* (2008)—turned to divinity and mysticism. Following issuance of previously unpublished works, she refused workshop and speaking invitations and begged off attending the presentation of the National Humanities Medal. Handicapped by a broken hip, from 2004, she occupied a wheelchair at Rose Haven nursing home in Litchfield, Connecticut, and died of natural causes on September 6, 2007.

See Also: Friedan, Betty.

Reference

Marcus, Leonard S. *Listening for Madeleine: A Portrait of Madeleine L'Engle in Many Voices*. New York: Macmillan, 2012.

LEOPOLD, ALICE KOLLER (1906–1982)

Exemplary executive and civil servant Alice Koller Leopold sought opportunities for mature women and income equity for all female employees. An only child, she was born in Scranton, Pennsylvania, on May 9, 1906, to Leonora Edwards and artist and writer Edmund Leonard Koller, a designer of art books. At Goucher College in Baltimore, she explored extracurricular activities while earning degrees in English and economics and graduated at age 21.

Leopold entered the Baltimore business world as a clerk at Hutzler's department store and continued in retail for B. Altman in New York. Outside work, she led fellow saleswomen in a Young Women's Christian Association club. At age 22, her enthusiasm for staff won her a promotion to personnel manager.

In 1931, Alice married Joseph Leopold, a New York advertising executive, and reared sons Robert and John on a 10-acre estate in Weston, Connecticut. She advanced from department store management to toy designer of theme complexes, beginning with a garage and fire station and extending to a rail depot and plane hangar. Her organizational talents invigorated Connecticut Republicans and the PTA, for which she led a cooking squad to produce hot lunches and serve them at her son's school. For the League of Women Voters, to entice more women to run for local offices, she composed the leaflets "Value Your Vote" and "Don't Be an Armchair Citizen." During World War II, she sold war bonds, raised vegetables and livestock, and volunteered with the Red Cross, ration board, and two hospitals.

Elected Official

After Leopold won election to the Connecticut General Assembly in 1949, she spoke frequently to political rallies, social clubs, and professional organizations. As a freshman member of the education and labor committees, she fostered equal pay for women, standards for cleaners and laundry workers, funding for vocational schools, and a 75-cent minimum wage. In retrospect of a life of juggling marriage, motherhood, and public affairs, she urged women to ready themselves to rear educated children.

Leopold's rise to Connecticut Secretary of State in 1951 preceded appointment two years later to federal offices during the Eisenhower administration, for which she advocated passage of the Equal Rights Amendment. On July 10, 1953, she accepted membership on the Commission on Intergovernmental Relations, a congressional panel exploring waste, duplication of services, and division between state and federal regulations. At the time, she determined from national demographics that 32.1 percent of women held jobs.

As a traditionalist and the first married female director of the Women's Bureau of the U.S. Department of Labor, Leopold accepted the post in Washington on condition that she fly home each Friday to her family. She recognized that she joined the 25.8 percent of married women who held jobs outside the home. From her nomination on November 19, 1953, to 1961, she encouraged young mothers to devote some time to civic clubs and community betterment as sources of personal satisfaction. Although she labored to raise salaries for nurses, teachers, and female professionals in defense, aerospace, and substandard communities needing social and health workers, her oration in Washington, D.C., to the 1954 Girl's Nation stressed the value of home and family to ambitious young women.

In the speech "New Horizons for the Future" on September 8, 1954, the Women's Organization Day at the New York State Fair in Syracuse, Leopold outlined increasing demands on the female workforce. During the Cold War, she promoted female talent in Toronto at the 1955 Altrusa International Biennial convention. She lauded women's willingness to aid the country in the speech "The Effective Use of Womanpower," a term for political and community volunteerism.

An Influence on Women

Leopold filled her speeches and reports with data substantiating conservatism. By analyzing U.S. labor statistics drawn from jobs in insurance, accounting, statistics, law, biology, and technology, she aimed to assist older women in returning to the labor market and proposed a commission to investigate federal regulation of women's employment standards. In "What Becomes of Women College Graduates?"—an address to the 1956 National Vocational Guidance Association assembly at the Shoreham Hotel in Washington, D.C.—she acclaimed education as a completion of the self rather than a source of higher income.

Appointed director of women's affairs under Secretary of Labor James P. Mitchell on September 30, 1954, Leopold lauded a period of women's peacetime contribution to the national economy unequaled in American history. She masterminded an exchange program with France and Italy and scheduled speeches for March 10 and 11, 1955, at the Women's Bureau Conference on the Effective Use of Womanpower. In addition to studying future needs for teachers in April 1955, she surveyed employment of female engineers and investigated data on worker absenteeism.

Leopold explored a variety of venues in which to influence the thinking of women on education and the professions. She presented "Your Role in Tomorrow's World," a prophecy of female achievement at her alma mater on January 25, 1956. In Chicago on April 23, 1956, she rallied female intellectuals from Illinois, Indiana, Michigan, Ohio, and Wisconsin at the Northeast central regional convention of the American Association of University Women. In Boston on May 10, 1956, she spearheaded a job-finding forum for middle-aged women.

Avoiding the feminist philosophy of gender equality, Leopold envisioned female citizenship as the foundation of patriotism and culture rather than as wage earners competing against men. She emphasized knowledge of current events and foreign policy as ways to adapt to shifts in American values. As a mother and bureaucrat, in May 1957, she refuted claims by the National Education Association, Family Life Bureau, National Manpower Council, and Federal Bureau of Investigation director J. Edgar Hoover that workingwomen neglected their children and abetted juvenile delinquency. She declared to the press that such broad accusations unfairly targeted female workers as scapegoats of mid-20th century social ills. She demanded statistics on delinquency to prove that employed women cared less for their children.

Leopold compiled *Job Horizons for the College Woman* (1956), *Spotlight on Women in the United States, 1956–1957, What Social Security Means to Women* (1957), and *Handbook on Women Workers* (1958), a reference source for use in labor mediation, employment, education, and counseling of high school graduates. The text and accompanying charts summarized female progress in the labor force as well as education, income, and laws regulating female employment. In the article *Marriage and Family Living* (1958), she outlined the typical merger of work, home, church, and community activities in the life of a typical high school graduate.

Campaigning for the continued emergence of American women from domestic lethargy, Leopold predicted that part-time hiring of women from 1959 to 1964 would rise 18 percent and, by 1969, another 30 percent. Advocacy of the working-woman in such publications as *Future Jobs for High-School Girls* (1959) won her the 1960 Jane Addams Medal from Rockford University. At Leopold's death in New Jersey in 1982, women's historians acknowledged her convictions that women could get an education, rear a family, and involve themselves in community organizations and careers without endangering quality of life for themselves or their mates and children.

References

Leopold, Alice K. *The Effective Use of Womanpower.* Washington, DC: U.S. Government Printing Office, 1955.

"Women's Bureau Director Likes Woes of Others." *Corpus Christi* (Texas) *Caller-Times,* January 10, 1954, 10.

LEVERTOV, DENISE (1923–1997)

In 24 published collections, Guggenheim Award–winning poet Priscilla Denise Levertov debated the barbarity and pervasiveness of war in human suffering. She was born in Ilford, Essex, on the northeastern outskirts of London on October 24, 1923, to Beatrice Adelaide Spooner-Jones and Paul Philip Levertoff. Along with home schooling by BBC radio, Denise absorbed Paul's Judeo-Christian eloquence and Talmudic mysticism, Beatrice's folklore and reading aloud from Charles Dickens's novels, and verse from older sister Olga.

After classes in French, ballet, and art, in 1933, Levertov considered herself an artist in the making as well as a budding leftist who sold copies of the *Daily Worker.* In 1940, she published verse in *Poetry Quarterly* during a period when her family rescued Austrian and German refugees from the Nazis. For three years during World War II bombardments, she volunteered as a nurse and took as her mission sanitizing the baths and scrubbing the sheets of Blitz victims at a civilian hospital.

A procurer of rare books, Levertov supported herself by selling antique literature while she assembled poems for a first collection, the neo-romantic *The Double Image* (1946). Critic Kenneth Rexroth chose some of her verse for *New British Poets* (1949). After an English wedding on December 2, 1947, she lived in Paris, Provence, and Genoa as the wife of pamphleteer and social reformer Mitchell Goodman. The couple toured Guadalajara and Oaxaca, Mexico, before immigrating to Greenwich Village, where they produced son Nikolai.

In an era of antinuclear demonstrations, while working part-time at St. Vincent Hospital in the early 1950s, Levertov marshaled New Yorkers against bomb tests and air raid drills. She achieved naturalization in 1955, an influence on her submissions to the *Black Mountain Review* and to the American anthology *Here and Now* (1956). In the poem "Illustrious Ancestors" (1958), she celebrated White Russian forebears.

For protests, Levertov incurred occasional arrests. On October 21, 1967, she dramatized anti-Vietnam War demonstrations by reading pacifist verse at rallies, publishing *The Sorrow Dance* (1967), and editing *Out of the War Shadow: An Anthology of Current Poetry* (1967). She and her husband coordinated a draft protest at March on the Pentagon, which began with the mustering of 70,000 dissidents at the Lincoln Memorial. She and fellow signatories of the War Resisters League issued a 1968 antitax resolution by which they ceased supporting the Southeast Asian war.

With clear, precise oratory, on April 15, 1970, Levertov lectured protesters at the University of Massachusetts at Amherst on "Great Possessions," stressing links between America's racial divide and global wars. She made a telling connection between napalm and greedy capitalist corporations. In a salute to militancy and solidarity, she mustered hearers to action on behalf of social justice: "The days of mere protest are over, and the days of separating war, and racism and pollution of natural resources, and social injustice, and male chauvinism, into neat little compartments are over" (Levertov 1970).

Relocated to Somerville, Massachusetts, Levertov translated the compressed, evocative poetry of Eugène Guillevic, an advocate of communism during the Spanish Civil War. She taught English and the poetic craft at Brandeis, MIT, Vassar, University of Cincinnati, and Tufts University. While on staff at Stanford, she lived in Palo Alto, California.

Levertov's antiwar writings appeared in *To Stay Alive* (1971), a year before she joined poet Muriel Rukeyser and Jane Briggs Hart from October 29 to November 5, 1972, in a fact-finding trip to Hanoi. Levertov's writings honored the courage and resilience of American pilot prisoners of war and North Vietnamese noncombatants living with ongoing devastation, maiming, and death. On a campus speaking tour and in a speech composed for NBC in May 1972, she reported the loss of hospitals and schools from U.S. bombing raids, which she charged to the Nixon administration and the Central Intelligence Agency (CIA).

Levertov divorced at age 52 and moved to Seattle to lecture at the University of Washington and edit verse for *Mother Jones* magazine. Her pacifist oratory included the lyrical text of "A Speech: For Antidraft Rally, D.C., March 22, 1980." In retirement, she read verse during a tour to England and published the speech "The Writing of Poetry by Denise Levertov" (1981), a description of the communication between writer and reader. At the fall of 1982 Institute on War and Conscience at Santa Clara University, California, she delivered "Poetry on War," a lecture on the need for political verse.

As a newly converted ecumenical Catholic in 1984, Levertov chose stalwart images of God and immortality. She translated Jean Joubert's *Black Iris* (1989) and, on February 7, 1990, returned to the Santa Clara University dais at the Institute on Human Rights and Social Justice to speak on homelessness. She charted a religious coming-of-age in *The Stream & the Sapphire* (1997) and revived civil disobedience by denouncing U.S. combat in Iraq.

In her last three years, while seeking treatment for laryngitis, pneumonia, and lymphoma, Levertov composed mystic verse. She died in Seattle on December 20, 1997, from intestinal necrosis and heart failure brought on by lymphoma.

References

Levertov, Denise. "Rally at the University of Massachusetts Amherst, April 15, 1970." Modern American Poetry. Accessed December 30, 2014. http://www.english.illinois.edu/maps/poets/g_l/levertov/speech.htm.

Levertov, Denise. "Statement for a Television Program." May 1972. Gifts of Speech: Women's Speeches from Around the World. Accessed December 31, 2014. http://gos.sbc.edu/l/levertov2.html.

ON GENOCIDE AND THE VIETNAM WAR
BY DENISE LEVERTOV
NBC
MAY 1972

Poet and activist Denise Levertov debated the barbarity and pervasiveness of war in human suffering. After officials at NBC invited her to speak, then rejected her speech on the Vietnam War, she published her protest. Her writings honored the courage and resilience of American pilot prisoners of war and North Vietnamese noncombatants living with ongoing devastation, maiming, and death, which she charged to President Richard Nixon and the CIA.

I have been asked to speak on this program because I am a poet. One of the obligations of the writer, and perhaps especially of the poet, is to say or sing *all* that he or she can, to deal with as much of the world as becomes possible to him or her in language. I and most of my fellow American poets nowadays find ourselves inevitably—of necessity—writing more and more poems of grief, of rage, concerning the despoilment of the earth and of all life upon it, of the systematic destruction of all that we feel passionate love for, both by the greed of industry and by the mass murder we call war.

We are living at war: the shame and horror of being citizens of the country which, in its ruthless imperialism, is not only ravaging Southeast Asia but, with its military bases, its Polaris submarines, the machinations of its CIA, and the tentacles of its giant corporations, is everywhere the prime force of antilife and oppression—this shame and horror cast their shadow over all we say, feel, and do. The spring sunshine, the new leaves: we still see them, we still love them: but in what poignant contrast is their beauty and simple goodness to the evil we are conscious of day and night.

And this evil, this blight, this war in which our whole lives are being spent, is present at home, here in the U.S., as well as abroad, in the form of racism, of gross injustice, of poverty and hunger in the midst of the very richest country in the world. As corrupt and self-seeking politicians erode the Constitution and bring us daily closer to outright fascism, the poet is turned away from his impulse to sing, to testify in patterns of words to the miracle of life, and is driven willy-nilly to warn, to curse, to gnash the teeth of language; and at the same time, living always in the war shadow, to celebrate the courage and high spirit of all who dare to struggle, Davids to the Goliaths of capitalism (the expression of man's greed) and imperialism (the expression of man's lust for power); to celebrate the courage and tenacity of the so-called "enemy" in Southeast Asia, and of all who here at home resist the system—people like Angela Davis, Dan and Phil Berrigan, Cesar Chavez; and to declare solidarity with them and with all who share their struggle.

Poets differ from other people only in having a specially intimate relation to words. When I say I speak as a poet, it is the same as to say I speak as a human being. In the name of humanness, then, I call on my fellow humans to *stop the war*; but not to think that by stopping the present slaughter in Vietnam we will have done the job—for that slaughter is only one manifestation of the total war that surrounds us. We could *begin* if we wanted to: we could stop the bombing tomorrow if every individual who would like to see an end to U.S. involvement would say *No Business as Usual* and ACT on those words.

It is our own timidity that makes us feel powerless. If we acted to bring about a general strike and economic boycott, we would see we have more power than we think. But even if we stop the bombing and get rid of Nixon, let us understand that though it would be a beginning—and a good one—it would be ineffectual unless it led to a thorough change—outward and inward, institutional and personal—of the system Nixon and his bombs are part of.

Stop the bombing. Declare peace. Change the system.

LIVERMORE, MARY ASHTON (1820–1905)

Essayist and lyceum lecturer Mary Ashton Rice Livermore promoted full involvement of women in volunteerism, citizenship, and moral reform. She was born in a Boston family of seven siblings on December 19, 1820, to strict Baptists, Zebiah Vose Glover Ashton and Timothy Rice. The family briefly experimented with farming in Arcade, New York, in 1832 before buying a stagecoach ticket and Erie Canal passage back to Boston and occupying a house near Old North Church.

In her teens, Livermore fantasized about preaching sermons and became an avid scripture reader. After winning medals for excellence at the Hancock School, she apprenticed in dressmaking. In 1836, she studied metaphysics, astronomy, French, and Latin at the Charlestown Female Seminary.

The dour Calvinism of the Rice household convinced Livermore that her deceased sister Rachel never entered heaven. As a result, in her late teens, Livermore edged away from orthodoxy toward progressivism and taught herself Greek for readings of the New Testament. During membership on the Charlestown seminary faculty for the next two years, she heard abolitionist and reformer Angelina Grimké's pro-woman oratory and became a feminist.

Supporting Human Rights

From 1839 to 1842, in Virginia, Livermore's observations of the lashing of a slave cooper expanded her humanity and outrage at human bondage. She devoted herself to abolitionism and to compiling temperance fiction in *The Children's Army* (1844). After marriage in May 1845 to Universalist clergyman Daniel Parker Livermore, she organized medical care and education for industrial workers while tending parishioners in Stafford, Connecticut; Auburn, New York; and Malden and Weymouth, Massachusetts.

In the early years of activism, Livermore fought the spread of alcoholism by issuing *Thirty Years Too Late: A Temperance Story* (1845) and refuted fundamentalist scare tactics with a novel, *A Mental Transformation* (1848). In 1857, she made a home in Chicago and volunteered to aid victims of a summer cholera epidemic caused by polluted drinking water. She and Daniel published the *New Covenant*, a Universalist reform paper, and advanced Universalism and the campaign of presidential candidate Abraham Lincoln.

During the Civil War, Livermore rejoiced at President Lincoln's able response to a military crisis and to the departure of the Sixth Massachusetts Regiment. She joined the Chicago division of the United States Sanitary Commission as a combat nurse, visitor of military camps, and collector of food, clothing, blankets, and medical supplies for the Union army. On appointment by head nurse Dorothea Dix as a recruiter of female volunteers for the Northwest Commission, Livermore became adept at addressing members of 3,000 aid societies and demonstrating how to circumvent military bureaucracy. To relieve the domestic problems of female volunteers, she and other nurses formed a cooperative laundry and daycare.

After the Battle of Fort Donelson, Tennessee, from February 11 to 16, 1862, Livermore aided herbalist Mary Ann Bickerdyke in loading boats evacuating the severely wounded to Louisville and St. Louis. Having conquered queasiness at the sight of mutilation, Livermore brightened wards of military hospitals in Helena, Arkansas, and Cairo and Mound City, Illinois. On April 6, 1862, she aided staff field hospitals overrun by men shot at the Battle of Shiloh, Tennessee.

The following November, Livermore met President Lincoln, who despaired at the high number of desertions from Union ranks. At a low point in wartime morale, she buoyed patriotism by assembling treatment packets and mailing surprises to Union soldiers. She appealed for funds to create Chicago's Soldiers' Home, a rehabilitation center that remained in use until 1877.

Postwar Reform

As a colleague of organizers Julia Ward Howe and Lucy Stone, Livermore cofounded the American Woman Suffrage Association, a drive for full female citizenship, and engaged audiences to support the Woman's Christian Temperance Union. In 1868, she chaired the Illinois Woman Suffrage Association and managed Chicago's first Woman Suffrage Convention. After her friend Anna Elizabeth Dickinson spoke to delegates, Livermore depicted suffrage as a wildfire spreading throughout Illinois. She successfully lobbied state legislation to grant women control of their finances and property. In January 1869, she, Stone, and Howe began publishing a women's newspaper, *The Agitator*, while Daniel Livermore managed the business affairs.

On relocating to Melrose, Massachusetts, in 1869, Livermore co-edited *The Women's Journal* and issued essays in the *Chautauquan*, *North American Review*, and the *Independent*. A schedule of five speeches per week took her some 25,000 miles annually from Maine to California to demand equal rights, health care, and education for females. Her subject matter included the gender equality speeches "The Reasons Why," "Concerning Husbands and Wives," and the temperance topic "Does the Liquor Traffic Pay?" She spoke extemporaneously and held the platform for up to two hours at a time. In 1883, she published her most popular address, "What Shall We Do with Our Daughters: Superfluous Women," which she delivered some 800 times. The theme impressed men and women with the absence of choice in young women's lives.

With anti-alcohol campaigner Frances E. Willard, Livermore publicized female achievements by compiling *A Woman of the Century: Fourteen Hundred-Seventy Biographical Sketches Accompanied by Portraits of Leading American Women in All Walks of Life* (1893). Daniel Livermore's death in 1899 dampened her buoyancy and left her pining for a reunion with her mate through spiritualism. She died of bronchitis and heart disease in Melrose on May 23, 1905.

See Also: Barton, Clara; Dickinson, Anna; Howe, Julia Ward; Stone, Lucy.

Reference

Venet, Wendy Hamand. *A Strong-Minded Woman: The Life of Mary Livermore*. Amherst: University of Massachusetts Press, 2005.

INDUSTRIAL GAINS OF WOMEN DURING THE LAST HALF-CENTURY (EXCERPT) BY MARY ASHTON LIVERMORE INTERNATIONAL COUNCIL OF WOMEN ALBAUGH'S OPERA HOUSE, WASHINGTON, D.C. MARCH 25, 1888

A former volunteer nurse during the Civil War, Mary Ashton Livermore of Boston addressed a Washington, D.C., audience on the exemplary patronage of women during four years of war. In an 1865 accounting of women's organization and administration, fairs raised $3 million in funds in Chicago, Boston, Brooklyn, New York, Cincinnati, Cleveland, Philadelphia, Albany, and Pittsburgh for the U.S. Sanitary Commission to supply field hospitals and rehabilitation centers.

Livermore deplored the fact that, when the nation reunited, females returned to an infantile state of dependency on males for the management of their land and money and even the parenting of their children.

The transition of the country from peace to the tumult of war was appalling and swift, but the regeneration of its women kept pace with it. They lopped off superfluities, retrenched in expenditures, became deaf to the calls of pleasure, and heeded not the mandates of fashion. Their work was that of relief and philanthropy, and for the first time in the history of the world the women of America developed a heavenly side to war. They cared for the needy families of soldiers, nursed the sick in camp and the wounded in hospitals, ministered to the dying in the rear of battlefields, and kept full to overflowing the channels of beneficence which extended from Northern homes to the army at the front. For their multiform work they needed immense sums of money, and now the latent business abilities of women began to show themselves.

They came to Washington and competed with men for government contracts for the manufacture of army clothing and obtained them. When their accounts and their work were rigorously inspected by the War Department, they received commendation and not a word of criticism and were awarded larger contracts. They planned great moneymaking enterprises, whose vastness of conception and good business management yielded millions of dollars to be expended in the interest of sick and wounded soldiers.

The last two of the colossal sanitary fairs held in New York and Philadelphia yielded, respectively, one million dollars and one million two hundred thousand dollars. Women were the inspiration, the creators, the great energizing force of these immense fairs, and also from first to last of the Sanitary Commission. . . . Men awoke to the consciousness that there were in women possibilities and potencies of which they had never dreamed.

The old-time theory that "all men support all women" led to the enactment of laws which gave all the earnings of the married woman to her husband; in most instances gave him control of her property, always legal possession of her person, and legal ownership of her minor children; the right to decide the location of their joint domicile; the power, in short, to become the arbiter of her fate; while the husband, in return for the service rendered him by the wife, was to give her such shelter, food, and clothing as was compatible with his means or inclination. While the woman remained unmarried and a minor, all her earnings belonged to her father, who did not hesitate to demand and retain them.

Usually, if she remained unmarried through life, she continued to share the labors of her father's household without other compensation than shelter, food, and clothing, as in the days of her minority, sometimes receiving a meager stipend from her father's estate when he died. Generally, however, the property of the father was left to the sons with the exception of the mother's right of dower, and the mother and sisters became then the dependents of sons and brothers as they had formerly been of the father and husband. In some sections of the country this unjust and iniquitous condition of things remains still unchanged. . . .

Source: Livermore, Mary A. "Industrial Gains of Women during the Last Half-Century." In *Report of the International Council of Women*. Washington, DC: Rufus H. Harby, 1888, 131–136.

LORDE, AUDRE (1934–1992)

Radical New York polemicist and poet Audre Geraldine Lorde focused her writings and lectures on the overthrow of oppressors who classified her as "other." Born in Harlem on February 18, 1934, to Linda Gertrude Belmar and Frederick Byron Lorde, she attended St. Mark's and St. Catherine's parochial schools, both run by hostile nuns, and balanced her first and last names by dropping the y from Audrey. She began writing verse at age 13 and viewed her talent as an obligation to human survival.

At age 17, Lorde lived apart from her parents, supported herself as a nurse's aide at Bellevue Hospital, and allied with fellow social outcasts. In 1951, Lorde published verse in *Seventeen* magazine and the *Harlem Writers' Quarterly*. At Hunter College, she worked toward a degree in literature and philosophy and edited the campus magazine *Echo*. To escape a racist trade union and the antihomosexual persecution of the McCarthy era, she lived publicly as a lesbian in Cuernavaca from 1952 to 1953 while working as a clinic clerk and studying at the National University of Mexico.

While investigating child welfare in 1959, Lorde questioned Christian and radical moral authorities who alienated black lesbians. As a prominent spokesperson for women, she differed from Betty Friedan, Mary Daly, and other white feminists over the patterning of the women's movement after the lifestyles and aims of privileged white females. Lorde maintained individualistic theories of feminism that cast her as an isolationist.

The poet issued her first self-analytical collection, *The First Cities*, in 1968. While seeking a divorce and coping with outrage at the assassinations of Dr. Martin Luther King Jr., and Robert Kennedy, she served Tougaloo College in Jackson, Mississippi, as poet in residence and editor of *Pound* magazine. During the compilation of a second anthology, *Cables to Rage* (1970), while she raised a family on Staten Island, she centered writing themes on love, motherhood, and authentic lesbian romance. A subsequent anthology, *From a Land Where Other People Live* (1972), won a National Book Award nomination. For *Coal* (1976), she explored the layering of identities through the metaphor of coal transformed into diamonds.

Lorde exhibited literary prominence with the paper "Self-Definition and My Poetry" (1976) in December 1976; with commentary at the First Black Feminist Retreat at South Hadley, Massachusetts, on July 6, 1977; and with an undated lecture at her alma mater, "Difference and Survival: An Address at Hunter College," which claimed differences as assets. She made a lasting contribution to women's oratory with "The Transformation of Silence into Language and Action," an address to the Modern Language Association in Chicago on December 28, 1977. She spoke on "Blacks and the Sexual Revolution" at Spelman College and reflected on her part in the Dahomeyan diaspora in *The Black Unicorn* (1978). For the keynote address on October 13, 1979, at the First National Third World Lesbian and Gay Conference in Washington, D.C., she posed a poignant question, "When Will the Ignorance End?"

Lorde assembled uncensored observations on passion as a creative life force in *Uses of the Erotic: The Erotic as Power* (1981). The Gay Caucus award-winning text *The Cancer Journals* (1981) expounded on the importance of sisterhood to cancer survivors. She made an issue over the value of silicon prosthesis to the plastic surgery industry and to women who fear being judged as maimed females. She next rallied black poets at the 1981 Women Writers Symposium in St. Croix and overlaid autobiographical cross currents with African goddess myths in a memoir, *Zami: A New Spelling of My Name* (1982).

Although burdened with treatments for liver cancer, Lorde accepted a professorship at the Kennedy Institute for North American Studies at the Free University of Berlin, a research center for the humanities. Her encouragement aided the development of a gay publishing group, Orlanda Frauenverlag, which exposed the murderous Nazi attitude toward mixed-race German children. As an expatriate in St. Croix during her last six years, she won a National Book Award for *A Burst of Light* (1989). As recipient of the Walt Whitman Citation of Merit, she looked to the future of books with "What Is at Stake in Lesbian and Gay Publishing Today" (1990).

Before her final decline, Audre Lorde chose a ritual African name, Gambda Adisa, meaning Warrior: She Who Makes Her Meaning Known. In 1991, she served New York as state poet laureate. Following an honorarium from the Publishing Triangle, she died of liver cancer in St. Croix on November 17, 1992. Her last poems appeared in a posthumous collection, *The Marvelous Arithmetics of Distance: Poems 1987–1992* (1993).

See Also: Friedan, Betty.

References

Griffin, Ada Gay, and Michelle Parkerson. *A Litany for Survival: The Life and Work of Audre Lorde* (film). New York: Third World Newsreel, 1995.

Lorde, Audre. "The Transformation of Silence into Language and Action." December 28, 1977. The Incredible Shrinking Phallus. Accessed March 24, 2015. https://shrinkingphallus.wordpress.com/the-transformation-of-silence-into-language-and-action-by-audre-lorde/.

WHAT IS AT STAKE IN LESBIAN AND GAY PUBLISHING TODAY (EXCERPT) BY AUDRE LORDE BILL WHITEHEAD AWARD CEREMONY MAY 15, 1990

A radical Harlem polemicist and poet, Audre Lorde lectured on the overthrow of oppressors who classed her as "other." As a creator of Kitchen Table: Women of Color Press, she recognized the triple jeopardy of the black lesbian author, especially in a profession dominated by white males. In addition to promoting inclusion in American publishing, she taught at Berlin and exposed the murderous Nazi attitude toward mixed-race German children.

What is at stake in lesbian and gay publishing today basically is what has always been at stake—our survival—our future: for each one of us and collectively, the question—how do we define ourselves and how do we put who we are behind what we say we believe?

We are lesbians and gay men helping to shape a future for ourselves and for those various communities of which we are a part and within which we must define the meaning of being lesbian and gay. For without community, whatever we do can be only a temporary armistice between an individual and his or her particular situation.

Lesbian and gay publishing does not exist in a vacuum, however, and we are not one great vat of homogenized milk. We are lesbian and gay in a world growing increasingly hysterical with denial and contradiction—a world where the increasing disparity between the haves and the have-nots threatens to detonate in each one of our dooryards. Of course, you say, we all recognize the importance of a world-view—we know the ozone layer is disappearing, nuclear proliferation is poisoning our planet. But to an increasing percentage of people upon this earth, watching their children starve to death in Lahore and the Sahel, lost to drugs in L.A. and New York, stomped to death in Leipzig and Berlin and Brooklyn because of the color of their skin, nuclear holocaust and ecological disaster is of little concern. What does lesbian and gay publishing have to offer them?

I am a black lesbian feminist warrior poet mother, strong for all my identities, and I am indivisible. Out of the insights and power of those identities have come the work which you honor here tonight.

The increase in racist, anti-Semitic, heterosexist attacks here in North America is being mirrored throughout Europe by the rise in neo-fascist activity against Afro-Europeans, Jews, homosexuals, and foreign workers.

There are lesbian and gay writers of color in this country articulating in their work questions and positions which must be heard if we are to survive into the 21st century . . . There are lesbian and gay writers of color across Europe chronicling what the current political changes on that continent can mean for people of color, that is, for the majority of people upon this earth. How many of these writers are known to you? How do you use your power when their manuscripts come across your desk, the modest announcements of their books appear in your mail?

What is at stake in lesbian and gay publishing in 1990, quite simply, is: how will you define yourselves in the 21st century in a world where seven-eighths of that world's population are people of color? And how will you use the power that definition engenders?

I recognize the honor you do me with this award. But honors are most meaningful when they include peer decisions. How many lesbians and gay men of color are included in your group? How many were polled for this award? Or even, how many writers of color have you published or encouraged or helped to voice in any way? At the National Lesbian and Gay March on Washington, D.C., the largest gathering of lesbian and gay men to date, the one book exhibit at the march ignored the works of gay people of color. Lesbian and gay writers of color, our work and our concerns, are consistently invisible within the publishing and literary newsletters circulating in the lesbian and gay communities.

. . . If this group wishes to truly honor my work, built upon the creative use of differences for all our survivals, then I charge you as a group in some way to include and further expose the work of new lesbian and gay writers of color in the coming year, and to report on what has been done at next year's award ceremony.

That will be a truly bold and meaningful gesture and one reflective of the growing vision and power of lesbian and gay publishing in the 1990s.

LOTZ, ANNE GRAHAM (1948–)

A reflective writer and evangelist, Anne McCue Graham Lotz addresses Christian gatherings with her own style of revivalism. A North Carolinian born in Montreat on May 21, 1948, she is the daughter of meditation author and poet Ruth Bell and

William Franklin "Billy" Graham Jr., a conservative Protestant preacher of global renown. She grew up in a structured moral environment, with her grandmother setting the traditional example of womanhood as the fount of home rule and child care.

Ruth Graham disciplined the children with tough love, ruled out long hair and loud music, and led welcoming celebrations at the railroad station when Billy returned home. In 1958, Ruth gave Anne *Daily Light*, a collection of one-page scriptural meditations. The guidebook remained a source of wisdom into adulthood. At Easter, a television viewing of Cecil B. DeMille's biblical epic *King of Kings* inspired her to accept Christianity.

A Bible Reader

On finishing high school, in 1964 at age 17, Anne attended a Fellowship of Christian Athletes conference at which she encountered dentist Daniel Milton "Dan" Lotz, a former University of North Carolina at Chapel Hill basketball star 11 years her senior. After Daniel joined the Billy Graham crusade to Earl's Court in London, he proposed marriage. She and Daniel wed in a ceremony at the Gaither Chapel in Montreat on September 2, 1966, conducted by Billy Graham and Daniel's father, a street corner Baptist preacher.

After a weeklong honeymoon in Palma Valley, California, Lotz proposed entering UNC-Chapel Hill in January 1967. For a decade, housewifery and motherhood of three children—Jonathan, Morrow, and Rachel-Ruth Lotz—absorbed her but plunged her into depression. In 1974, while she attended an evangelism conference in Lausanne, Switzerland, and went on vacation to Cape Cod, she pondered undertaking an independent ministry.

Through Bible Study Fellowship (BSF), a nondenominational lay study structured by a British missionary to China, in 1975, Lotz underwent intensive reading of Genesis. The basis of Judaism, Christianity, and Islam fed her fascination with the patriarchy of Abraham, a human hero who struggled with issues of faith. The BSF syllabus included Exodus, prophecy, and the New Testament, particularly Matthew, Acts, and Revelation. Her venture inspired her sister Bunny, who launched her own BSF class.

Lacking religious ordination, in the spring of 1977, Lotz made visits to prison cells and taught BSF to some 200 members. Over 12 years, attendance grew by 150 percent and directed her concentration toward guiding Christians of dwindling or lapsed faith. In 1983, she became the only female speaker at a plenary session of the International Congress of Itinerant Evangelism in Amsterdam.

World Fame

In 1988, Lotz initiated a speaking career with the nonprofit AnGeL Ministries, of which she directed. As a Christian messenger, she rallied seminaries, colleges, and conferences for ministers, women, and world evangelism in 30 cities in Norway, Wales, England, Ireland, Moldova, Ukraine, Philippines, South Korea, India, Paraguay, Panama, Puerto Rico, and Canada. At her father's seminars at the Billy Graham Training Center at the Cove, she led sessions that preceded commitment services and communion.

Less controversial and opinionated than her brother Franklin, Lotz crafted her lectures on scriptural exegesis and unwavering fundamentalism that condemned abortion and homosexuality. In addition to speaking 100 times per year, she appeared on *The Today Show*, *The Early Show*, *Larry King Live*, and *60 Minutes*. In 1989, she and sisters Gigi and Bunny traveled with their mother to Huaiyin, China, Ruth's birthplace. A decade later, the *New York Times* listed Anne among the top five U.S. preachers. She informed a reporter that God forbade her seeking ordination or a senior pastorate.

As a result of deep scriptural study, Lotz published *The Vision of His Glory* (1997), an updated seven-volume video series with study guides and workbooks. Personal struggles did not dim her enthusiasm for oratory. At Easter 1999, she energized a sermon in Charlotte before 1,900 in the convention center. Standing behind a cruciform lectern she elevated both fists in a gesture of control and power. At her height, she composed *Just Give Me Jesus* (2001), a title she applied to urban revivals. Two years later, she issued *My Heart's Cry* (2002), winner of her fourth Gold Medallion Book Award for excellence.

In addition to marketing books, scriptural reading guides, CDs, and DVDs, Lotz traveled internationally to urban arenas and hotel ballrooms and spoke daily over the global radio program *Daily Light for Daily Living*. For books such as *I Saw the Lord: A Wake-up Call for Your Heart* (2006), she interpreted worrisome events such as the O. J. Simpson trial, Timothy McVeigh's bombing in Oklahoma City, murder of child beauty queen JonBenet Ramsey, and Hurricane Katrina as warnings from God.

Lotz's 21st-century writings featured *The Magnificent Obsession: Embracing the God-filled Life* (2009), a disclosure of her parents' disapproval of her radical departure from organized faiths. She justified disdain for educated religionists and for ritual, creeds, and church traditions that breed judgments and hostility. She followed with *Expecting to See Jesus: A Wake-up Call for God's People* (2011) and interpretations of the 9/11 disasters a decade later in the September 2011 issue of *Christianity Today*.

In 2012, Lotz weathered another challenge after Daniel entered the hospital for treatment of MRSA, a blood infection. On experiences with officious organized religions, she wrote *Wounded by God's People* (2013). On the National Day of Prayer, May 7, 2014, she proposed citizen repentance. In June 2014, she issued a revelation that the world was about to end and called followers to begin a fast and daily prayer over July 1–7 for the nation's salvation.

In 2014, Lotz completed a children's book, *Heaven, God's Promise for Me*, and composed her "Prayer for Jerusalem," a long address to the god of Abraham, Isaac, and Jacob, the first patriarchs of the Old Testament. The text declared the House of Israel desperate from the effects of war and greed. She identified Pharaoh's army in Exodus with contemporary animosities of Hamas, Hezbollah, ISIS, Taliban, Al Qaeda, the Muslim Brotherhood, and Boko Haram. In May 2015, she predicted that gay marriage, abortion, white police shooting black suspects, and the abandonment of Israel signified the coming of the end time. In recovery from the death of her husband in August 2015, she greeted New Year 2016 with visions of increased world conflict and chaos.

Reference

Nüesch, Hanspeter. *Ruth and Billy Graham: The Legacy of a Couple*. Grand Rapids, MI: Baker Books, 2014.

ONE VOICE, UNITED IN PRAYER
BY ANNE GRAHAM LOTZ
NATIONAL DAY OF PRAYER, WASHINGTON, D.C.
MAY 1, 2014

Evangelist Anne Graham Lotz used the National Day of Prayer as preface to a warning to Americans that the world would end soon. To rescue citizens, she proposed repentance, fasting, and prayer. Incorporated in the text, reminders of terrorism connected cosmic fears with real national enemies. A year later, she prophesied that gay marriage, abortion, white police shootings of black suspects, and the political abandonment of Israel signified the coming of an apocalypse.

Lord of the Universe. Lord of this planet. Lord of the nations. Lord of our hearts. On this National Day of Prayer, we look to You.

In the darkness, You are our Light.

In the storm, You are our Anchor.

In our weakness, You are our Strength. In our grief, You are our Comfort.

In our despair, You are our Hope.

In our confusion, You are our Wisdom. In time of terrorism, You are our Shield. In time of war, You are our Peace.

In times of uncertainty, You are the Rock on which we stand.

We make our prayer to You using the words of the prophet Daniel:

O Lord, You are the great and awesome God, who keeps His covenant of love with those who love Him and keep His commandments. You are merciful and forgiving. You are righteous, but this day we are covered with shame because we have sinned against You, and done wrong. We have turned away from Your commands and principles. We have turned away from You.

Yet You have promised in 2 Chronicles 7, that if we—a people identified with You—would humble ourselves, pray, seek Your face, and turn from our wicked ways, then You would hear our prayer, forgive our sin and heal our land.

So we choose to stop pointing our finger at the sins of others, and examine our own hearts and lives. We choose to acknowledge our own sin—our neglect and defiance and ignorance and even rejection of You. This day we choose to repent.

In response to our heartfelt repentance, God of Abraham, Isaac and Jacob, Father of Jesus Christ, in keeping with all Your righteous acts and according to Your promise, turn away Your anger and Your wrath from the United States of America. Hear the prayers and petitions offered to You on this National Day of Prayer, as we give You our full attention. Give ear, our God, and hear; open Your eyes and see. We do not make requests of You because we are righteous, but because of Your great mercy.

For the glory of Your Name hear our prayer, forgive our sin, and heal our land.

We ask this in the name of Your Son Jesus Christ who offers us salvation from Your judgment, forgiveness for our sin, and reconciliation with You through His own blood shed on the Cross. Amen.

LUCE, CLARE BOOTHE (1903–1987)

An exemplary orator and satirist of the modern era, Ann Clare Booth Luce was a playwright, politician and the first female ambassador to a major world power. She was born on March 10, 1903, in New York City to typist and dancer Anna Clara Schneider and violinist William Franklin "Frank" Boothe. She understudied actor Mary Pickford's part in *A Good Little Devil* (1912–1913) and performed in the silent film *The Heart of a Wolf* (1915).

After Frank deserted his family, Luce attended St. Mary's Catholic School in Garden City, New York. In 1917, she studied modern foreign languages and rhetoric at Miss Mason's School at the Castle in Tarrytown, New York. On graduating valedictorian in May 1919, she looked for avenues to fame. On return from a European tour, while enrolled in Clare Tree Major's School of Theatre in New York, she recruited volunteers and donors for the Red Cross and the National Woman's Party.

In Greenwich, Connecticut, on August 10, 1923, Luce married George Tuttle Brokaw, a wealthy garment manufacturer. With their daughter Ann, the family lived in Newport, Rhode Island, until 1929, when Luce eluded George's drunken rages by divorcing him. Publisher Condé Nast hired her to write captions for illustrations in *Vogue*. For *Vanity Fair*, she phrased sassy remarks about social climbers and, after publishing *Stuffed Shirts* (1931), wangled a promotion to manage the magazine. She quit the post to accept appointment to the National Recovery Administrations' Code Authority for the Motion Picture Industry.

Following the failure of a first play, *Abide with Me* (1935), on November 23, 1935, Clare married Henry Robinson Luce, publisher of *Fortune*, *Sports Illustrated*, and *Time*. At her suggestion, he initiated *Life* magazine, for which she wrote articles on celebrities and European culture. She gained literary fame as dramatist of the satiric *The Women* (1936), which flourished in Europe. She followed with the Hollywood romp *Kiss the Boys Goodbye* (1938) and *Margin for Error* (1939), in which she denounced Nazi anti-Semitism.

To witness World War II as a combat reporter for *Life*, in the winter of 1939–1940, Luce traveled to Great Britain and toured through battlefields in France, Belgium, Holland, and Italy. Her publication of *Europe in the Spring* (1940) convinced Americans that the United States could not isolate itself from the mounting furor. She extended wartime coverage for *Life* in 1941 with an insider's glimpse of conditions in China, Burma, India, the Philippines, and Egypt and interviewed Douglas MacArthur, Chiang Kai-Shek, George S. Patton, and Jacques Phillipe Leclerc. From Radio City, she raised hopes that the Sino-Japanese War would prove disastrous for the invaders. In collaboration with Madame Chang at Chungking, Luce elevated U.S. concern for Chinese war orphans.

In November 1942, Luce gained a seat in the U.S. Congress as a representative from Connecticut. She proposed desegregation of the military, championed formation of the Atomic Energy Commission, and advocated peace, postwar employment, and aid to the wives of soldiers and sailors. Globally, she denounced communism and scolded Republican presidential candidate Wendell Willkie for ignoring the totalitarian guile of Russian dictator Joseph Stalin.

Early in service on the House Military Affairs Committee, Luce surprised members of the 78th Congress with the speech "America's Destiny in the Air" (1943), a proposal that the United States could stave off another world war by dominating both military and commercial flight. Her facile delivery varied the tone from patriotic highs to respectful lows for military losses and the collapse of the U.S. Merchant Marine. Clever and glib, she balanced opinions with fact and predictions that young Americans anticipated greatness in aeronautical advancement. Within hours, the media broadcast her ebullient address, picking for posterity her made-up term "globaloney" to skewer the thinking of Vice President Henry A. Wallace.

Luce's fractious orations at national political conventions generated memorable quotations ridiculing presidents Roosevelt and Harry S. Truman. From 1944 to 1945, she witnessed the freeing of prisoners from Nazi death camps with a U.S. delegation. She lectured Congress on October 4, 1945, about the need for a holistic policy toward rehabilitating war-torn Europe. Her postwar correspondence proposed solutions to demobilization, wartime shortages of nylon and rayon, price controls, and reshaping the draft during peacetime.

During the Eisenhower administration in March 1953, Luce accepted presidential appointment as a U.S. ambassador to Italy. As a resident of Villa Taverna in Rome, she mastered Italian and negotiated a compromise between Italy and Yugoslavia on postwar possession of Trieste. With poise and charm, she cultivated the good will of Pope Pius XII and persuaded Giovanni Gronchi, Italy's first Catholic president, to allow the U.S. military to build an Italian base at Camp Darby in Pisa.

Luce maintained a speaking schedule that included "Ambassadors: Professionals or Amateurs" in October 1957 and "American Diplomacy at Work" (1958). In 1961, she addressed the National War College on "Population Explosion or Population Annihilation." As both journalist and Catholic, she found fault with the liberal media for endorsing free sex.

At Wilson College in Chambersburg, Pennsylvania, in 1961, Clare questioned the morality of the Cold War arms race, a topic she pursued in February 1962 with "American Morality and Nuclear Diplomacy." Because of anti-Communist oratory, she achieved the 1971 American Statesman Medal from the Freedoms Foundation at Valley Forge. President Ronald Reagan appointed her to the Foreign Intelligence Advisory Board, a position she held from 1973 to 1977 and returned to in 1981. A high point of her oratory, "Is the New Morality Destroying America?" (1978), expressed a conservative's distaste for licentious behavior, a topic she pursued after Jimmy Carter's remarks on *Playboy* magazine.

In 1983, when Luce occupied an apartment at the Watergate in Washington, D.C., Reagan presented her the Presidential Medal of Freedom. In the months before her death, the National Women's Party awarded her the Alice Paul Pioneer Achiever citation, an honor named for a suffrage strategist. She also accepted the 1986 Eleanor Roosevelt Humanitarian Award from the National Women's Forum. Luce died of brain cancer at her Washington home on August 9, 1987.

References

Luce, Clare Boothe. "A Greater and Freer America: G.I. Joe's Future." June 27, 1944. Accessed December 4, 2014. http://www.ibiblio.org/pha/policy/1944/1944-06-27a.html.

Morris, Sylvia Jukes. *Price of Fame: The Honorable Clare Boothe Luce*. New York: Random House, 2014.

AMERICA'S DESTINY IN THE AIR (EXCERPT) BY CLARE BOOTHE LUCE HOUSE MILITARY AFFAIRS COMMISSION HOUSE OF REPRESENTATIVES, WASHINGTON, D.C. FEBRUARY 9, 1943

A former combat journalist, U.S. Congresswoman Clare Boothe Luce of Connecticut proposed the desegregation of the U.S. military and the formation of an atomic energy agency. As a member of the House Military Affairs Commission, she looked beyond World War II to the future need of air power and the technological advancement of aerial combat. Her proposal preceded formation of the U.S. Air Force on September 18, 1947, and the deployment of planes to deter nuclear attack, recover missing personnel, support ground and naval forces, and probe outer space.

. . . The time has come for the administration to redefine clearly what it believes our air policy is, or should be. Then it is up to the people to decide that they approve of it, and the State Department to negotiate those policies with all United Nations countries, in a generous manner, a manner consistent with our new and grave responsibility as the world's leading air power. And above all, it is for us here to review laws and make appropriations which will implement this responsibility forcefully. To this end, we must assemble here in this House that able body of men of aviation-minded experts who already exist and allow them relentlessly to apply their full energies, time, and thought to this all-important question.

If in the next few years thousands upon thousands of our young men who have flown the highest mountains, the deepest rivers, and widest jungles, who have navigated the seven green seas, dyeing them red with their blood; if the great air ground personnel which has sustained them overseas, and the hundreds of thousands employed in our aircraft factories suddenly find that a new national air policy has robbed them of their professions and jobs—well, my colleagues, we and this administration shall answer at the bar of history rather sooner than we expect to young America.

Furthermore, I do not hesitate to say, if out of indifference or lack of foresight, this administration and this Congress espouse the wrong air policy for this Nation, we shall have most efficiently laid the groundwork for America's certain defeat in World War No. 3. Then indeed the air over our heads will be full of the sound of wings—the wings of the chickens coming home to roost, but to roost uncertainly in these steel girders above us, as the bombs of the enemy send them squawking in terror, and us squealing with shame out of this great hall.

To paraphrase the words of our gallant ally and that greatest of patriots, Winston Churchill, who sees, as he should see, nothing inconsistent between fighting a war for democracy and defending the interests of the noble nation which nobly sired him, "We, gentlemen, were not elected by our constituents on either side of this aisle, to preside over the liquidation of America's best interests, either at home or abroad." The sky's the limit of those interests. The time is now.

Source: Luce, Clare Boothe. "America's Destiny in the Air." *Congressional Record, House.* 78th Cong., 1st sess., February 9. Washington, DC: U.S. Government Printing Office, 1943, 759–764.

M

MANKILLER, WILMA (1945–2010)

A pacesetting social visionary and politician, Wilma Pearl Mankiller led the Cherokee nation for a decade, setting an example of Indian culture and female leadership for Indian girls. A native of Oklahoma, she was born in the Hastings Indian Hospital in Tahlequah on November 18, 1945, to Clara Irene Sitton, a Dutch-Irish mother of 11 children, and union organizer and warehouse laborer Charley Mankiller, a Cherokee landowner. In winter 1838–1839, her great-grandfather, John Mankiller, survived the Trail of Tears, which forcefully reoccupied 16,000 Cherokee from the Carolinas, Georgia, Tennessee, and Alabama; around 4,000 died along the way.

From first to sixth grade, Mankiller made a six-mile round-trip on weekdays to Rocky Mountain School. After the U.S. Army uprooted the family from a tight-knit neighborhood in fall 1957, the Bureau of Indian Affairs (BIA) relocated the Mankillers to San Francisco's Keys Hotel near the American Indian Center. From a racist urban environment that inflicted emotional distress and physical damage, the family migrated to a housing project in Daly City.

An activist in the pan-Indian Red Power Movement, Mankiller joined 89 college students from 13 tribes on November 20, 1969, in the 19-month occupation of Alcatraz Island, an abandoned federal prison. To feed and supply the dissidents, with siblings Richard, James, Vanessa, and Linda, Mankiller raised funds. At headquarters at the American Indian Center, she maintained communications and defended civil rights.

By establishing the Cherokee Nation Community Development Department and writing grant requests, Mankiller experienced a spiritual rejuvenation that targeted tribal hopelessness, environmental damage, and antifemale sentiment. In August 1983, she won election to deputy chief of the Cherokee and president of the 15-member Tribal Council. On the resignation of head chief Ross Swimmer in early December 1985, she achieved a victory for women's history by replacing him. In an inaugural speech, she dispelled fears of change and promised to focus on developing the rural economy to end poverty.

Through pragmatic collaboration, Mankiller restored historic two-gender leadership by mustering work crews to tackle such community needs as Head Start, Job Corps training, housing, sanitation, health clinics, and burial assistance. By securing control of tribal funds from the BIA for internal improvements, she facilitated 1,200 employees in establishing women's businesses, native ranches, lumberyards and factories, and a hydroelectric plant on the Arkansas border at Bell, Oklahoma. After a tribal election in July 1987, she shared power with six female tribal council members. Her ambitious agenda involved expelling black freedmen's families from the Cherokee enrollment and admitting only blood Indians. During her three terms as head chief, the Cherokee population nearly tripled in number, comprising the nation's second largest tribe.

At Sweet Briar College on April 2, 1993, Mankiller delivered the witty oration "Rebuilding the Cherokee Nation," which outlined tribal resurgence through hands-on projects. She described a long tradition of constitutional law and governance once symbolized by a wampum belt and the applicability of old treaties to current Indian nations. By characterizing collaboration among 140,000 people spread over 7,000 square miles, the speech defeated media stereotypes of Indians as unable and unwilling to accept self-sufficiency. She informed readers of tribal accomplishments with a best-selling memoir, *Mankiller: A Chief and Her People* (1993), which she dedicated to all Cherokee, especially women, the founts of harmony and balance. Capping the chief's rise to power, President Bill Clinton presented her a 1993 Medal of Freedom.

In support of tribal self-governance, Mankiller organized a panel in Tahlequah for the January 20, 1994, Oversight Hearing on Natural Resources by the U.S. Congress to discuss underfunding of Indian health and education. Central to her concerns, the closure of one of the federal offices serving the Cherokee created a serious inconvenience. Her straightforward statements accentuated shortfalls in funds for essential services from clinics and schools.

On retirement from politics in 1995 to recover from breast cancer and lymphoma, Mankiller retained homage as counselor, judge, and articulate spokesperson for the Cherokee. In 2004, she cowrote *Every Day Is a Good Day: Reflections by Contemporary Indigenous Women.* Terminal pancreatic cancer ended her activism in March 2010. Before she died at home on April 6, 2010, she helped plan a biographical film, *The Cherokee Word for Water*, directed by her husband. In 2015, proposals for a female portrait to replace Andrew Jackson on the $20 bill suggested Mankiller, whose family survived Jackson's removal of the Cherokee to Oklahoma.

References

Adams, Nicole, Tashina Etter, and Sarah Hernandez. *Relationships, Respect and Revitalization: Grantmaking Strategies.* Portland, OR: Grantmakers for Education, 2006.

Marshall, Brenda DeVore, and Molly A. Mayhead, eds. *Telling Political Lives: The Rhetorical Autobiographies of Women Leaders in the United States.* Lanham, MD: Lexington Books, 2008.

OKLAHOMA TRIBAL CONCERNS
BY WILMA MANKILLER
OVERSIGHT HEARING BEFORE THE SUBCOMMITTEE ON NATIVE AMERICAN AFFAIRS OF THE COMMITTEE ON NATURAL RESOURCES
TAHLEQUAH, OKLAHOMA
JANUARY 20, 1994

The first female chief of the Cherokee, Wilma Mankiller of Tahlequah, Oklahoma, applied her knowledge of social services to Indian needs. She invigorated reservation members to update community housing, sanitation, health clinics, schools, and burial assistance. By securing tribal control of federal funds, she enhanced minority education, expanded preventative medicine, and initiated native industry and commerce, including women's businesses. She chose self-help as a core concept for tribal welfare in the future.

I would like to thank you, Congressman Synar, and also thank the staff, your staff and Congressman Richardson and his staff for doing this field hearing in the state of Oklahoma. All too often, Oklahoma is neglected and we have to fight to be included in many of the things in Washington, D.C. As you know it is an ongoing problem in many federal programs to make sure that Oklahoma is included and not excluded because it is not considered to be a reservation state. So it is an important signal to all of us in Oklahoma that you are here.

One of the issues that I wanted to comment on, and probably the most important issue today for the record, is the issue of self-governance. Our tribe is one of the first tribes that entered into the self-governance compact, along with a number of other tribes, and the self-governance program has allowed us to have control over the allocation of our own resources. We are very concerned that the U.S. government will see this as just another demonstration project and will not make this legislation permanent.

I know that Congressman Richardson in the House and Senator McCain in the Senate have both been interested in making this legislation permanent, and we strongly support that. It has allowed us to allocate the resources where they are most needed, and respond to local needs, and it has been successful from our standpoint. So we wanted to make sure that we are very strongly supporting that.

I also believe that the self-governance project or demonstration project, as it is now known, should include both the Bureau of Indian Affairs and the Indian Health Service. This piecemeal way of dealing with self-governance just through the BIA is not going to work. I think it has to be kind of across-the-board.

Briefly, one of the other issues—and this is explained much more fully and at length—is the fact that still in the allocation of resources for health care, Oklahoma tribes and tribal people are underfunded. There has to be more equity in the funding for tribal people in Oklahoma. Governor Anoatubby has taken a leadership role in making sure that we are funded.

Just to give you an example, in Oklahoma, the average health care cost per person is about $2700 per year. Less than $900 is available, however, to individual Indian clients through IHS and other federal programs. So that is a huge issue.

We are also very, very concerned that the message of self-governance that the United States Congress puts forward in these bills gets filtered down to every level of the bureaucracy. Always there are these great speeches about supporting tribal governments and that sort of thing in Washington from the leadership, but it needs to permeate every layer of these agencies, people we deal with on a day-to-day basis. I think that is very, very important. As you know, we have had chronic funding problems in Indian health care, which limits our ability to provide health care. And that is also more fully explained in the written testimony.

Health care is not the only issue we are concerned about. The BIA funds for operating Indian schools are terribly insufficient. The fact that our school, Sequoyah Indian School, has managed to provide a decent education to students with the kind of funding we receive today is nothing short of a miracle. And if we did not have the kind of dedicated teachers that we have and staff there working with the students, then we would not be able to do the kinds of things that we are doing now. Almost every year, the Cherokee Nation Tribal Council augments the funding there.

Let me sum up by also pointing out that finally and most importantly, that the Bureau of Indian Affairs now has a consolidation program that would consolidate the Muskogee and the Anadarko offices, which is both unfair to the tribes on the western part of the state and to the tribes in this part of the state. If they choose Tulsa, the people on the west side will have to drive across the state to go to Tulsa. If they choose Anadarko, we will have to drive across the state to go to Anadarko. There surely is a way of streamlining those offices in a more efficient way so that the tribes on the west side are served and we are served. I think that is very, very important.

Source: Mankiller, Wilma. "Oklahoma Tribal Concerns." *Oversight Hearing before the Subcommittee on Native American Affairs of the Committee on Natural Resources, House of Representatives.* 103rd Cong., 2d sess. Washington, DC: U.S. Government Printing Office, 1995, 8–10.

MCPHERSON, AIMEE SEMPLE (1890–1944)

Canadian-American evangelist Aimee Elizabeth "Beth" Kennedy Semple McPherson raised the popular appeal of pulpit sermons by preaching Christian principles on street corners and over radio broadcasts and phonograph records. A native of Salford outside Ingersoll, Ontario, she was born on October 9, 1890, to Mildred Ona "Minnie" Pearce and James Morgan Kennedy. While she grew up on a small farm, she developed no affinity for her father's fundamentalist spirituality.

In her teens, McPherson competed for drama and speaking medals from the Women's Christian Temperance Union and studied science at the Ingersoll Collegiate Institute. At a storefront mission in Stratford in December 1907, she met foundryman and revival leader Robert James Semple of Magherafelt, Ireland, and converted to Pentecostalism. Her newfound faith created order and discipline by welcoming all ethnicities and demanding adherence to scripture, a personal acceptance of Jesus as savior, and baptism by immersion.

McPherson married Robert on August 12, 1908, in an outdoor farm wedding. Late in the year, they moved from Stratford to London, Ontario, while building a church. In January 1909, they relocated to Chicago to support Holiness theologian William Durham's Full Gospel Assembly, where they received ordination. She served the mission as interpreter of congregational *glossolalia*, or speaking in tongues, and spoke her first sermon, "Lost and Restored" (1908), which described immersion in a supernatural realm.

Joining Semple in a mission to London, at Victoria and Albert Hall in March 1910, McPherson preached a self-revelatory vision in "The Dispensation of the Holy Spirit." Members of an Italian congregation bankrolled their planned mission, which took them through the Suez Canal, Ceylon, and Macau to Hong Kong on June 1, 1910. At Matilda Hospital, Robert died of malarial dysentery on August 19, 1910. Aimee gave birth to their only child, Roberta Star Semple, on September 17. After a difficult passage through Shanghai in November for mother and infant, they reached San Francisco.

The young widow labored for the Canadian Salvation Army and the New York City Rescue Mission, where she met restaurant cashier Harold Stewart McPherson.

The two wed in Chicago on February 5, 1912, and in spring 1913 moved to a home in Providence, Rhode Island. At age 25, she resolved to preach across country, beginning with a revival at Mount Forest, Ontario. She abandoned Harold and took her infant son Rolf and daughter on tent revivals and faith healing in Florida. For appearances, she dressed in white topped by a navy blue cape and gradually incorporated staging and dramatic techniques from theater. Her outreach included publication of a women's monthly, *The Bridal Call*, which, in 1917, merged faith with feminism.

McPherson sought credentials in 1919 from the Assemblies of God. A Kimball pipe organ, brass band, massive choir, and parade floats set the stage for her most popular sermons—"Big Bad Wolf," "I Found the Keys," "Live Wire," "The Storm and the White Lambs," and "Zero Hour." At the height of charisma in the 1920s, "Sister Aimee" allied with mainstream Baptists and the Methodist Episcopal Church. Her sermons reached home phonographs on the Foursquare Religious Recordings label and in a collection, *Divine Healing Sermons* (1921). She addressed the Ku Klux Klan and, on a campaign in Australia in August 1922, preached a signature exhortation, "The Four Square Gospel," a holistic union of body, soul, spirit, and eternity.

The 5,300-seat Angelus Temple, McPherson's Los Angeles church, developed into the International Church of the Foursquare Gospel headed by the "first lady of Pentecostalism." The budget required constant fund-raising strategies to finance a flamboyant wardrobe, chauffeur and bodyguard, and holiday events. In 1925, she added the Lighthouse for International Foursquare Evangelism (LIFE) Bible College to the complex as a means of refining uneducated black and Hispanic fundamentalists.

McPherson's revivals and newsreel footage took on the themes of pacifism and antimilitarism, beginning with "The Way to Disarm Is to Disarm" (1932) and "God in American History" (1934). During the Red Scare of 1939, the sermons "Signs of the Times" (1938), "America—Whither Bound?" (1939), "Blessed Is the Nation Whose God Is the Lord" (1939), and "The Trojan Horse" (1940) warned listeners of un-American influences that contradicted the Bible.

During World War II, McPherson's *Foursquare Crusader* magazine and "Four Freedoms" sermons advocated volunteerism, war bonds, and blood donations to the Red Cross. She supported President Franklin D. Roosevelt in the incarceration of Japanese Americans in concentration camps as a means of relieving Americans of fear and tied her ministry to patriotism with "Foursquaredom and Uncle Sam" (1942). While refining the speech "Story of My Life," in Oakland, California, at age 53, she died in her hotel room on September 26, 1944. An autopsy traced her unexpected death to an overdose of barbiturate sleeping pills that hastened kidney failure.

References

McPherson, Aimee Semple. "Lost and Restored." In *This Is That: Personal Experiences, Sermons and Writings*, 380–382. Los Angeles: Bridal Call Publishing, 1919.
Sutton, M. A. *Aimee Semple McPherson and the Resurrection of Christian America.* Cambridge, MA: Harvard University Press, 2007.

LOST AND RESTORED (EXCERPT) BY AIMEE SEMPLE MCPHERSON FULL GOSPEL ASSEMBLY, CHICAGO, ILLINOIS MARCH 1908

Canadian American evangelist Aimee Elizabeth Kennedy Semple McPherson raised the popular appeal of pulpit sermons by preaching Christian principles on street corners and over radio and phonograph records. Her maiden oratory displayed a faith in supernatural powers that gave her the words to speak to an audience.

I found that this whole building was packed with people, and I was to speak to them at once. My attendant whispered into my ear that we were late, and then I heard the voice of the man on the platform saying: "Now our sister will speak to us and bring the message."

Before I realized it, I was standing, dazed and confused before the largest audience I had ever spoken to. The gallery, the balcony, the pit, and the rostrum were all filled; and to add to my confusion, just then the footlights flashed into brilliancy all around me and there I stood, a slip of a girl, with my bible in my trembling hands. I had prepared no sermon, trusting God to speak through me at the moment. But not a thought came to me. Lifting my heart to God in silent prayer, I said: "O God, if you ever helped me in my life, help me now!"

Just then something happened. The power of God went surging through my body, waves of glory and praise swept through my soul, until I forgot the throng of eager faces that had, a moment before, seemed to swim before me, forgot the footlights, and the learned men with their long-tail coats, forgot that I was only a child of eighteen, and that many there with their gray hair knew more in a moment than I in the natural course would know in a lifetime, and "I was in the Spirit."

All this takes a long time to write, but it happened in a moment, for those who put their trust in God shall never be put to shame. My mouth opened; the Lord took control of my tongue, my lips and vocal organs, and began to speak through me, not in tongues, but in English. The Spirit spoke in prophecy, and as He spoke, I did not know what the next word was to be; certainly the water did flow, not from my head but from the innermost depths of my being, without my having aught to do with it.

As I spoke thus for one hour and a quarter, there did not seem to be a stir in all that vast audience, and as I spoke I saw a vision of a great circle. . . . This big circle seemed so big that its top reached the sky; it was the dispensation of the Holy Spirit, from its opening on the day of Pentecost to its closing at the coming of the Lord Jesus. The vision was so indelibly stamped upon my mind that I have had my husband draw it from my description that all may see it as simple and plain as the Lord showed it to me. Before starting to speak, I opened my bible with closed eyes, trusting God for my text, and my finger was guided to a certain verse; when I opened my eyes and read it this was the verse the Lord had given me: "That which the palmerworm hath left hath the locust eaten; and that which the locust hath left hath the cankerworm eaten; and that which the cankerworm hath left hath the caterpillar eaten." Joel 1:4.

Just so when I came to the bottom of the circle, and the dark ages were pictured in their horror, my hand automatically turned the page over to the second chapter and placed my finger upon the following verse: "I will restore to you the years that the locust hath eaten, and the cankerworm, and the caterpillar and the palmerworm, my great army which I sent among you." Joel 2:25. . . It is He, not I, who is worthy of praise forever. . . .

Source: McPherson, Aimee Semple. "Lost and Restored." In *This Is That: Personal Experiences*, 380–382. Los Angeles: Bridal Call Publishing House, 1919.

MEIR, GOLDA (1898–1978)

The first female prime minister of Israel, Ukrainian-American politician Golda Mabovitch Meir spent much of her adult life negotiating for a secure Jewish homeland. During an era of Cossack-led pogroms in Kiev, she was born May 3, 1898, to carpenter and cabinetmaker Moshe Itzhak Mabovitch and Blume "Bella" Neiditch, the rebellious daughter of a soldier conscripted into the Russian army. Blume suffered cyclical miscarriages and produced four sons and a daughter who died from poverty and disease in early childhood, leaving Golda the middle of three surviving girls.

At age five, Meir lived with her maternal grandparents in Pinsk, Belarus, while her father sought a start in New York. The family fasted to protest the Kishinev Pogrom, a lethal attack by 5,000 soldiers on April 19, 1903, sanctioned in St. Petersburg by Tsar Nicholas II. By 1906, she, her sisters Sheyne "Shana" and Zipke "Clara," and their mother immigrated to Quebec.

Under false names, the trio traveled by train to Milwaukee, Wisconsin, to unite with Moshe, who constructed projects for the municipal railyard. While studying English at the Fourth Street Grade School, Meir helped her mother sell groceries each morning. Although she often arrived late, she graduated first in the class and, in 1912, entered North Division High School.

Because Meir and her mother quarreled over the choices of a matchmaker, Meir ran away. To pay for a train ticket away from Milwaukee, in 1912, she gave English lessons for a dime each and traveled to the home of her sister, Sheyne Mabovitch Korngold, a Zionist who received treatment for tuberculosis in Denver, Colorado. Amid lively conversation at the Korngold home, Meir absorbed opinions from suffragists, trade unionists, socialists, Marxists, and Zionists.

Zionism and Refugees

On return to Milwaukee in 1913, Meir continued high school and allied with the Socialist Zionist youth movement, which promoted the pioneering of a Jewish laboring class in Palestine. She worked while attending classes and refused her mother's suggestion that she quit school to enter an arranged marriage. Meir asserted her convictions through speeches and relief work among Jewish refugees fleeing World War I.

With a teaching certificate from Milwaukee State Normal School, in 1917, Meir taught adults at a Yiddish folk school, led protest marches, and became a U.S. citizen. At a home wedding on December 24, 1917, she married the man of her choice, sign painter Morris Meyerson, whom she had first encountered in Denver. Inspired by the 1918 American Jewish Congress in Philadelphia, she solicited donations to the Zionism movement in Chicago and Canada.

In a second immigration, in 1921, Golda journeyed to Tel Aviv with Morris, Sheyna, and Sheyna's daughter to work at a Merhavia Kibbutz in Afula, southeast of Nazareth. For three years, Meir moved stones, cut brush, planted trees, harvested almonds, and tended hens. She accepted a promotion to cooking and improved the kibbutz menu. Before her election as a delegate to the General Federation of Labour, she moved Meyerson to Tel Aviv to improve his health.

The couple relocated in the mid-1920s from Tel Aviv to Jerusalem, where they raised their children, Menahem and Sarah Meyerson. As secretary of the Working Women's Council in 1928 and co-founder of the Labor Party in 1930, Meir and her son and daughter traveled to the United States in 1932 for a two-year posting, during which she sought medical care for Sarah's kidney disease. Meir made frequent addresses for the Pioneer Women's Organization of America before returning to Jerusalem in 1934.

In July 1938, Meir attended the Évian Conference in France, a consortium led by President Franklin D. Roosevelt to decide the future of 450,000 European Jews escaping Nazi persecution by fleeing to Palestine. She regretted the British rejection of wholesale migration to Palestine for Jews. In 1940, she formally separated from Meyerson. While grieving her father's death and recovering from gall bladder infection at the end of World War II, she led negotiations between Palestinians and Jews and facilitated creation of the state of Israel.

Diplomat and Tactician

On the strength of "The Speech That Made Possible a Jewish State" in Chicago on January 2, 1948, Meir convinced listeners, "If these 700,000 Jews in Palestine can remain alive, then the Jewish people as such is alive" (Meir 1948). On May 10 before the official opening of the Israeli government, she disguised herself in Arab dress to enter Amman to establish diplomatic relations with Jordanian monarch Abdullah I. She guided talks with the Soviet Union and secured the assimilation of Russian Jewish immigrants into jobs, housing, and schools.

After a successful compromise among families seeking entry to Palestine, at the Tel Aviv Art Museum on May 14, 1948, Meir signed the Declaration of Independence. With stirring phrases honoring her daughter in the Negev and the military Israelis hurling stones at aggressors, she secured $50 million from U.S. citizens to arm Israel with modern weapons. During solicitation of donations in New York, she weathered a serious leg fracture caused by a car accident.

In 1949, Meir jockeyed for the position of labor minister and worked diligently for the Israeli parliament in 1951 after the deaths of her husband and mother. A campaign for mayor in 1955 failed because intransigent males refused to vote for a woman. As a symbol of loyalty, she altered the spelling of her American name to the Hebrew "Meir."

As foreign minister during the 1956–1957 Suez Crisis, on January 17, 1957, Meir addressed the U.N. General Assembly on the political situation in the Gulf of Aqaba. To solidify support for Israel in the Sinai, she cultivated Israeli alliances with emerging African states. She suffered a shrapnel wound to the left foot on October 30, 1957, when an Iraqi terrorist hurled a grenade into the Israeli legislature. To justify the capture of Nazi war criminals in Argentina, in 1960, she delivered a major address on the villainy of Adolf Eichmann, designer of the Holocaust.

Although Meir suffered from lymphoma from 1963, she remained active in the Israeli cabinet until age 68. Still a vital proponent of Israel, she headed the Mapai party until March 17, 1969, when she unified Israelis as prime minister during the Six-Day War. With orations such as "The War of Attrition and Cease Fire" on May 5, 1969, and "For the Attainment of Peace," a rally of the legislature on May 26, 1970, she upheld the military with prudent control during the conflict against Egypt.

Meir conducted ongoing talks with King Hussein of Jordan in 1970. She bolstered morale in the wake of terrorist murders of 27 people in Lod Airport in Tel Aviv and at the Munich Olympics in September 1972 and after the October 6, 1973, Yom Kippur War. In retirement in 1974, she compiled a best-selling memoir, *My Life* (1975). Sapped by extensive radiation treatment, she lapsed into a coma and died of lymphatic cancer in Jerusalem's Hadassah-Hebrew University Medical Center on December 8, 1978.

References

Meir, Golda. "The Speech That Made Possible a Jewish State." January 2, 1948. Tamilnation.org. Accessed December 15, 2014. http://tamilnation.co/ideology/golda.htm.

Provizer, Norman. "Golda Meir: An Outline of a Unique Life." Metropolitan State University of Denver. Accessed December 15. 2014. https://www.msudenver.edu/golda/goldameir/chronologyofgoldameir.

MICHELMAN, KATE (1942–)

A political consultant and champion of women's reproductive rights, Kate Michelman presses for repeal of regulations and laws prohibiting women from managing their own health decisions. Born to a Catholic family on August 4, 1942, in New Jersey, she was the daughter of a superintendent of the Campbell Soup Company. She grew up in Defiance, Ohio, and developed keen insights into social justice.

At the University of Michigan, Michelman majored in classical archeology and developmental psychology and specialized in early childhood development for the disabled. In 1964, she protested the Vietnam War and joined the civil rights march from Selma to Montgomery, Alabama.

From late 1985 to 2004, Michelman chaired the National Abortion and Reproductive Rights Action League (NARAL) Pro-Choice America and initiated a vigorous campaign, "Silent No More." While opposition imperiled *Roe v. Wade*, she increased her influence as an expert on women's issues. Following a ban on late-term pregnancy termination in 1996, she tackled a melodramatic antichoice challenge.

To cut through obfuscation by the religious right, Michelman delivered the speech "Partial Birth Abortion: The Truth" to a joint congressional hearing on March 21, 1997. She declared that a federal ban endangered women's lives while violating rights to crucial medical treatment and privacy. The speech declared the decision of late-term intervention an ethical and moral decision of the woman on the advice of her doctor.

In part for a stance against prohibition of partial birth abortion and the possible overturn of *Roe*, in 2003, Michelman attained listing among Pennsylvania's most politically powerful women. During the November 2004 elections late in her presidency, NARAL officials flooded voters with media and mailings forcing presidential candidates George W. Bush and John Kerry to prioritize reproductive rights and the appointment of pro-female Supreme Court candidates on political platforms.

In retirement, Michelman remained assertive as a writer and lecturer at campuses nationwide. For the Democratic National Committee, she masterminded the 2004 Campaign to Save the Court, a rally to defy conservative control of Supreme Court appointments. Her essays in the *Washington Post* and *New York Times* crusaded for privacy. On January 12, 2006, she testified before the Senate Judiciary Committee against nominee Samuel Alito for opposition to women's abortion rights.

To inspire the next generation of female advocates, in December 2005, Michelman issued an autobiography, *With Liberty and Justice for All: A Life Spent Protecting the Right to Choose* (2005), a text that earned the regard of former secretary of state Madeleine Albright. Michelman followed with *Protecting the Right to Choose* (2007). Unrestrained by politics and NARAL, in early widowhood, she maintained a Washington, D.C., office and empowered get-out-the-vote initiatives in Pennsylvania aimed at youth, elderly, unmarried, and minority women voters. While backing laws against domestic violence and against unnecessary ultrasounds, she fostered a clearer understanding of pro-choice philosophy. She empowered Women Vote PA, a nonpartisan drive for more female representation in government to protect the health, safety, and economic security of women, especially minorities.

For the Women's Law Project in Philadelphia, in 2015, Michelman directed policy on female health initiatives and contributed to an Internet blog such information as the rise in infant and maternal mortality and premature births among ethnic groups who lack access to medical treatment. She crusaded for an expansion of state Medicaid coverage and for legislation protecting the comfort and safety of pregnant and lactating workers. A major issue, gag laws forcing doctors to politicize their instructions to patients according to antichoice policies, informed her op-ed advice to Pennsylvania's governor-elect Tom Wolf.

See Also: Albright, Madeleine.

Reference

Weeks, Linton. "Kate Michelman, the Public Face of a Woman's Right to Privacy." *Washington Post*, January 12, 2006.

PARTIAL BIRTH ABORTION: THE TRUTH BY KATE MICHELMAN JOINT HEARING BEFORE THE SENATE COMMITTEE ON THE JUDICIARY AND THE SUBCOMMITTEE ON THE CONSTITUTION OF THE HOUSE COMMITTEE ON THE JUDICIARY U.S. HOUSE OF REPRESENTATIVES, WASHINGTON, D.C. MARCH 11, 1997

A political consultant from New Jersey, Kate Michelman fights conservative politicians and Catholics who protest reproductive choice by romanticizing the fetus. As chair of NARAL Pro-Choice America, for two decades, she forced political candidates to confront women's real-life dilemmas. She continues to promote women's health initiatives and to denounce gag laws forcing doctors to politicize their instructions to patients according to antichoice policies.

I welcome the opportunity to bring NARAL's perspective to this debate, one with enormous consequences for American women's reproductive health and privacy—and, for some women, their very lives.

Whether the number of women whose doctors recommend this procedure is five, five hundred, or five thousand a year, each one of these numbers represents the real life of an individual woman. A wife. A mother. A daughter. A sister. Many face agonizing circumstances. And under your legislation, each and every one of them would be denied the treatment her doctor believed to be the safest and most appropriate for her.

This debate must focus on the lives of those women. And it requires discussing the hazards this legislation would pose to the health of American women and to their constitutionally protected reproductive choices.

For the record, let me note that ninety-nine percent of all abortions in this country are performed prior to 20 weeks of pregnancy. The procedure at issue here is essentially a subset of that other one percent of abortions. It is rare.

But a federal ban on even this rare abortion method also poses an unprecedented threat to a woman's constitutional right of choice. The law of the land for the past 24 years, *Roe v. Wade*, has been a careful balance between the right of a woman to choose and the right of a state to protect potential life. This legislative ban is a threat, too, to women's health—putting politics above the sanctity of the doctor-patient relationship.

We as a society—and as a nation of laws—have asked the question "who decides?" for a generation now. Time and again, the majority of Americans have agreed that only a woman, consistent with her moral and ethical values, should make that decision along with her family and her doctor. NARAL has worked to protect that choice. Consistent with *Roe*, we've kept government officials out of this most profound and intimate territory.

Under *Roe v. Wade*, prior to the point at which a fetus can live outside the woman, decisions about her pregnancy are beyond the reach of politicians and bureaucrats. These choices are personal and private under the U.S. Constitution. After viability, the *Roe* decision says that a state may "regulate, and even proscribe, abortion" except when a woman's life or health is threatened. This ban—without any concern for a woman's health or privacy—rejects the basic principles of *Roe*.

Senator Hatch, Congressman Hyde, Congressman Canady, you all have strong records—based on deeply held convictions—opposing a woman's right to choose under any circumstance using any procedure. You believe that *Roe v. Wade* was fundamentally wrong, that politicians and government officials should control decisions now made by women, their families, and their doctors.

But let me address myself for a moment to those members of Congress whose minds are open, who fundamentally believe in the principles of Roe, but are uncomfortable with what they've heard about the procedure at issue today. As you struggle with your vote on this legislation, there are two crucial questions I urge you to consider: first, are you ready, as a member of Congress, to dictate medical decisions surrounding this constitutionally protected choice, even when a doctor considers this procedure the safest and most medically appropriate? And second, does this legislation protect the lives and health of those women whose wanted pregnancies have become medical nightmares?

In our nation of laws, legislation profoundly affects the lives of individuals. Listen to the testimony of Coreen Costello, a California homemaker, who addressed your subcommittee last year, Congressman Canady. She is a conservative Republican, a deeply religious Christian, personally opposed to abortion. Yet in the seventh month of her third pregnancy, she discovered that the child she was carrying had a lethal neurological problem.

Her doctor recommended terminating the pregnancy to preserve her health, and, very reluctantly, the Costellos came over a period of weeks to agree. Her obstetrician advised that the safest way to end this tragedy was the very procedure your legislation would outlaw. As Coreen testified last year, "Because of the safety of this procedure, . . . I will have another baby in June. . . . If you outlaw this surgical procedure, other women like me will be denied that gift, that joy. They may lose their ability to have more children—they may lose their health. They may lose their lives."

With all due respect, Senator and members of the committees, is this a choice you should be making instead of Coreen Costello's doctor? For 25 years we have raised and maintained a standard on which women, their doctors, and families could rely. Are we now prepared as a nation to tear down that standard and place this most personal decision in the hands of politicians?

Source: Michelman, Kate. "Partial Birth Abortion." *Joint Hearing before the Senate Committee on the Judiciary and the Subcommittee on the Constitution of the House Committee on the Judiciary.* 105th Cong., 1st sess. Washington, DC: U.S. Government Printing Office, 1997, 19–20.

MINK, PATSY T. (1927–2002)

A Hawaiian feminist and supporter of working families and trade unions, Patsy Matsu Takemoto Mink set records in American history as the first nonwhite U.S. congresswoman and a proponent of social and economic justice for women. A Sansei Japanese American, she was born in Hamakua Poko, Maui, on December 6, 1927, to Mitama Tateyama and Suematsu Takemoto. Her maternal grandparents, Tateyama and Tsuru Gojiro, emigrated from Japan in the late 1890s to work as sugar plantation laborers.

While finishing her senior year at Maui High School, Mink served as school president and advanced to valedictorian of the class of 1944. At age 18, she settled with her parents in Honolulu, Oahu, where her father opened a surveying firm. She studied chemistry and zoology at the University of Hawaii before transferring to Wilson College in Chambersburg, Pennsylvania, for a semester in 1946. Another transfer to the University of Nebraska placed her at the forefront of an integration movement that ended racial segregation of campus dormitories.

To battle discrimination against women in medical colleges, from 1948 to 1951, Mink completed a degree from the University of Chicago Law School. She became the first Japanese-American female admitted to the Hawaii bar but encountered male diminution of a female lawyer. She wed geophysicist and hydrologist John Francis Mink in 1951.

In 1956, Mink won election to the Hawaii territorial legislature and held office during the establishment of Hawaii as the 50th U.S. state on August 21, 1959. Defeated in a first run for the U.S. Congress by war hero Daniel Inouye, in 1962, she advanced to the Hawaii senate. In these formative years, she joined the League of Conservation Voters, American Civil Liberties Union, and National Association for the Advancement of Colored People.

In 1965, Mink began a 12-year stint in the U.S. House of Representatives, where she advised the Committee on Education and Labor. At a peak of fame, she helped draft Title IX, an amendment to education legislation that promised girls and women equal educational opportunity in the classroom and intercollegiate sports. On January 22, 1970, she became the first female Democrat to respond to a presidential State of the Union address, at which Richard Nixon outlined an environmental initiative.

To stress the needs of women and children, in 1971, Mink joined Bella Abzug, Shirley Chisholm, Betty Friedan, and Gloria Steinem in co-forming the National Women's Political Caucus. Mink's activism increased in 1975 during the U.N. International Women's Year, when congressional Democrats voted her secretary of the House Democratic Caucus and member of the powerful Budget Committee. She used her clout to sponsor an allotment of $5 million to the National Women's Conference, an event in Houston, Texas, in November 18–21, 1977, which tapped the ideas and vigor of Bella Abzug, Betty Ford, Maya Angelou, Rosalynn Carter, Betty Friedan, Lady Bird Johnson, and Barbara Jordan on such issues as gay and minority rights, child care funding, violence against women, national disarmament, and reviving the Equal Rights Amendment.

In 1976, President Jimmy Carter made use of Mink's speaking and organizing abilities as Assistant Secretary of State for Oceans and International Environmental and Scientific Affairs, a post she held until May 1, 1978. She returned home to Waipahu to chair the Honolulu city council until 1990, when she entered the last 12 years as a U.S. legislator and member of the Congressional Caucus for Women's Issues. At a crucial challenge to welfare in March 1995, in vain, she delivered "On Behalf of the Family Stability and Work Act." Her alert to cost-cutting Republicans indicted legislators for assaulting the poor and robbing low-income citizens of dignity and hope by slicing the school lunch program, child care, job training, and food stamps. Without success, she goaded President Bill Clinton to maintain the safety net that fed families with dependent children.

In Honolulu on August 30, 2002, Mink entered the Straub Clinic and Hospital for treatment of chicken pox and died of viral pneumonia on September 28, 2002. President George Bush renamed the Title IX amendment the Patsy Takemoto Mink Equal Opportunity in Education Act. President Barack Obama honored her illustrious career on November 24, 2014, by conferring a posthumous Presidential Medal of Freedom.

See Also: Abzug, Bella; Angelou, Maya; Carter, Rosalynn; Chisholm, Shirley; Friedan, Betty; Hill, Anita; Johnson, Lady Bird; Jordan, Barbara; Steinem, Gloria.

References

Gootman, Elissa. "Patsy Mink, Veteran Hawaii Congresswoman, Dies at 74." *New York Times*, September 30, 2002.

Mink, Patsy. "The Family Stability and Work Act." In *Journal of the House of Representatives, 1995*. Washington, DC: U.S. Government Printing Office, 1995.

ENGLISH LANGUAGE EMPOWERMENT ACT OF 1996 BY PATSY MINK HEARING ON THE LANGUAGE OF GOVERNMENT ACT OF 1995 SENATE COMMITTEE ON GOVERNMENTAL AFFAIRS, WASHINGTON, D.C. MARCH 7, 1996

As a U.S. congresswoman from Hawaii, Patsy Mink stated the obvious faults of a divisive conservative issue, the declaration that English was the official language of U.S. citizens. The bill passed in the House but never made it to the Senate before adjournment. Mink's background as representative of a multiracial state gave her leverage in denouncing language regulations as unnecessary and insulting to people who spoke other tongues, particularly Native Americans.

Mr. Chairman, thank you for the opportunity to appear today to speak against S. 356, which seeks to declare English as the official language of the United States Government.

According to the U.S. Census Bureau, 97 percent of Americans currently speak English "well" or "very well." Even among those immigrants who come to this country speaking other languages, most passionately desire to be proficient in English—for their own economic survival and to secure economic opportunity for their children. Today's immigrants are learning English faster than previous generations of immigrants; English classes are in such high demand that some stay open 24 hours a day, and statistics show that waiting lists are as long as 40 to 50 thousand. If this is so, why do we need a law to declare English to be our official language? It already is!

So maybe the reason for this bill is to save printing costs. A recent GAO report found that a mere six one-hundredths of one percent of federal documents produced since 1990 are in languages other than English; this works out to be only 256 out of 400,000 federal documents. I would also point out that most of those non-English documents were created to serve the Spanish-speaking residents of Puerto Rico. So I guess it is not the cost of publishing in other languages that justifies this limitation.

There is no evidence that this nation is threatened by "division among linguistic lines." English is far and away our nation's dominant, common language. There is no threat that English will be subsumed as a minor language. S356 has the potential of creating unwarranted division in this country. S356 is touted as a way to bolster the national unity, but I am troubled by the divisiveness it will create.

How will making English our official language promote unity when thousands of legal, tax-paying immigrants and citizens will be denied a fuller opportunity to gain needed information and services because they are of limited English? What is the overwhelming public policy need to punish the few?

The right to benefit from their government should not be limited by language barriers. Language communication via radio, television, and written material is essential for a basic understanding of an already intimidating political process for many non-native English speakers.

Under S.356, in my role as a government official, my hands would be tied when dealing with my own constituents, for many of whom English is a second language. To suggest that I cannot represent those constituents to the best of my ability and will be forced to essentially exclude them from the political process through English-only written communication is preposterous and insulting. The Constitution of the United States guarantees freedom of speech. Nowhere does it say that it has to be in English. If we enact this bill it will be a limitation of our free society.

The strength of our nation has always been its diversity. The right of each person to seek information from their government should not be limited by restrictions on the provider. To forsake immigrants this right is to deny the very principle on which this country was built, which is free and open access to our elected officials and our government.

S. 356 would also specifically prohibit Native American federal employees or officials from communicating with the native population in their native language, even though it would be a more effective means of communication. In addition, it could restrict the use of native languages by tribes and native organizations in implementing federal programs. It is clear that this legislation runs directly counter to overall efforts to preserve and promote the culture and history of the Native Americans.

Mr. Chair, I understand this particular piece of legislation does not specifically repeal bilingual education or multilingual ballot measures, however, its clear message of "English Only" is still exclusionary to those who do not speak English, implying that they are somehow less American than those who do. Whether or not it is its intention, linguistic elitism often gives way to the social forces of resentment and intolerance, and this bill panders to the wave of anti-immigrant sentiment that has become increasingly prevalent. Worst, this official act of exclusion by the government delivers a hostile message to hard-working and patriotic non-native Americans who come to this country and ultimately contribute to its greatness—a slap in the face I am not willing to deliver or support.

For a bill which has no ostensible purpose or meets no urgent need, the price is too great. I urge the committee to reject it.

Source: Mink, Patsy. "English Language Empowerment Act of 1996." *Hearings before the Committee on Governmental Affairs, United States Senate.* 104th Cong., 1st and 2d sess., December 6, 1995 and March 7, 1996. Washington D.C., U.S. Government Printing Office, 1996, 56–57.

MONK, MEREDITH (1942–)

A creative maverick, Meredith Jane Monk creates cinema music and gynocentric performances featuring introspective polyphony, instrumental melody, timeless scenarios and visual designs, and dance. Born during her mother's singing tour in Lima, Peru, on November 20, 1942, she came from an artistic family. From an early age she developed a broad vocal range and learned to read music.

Monk trained in classical singing and the folk and rock genres in Bronxville, New York, composing *And Sarah Knew* (1962) while a sophomore at Sarah Lawrence College. She completed a degree in modern dance in 1964. In 1968, she incorporated an avant-garde performance company, the House Foundation for the Arts, which integrated 20 young performers in dance and tune at numerous expositions and festivals.

Into the 1970s, in France, Italy, and Japan, Monk pioneered the sounds of unaccompanied voice, numerous instruments, and the rim tones of a wine glass, the featured instrument on the album *Our Lady of Late* (1973). In 1978, she initiated the Meredith Monk and Vocal Ensemble, presenting radical compositions in multiple states, Canada, and Israel. Critics classified her unique style as demotic or folk based, reflecting ancient vocals expressing communal joys and sorrows and individual experience.

In the early 1980s, Monk introduced new instruments to compositions, such as bagpipes, Chinese horn, and didgeridoo. To express her artistry to college seniors, she presented the commencement address at Sarah Lawrence to the class of 1985. Extolled globally by aficionados of the progressive arts, she lectured in Tokyo in 1988. In April 1990, she delivered the oration "Art, America and Jumping Off the Cliff" as a testimonial to U.S. Congress on behalf of the National Endowment for the Arts. The speech affirmed risk-taking that transcended boundaries between culture and citizens.

Monk expanded musical skills to the richly varied dance opera *Atlas: An Opera in Three Parts*, an epic tale of the traveler Alexandra David-Neel, the first Western female to explore Lhasa, Tibet. The multidisciplinary opera, composed for 22 voices and 14 instruments, opened on February 22, 1991, at the Houston Grand Opera. The composer applied concepts of "Dancing Voice/Singing Body" in coaching workshops at Bucknell and the University of Illinois on the program of the Apple Hill Summer Festival and the Jacob's Pillow Dance Festival. In 1993, she researched the arts in Bali and Nepal.

As artist in residence, in 1995, Monk taught at the University of Wisconsin. Following honoraria from the Scripps American Dance Festival, New York Foundation for the Arts, and MacDowell Colony, she intrigued opera fans on college campuses in Pennsylvania and Georgia and in Prague and Budapest with the percussive *Magic Frequencies* (1998). She provided the Coen brothers with "Walking Song" for the background of the film *The Big Lebowski* (1998) and, in October 1999, honored the Dalai Lama in Los Angeles with *A Vocal Offering.*

Monk's kudos include listing among National Public Radio's 50 Great Voices, three Obies, a Doris Duke Artist Award, the 2011 Yoko Ono Lennon Courage Award, a MacArthur Genius Grant, two Guggenheim fellowships, a *Premio Arlecchino d'Oro*, the 2012 *Musical America* composer of the year following performance of *Realm Variations* with the San Francisco Symphony, and a 2013 French Officer of the Order of Arts and Letters. In 2014, she achieved the Debs Composer's Chair at Carnegie Hall.

References

Monk, Meredith. "Some Thoughts about Art, America and Jumping Off the Cliff." April 1990. Gifts of Speech: Women's Speeches from Around the World. Accessed May 5, 2015. http://gos.sbc.edu/m/monk1.html.

Stearns, David Patrick. "Arts Abounding." *Philadelphia Enquirer WKND*, February 4, 2011, 16, 18.

SOME THOUGHTS ABOUT ART, AMERICA AND JUMPING OFF THE CLIFF BY MEREDITH MONK U.S. CONGRESS, WASHINGTON, D.C. APRIL 1990

A multidisciplinary maverick, Meredith Jane Monk composes movie music and gynocentric performances. In 1990, she defended the National Endowment for the Arts with a speech to U.S. legislators about the need for imaginative stimulus for human wholeness.

When I began writing this article there was talk of a strong lobby of members of Congress who wanted to eliminate the National Endowment for the Arts completely. I pondered upon what that would mean to this country and further, what exactly does art mean to this country at this time? And even further, what is the role of the artist in this society?

I often go on tour as a "cultural ambassador" representing the United States in festivals and concert halls in countries as far reaching as Finland, Morocco, Japan, Italy, France, Portugal, Israel, Norway, Germany, and Yugoslavia. I am proud to be called an American artist (although I feel actually more like a citizen of the world), and I am moved by the responses of the audiences to art. It seems then that art really speaks from heart to heart and that it can eloquently communicate the deepest human mysteries, insights, and expression regardless of differences in culture and language. In a way, I am fortunate in that my work is non-verbal in nature so that the smokescreen of language does not have to be bypassed or passed through. Nevertheless even in work in which there is a great deal of text (which needs to be translated), art is basically a language of perception and spirit and feeling which at its best can transcend the particularities of culture.

I was recently on a panel in Boulder, Colorado, about the Artist in Society. Steve Durland, an artist and writer from Los Angeles, stated eloquently that "the artist is the conscience or soul of a culture." As our society becomes more fragmented, more bombarded with images, more numbed to feeling, more restless and impatient, what the artist has to offer becomes more and more essential to the health of the community. In a sense, there are three basic artistic strategies which fulfill this function. One is to make art which states the problems or wounds of society; which makes people aware of the underpinnings of the society and wakes them up to act or make changes in their lives or in their communities. The second is to make art which offers an alternative; that demonstrates human behavior which becomes a paradigm for what creativity, cooperation, freedom, and playfulness could be. The third is to make art which in itself provides glimpses of a larger consciousness or reflects upon the inexplicable. Some artists mirror the time in which they live. Others convey in their work a sense of timelessness and continuity. That we have this variety of approaches is healthy and meaningful.

What I am always struck by when I return to the United States after having been away for a while is the misguided perception (or non-perception) of art as a marginal concern in our contemporary life. It saddens me to think of how a country filled with energy, ingenuity, and originality can have so little care about something which is ultimately so nourishing and life affirming. In other countries, art is still a vital forum. Quality is appreciated; communication and involvement are respected and taken in deeply. Here, art has become a commodity rather than a way of life. It is thought of as a diversion rather than an essential need. It is true that it takes a lot of effort to go somewhere after a day of working at a job that might not be very satisfying and take a chance on seeing or hearing something that might be beautiful but could also be disturbing or provocative. At the least, it would probably take some commitment or mental participation to fully enjoy it. It is easier to stay home and watch TV, listen to music, or read a magazine. Media satisfy the restlessness and impatience that come from speed, fragmentation and exhaustion with instant gratification and no effort. Media provide an image of experience rather than grounded experience itself. Art offers something else—depth, involvement, a new way of looking at the world that we live in, a fresh approach to what we take for granted, a chance to experience freedom of the imagination.

I've been thinking about why freedom of the imagination could seem so dangerous to some of the "powers that be." Imagination seems like such a quiet but inalienable right. It is true that the more ignorant a people becomes, the more it can be manipulated from above. You don't miss what you don't know. If you don't know what you are missing, you don't know that you miss it. It is important that future generations can still partake of the process and the riches of art. That they can be exposed to the adventure of creativity; that curiosity, trusting intuition, and taking risks are ways of keeping life a continually growing process.

For me as an artist, attempting to start at zero (trying to pretend that this is my first piece) with each piece that I begin, is a way of keeping me interested, curious, awake. I try not to take anything for granted. It's a little like being a detective—you have a few clues, but at the beginning, you are stumbling around in the dark. You follow each clue, hoping that it will lead to the next one; that what you sense internally will make itself known. At a certain point, you have to go to the edge of the cliff and jump (put your ideas into a form, share that form with others). Either you will fly or you might fall (then, for your next attempt you will have probably learned a great deal), but the courage of the jump is the creative act. Of course, the best times are when you feel that a piece already exists and that you are merely a medium for bringing it to life.

Those are blessed times creatively. In between, you continue working on your craft, struggling, learning so that you will be ready for the next inspiration or insight that comes to you. I think that what seems dangerous about this process to some prominent members of our society is the insistence upon following inner truth as opposed to obeying or giving into obligations coming from the world, which are in conflict with the inner reality of the individual. Joseph Campbell talked about "following your bliss." I guess for some people this can seem threatening to their sense of order or at best unrealistic. But in fact, this inner questioning, listening, awakening is one of the ways that we can each, in our own way, contribute to the future of the world.

Art, as one offering, provides an environment where people can experience magic and transformation; be part of a community; can feel wonder, awe, the full palette of emotion. We have lost contact with our inner life. Art becomes a paradigm for whole, integrated human beings using the fullness of their resources as artists and as audiences. Art stimulates perception, thought, feeling, physicality, spirit.

A few months ago, I was asked by an audience of presenters . . . "What does an artist want most from a presenter?" What came into my mind immediately was the word "love." When I said this, the audience was shocked and I, in turn, was surprised by their response. I guess what they thought I would say was "better hotel rooms, more meals, a limousine etc." What I meant was that what we need is the desire of sponsors to really have us there: that the sponsors know our work, know what we have to offer to their community; know that what we do is done with care. We spend our lives striving for a kind of perfection and even though we know that it is an illusion, we try nevertheless. Art, even the angriest, darkest variety, is created out of love.

In America, at this time, we are fortunate to have a handful of visionary presenters who understand this and perceive how important this is to their constituents. These hero/heroines have followed the field (and love the field), bringing artists because of their belief in quality and validity of the artists' work and the work's power to move, provoke, stimulate, and enrich the community. What has happened generally, in the past ten years, is that because of the economic climate, some of these brave souls have had to quit or to hand over their jobs to people who have no love for the arts and whose concern is merely for the bottom line. What this does is to cheat the public and particularly our children of expansive, lively experiences; experiences which stretch their perceptions and stimulate their own creativity as human beings. What they get is what they already know. Adventure is stripped away.

What we need in America right now is to fight for our right to jump off the cliff. That means to create a climate which affirms the ability to take risks; to demand recognition from the top, that art is a vital and pungent force in our lives. Art, even the most irreverent, is a vivid response to the time in which we live. As artists, presenters, audiences and lovers of art, we have a deep function and role in our society. We are responsible human beings.

To abolish the NEA would be an act of utter ignorance and destruction. It is almost inconceivable to think that a country whose artists influenced a generation of musicians, dancers, painters, writers, and directors in Europe and Asia could be so unappreciative of one of its finest resources (and exports). At the grass roots level, we need to encourage a renewal of energy, ideas and strategies of doing art and sharing it with our communities. We have the possibility of learning from each other, affirming each other, dissolving boundaries both between the art forms and between cultural communities. This is as it should be—a reflection of our rapidly changing world and our concern for the future of the planet.

Source: Monk, Meredith. "Some Thoughts about Art, America and Jumping Off the Cliff." Speech to U.S. Congress, April 1990. Reprinted by permission from Meredith Monk.

MORRISON, TONI (1931–)

American Nobel Prize winner Chloe Ardelia "Toni" Wofford Morrison speaks the truths of black America and probes the hurts of women and children. Born on Lake Erie in Lorain, Ohio, on February 18, 1931, to Ella Ramah Willis, a self-willed housewife, and George Wofford, a shipyard welder, she grew up in the Southern black diaspora that adapted to Ohio Valley urbanism and industrialization. Female dream interpretation and storytelling by her maternal great-grandmother, grandparents, and aunts about the Underground Railroad, Uncle Remus, and blacks who could fly back to Africa developed her courage and a reverence for black gumption.

Black lore did not nullify Morrison's envy of the child movie star Shirley Temple. As the only black first-grader at Hawthorne Elementary School, she encountered the homey white stereotypes of the reader *Dick and Jane.* She adopted the Catholic faith in 1943 and took the baptismal name Anthony.

When Morrison gained mature perspective, she pondered both sides of racial assertiveness from her tolerant mother and bitter, unforgiving father. While cleaning houses after school for $2.00 per week and working at the public library in her teens, she admired dancer Maria Tallchief and read novels by Jane Austen, William Faulkner, and Leo Tolstoy.

Before graduating top of her class at Lorain High, she started writing a short story about an unloved black girl—later named Pecola Breedlove—whose dusky skin sets her apart from lighter-skinned blacks.

At Howard University in Washington, D.C., Morrison majored in English, French, and Russian fiction and classics and toured with a theater group. With a thesis on the suicide motifs in the works of William Faulkner and Virginia Woolf, she finished postgraduate work in English literature at Cornell at age 24. At Texas Southern University and Howard, she taught English and humanities to Claude Brown, Stokely Carmichael, and Andrew Young.

Married in 1957 to Kingston, Jamaica, architect Harold Morrison, the author produced sons Harold Ford and Slade Kevin Morrison. After a sojourn in Europe and a divorce, in 1965, she returned home temporarily before relocating to Syracuse to edit textbooks for Random House during the Black Power movement, when black works entered the mainstream. While readying trade books in New York, she groomed the writings of Angela Davis, Toni Cade Bambara, Huey Newton, and Muhammad Ali.

A Late Start

Juggling motherhood and writing, Morrison issued *The Bluest Eye* (1970), a psychosocial novel on incest and madness that doom a pathetic, unloved black girl. The writer moved to Nyack on the Hudson River in 1971 to teach humanities at the State University of New York. She completed a romance, *Sula* (1973), and *The Black Book* (1974), a compendium of slave recipes, biography, advertising, photos, and patent applications.

A substantive lecturer from early times, Morrison enlarged on the American dream at a panel discussion at Portland State University in May 1975 with "A Humanistic View." She characterized murderous racism, such as that of Andrew Jackson and General William Sherman against Native Americans, as a distracting phantom and con game. She lionized black music for its uniqueness and boasted of dealings with bigots, whom she left unchallenged and ignorant.

During employment on the faculty at the Bread Loaf Writer's Conference and at Yale, Morrison composed a successful novel, *Song of Solomon* (1977), winner of a National Book Award and Ohioana commendation, the Barnard Medal of Distinction, and a Book-of-the-Month Club selection. In 1980, President Jimmy Carter appointed her to the National Council on the Arts.

Following publication of a metaphorical Caribbean novel, *Tar Baby* (1981), Morrison appeared on the cover of *Newsweek*. She delivered the keynote address to the American Writers' Congress that anticipated an era of heroic writers who ventured into the fray to influence American consciousness and morality. She lectured at the State University of New York at Albany and wrote *Storyville* (1984), a musical dramatizing the ebullient black district of New Orleans in 1917. She taught at Bard College and wrote the unpublished play *Dreaming Emmett* (1986), a reflection on the murder of a 14-year-old black boy in Mississippi by unrepentant white extremists.

From newspaper clippings, Morrison saved the source of her lyrical, tragic novel, *Beloved* (1987), the mythologized saga of Margaret Garner, a Kentucky domestic who escaped over the Ohio River to free territory. A deluge of honoraria elevated the novelist to global status, including a Pulitzer Prize and citations from the New York Governor's Arts Council, Robert F. Kennedy and Melcher book citations, the American Academy and Institute of Arts and Letters, Modern Language Association Commonwealth Award, Langston Hughes Festival, Anisfield Wolf Book Award for Race Relations, and three listings among the Public Library Books for the Teen Age. She accepted invitations to lecture at Bowdoin College, the University of California at Berkeley, and the University of Michigan and began a permanent relationship with Princeton.

Morrison extended her career with the treatise *Playing in the Dark* (1992) and *Jazz* (1992), a retrospect on Harlem violence in the 1920s, and commented on national events with *Race-ing Justice, En-gendering Power: Essays on Anita Hill, Clarence Thomas, and the Construction of Social Reality* (1992). In an acceptance parable on October 7, 1993, for a Nobel Prize worth $825,000, she listed humor along with sympathy and humanity as the lasting qualities of fictional characters.

Virginia, delivering 15 sermons and 34 speeches. With companion Elizabeth Cady Stanton, Mott proposed a suffrage movement in 1848. She and 18 associates composed the Declaration of Sentiments, a manifesto of gender equality based on the Declaration of Independence.

Mott's skill at discourse included the parsing of diction and translation and a systematic revelation of the "inner light" as a deterrent to female and slave debasement. In Philadelphia's Assembly building on December 17, 1849, she delivered her chief oration, "Discourse on Women," which she published in pamphlet form the following year. She grounded her faith in women on scripture. In refuting notions of female inferiority, she expounded feminist tenets of rights to children, property, and a college education.

In her sixties, Lucretia Mott's crusades escalated. In 1854, she rebuked male clergy for declaring women inferior to men in intellect. Citing the Salem witchcraft slaughter as an example of misguided piety, she quoted Saint Paul's assertion that godly women were capable of prophecy. Near the end of the Civil War, she co-founded Swarthmore College in Pennsylvania and opened its classes to men and women. Despite mounting digestive ills, in 1866, she presided over the American Equal Rights Association and the Pennsylvania Peace Society and held the vice presidency of the Universal Peace Union. She died from pneumonia on November 11, 1880, in Cheltenham, Pennsylvania.

See Also: Stanton, Elizabeth Cady.

References

Mott, Lucretia. "Cherry Street Friends Meeting, Philadelphia." *Inter Ocean*, January 24, 1881, 3.

Mott, Lucretia. *Lucretia Mott's Discourse, at the Friend's Quarterly Meeting, in the Hester Street House.* New York: Ross & Tousey, 1850.

DISCOURSE ON WOMAN (EXCERPT) BY LUCRETIA COFFIN MOTT ASSEMBLY BUILDING, PHILADELPHIA, PENNSYLVANIA DECEMBER 17, 1849

A self-educated Quaker theologian and revered abolitionist, Lucretia Coffin Mott of Nantucket, Massachusetts, displayed skill at logic in refuting Lyceum lecturer Richard Henry Dana Sr. of Boston. In a speaking tour to major cities, he had delivered "An Address on Woman," which demeaned women as physically, mentally, and morally inferior to men. Quoting the Bible, Shakespeare, and Milton, he had charged that suffrage would "unsex" the female, whom God created to stand in awe of males. After hearing his lecture several days earlier, Mott cited the faulty claims by laypersons and the clergy that males were innately superior to women. Her sermon charged men with mocking females and ignoring biblical affirmation of women's ability to prophesy. She anticipated social progress as a result of full citizenship for women, which she claimed that females had deserved from the beginning of creation.

There is nothing of greater importance to the wellbeing of society at large—of man as well as woman—than the true and proper position of woman. Much has been said, from time to time, upon this subject. It has been a theme for ridicule, for satire and sarcasm. We might look for this from the ignorant and vulgar; but from the intelligent and refined we have a right to expect that such weapons shall not be resorted to—that gross comparisons and vulgar epithets shall not be applied, so as to place woman, in a point of view, ridiculous to say the least.

This subject has claimed my earnest interest for many years. I have long wished to see woman occupying a more elevated position than that which custom for ages has allotted to her. It was with great regret, therefore, that I listened a few days ago to a lecture upon this subject, which, though replete with intellectual beauty, and containing much that was true and excellent, was yet fraught with sentiments calculated to retard the progress of woman to the high elevation destined by her Creator. I regretted the more that these sentiments should be presented with such intellectual vigor and beauty, because they would be likely to ensnare the young.

The minds of young people generally, are open to the reception of more exalted views upon this subject. The kind of homage that has been paid to woman, the flattering appeals which have too long satisfied her—appeals to her mere fancy and imagination, are giving place to a more extended recognition of her rights, her important duties and responsibilities in life. Woman is claiming for herself stronger and more profitable food. Various are the indications leading to this conclusion. The increasing attention to female education, the improvement in the literature of the age, especially in what is called the "Ladies' Department," in the periodicals of the day, are among the proofs of a higher estimate of woman in society at large. Therefore we may hope that the intellectual and intelligent are being prepared for the discussion of this question, in a manner which shall tend to ennoble woman and dignify man. . . .

This age is notable for its works of mercy and benevolence—for the efforts that are made to reform the inebriate and the degraded, to relieve the oppressed and the suffering. Women as well as men are interested in these works of justice and mercy.

They are efficient co-workers, their talents are called into profitable exercise, their labors are effective in each department of reform. The blessing to the merciful, to the peacemaker is equal to man and to woman. It is greatly to be deplored, now that she is increasingly qualified for usefulness, that any view should be presented, calculated to retard her labors of love.

Why should not woman seek to be a reformer? If she is to shrink from being such an iconoclast as shall "break the image of man's lower worship," as so long held up to view; if she is to fear to exercise her reason, and her noblest powers, lest she should be thought to "attempt to act the man," and not "acknowledge his supremacy;" if she is to be satisfied with the narrow sphere assigned her by man, nor aspire to a higher, lest she should transcend the bounds of female delicacy; truly it is a mournful prospect for woman. We would admit all the difference, that our great and beneficent Creator has made, in the relation of man and woman, nor would we seek to disturb this relation; but we deny that the present position of woman, is her true sphere of usefulness: nor will she attain to this sphere, until the disabilities and disadvantages, religious, civil, and social, which impede her progress, are removed out of her way. These restrictions have enervated her mind and paralyzed her powers. While man assumes that the present is the original state designed for woman, that the existing "differences are not arbitrary nor the result of accident," but grounded in nature, she will not make the necessary effort to obtain her just rights, lest it should subject her to the kind of scorn and contemptuous manner in which she has been spoken of. . . .

Woman has never wakened to her highest destinies and holiest hopes. The time is coming when educated females will not be satisfied with the present objects of their low ambition. When a woman now leaves the immediate business of her own education, how often, how generally do we find her, sinking down into almost useless inactivity. To enjoy the social circle, to accomplish a little sewing, a little reading, a little domestic duty, to while away her hours in self-indulgence, or to enjoy the pleasures of domestic life—these are the highest objects at which many a woman of elevated mind, and accomplished education aims. . . .

A new generation of women is now upon the stage, improving the increased opportunities furnished for the acquirement of knowledge. Public education is coming to be regarded the right of the children of a republic. The hill of science is not so difficult of ascent as formerly represented by poets and painters; but by fact and demonstration smoothed down, so as to be accessible to the assumed weak capacity of woman. She is rising in the scale of being through this, as well as other means, and finding heightened pleasure and profit on the right hand and on the left. The study of physiology, now introduced into our common schools, is engaging her attention, impressing the necessity of the observance of the laws of health. The intellectual Lyceum and instructive lecture room are becoming, to many, more attractive than the theatre and the ballroom. The sickly and sentimental novel and pernicious romance are giving place to works calculated to call forth the benevolent affections and higher nature. . . .

The question is often asked, "What does woman want, more than she enjoys? What is she seeking to obtain? Of what rights is she deprived? What privileges are withheld from her? I answer, she asks nothing as favor, but as right, she wants to be acknowledged a moral, responsible being. She is seeking not to be governed by laws in the making of which she has no voice. She is deprived of almost every right in civil society and is a cypher in the nation except in the right of presenting a petition. In religious society her disabilities, as already pointed out, have greatly retarded her progress. Her exclusion from the pulpit or ministry—her duties marked out for her by her equal brother man, subject to creeds, rules, and disciplines made for her by him—this is unworthy her true dignity. In marriage, there is assumed superiority, on the part of the husband, and admitted inferiority, with a promise of obedience, on the part of the wife. This subject calls loudly for examination, in order that the wrong may be redressed. . . .

May these statements lead you to reflect upon this subject, that you may know what woman's condition is in society—what her restrictions are, and seek to remove them. In how many cases in our country, the husband and wife begin life together, and by equal industry and united effort accumulate to themselves a comfortable home. In the event of the death of the wife, the household remains undisturbed, his farm or his workshop is not broken up, or in any way molested. But when the husband dies, he either gives his wife a portion of their joint accumulation, or the law apportions to her a share; the homestead is broken up, and she is dispossessed of that which she earned equally with him; for what she lacked in physical strength, she made up in constancy of labor and toil, day and evening. The sons then coming into possession of the property, as has been the custom until of latter time, speak of having to keep their mother, when she in reality is aiding to keep them. Where is the justice of this state of things? . . .

Women's property has been taxed, equally with that of men's, to sustain colleges endowed by the states; but they have not been permitted to enter those high seminaries of learning. Within a few years, however, some colleges have been instituted, where young women are admitted, nearly upon equal terms with young men; and numbers are availing themselves of their long denied rights. This is among the signs of the times, indicative of an advance for women. The book of knowledge is not opened to her in vain. Already is she aiming to occupy important posts of honor and profit in our country. . . .

Let woman then go on—not asking as favor, but claiming as right, the removal of all the hindrances to her elevation in the scale of being—let her receive encouragement for the proper cultivation of all her powers, so that she may enter profitably into the active business of life; employing her own hands, in ministering to her necessities, strengthening her physical being by proper exercise, and observance of the laws of health. Let her not be ambitious to display a fair hand, and to promenade the fashionable streets of our city, but rather, coveting earnestly the best gifts, let her strive to occupy such walks in society, as will befit her true dignity in all the relations of life.

Source: Mott, Lucretia. *Lucretia Mott's Discourse, at the Friend's Quarterly Meeting, in the Hester Street House.* New York: Ross & Tousey, 1850.

N

NATION, CARRY (1846–1911)

Kentucky-born visionary and radical exhorter Carry Amelia Moore Gloyd Nation turned the campaign against alcohol into a media circus on street corners and at smashed saloons and bars. Born Caroline Amelia Moore, the first of six children, on November 25, 1846, she grew up on a farm in Belton, Missouri. Nation studied at the Baconian Institute in Midway, Kentucky, in 1854 and at Mrs. Tillery's academy in 1859 in Independence, Missouri. Before the outbreak of the Civil War in April 1861, the Moores lived in Cass County, Missouri. After the war started, they avoided regional hostilities over slavery by boarding a wagon train on a six-week journey crossing the Oklahoma border into Grayson County in northern Texas.

On November 21, 1867, Nation wed a military surgeon, Charles Gloyd, a war veteran and alcoholic who boarded at the Moore residence. The couple built a small house in Holden, Missouri, but separated during her pregnancy. At his death from alcoholism in 1870, she and her toddler, Charlien Gloyd, lived with his mother while Nation took classes at the Warrensburg State Normal Institute.

After four years of teaching primary grades in Holden, on December 30, 1874, Nation married widowed lawyer and newspaperman David A. Nation, a Union army captain from Henry, Indiana. In 1880, the couple moved with his five children—Mary Jane, Oscar O., Cathus, Mariah, and Lola Nation—to Missouri, where David opened a saddlery. She began managing an inn at Columbia, where she supported Gloyd's mother and Nation's sister Lola.

Temperance Campaign

The couple took control of a hotel in Richmond, Texas, in February 1881. Because of David's involvement in political outlawry, the family moved once more to Medicine Lodge, Kansas, in 1890, when Nation returned to innkeeping while

David preached. She fostered hostility toward drinkers, grog shops, and clubs and denounced pharmacists who sold alcohol.

In May 1892, Nation co-formed a Kansas branch of the Women's Christian Temperance Union to evangelize drunkards in jail cells with unscripted "moral suasion" (Grace 2001, 138). At Medicine Lodge in December 1894, she joined a cadre of militant "home defenders" in raiding a pharmacy for dispensing whiskey. In 1896, she and David homesteaded near Seiling in northwestern Oklahoma. They added to their family a 13-year-old niece, Callie Bell Moore, a potential successor to Nation's fight for universal sobriety.

Returned to Medicine Lodge by 1899, Nation abandoned gentility for direct action against liquor parlors, beginning in Kiowa with the Dobson Saloon on June 6, 1900. Her memoir recorded the extempore sermon, which she delivered as a warning. Certain of the dictates of state law, she declared owners of saloons criminals and offered herself as a sop to the sheriff if a court should charge her with vandalism. A witty conclusion, a recitation of the angelic benediction from the Christmas story in Luke 2:14, rid the sermon of personal animus and directed anti-alcohol violence at the sin of selling and serving liquor.

On February 16, 1900, Nation led the temperance cadre to O. L. Day's pharmacy in Medicine Lodge. Alone on June 6, 1900, she assailed several rumhouses in Kiowa. In obedience to a heavenly vision, at the Hotel Carey bar on December 27, 1900, she harangued inebriates while setting fire to beer kegs and throwing rocks at mirrors, windows, glassware, and lascivious paintings. For demolishing private property, she served time in the Wichita jail, the first of 30 arrests in the next 10 years. She paid court fines out of fees for delivering prohibition lectures.

Following more temperance forays in Wichita and Enterprise, on January 27, 1901, Nation carried civil disobedience to the Senate Saloon at Topeka. In a speech before the combined houses of the Kansas legislature, on February 7, she admonished Governor William E. Stanley for flouting prohibition laws. On February 17, 1901, she wrecked eight Topeka saloons, followed in April by incarceration for more vandalism and disturbing the peace. The chain of lawlessness interested Hearst investigative reporter Dorothy Dix, who spread the legend of the Kansas virago and her violent band. Nation further tainted her reputation by celebrating the assassination of President William McKinley, whom she considered a proponent of liquor.

After David divorced his wife for cruelty and desertion in November 1901, Nation chose prayer and preaching as safer methods of winning converts to abstention from alcohol and tobacco. Her roving spread to warehouses and beer joints in Chicago, Muscatine, Iowa, and Peoria, Illinois, and, in 1902, to lectures at Harvard and the universities of Texas, Kansas, and Missouri. In Washington, D.C., in November 1903, she failed to get an appointment to proselytize President Theodore Roosevelt.

Lecture Tour

Over a decade, Nation incurred 32 arrests for waving a hatchet, squashing cigars, and hurling bricks at ale bottles and barkeeps. As a representative of the Furlong Lyceum Bureau in Rochester, New York, she targeted audiences from Atlantic to Pacific, covering churches, theaters, and Salvation Army halls. At Guthrie, Oklahoma, in 1905, she lobbied for federal prohibition of alcohol. In addition to admission prices of a quarter or half dollar, she financed abstinence lectures and women's suffrage campaigns with sales of souvenir pewter hatchets, photos, the autobiographical *The Use and Need of the Life of Carrie A. Nation* (1905), and three propaganda publications—*Home Defender*, *The Hatchet*, and the biweekly *Smasher's Mail*.

To legitimize campaigning on the campus of the University of Texas, Nation informed the principal that she was alerting boys to debauchery, a proactive strategy that she had initiated at Yale, Harvard, and the University of Michigan. At Hartford, Connecticut, she blasted alcohol as a demonic poison that "rots the brain, rots the body, and rots the soul" (Nation 1905, 133). In San Francisco, she proclaimed whiskey a drug that degraded and robbed its victims and left them "the sorrows in this bottle, the headaches, the heartaches, the desolation" (134).

In the last six years of her life, Nation wrestled with Charlien's mental illness and remanded her daughter to the Texas State Lunatic Asylum. After planning an anti-vice crusade in Orleans, Nebraska, in 1907, Nation altered direction to the nation's capital. In Columbus, Ohio, in July 1908, she attended the National Prohibition Party as a delegate. Her orations declined but included a scriptural blast at the boozer in the essay "Prohibition or Abolition—What It Means" (1908), a paean to the sanctity of American homes.

In winter 1908, Nation campaigned for sobriety in England, Scotland, and Ireland. With proceeds from civil disobedience, a 1909 comedy act in Great Britain, and lectures in Canterbury, England, she invested in a Kansas City women's shelter. In January 1910, a bartender assaulted her.

Following collapse on January 13, 1911, at a lecture in Eureka Springs, Arkansas, Nation retired to Hatchet Hall, a home she opened in the Ozarks for abused and homeless women. She sank into a coma and died on June 9, 1911, in Evergreen Place Hospital in Leavenworth, Kansas. Nine years later, the 1920 National Prohibition Act legitimized temperance.

References

Grace, Fran. *Carry A. Nation: Retelling the Life*. Bloomington: Indiana University Press, 2001.

Nation, Carry Amelia. *The Use and Need of the Life of Carry A. Nation*. Topeka, KS: F.M. Steves & Sons, 1905.

THIS DEN OF VICE
BY CARRY A. NATION
DOBSON SALOON, KIOWA, KANSAS
JUNE 6, 1900

One of the most colorful orators in women's history, Carry Nation of Garrard County, Kentucky, led a state branch of the Women's Christian Temperance Union in evangelizing drunkards and terrorizing saloon and warehouse owners. On her first attack in Kansas, she sang hymns to the accompaniment of a portable organ, threw rocks through windows and mirrors, and set fire to beer kegs. After demolishing bars with hatchets from Missouri to California, she campaigned in Great Britain and toured U.S. college campuses warning young men of the dangers of intemperance.

Mr. Dobson, I told you last spring, when I held my county convention here, to close this place, and you didn't do it. Now I have come with another remonstrance. Get out of the way. I don't want to strike you, but I am going to break up this den of vice. . . . I have destroyed three of your places of business, and if I have broken a statute of Kansas, put me in jail. If I am not a lawbreaker, your mayor and councilmen are. You must arrest one of us, for if I am not a criminal, they are. . . .

As Jail Evangelist of Medicine Lodge, I know you have manufactured many criminals and this county is burdened down with taxes to prosecute the results of these dives. Two murders have been committed in the last five years in this county, one in a dive I have just destroyed. You are a butcher of hogs and cattle, but they are butchering men, women and children, positively contrary to the laws of God and man, and the mayor and councilmen are more to blame than the jointist, and now if I have done wrong in any particular, arrest me. I'll go home. . . .

You are a partner of the dive-keeper and the statutes hold your building responsible. The man that rents the building for any business is no better than the man who carries on the business, and you are *particeps criminus* or party to the crime. Peace on earth, good will to men.

Source: Nation, Carry Amelia. *The Use and Need of the Life of Carry A. Nation.* Topeka, KS: F.M. Steves & Sons, 1905, 71–72 passim.

NOOR, QUEEN (1951–)

Pacifist Elizabeth "Lisa" Najeeb Halaby al Hashimi, the widowed Queen Noor of Jordan, promotes religious tolerance, social rights, and global justice. She was born in Washington, D.C., on August 23, 1951, to Doris Carlquist and U.S. Navy test pilot Najeeb Elias "Jeeb" Halaby Jr., a veteran of World War II, the CEO of

Pan-Am Airlines, and aide to the U.S. Department of Defense. Privately educated at the National Cathedral School during the Kennedy administration and in New York City at the Chapin School, she vacationed at her grandmother's Virginia farm and rode horses. Miserable at Chapin, she completed high school in Massachusetts at Concord Academy while debating, writing for the newspaper and yearbook, and playing field hockey, lacrosse, and basketball. She enrolled in architecture and urban planning in the first co-ed class at Princeton, played on the first women's ice hockey team, and joined the cheerleading squad.

In Iran's Qajar era in the mid-1970s, Noor worked for British designers at Llewelyn-Davis to supply Reza Shah with a modernist capital and an Arab Air University. The architectural team revitalized Tehran to rid it of water and air pollution and provide public space, jobs, and housing for rural Arabs moving to the city. In 1976, she joined the managerial staff of Arab Air Services to design modern headquarters for Royal Jordanian Airlines in New York.

In Jordan, Noor explored the ancient stone city of Petra, an historic site that needed protection for its architectural integrity. While designing Queen Alia International Airport at Zizya, east of central Amman, in spring 1977, she attended a ceremony honoring Jordan's first Boeing 747. At the event, she displayed fresh beauty and restrained fashion sense.

During events honoring increased air travel, Noor met Hussein bin Talal, a widower and king of Jordan. In early April 1978, she accepted his invitation to lunch at Al Nadwa Palace to meet the royal children and tour a stable of fine Arabian horses. In exchange for hospitality, she detailed structural weaknesses in the palace architecture. On May 13, 1978, she accepted his proposal of marriage, an alliance that resonated through the world media.

In a traditional Arab ceremony at Zaharan Palace, on June 15, 1978, Noor became Hussein's fourth wife and the first American monarch of an Arab nation. The wedding necessitated her union with the Hashemite clan and induction into Islam as Noor, Arabic for "light." She began chairing committees to build parks, support children's reading, and immunize babies.

The mother of the royal children and manager of the palace, the queen reared four-year-old princess Haya; an adopted daughter, five-year-old Abir; and three-year-old Prince Ali, the only son of Queen Alia. In 1980, Noor gave birth to Crown Prince Hamzah, who preceded three siblings, Prince Hashim and Princesses Iman and Raiyah.

Noor's influence on royal pronouncements derived from her fluency in English, French, and Arabic and a daunting series of speaking tours across the United States by which she refuted misconceptions about Arabs. As head of the Noor Al Hussein Foundation, in 1985, she coordinated the Jerash Festival of music and worked to alleviate poverty, illness, and unemployment through microcredit. She devoted volunteer time to human rights and archaeological and ecological preservation through collaboration with the International Union for the Conservation of Nature and Bird Life International. Blaming the queen, Americans raised objections to Hussein's denunciation of the U.S. alliance with Israeli prime minister Itzhak Shamir.

After Hussein's kidney removal at the Mayo Clinic, in Rochester, Minnesota, Noor took on heavier responsibilities at home and globally. In 1995, she accepted a U.N. Environment Program Global 500 Award for protecting Jordanian culture and heritage along with global honors from Brunei, Egypt, Italy, Sweden, Denmark, and Austria. At an oration to the Greater Washington Society of Association Executives on March 4, 1996, she talked at length about the name "Noor" and her intent to illuminate current events and foster peace in the Middle East.

Without warning, in spring 1998, the king's health deteriorated from fever, pain, and exhaustion. Chemotherapy increased fatigue, limiting Hussein to drives in the country, garden walks with a cane, and bedside visits from Hamzah. Noor continued public speaking by opening the First Middle East Conference on Landmine Injury and Rehabilitation on July 11, 1998, with the clearing of 64,000 mines from the Jordan Valley to free land for farming, mining, and tourism. In the address "Surviving the Scourge of Landmines," she disclosed the news of Jordan's signing of the Ottawa Convention and pledged that Jordanians would not export antipersonnel mines.

After the king succumbed to lymphatic cancer on February 7, 1999, ending a 47-year reign, the widowed queen honored his interment in the Royal Mausoleum at Raghdan Palace in Amman. She retained limited power in Jordan as mother of the crown prince and stepmother of King Abdullah II. She founded the King Hussein Foundation, a humanitarian agency supporting economic empowerment of girls and women and sustainable development.

Noor compiled a biography of her husband, *Hussein of Jordan* (2000). She followed with a best-selling retrospect on her progression to royalty, *Leap of Faith: Memoirs of an Unexpected Life* (2003). A year later, Abdullah replaced Hamzah's birthright with the birth of a new heir to the throne, Hussein bin Abdullah.

Noor's positive outlook energized Refugees International and the International Union for Conservation of Nature and boosted international exchange at the 2010 Rotary International Convention. At the Skoll World Forum in Oxford, England, on April 13, 2011, her lecture, delivered with a warm intimacy, invigorated entrepreneurship.

On receipt of the Woodrow Wilson award on February 21, 2015, Noor gave an acceptance speech at Princeton, where alumni celebrated the university centennial. The oration stressed the uselessness of bombing to end world tensions with Islam and the breeding of extremist hatred through ongoing militarism. The text advanced to Middle Eastern women and their oppression by sexists.

Noor's speeches incubated gendered innovations, such as investment in food processing and tourism through the training of women in management. Mentoring aided youths, women, and displaced Iraqis to find jobs offering substantial earnings. A policy assessment initiated reception of Syrian refugees through legal asylum, reunion of parents and children, and rehabilitation of torture victims. For the 2016 World Leaders Forum at Judson University, she appeared as keynote speaker.

Reference

Noor, Queen. *Leap of Faith: Memoirs of an Unexpected Life*. Waterville, ME: Wheeler, 2003.

BILL OF RIGHTS FOR LANDMINE SURVIVORS BY QUEEN NOOR OF JORDAN REGIONAL MEETING ON LANDMINE INJURY AND REHABILITATION AMMAN, JORDAN JULY 11, 1998

The widowed Queen Noor of Jordan promotes pacifism, religious tolerance, social rights, and global justice. Her drive to eliminate landmines from weapons of war resulted in efforts to rid the globe of antipersonnel explosives and to compensate victims with humane care, education, and employment to enable them to live normal lives. As of 2004, 13 nations continued to manufacture mines, a consortium of states that placed the United States among some of the world's most hostile governments, including Burma, North Korea, Pakistan, Iran, Iraq, Russia, Cuba, and China.

I have a particular interest in this issue because I come from one of the most mine infested regions of the world, where mines planted since World War II and during more recent conflicts are killing innocent men, women, and children daily and endangering the agricultural and economic productivity.

One hundred thousand American soldiers and civilians have been injured and killed by landmines in this century alone. Thirty-four percent of American casualties in the Gulf War and 33 percent in the Vietnam War were all landmine casualties. Some 300,000 people around the globe are living with shattered limbs and lives and the number is growing. Every month around 800 people are killed and 1200 maimed by landmines. Anti-personnel land mines harm primarily civilians. They contravene international humanitarian law because they are designed to injure rather than kill; to maximize suffering.

Landmines are generally placed in rural villages in order to shatter the morale and integrity of family, clan, tribe, and village. These weapons have proliferated into a source of random terror that respects neither time nor territory and does not distinguish between hostile combatants and schoolboys playing football.

Consistent with the Universal Declaration of Human Rights; based on the collective wisdom of world religions; in conformance with United Nations Standard Rules on the Equalization of Opportunities for Persons with Disabilities; recognizing that hundreds of thousands of men, women, and children injured by mines urgently need care and support to resume productive lives; believing that landmine survivors should share the same rights and protections that should be enjoyed by all persons, Landmine Survivors Network advocates:

- The right of survivors to participate fully in all decisions concerning their health and well-being.
- The right to comprehensive rehabilitation and access to reliable information of physical, psychological, social, and economic aspects of recovery.
- The rights of survivors, born free and equal in dignity and rights, to participate fully in their society.
- The right to education commensurate with ability.
- The right to obtain such aids, equipment, and materials that assist in education, training, movement, and transportation.
- The right to an environment that allows freedom of movement and transportation in a safe and secure manner.
- The right to employment commensurate with capabilities and qualifications.
- The right of families of mine victims to necessary relief and support services.
- The right to peer support, recreation, and vocational resources to promote social and economic integration.
- The right to select qualified health practitioners, voice concerns about quality care, and seek redress if services or products do not meet high quality standards.

Source: Busé, Margaret S. "Her Majesty Queen Noor of Jordan: A Commitment to Landmine Awareness and Victim and Survivor Assistance." *Journal of ERW and Mine Action* 3, no. 3 (1999). Accessed September 10, 2015. http://www.jmu.edu/cisr/journal/3.3/index.htm. Reprinted by permission from James Madison University.

O

OBAMA, MICHELLE (1964–)

The 44th first lady, Michelle LaVaughn Robinson Obama advocates for numerous issues, such as nutritional health, veterans' sacrifices, and empowering young women with greater opportunities. A Chicagoan, she was born on January 17, 1964, to Marian Shields and Fraser Robinson III. With degrees in sociology and African-American studies, she graduated from Princeton in 1985 and, over the next three years, completed a law degree from Harvard.

Obama's advocacy focused on the employment of more nonwhite teachers at the university and pro bono representation of the poor for the Harvard Legal Aid Bureau. On staff at Sidley Austin as an associate in marketing and royalty law, she met Barack Hussein Obama, a fellow Harvard alumnus. After marriage at the Trinity United Church of Christ on Chicago's South Side on October 3, 1992, she directed the Office of Public Allies as a youth mentor and fundraiser for AmeriCorps and produced Malia Ann and Natasha "Sasha" Obama.

While her husband ran for the Illinois Senate in 1996, Obama joined the student services staff at the University of Chicago and created community aid programs. She advanced over the next decade to university hospitality director and vice president of community affairs. She also advised TreeHouse Foods and the Chicago Council on Global Affairs, which analyzed U.S. involvement in world food markets.

In mid-February 2007, Obama balanced stumping for her husband's first presidency with home duties to the two girls, who enrolled at the University of Chicago Laboratory Schools. In Denver on August 25, 2008, she directed to delegates of the Democratic National Convention the keynote address "One Nation." Themes stressed an end to the Iraq War and a more robust economy. To ensure prosperity to families, the text named hard work, health, and college education as the foundations of well-being and success.

At the White House, the first lady planted a kitchen garden and mounted beehives to provide organic vegetables and honey for the family table. Additional efforts to shield homosexuals from hate crime and prejudice in the military included invitations to gay service members for Washington events and verbal backing of same-sex marriage.

Obama's crusade for healthy weight resulted in *Let's Move*, a program she originated in February 2010. She laced television interviewers with tips on obesity prevention via a broad-based diet, safer places to play, and everyday exercise through walking, dance, hula hoop games, and tennis. In the spirit of fun, she demonstrated jumping rope.

During her husband's 2012 campaign against Republican candidate Mitt Romney, Obama continued traveling and promoting her aims to audiences and on camera. In June 2012, she informed Philadelphians about her resolve to raise health and wellness standards. Her physical activity campaign included more individual attention to food labels and the consumption of affordable fresh produce, especially in school cafeterias, concepts she proposed in *American Grown: The Story of the White House Kitchen Garden and Gardens Across America* (2012). She made extensive television appearances praising the involvement of 23 fifth-graders in cultivating 1,100 square feet of garden and promoting the investment of her book royalties in the National Park Service. After harvest, the children assembled for lessons on cooking and serving their bounty.

On a second residency in the White House on November 6, 2012, Obama proved an equal marriage partner by backing the president's drives for pay equity and family leave for women in the workplace. She directed personal support toward cabinet agencies, wellness and diet, and the Joining Forces program, a national rally for military households and veterans. The Obamas recruited children to participate in Olympic and Paralympic sports and appeared together serving meals at free kitchens for the homeless.

At the Conference on Ending Homelessness in Washington, D.C., on July 31, 2014, Obama presented the speech "Homeless Veterans." Her outline included partnership with the Veterans Administration, housing rental assistance from the Department of Housing and Urban Development, and a challenge to 250 governors, mayors, and county commissioners to rescue veterans from the street by December 2015. In straightforward rhetoric, she lauded as an example the housing of all 227 homeless veterans in New Orleans and projected hope for similar rescue of ostracized gay teens and poor families migrating from motel to motel.

The Reach High Initiative of 2014 engaged Obama in recruiting high school graduates to skills training or higher education. The program nurtured academic planning and the possibility of financial aid by providing public school counselors with source material. The following year, she conceived Let Girls Learn, a global effort to keep female students in class.

With an emphasis on personal experience, in spring 2015, Obama addressed several commencements, including Tuskegee University, Oberlin College, and Martin Luther King College Preparatory High School in southern Chicago. She acknowledged the sting of racist caricatures and taunts and declared them badges of pride for disproving myths about black Americans. Her remarks to graduates encouraged an embrace of challenges and a commitment to fairness and equality.

In July 2015, Obama's acceptance of challenge included editing *More* magazine, a commentary on America's monuments and national parks. Of women's lives, she saluted the ability of females to multitask. In January 2016, she exemplified respect for Islam by visiting a mosque in Jakarta, Indonesia.

Reference

Slevin, Peter. *Michelle Obama: A Life*. New York: Knopf Doubleday, 2014.

HOMELESS VETERANS (EXCERPT)
BY MICHELLE OBAMA
NATIONAL ALLIANCE TO END HOMELESSNESS
RENAISSANCE HOTEL, WASHINGTON, D.C.
JULY 31, 2014

In her second term as first lady, Michelle Obama directed national attention to homeless veterans, who made up 20 percent of male homeless Americans. In challenging 250 governors, mayors, and county commissioners to rescue veterans from the streets by December 2015, she set an example of citizen resolve to end an ongoing misery for all Americans. Her speech preceded a government effort in summer 2015 to employ more homeless veterans and to supply health care and support services.

I want to thank all of you—the leaders who are fighting every day to end homelessness in communities across this country. The work you are doing is so critically important. You are helping folks meet one of their most basic human needs. You're making sure our communities reflect our shared values of compassion, empathy, and service. And you're doing the hard work to show that here in America, we take care of our own.

So given your extraordinary contributions, it is disappointing that you often don't get the support, respect, and appreciation you need to get the job done. Whether you're running a shelter or raising money for a community organization or managing a citywide anti-homelessness campaign, you all are working long hours to keep it all together. You're fighting each year for every single penny in your budgets. But inevitably the cuts come and it's up to you to figure out how to salvage what's left of your programs.

And day after day, as you fight for more resources, you encounter too many folks who don't take you seriously because they don't believe that we'll ever truly be able to solve this problem; or even worse, because they feel like our homeless brothers and sisters have brought these problems on themselves.

Yet, when so many others accept homelessness as a fact of life, you refuse to give up. When they scoff at your idealism, you show them the data and evidence that prove that we can solve this problem. And when they still throw up their hands and walk away from this challenge, you roll up your sleeves and get back to work.

So today, before I say anything else, I just want to say thank you. Thank you. Thank you for taking that gay teenager whose parents kicked him out of the house. Thank you for connecting that low-income family with resources that keep them from being evicted. And thank you for showing veterans like Leon [who spoke earlier] that the country they served still has their backs.

I don't know if you hear that enough. But it's veterans like Leon that's actually what I'd like to focus on my discussion with you today on. I'd like to talk about how we're serving our veterans in this country, particularly when it comes to the issue of homelessness.

As you know, as First Lady, I've been blown away by the stories of courage and selflessness that define our veterans and their families. I have met wounded warriors who have lost legs to an IED and then fight through recovery to run marathons. I've met veterans who have run into sniper fire and explosions to save their friends. Every single time they're asked, these men and women answer the call and give this country everything they've got.

And so when I hear that these folks don't even have a place to go when it rains, like all of you, I am outraged. And the fact that right now, our country has more than 58,000 homeless veterans, well, that's a stain on the soul of this nation.

Now, I always try to be very clear that the vast majority of our veterans are tremendously resilient and never experience homelessness. They transition back in good health and good spirits and go on to build successful careers and strong families. But as Americans, the idea that anyone who has worn our country's uniform spends their nights sleeping on the ground should horrify us. And so it is truly our duty to right this wrong and put an end to veteran homelessness once and for all.

But that moral and patriotic duty is only part of the reason why ending veteran homelessness is so critical. As we all know, ending homelessness for our veterans can also be a crucial first step—a proof point—to show that we can end homelessness for everyone in this country, too. . . .

Source: Obama, Michelle. "Remarks by the First Lady at the National Alliance to End Homelessness Annual Conference." July 31, 2014. The Office of the First Lady. Available at: https://www.whitehouse.gov/the-press-office/2014/07/31/remarks-first-lady-national-alliance-end-homelessness-annual-conference.

OLSEN, TILLIE (1912–2007)

A focused writer, lecturer, and earnest labor agitator, Tybile "Tillie" Lerner Olsen dramatized how housework and motherhood disempowers women and shreds their dreams. Born on a tenant farm on January 14, 1912, in Wahoo, Nebraska, she was the daughter of feminist writer Hashka Ida Goldberg and Samuel "Sam" Lerner, a painter and secretary of the Nebraska Socialist Party. A stutterer in classes at Kellom Elementary School and Long School, she outlined skits for the Young Socialist League and recited Spartacus's harangue to Roman slaves and William Wadsworth Longfellow's literary epic *Hiawatha*.

Olsen left Omaha Central High in 1927 to labor in ill-paid jobs at cafés, a hotel, a tie factory, and laundries. Employment in meat processing plants filled her with disillusion at the unsatisfying lives of blue-collar workplaces. Lifelong socialism edged her toward union and political speech writing on behalf of out-of-work meat packers in Kansas City and Omaha.

On February 14, 1931, Olsen married Abraham Jevons Goldfarb in Reno, Nevada, and settled in Stockton, California. A five- to six-week jail term in Kansas City in winter 1931–1932 for vagrancy and distributing handbills precipitated her decline from pleurisy and tuberculosis and a beating by an inmate. While recovering from childbirth in Faribault, Minnesota, she worked as a maid at the Palace Hotel while she wrote *Yonnondio* (1932), a survey of domestic abuse and debt among underpaid workers in a reeking meatpacking house.

In the midst of the Great Depression, Olsen's harangues on racism, homelessness, civil rights, schools and libraries, and peace energized Bay Area picketers and demonstrators for the American Communist Party. She described the struggles of have-nots in the poem "There Is a Lesson" for *The Daily Worker* and in the essays "Thousand-Dollar Vagrant" for *New Republic* and "The Strike," "I Want You Women Up North to Know," and "The Iron Throat" for *Partisan Review*.

In 1935, Olsen relocated to Los Angeles to write for editor Bennett Cerf at Random House and organize Southern California stoop laborers. While living in San Francisco in 1936, she began a common law relationship with Kiev-born warehouseman Jack Olsen. She presented diatribes against fascism in Catalonia, Germany, and Italy and rallied trade unions with the Congress of Industrial Organizations (CIO) over the American Federation of Labor (AFL). Her rousing speeches encouraged California sailors to join the Abraham Lincoln Brigade, volunteers to Spain's rebel forces.

Prior to his deployment in World War II, Jack married Olsen on February 29, 1944. In 1947, she advanced to chair of the CIO War Relief, but later investigations by the House Committee on Un-American Activities cost her several jobs. Despite Federal Bureau of Investigation surveillance, she completed coursework in 1954 at San Francisco State University and crafted the classic feminist short fiction "I Stand Here Ironing," a scenario of futile female chores anthologized in *Tell Me a Riddle* (1961), winner of the O. Henry Prize.

As a consultant to Feminist Press, Olsen earned the nickname "Tillie Apple Seed" for reviving works by little-known female authors, including Lillie Devereux Blake's feminist classic *Fettered for Life, or Her Lord and Master: A Story of Today* (1872). A late-in-life recipient of critical recognition as a Guggenheim Fellow and National Endowment for the Arts honoree, Olsen composed *Silences* (1978), a summation of the intrusions of mothering, housekeeping, political involvement, and publishing difficulties on women's writing careers. She taught creative writing and women's literature and film at Amherst College, Stanford University, Massachusetts Institute of Technology, University of California at San Diego, and Kenyon College.

As Olsen's international reputation for oratory expanded, she spoke on "Comprehensions" at Radcliffe on March 13, 1979, and appeared for two weeks in Norway at Bergen, Oslo, Trondheim, and Tromsø universities as the 1980 visiting scholar. On March 16, 1982, she lectured on "Responding to the Nuclear Threat," a topic she developed with author Alice Walker, and began collecting works by 120 authors for *Mother to Daughter, Daughter to Mother* (1984). At the University of Northern Iowa in April 1984, Olsen's speech "The Word Made Flesh" honored students for their language and experiences.

In widowhood after 1989, Olsen continued crusading for blue-collar workers and contesting racial bias, political silencing in Beijing, and the classism and elitism of charter schools. She received the 1994 Rea Award for short fiction, the Marie Sandoz Award for Nebraska authors, and multiple honorary doctorates. Cared for by daughter Laurie Olsen Margolis during years of decline from Alzheimer's disease, the activist died in an Oakland, California, hospital on January 1, 2007.

See Also: Blake, Lillie Devereux; Walker, Alice.

Reference

Reid, Panthea. *Tillie Olsen: One Woman, Many Riddles*. New Brunswick, NJ: Rutgers University Press, 2010.

INTERVIEW WITH ANNE-MARIE CUSAC BY TILLIE OLSEN *THE PROGRESSIVE*, MADISON, WISCONSIN NOVEMBER 1999

An intensely focused writer, lecturer, and labor agitator, Tillie Olsen dramatized the disempowerment of women and the diminution of the working class. Through her promotion of democracy in education and social opportunity, she developed a following for her lectures and writings. Her example encouraged citizens, especially women, to involve themselves in public debate and to express their outrage at preferential treatment for the upper class.

. . . The silences go on. The first silencing is the inequality of the educational system. We still have a strong class system in this country. Look at what's happening with most public schools. Think of the future writers who are being lost all along. Future writers. In [my novel] *Yonnondio*, the kids really hate school, and their mom wants them to get a good education, but instead they are turned against it. And as I write in there, "For was it not through books they had been taught that they were dumb, dumb, dumb?"

. . . That process is exactly what is happening in the public schools now for many children—the doing in of bilingual programs, for instance. I'm enraged by charter schools. Every school should be a good school. We are just setting up more educational class systems.

The second silencing is the workload so many have to carry, the problem of time. You may use spoken speech marvelously, people love to listen to you. Or you are a great gossiper, or somebody who is empathetic to what others are thinking and feeling, but none of that gets written.

. . . The century has also been full of resistance. Why is it that the resistance movements—often so heroic and so ingenious—get obliterated from consciousness?

There's always been resistance, and there comes a time when changes are made. The fact that human beings do not put up forever with misery, humiliation, degradation, actual physical deprivation but act is a fact which every human being should know about. We are a species that makes changes.

I have a lot of faith in the American people if they have access to truth. I buy 100 copies at a time of the Universal Declaration of Human Rights. It was Eleanor Roosevelt's great work. And it happened in San Francisco, at the first meeting of the United Nations. I was there because I was head of CIO [Congress of Industrial Organizations] War Relief, and also I was president of the California CIO state auxiliary. So since labor was big and important because it was needed in the war, I was invited to U.N. gatherings.

It was such a time of hope.

The Universal Declaration of Human Rights includes economic rights. It also has a clause that the son-in-law of Karl Marx would have loved. He wrote a book called *The Right to Be Lazy*, one of my favorite revolutionary pamphlets—the right to vacations with pay, what Walt Whitman called "loafing and inviting one's soul."

I sometimes, if it's an adult audience, ask how many of them are familiar with the Universal Declaration of Human Rights. Most highly educated people have never read it. It's a tragic erasure of our heritage.

. . . There's been some change, as is evident by the number of women writers who are read. And education itself has somewhat changed. There's a lot more encouragement, a lot more writing classes. It was the women's movement that gave women in academe a certain strength. If you'd look at the old reading lists, maybe George Eliot, the Brontës, Virginia Woolf might be taught.

At Stanford, I think it was 1971, they needed somebody [to teach their first-ever course on women's literature], and my name was suggested. Well, I had no credentials. I had never gone to college. And there was quite a to-do about whether or not I had the qualifications. It was supposed to be a small class. I went into this auditorium. It was jammed. There were, I think, four guys, one of whom went out and then came back again and then went out and then came back again. There were over 100 women there, including faculty wives. By and large, none of this had ever been taught at Stanford before.

. . . I have a lot of hope from young people, too, with that flame of freedom and light of knowledge, as well as from some of the old people, whom I honor a lot. There's the Abraham Lincoln Brigade, who fought in Spain, what's left of them, and there's no bitterness, there's no cynicism. They believe, too, as I do, that it's in human beings not to put up with what is harming and depriving. I am a believer, but the U.S. *über alles* psychology is very strong now and our bombings from the air. I don't want to die leaving the world as it is right now.

Source: Cusac, Anne-Marie. "Interview with Tillie Olsen." *The Progressive*, January 4, 1999. http://www.progressive.org/news/1999/01/4386/tillie-olsen-interview. Reprinted by permission from *The Progressive*.

P

POLLITT, KATHA (1949–)

Humanist poet, pundit, and humorist Katha Pollitt focuses social critiques on poverty, bigotry, gendered violence, and individual worth. Born October 14, 1949, in Brooklyn Heights, New York, she grew up in an intellectual, communist household. In her bedroom in fourth grade, she began regularly writing poems. In 1975, she completed an MFA in composition from the Columbia School of Arts and submitted poems to the *Atlantic* and *New Yorker.*

In 1982, Pollitt joined the staff of Barnard College as creative writing professor and poet in residence. She laced a verse collection, *Antarctic Traveler* (1982), with realistic detail, a reason for the 1983 National Book Critics Circle Award, a National Endowment for the Arts grant, and a 1984 Lavan Younger Poets Award. On June 6, 1987, she wed dramatist and humor columnist Randy Cohen, a writer for David Letterman's television show.

In December 1988, Pollitt stressed "Children of Choice," a valorization of babies planned by stable couples. Her pro-family essay "Contracts and Apple Pie" deflated the gooey hallowing of "motherhood" popularized by the Moral Majority. A year later, she attacked "fetal rights" as a punitive reduction of expectant women to two-legged wombs.

In Denver on September 29, 1995, at the annual assembly of the Freedom from Religion Foundation, Pollitt reflected on a confession on *Crossfire* that she grew up atheist. In the speech, "Fundamentalism," rapid-fire reasoning linked fundamentalist illogic with demands for school prayer, an end to abortion clinics, and withdrawal of welfare funds from teenage mothers. She concluded that politicians screened issues through scriptural exegesis, an obfuscation based on ignorance. At a speech to the Women's Leadership Conference at George Mason University on March 22, 1997, she named women's work and citizenship objectives as the prime movers of feminist progress.

Covering a range of topics from school prayer to domestic violence and absent fathers, Pollitt anthologized 88 columns in *Subject to Debate: Sense and Dissents on Women, Politics, and Culture* (2001). In protest of jingoism and hawkish Pentagon policies, after 9/11, she composed her most controversial opinion, "Put Out No Flags" (2001), a refusal to endorse a push for bombing in the Middle East.

Pollitt's op-ed pieces began appearing in college composition and debate texts as models of persuasive writing. She collected personal themes, including "Sisterhood" and "Webstalker," in the prose anthology *Learning to Drive: And Other Life Stories* (2007), the source of a 2014 film. In August 2008, she spoke on the advances Senator Hillary Clinton made for women in politics by vying for the Democratic presidential nomination. She accepted the American Sociological Association invitation to deliver a keynote speech, "What Do You Mean I'm Not Equal Yet," at a 2012 assembly in Denver and received acclaim as a 2013 heroine of the American Humanist Association.

Pollitt recast pregnancy termination from an agonizing dilemma into a pressing and private decision in the female reproductive life. She described womb cleansing of fertilized eggs as a force for good among the poor, immature, and over-burdened. She listed lies embedded in government-scripted advice parroted by doctors that abortion can cause infertility, breast cancer, and insanity. Of the judgmental, antiwoman laws that restricted, postponed, and dissuaded parturient women from ending pregnancies, she characterized such legislation as 21st-century methods of stifling women's autonomy.

See Also: Clinton, Hillary; Dworkin, Andrea; Friedan, Betty.

References

Pollitt, Katha. "Hers: The Smurfette Principle." *New York Times Magazine*, April 7, 1991.

Snodgrass, Mary Ellen. *Encyclopedia of Feminist Literature*. New York: Facts on File, 2006.

WHAT IT'S LIKE TO WRITE A WOMAN'S LIFE NATIONAL PUBLIC RADIO INTERVIEW BY KATHA POLLITT WASHINGTON, D.C. MARCH 12, 2012

In a radio interview for NPR, Katha Pollitt displayed an agile knowledge and analysis of women's history ranging from the Virgin Mary and Ruth to life stories of Zora Neale Hurston, Cleopatra, and Margaret Sanger. Verbally graceful and detailed, Pollitt encouraged a thoughtful return to scripture and history to evaluate events impacted by female action and ethics.

MICHEL MARTIN, HOST: I'm Michel Martin and this is Tell Me More from NPR News. . . We wanted to kick off Women's History Month, which starts today, by taking a closer look at the stories by and about women. As women around the world are rethinking and rewriting their roles in society, we decided to take a look at how the biographies of notable women reflect those changes.

In the coming weeks, we are going to dig into biographies of divas and dancers, leaders of nations and queens of fashion, but before we hear from these authors, we have called upon two scholars to help us get started by talking about how women's lives have been written about and why that matters.

With us now is Katha Pollitt. She's an award-winning essayist, author and poet. Among many books, she is the author of "Reasonable Creatures: Essays on Women and Feminism," and she's a columnist for the magazine *The Nation*. Welcome, Katha Pollitt. Thank you so much for joining us.

KATHA POLLITT: Thanks so much for having me.

MARTIN: Also here with us once again, Dana Williams. She is the chair of the department of English at Howard University and a professor of African-American literature. Welcome back to you. Thank you for joining us once again.

DANA WILLIAMS: Hello, Michel. Thank you.

MARTIN: So Katha Pollitt, I'm going to start with you because your 1995 book "Reasonable Creatures" is titled after a quote by the author Mary Wollstonecraft, who said that women are, quote, "neither heroines nor brutes, but reasonable creatures," which leads me to wonder whether—is that kind of a defensive title in that women—have women traditionally been just depicted as either heroines or brutes and not reasonable?

POLLITT: Well, it's interesting. What Mary Wollstonecraft actually said was, I wish to see women neither heroines nor brutes but reasonable creatures. And she was talking about everything from the—you know, the virgin/whore dichotomy, to putting women on a pedestal, but also condemning them as prostitutes and sluts. These are things we still see today.

And you can really see that in the way women's biography has developed, including biographies of her, because after her death she was demonized as—you know, she'd had a child out of wedlock, she led this riotous life, she did things women weren't supposed to do.

And it was only much, much later in our own time that you begin to see biographies of Mary Wollstonecraft that take her very seriously as a philosopher, which she was, as a major political figure in her time, as part—a big part of the Romantic movement and so on.

So one thing that women's biography has done in our time is to put women back in history as historical actors, not just the wife of, the girlfriend of, someone who died a dramatic death and wrote a book no one reads anymore, that kind of thing.

MARTIN: Well, couldn't you make an argument, though, that sacred books have always, in fact, had in a way a biography of women? Or maybe that kind of just reinforces the existing point that they exist to tell a point as opposed to be people on themselves. I'm just thinking about, like, in Hebrew and the Hebrew Scriptures, like the book of Ruth. You could argue that's a biography, in a way.

POLLITT: Well, it's—I guess it sort of is a story about a woman. Yes.

MARTIN: OK. You don't have to agree with my theory, but that's . . .

POLLITT: Yeah. But, you know, on your point, it's very interesting, if you read the New Testament, how little there is about the Virgin Mary. You know, she really doesn't have a lot—have a big speaking part, and yet, you know, there is such a need for women as heroes, as important actors in history, that a whole—you know, a whole myth and scholarship and folklore about the Virgin Mary has grown up that is part of religion now, but a lot of it is—comes after the New Testament or is extracted from tiny little hints in the New Testament.

MARTIN: Professor Dana Williams, you specialize in African-American literature and you were part of our conversation last month where we kicked off our investigation of black memoirs. And you noted that formerly enslaved Americans set down memoirs and that African-American women were certainly a part of that. But what about biography?

WILLIAMS: We see black women's lives written about a lot and especially, as of late, just in the last two or three years we see three different biographies on Michelle Obama, for instance. So we see books about literary figures. There are several biographies of Zora Neale Hurston, and as we were talking a little bit earlier, there are several biographies of Ida B. Wells, for instance. And those are all very good and interesting.

MARTIN: Is this new, though? Is this presence of African-American women in biography a pretty new phenomenon?

WILLIAMS: I don't think so. I think there's a long kind of genealogy or history of black women being written about. The newer aspect may be having black women tell the stories of other black women.

MARTIN: Have you noticed a shift in the way these women are written about? Because one of the things I'm interested in digging into further is—can people really tell the truth of their lives or is it always through a lens of whatever the politics are of the time? For example, noting those biographies of Ida B. Wells-Barnett, we reported on, you know, a major work by Professor Paula Giddings when it was published. And one of the things that I was noting was how she grappled with the question of how much of a public role she should play—of course the great anti-lynching activist, a newspaper publisher, very significant figure, and also a wife and a mother.

So we're thinking—is she the original work/life balanced person, kind of angst-ing about that? Or is it that she felt she had to—she couldn't own her own interests in being a public figure because she felt like she had to pretend to be reluctant? I mean, and you don't really know. So Dana, what do you think?

WILLIAMS: In that regard, we do see a shift, indeed, particularly because now there are limitations of privacy. With the kind of multimedia age, the things that Ida B. Wells would have been able to keep to herself or to keep private just aren't an option anymore, so you have everything from the Internet to women writing journals that they're making public or allowing other people to read, to a letter.

So one of the biographies of Zora Neale Hurston, for instance, is actually a life in letters, where we begin to try to figure out who she is based on the letters that she wrote. Hurston is a good example, also, of women not telling everything about themselves. Hurston lied about her age, everything from when she was born to what she was interested in and what moved her. So now that we have these letters that are collected, we can begin to recreate her life and so in that regard too we see as much about the person who's writing the biography as about the person that the biography is about.

How are they choosing to frame the story? What are they imagining to be true about the person? What are they choosing to focus on?

MARTIN: But just briefly, why did she lie about her age, by the way?

WILLIAMS: I think it was just vogue for women to not tell their ages and so, you know, it's still taboo now in most communities where you ask a woman her age and she'll say, well, I can't tell you that.

(SOUNDBITE OF LAUGHTER)

MARTIN: Katha Pollitt, what do you think? Do you think that there is a—have you observed a difference in the way that women's stories are told? And it's been said that the biographies say as much about the biographer as they do about the subject.

POLLITT: Well, I think we need to see women's biographies now in the context of the revitalization of feminism and the effect it had on the teaching of history and our sense of what is history and also the tentative remaking or opening up of the literary canon.

And Zora Neale Hurston is a really good example of that because she was incredibly famous during the Harlem Renaissance. She was a big deal, both as an anthropologist and as a folklorist and as a writer of fiction. But by the time she died, which I think was in the '60s, she was completely forgotten. She was working as a cleaning woman, and it was left to Alice Walker and other black writers that came up in the '60s and '70s to rediscover her.

And then we started getting this intense interest in her, where she had been seen by, for example, Richard Wright, you know, a very left-wing political black writer, as she was seen as—well, she's telling stories we don't want told. This is all making black people look primitive.

When Zora Neale Hurston came back into favor at a different historical moment, she was seen as a very important figure, partly because she wasn't so time-bound to, you know, the struggles of the Communist Party in the '30s, and I think that, you know, now we're getting this wealth of information and interest in her that would never have happened if it hadn't been for the political developments of the '60s, '70s, '80s and ongoing to now.

MARTIN: You're right, by the way. Zora Neale Hurston died in 1960, according to our information. That's essayist and columnist for *The Nation*, Katha Pollitt. Also with us, Professor Dana Williams of Howard University. We're talking about women's biographies. And just briefly, to tie a bow on that, Professor Dana Williams, do you think that the—I'll just say the word lies or fibs—let's say fibs that women have been moved to tell about their lives—are they really any different from the ones that men have told to shape their narratives—to shape the narratives around men? Because I was just thinking, if you were sort of a male political leader, would you really want it known that you might have been, like, afraid to do something? Like, you know, that you didn't really want to go into the service or something, that you were scared or something like that?

Or a latter-day . . . I just wondered if you think that there is just more shading. Do you think that—and I'm asking for your opinion—more shading around the story of women than the stories of men?

WILLIAMS: I don't think so.

MARTIN: More of a dissonance?

WILLIAMS: I don't think so. I think if we look at the stories that men tell or stories that are told about men, we see the same kind of dissonance that we see with women's stories. One kind of interesting distinction, to go back a little bit on something that Katha was suggesting, might be in looking at the lives of black women and their biographies and the way that they tend to focus more on an institution or an organization or the community as opposed to the individual life.

So we do see that shift from a kind of traditional biography, and even with the resurgence of feminism in, say, the last 10 or 15 years or so, we still see a distinct difference between the biography of Ella Baker, for instance, where even the title tells us it's the black freedom movement, so it's Baker's lens through which we're looking at the black freedom movement.

"For Freedom's Sake," again, with Fannie Lou Hamer, the idea is to look at a particular type of movement or a way of being that impacts the community, and one of the—I know you'll talk to the author of "Joan Myers Brown and the Audacious Hope of the Black Ballerina." So again, we're talking about Philadanco and what it meant to try to assert a place for black ballerinas in a civil rights kind of environment that wasn't as friendly to black ballerinas, everything from color to body type.

So it's interesting to see how black women's lives focus probably a little bit more on a communal kind of aspect, much more so than the kind of traditional white male story that takes on a different framework completely.

MARTIN: Interesting. To that end, here's a—I just want to play a short clip from a conversation with author Rebecca Skloot, whose book "The Immortal Life of Henrietta Lacks" has been a huge bestseller about an African-American woman whose cells, cancer cells were used in medical research, had a profound effect on medical research. And this is Skloot speaking to NPR's Neal Conan in 2010.

(SOUNDBITE OF ARCHIVED RECORDING)

REBECCA SKLOOT: I just sort of became obsessed with this question of who was she and did she have any kids and what did they think about all this stuff that was done with her cells. You know, I spent many years trying to sort of uncover the story of both the science and the person behind it all.

MARTIN: I'll ask each of you. Katha Pollitt, I'll start with you. What do you think it means that a woman like Henrietta Lacks has now been given voice in this time? What do you think it means?

POLLITT: Well, I think it's fascinating. I think it shows that—a kind of democratization of the notion of history and, even in this case, maybe the notion of science, and that all these people that were considered to be completely unimportant, like the person whose cells are used for medical discoveries, turn out to be absolutely fascinating and turn out to be part of the story.

For example, you might find that the model for a great painting is an interesting person and that that model then, through that lens, you could see, well, you know, models played a more important role in the development of art than we might think, and I think that's happening all over and it's really great. I'm really happy that we live in this time of biography, when we find out so much that was hidden before.

MARTIN: Professor Dana Williams, what do you think it means?

WILLIAMS: I think it, again, raises that conversation that we were talking about, in terms of the distinction or the way that biography teaches us something about the biographer as much as it teaches us about the person. So I think we come to know more about the person and the choice of framing the story of Henrietta Lacks, probably—I wouldn't say more than we learn about Henrietta Lacks, because indeed we do.

But the tension that was present between the family and the biographer is an interesting conversation that even reminds me a little bit of the tension around "The Help," for instance, where—what do you do when the person whose story it is is not necessarily excited about the story being told in this particular way?

Or, in some instances, the lawsuit that happens, where the woman based on the story is saying, this isn't what I agreed to. So what do you do with that tension in terms of the person who's telling the story versus the family?

MARTIN: But wouldn't you rather know?

WILLIAMS: Sure.

MARTIN: Wouldn't you rather know than not know?

WILLIAMS: Absolutely.

MARTIN: I was fascinated when, in "The Immortal Life of Henrietta Lacks," the author, Rebecca Skloot, spent 12 years researching and writing this. She first discovered the cell line and that there was even a person's name that was known behind it when she was in high school or something crazy like that, and then the tension emerged well along in the story. And it is—would you rather know or not know or would you rather she'd kept that business out of it?

WILLIAMS: No. I think you certainly would rather know, I think. But what also has to happen is you have to understand how complicated the coming to knowing is about.

MARTIN: Before we let each of you go, we have to ask if you have a biography that you have read lately that you would like to recommend. This being Women's History Month, we'd prefer that it be of a woman, but we're not going to place restrictions on you. I know I'm springing this on you, but Professor Dana Williams, do you have a biography you'd like to recommend?

WILLIAMS: Yes. I'm actually thankful for the conversation with your producer, Anita(ph), and for your raising my attention to Joan Myers Brown and "The Audacious Hope of the Black Ballerina." I'm fascinated with Philadanco and I had known a little bit about Joan Myers Brown, so I'm looking forward to getting into that one.

MARTIN: All right. Katha Pollitt, what about you?

POLLITT: Well, I think you've got Stacy Schiff's "Cleopatra" on your list, which I was going to recommend. So let's see. I would say, since you have one biography of Margaret Sanger on your list, I would also recommend the earlier book by Ellen Chesler, which is really long and very magisterial and a very full and quite—you know, just exemplar of what a biography should be. Her book, her biography of Margaret Sanger.

MARTIN: All right. Well, thank you. Katha Pollitt is an award-winning essayist, author and poet. She is the author of "Reasonable Creatures: Essays on Women and Feminism," among other works. She is a columnist for the progressive magazine *The Nation*, and she was kind enough to join us from the studios at Radio Foundation in New York.

Here with us in our Washington, D.C. studios, Dana Williams, chair of the department of English at Howard University and a specialist in contemporary African-American literature.

Thank you both so much for joining us.

POO, AI-JEN (1974–)

Visionary and writer Ai-jen Poo nurtures the feeble and handicapped by coordinating disparate humanitarian agencies and nonprofit state and religious organizations. A first-generation Taiwanese American and the second of two daughters, she was born in Pittsburgh, Pennsylvania, to Taiwan immigrants—chemist and oncologist Wen-Jen Hwu and Mu-Ming Poo, a molecular neurobiologist at the University of California at Berkeley. During Wen-Jen's studies at Carnegie-Mellon University, Ai-jen spent summers in Taiwan with a grandmother and baked chocolate chip cookies to sell to aid Ethiopian famine relief.

While Mu-ming Poo held the rank of professor at Yale in New Haven, Connecticut, Ai-jen's paternal grandfather, Liang Shao Pu, taught tai chi to Asian Americans. Following his son's divorce and Wen-Jen's relocation to Irvine, California, to research skin cancer, Pu walked granddaughters Ting and Ai-jen home from school. Ai-jen regretted his stroke, decline, and death in 2007 in a dreary, malodorous nursing home.

Influenced by her mother and trained at Phillips Academy Andover, a private boarding school in Massachusetts, Poo volunteered at the New York Asian Women's Center, a shelter for battered women, and rallied for reproductive choice. She set an example of resistance in 1989 by boycotting a campus speech by President George H.W. Bush. Her advocacy focused on Women's Forum projects. She entered Columbia University in 1992 to major in women's and gender studies. She incurred arrest for a sit-in on the Manhattan Bridge to protest police brutality and the Bush administration's cuts in the federal education budget.

To end campus racism and call attention to the limited hiring of nonwhite professors, Poo strategized the overnight stay of 100 demonstrators at the Low Memorial Library rotunda. After a five-day seizure of the administrative buildings, she and 21 protesters entered police custody, a face-off preceding the establishment of the Center for the Study of Ethnicity and Race. On graduation in 1996, she aided the Committee against Anti-Asian Violence. Because historic labor regulations ignored the needs of domestics, initially black maids shut behind closed doors, she began leading nontraditional Asian domestics in efforts to secure higher pay, occupational safety, and worker benefits.

Activism for Housekeepers

To identify unwary immigrants and undocumented aliens, most of them people of color, in 1998, Poo canvassed parks, playgrounds, bus and train stations, and churches for women who lacked experience with the U.S. legal system and trade unions. In extreme situations, domestics incurred sexual bondage, house arrest, and human trafficking. Even under duress, they loved the children they reared and the elderly and crippled family members they fed and dressed.

Efforts of the Clinton administration met Republican opposition in 2000, when President George W. Bush repealed reimbursements for home care and failed to empower caregivers by setting guidelines and workplace standards to protect the vulnerable. To uplift two-income households, Poo's pioneering campaign preceded the 2000 alliance in the National Domestic Workers Alliance (NDWA) of African, Caribbean, Indian, and Central and South American maids, nannies, companions, and in-home aides of the chronically ill with diabetes, AIDS, heart disease, and Alzheimer's. As director of the NDWA, she rallied members to pursue self-determination, dignity, health care and maternity leave, training in elder care, travel allowance, and standard employment contracts. As part of her tactic of organizing with love, she proposed a Medicare Part C to cover home care, the third fastest growing industry in the United States.

Poo aided the formation of the U.S. Social Forum, a conference held in Atlanta from June 27 to July 1, 2007. To impress on Georgia state legislators the populist groundswell for rights of workers dismissed as marginal and expendable, she joined a Children and Families March from the capitol to the civic center and informed participants on "Domestic Workers." She continued public demonstrations in Albany and Harlem in a crusade she considers the unfinished business of the civil rights era.

Poo addressed domestics from an outdoor dais in Washington, D.C., and lobbied New York legislators to pass the 2010 Domestic Workers Bill of Rights, which ensured paid vacation and holidays, overtime, emergency leaves, and protection from exploitation and racial bias. After New York became the first state to enact legislation in September 2010, notice of Poo's advocacy derived from media articles on the *New York Moves* magazine "Power Woman" designation and a "40 under 40" tribute from the Feminist Press. Following successful legislative initiatives in California, Hawaii, and Massachusetts, in spring 2011, her high school honored her with a profile in the *Andover* alumni magazine.

Poo confronted the faults of a profession paying $9.40 per hour or around $15,611 per year. By initiating Caring across Generations in Washington, D.C., on July 12, 2011, she coordinated disparate campaigns to aid families and lone individuals to solve the social, economic, health, and nutritional needs of some 65 million elderly and disabled. Among participants, she collaborated with Department of Labor Secretary Hilda Solis, AFL-CIO secretary-treasurer Liz Shuler, and lobbyists from varied constituencies—Hand in Hand: The Domestic Employers Association, 9 to 5, Service Employees International Union, the American Federation of State, County and Municipal Employees, Family Values @ Work, the Alliance of Retired Americans, Direct Care Alliance, Young Women's Christian

Association, Bend the Arc: A Jewish Partnership for Justice, and the National Day Laborer Organizing Network.

In the midst of a care gap, Poo's lobbying emphasized the aging of post–World War II baby boomers at the rate of 10,000 per day and the stress of more retirees on the Social Security system. In justifying civil rights, women's rights, union solidarity, and gay rights, she reported a win-win situation by noting that long-term in-home care cost less than institutionalization in rehabilitation centers and nursing homes and, simultaneously, added jobs to the economy. Her patriotic example earned an American Express NGen Leadership Award, a listing among emerging power brokers in *Newsweek* and *Time*, and comparisons to the labor innovations of Jane Addams, Mother Jones, and Dolores Huerta.

By 2012, Poo allied 500,000 elderly and immigrants in the demand for semiprofessional elder care, a service dominated by female staffing. Within two years, the number grew by 50 percent and fueled an $84 billion industry. She posed in a public park with a bullhorn and poster labeled "Respect All Work." On April 30, *The Nation* publicized her Web speech "Caring across Generations," a national movement creating two million jobs tending frail and disabled people and hospice patients.

Poo's address predicted that, over the first half of the 21st century, the demand would more than double from 13 million to 27 million. Because workers had no federally recognized right to unionize and mediate demands, they flailed at disparities in programs from state to state and the isolation of caregivers from job to job. Complicating the employment picture were cuts to Medicaid and Medicare. To extend the coalition, she scheduled care assemblies in Los Angeles, Seattle, San Francisco, Dayton, New York, and San Antonio and chose as a cooperative model the heroism of caregivers following Hurricane Sandy on October 22, 2012.

For financial backing, Poo proposed taxing financial transactions and corporations, incentivizing with caregiver tax credits, and slicing the Pentagon budget. She anticipated that the "caring majority" would form a voting bloc composed of female and senior voters as well as the millennials and sandwich generation who rely on home staff. For championing the underdog, the *New York Times* called her the "nannies' Norma Rae" while the *Wall Street Journal* opposed her organizing crusades in Colorado, Oregon, Illinois, and Washington State.

For proposing holistic programs to transform the civic engagement, security, and well-being of old people and paid leave for caregivers, in 2014, Poo won a MacArthur genius grant of $625,000. Additional honoraria from the Union Square Award, Open Society Institute Community Fellowship, Leadership for a Changing World Award, *Ms.* Magazine Woman of Vision Award, Bannerman Fellowship for Organizers of Color, and Prime Movers Fellowship introduced her to more Americans. While living in an apartment in Woodside, Queens, with her cat Coco and relaxing with Buddhist meditation and yoga practice, she read the books of Thich Nhat Hanh to reflect on stages of life, aging, and dying. She compiled *The Age of Dignity: Preparing for the Elder Boom in a Changing America* (2015), a valuable prediction that preceded her listing among *Fortune*'s World's 50 Greatest Leaders. In 2016, her lectures focused on alleviating social isolation and fostering age-friendly cities.

See Also: Addams, Jane; Huerta, Dolores; Jones, Mother.

References

Ehrenreich, Barbara. "The Nannies' Norma Rae." *New York Times*, April 26, 2011.

Flanders, Laura. "Can 'Caring across Generations' Change the World?" *The Nation*, April 30, 2012, 21–25.

POWER, SAMANTHA (1970–)

An Irish-American scholar, advocacy journalist, and ambassador to the United Nations, Samantha "Sam" Power advanced from newsgathering to opposing genocide and advocating for global accountability for human rights abuses. She was born on September 21, 1970, in Dublin to Jim Power and Veronica B. "Vera" Delaney. She earned a history degree from Yale.

In 1989, images of protests in Tiananmen Square jolted Power into humanitarianism. From 1993 to 1996, while freelancing for *The Economist*, *New Republic*, *Boston Globe*, and *U.S. News & World Report*, she delivered news from war zones in Croatia, Bosnia, and Kosovo. She surveyed the conflict in Rwanda and the massacre of 800,000 Rwandans within 14 months of ethnic carnage. As a war correspondent, she reached a nadir of hope in July 1995 when Bosnian Serbs slew 7,000 male Muslim Albanians.

From 1996 to 1999, Power earned a law degree from Harvard Law School. Her research in the National Security Archive yielded *A Problem from Hell: America and the Age of Genocide* (2002), for which she won a Pulitzer Prize. In 2004, she delivered to the House committee on international relations a retrospective speech on an African massacre, "Rwanda's Genocide: Looking Back." The topic championed humanitarian intervention against suffering, even in the face of public disapproval. Despite military costs in lives and equipment, she embraced the concept of "responsibility to protect," a duty incumbent on world leaders. She charged the Clinton administration with an indelible genocidal stain and warned that Arab Muslims were plotting a similar ethnic liquidation for Sudan.

In 2005, Power joined U.S. senator Barack Obama's inner circle. As his policy adviser, she counseled on world affairs and the need for a proactive diplomacy in the 2008 campaign for the White House. In addition to serving as senior director of the Office of Multilateral Affairs and Human Rights, she aided the Obama transition by informing the State Department's Agency Review Team and National Security Council. In 2009, she joined the National Security Council, a post she held for six years.

To an audience at Columbia University in 2011, Power proposed U.S. military intervention and a no-fly zone over Libya to prevent Muammar Gaddafi from launching mass beheadings of Ethiopian and Coptic Christians. With support from Republicans and Democrats, on June 5, 2013, Obama named her the U.S. ambassador to the U.N. and the U.S. representative to the U.N. Security Council. Pro-Israeli factions backed the nomination and applauded her past record on international law and the prevention and adjudication of mass murder.

After resigning from the White House staff, in September 2013, in a crusade to increase global response to mass atrocities and genocide, Power outlined foreign options in situations calling for action. Her recommendations ranged from economic sanctions, jamming hate radio, and expulsion of ambassadors to mustering foreign alliances and deploying a military counterstrike, a solution she suggested to prevent conflict between Israelis and Palestinians. In 2016, she blamed Rwanda for furthering uprisings in Burundi.

References

Lockhart, Michele, and Kathleen Mollick, eds. *Global Women Leaders: Studies in Feminist Political Rhetoric.* Lanham, MD: Lexington Books, 2014.

Power, Samantha. "Rwanda's Genocide: Looking Back." *Hearing before the Subcommittee on Africa of the Committee on International Relations, House of Representatives.* 108th Cong., 2d sess. Washington, DC: U.S. Government Printing Office, 2004, 25–30.

U.S. PERMANENT REPRESENTATIVE TO THE UNITED NATIONS NOMINATION HEARING BY SAMANTHA POWER U.S. SENATE COMMITTEE ON FOREIGN RELATIONS, WASHINGTON, D.C. JULY 17, 2013

An Irish-American scholar, advocacy journalist, and ambassador to the U.N., Samantha Power advanced from newsgathering to advocacy against genocide. Her address to U.S. senators demanded moral accountability for global human rights abuses in Bosnia, Syria, and Mali. Her closing comments promised straight, nonpolitical dealings with the world's people and an honest evaluations of U.N. failures.

It is a great honor to appear before you as President Obama's nominee to serve as the United States Permanent Representative to the United Nations. Representing the United States of America would be the privilege of a lifetime. I am grateful to the President for placing his trust in me.

I would like to thank my friends and my remarkable family who are here with me today—my parents, who brought me here from Ireland, Vera Delaney and Edmund Bourke; my husband Cass Sunstein; and our children, four-year-old Declan, and one-year-old Rían, who may prove less interested in this hearing than others here today.

I would also like to thank Senator Chambliss and Senator Isakson for their generous introductions. Growing up as an Irish immigrant in Atlanta, Georgia, I cannot say that the United Nations was a popular topic with my classmates at Lakeside High School. But it was in Georgia, while working at a local television station, that I witnessed footage of the horrible massacres in Tiananmen Square and resolved that I would do what I could the rest of my life to stand up for American values and to stand up for freedom. My Georgia friends supported me every step of the way, and I am now very proud to count these two great public servants among them.

When I first came to this country, I viewed the United Nations as a place where people assembled to resolve their differences and prevent hunger and disease. It was the stage on which iconic Americans like Daniel Patrick Moynihan and Jeane Kirkpatrick stood up for what was right.

Unfortunately, when I travelled to the Balkans in 1993, I saw a different side to the U.N. The U.N. Security Council had sent peacekeepers to Bosnia to protect civilians. But in the town of Srebrenica, those Bosnians who sought the protection of the blue helmets were handed over to those who wished them harm. More than 8,000 Muslim men and boys were executed in cold blood, as the peacekeepers stood idly by.

A decade later, I travelled across the Chadian border into Darfur to document the genocide being carried out by the Sudanese government. After discovering a mass grave and many charred villages, I brought out some of the burnt remnants of those villages, which were exhibited at the U.S. Holocaust Museum. It was U.N. humanitarian workers who steered me to living witnesses, so eager were they to expose the regime-sponsored horror. I should note that, as the crisis in Darfur once again intensifies, U.N. peacekeepers on Saturday suffered a horrific ambush that killed seven soldiers and wounded seventeen others—a reminder of the risks that U.N. personnel face every day.

Elsewhere, today, we see physicians from the World Health Organization working with governments and local volunteers to provide polio vaccinations in Nigeria and Pakistan—determined to heal even as terrorists wage a campaign of assassinations against them. Just last Friday, the U.N. provided a platform for Malala Yousafzai—the brave young Pakistani girl who was shot in the head last year by Taliban gunmen on her way home from school—to inspire millions to stand up for girls' education.

Yet within this organization built in the wake of the Holocaust—built in part in order to apply the lessons of the Holocaust—we also see unacceptable bias and attacks against the State of Israel. We see the absurdity of Iran chairing the U.N. Conference on Disarmament, despite the fact that its continued pursuit of nuclear weapons is a grave threat to international peace and security. We see the failure of the U.N. Security Council to respond to the slaughter in Syria—a disgrace that history will judge harshly.

The U.N. is multi-faceted, and its record mixed. But sixty-eight years after the United Nations was founded in San Francisco, one fact is as true today as it was then: an effective U.N. depends on effective American leadership. The war in Bosnia didn't end because the U.N was shamed by the massacres in Srebrenica. It ended because President Clinton, backed by a bipartisan coalition in Congress, decided that American values and interests were imperiled and acted to end the war. It is now possible to imagine an AIDS-free generation in Africa not merely because of the essential work of UNAIDS, but because President George W. Bush decided to provide life-saving drugs on a massive scale.

I believe that America cannot—indeed, I know that America should not—police every crisis or shelter every refugee. While our goodwill knows no bounds, our resources are finite, strained by pressing needs at home. And we are not the world's police. We must make choices based on the best interests of the American people. And other countries must share the costs and burdens of fighting injustice and preventing conflict.

That is where the U.N. can be very important. There are challenges that cross borders that the United States alone cannot meet—terrorism, nuclear proliferation, and pandemics. There are cases—as with sanctions against Iran and North Korea—where U.S. efforts pack a far greater punch when we are joined by others. There are occasions—as in Mali today—when the U.N. has to step up to prevent state failure, which abets terrorism and regional instability.

An effective U.N. is thus critical to a range of U.S. interests, and strong American leadership at the U.N. is indispensable to advancing those interests. Under the leadership of President Obama, the U.N. supported action to save countless lives in Libya; assisted a peaceful referendum giving birth to an independent South Sudan; and established a new agency dedicated to the empowerment of women worldwide.

If I am confirmed by the Senate, I will remain clear-eyed about the U.N.'s flaws as well as its promise, and I will fight fiercely every day for what is in the best interests of the United States and the American people. The list of our challenges in New York is of course long, but let me highlight three key priorities.

First, the U.N. must be fair. The U.N. cannot focus disproportionate attention on a few, while giving a pass to others flouting their international obligations. There cannot be one standard for one country and another standard for all others. The United States has no greater friend in the world than the State of Israel. Israel is a country with whom we share security interests and, even more fundamentally, with whom we share core values—the values of democracy, human rights, and the rule of law. America has a special relationship with Israel. And yet the General Assembly and Human Rights Council continue to pass one-sided resolutions condemning Israel above all others. Israel—not Iran, not Sudan, not North Korea—is the one country with a fixed place on the Human Rights Council's agenda. Israel's legitimacy should be beyond dispute, and its security must be beyond doubt. Just as I have done the last four years as President Obama's U.N. adviser at the White House, I will stand up for Israel and work tirelessly to defend it.

Second, the U.N. must become more efficient and effective. In these difficult budget times, when the American people are facing tough cuts and scrutinizing every expense, the U.N. must do the same. This means eliminating waste and improving accounting and internal management. This means strengthening whistleblower protections and ending any tolerance for corruption. It means getting other countries to pay their fair share. And it means closing down those missions and programs that no longer make sense. As both the U.N.'s principal founding member and its largest contributor, the United States has the right and the duty to insist on reform. I will aggressively pursue this cause.

Third, the U.N. must stand up for human rights and human dignity, which are American and universal values. The U.N. Charter calls for all countries "to reaffirm faith in fundamental human rights and the dignity and worth of the human person." But fewer than half of the countries in the world are fully free. The Universal Declaration on Human Rights is universally hailed and yet only selectively heeded.

Taking up the cause of freedom is not just the right thing to do, nor is it simply the American thing to do; it is the smart thing to do. Countries that abuse their own people are unstable. Countries that violate the rights of women and girls will never approach their full potential. Countries that allow people to be trafficked provide safe haven to dangerous transnational criminal organizations. Countries that do not protect religious freedom create cleavages and extremism that cross borders and destabilize whole regions. Countries that fail to invest in the health and education of their citizens undermine our shared efforts to promote opportunity. Countries that are corrupt trample upon the dignity of their people, while scaring away investment. If I am given the honor of sitting behind the sign that says "United States," I will do what America does best: stand up against repressive regimes, fight corruption, and promote human rights and human dignity. I will also do everything in my power to get others to do the same.

This means pushing for democratic elections, but also pushing for the freedoms necessary for democracy to work—freedom of speech, freedom of the press, freedom of assembly, freedom of religion, independence of the judiciary, and civilian control over the military. It means contesting the crackdown on civil society being carried out in countries like Cuba, Iran, Russia, and Venezuela. It means calling on the countries of the world to unite against human trafficking and against grotesque atrocities of the kind being carried out by the Assad regime. It means ensuring that in places like the Democratic Republic of Congo, peacekeepers sent into harm's way have the resources and the will to protect civilians. It means bolstering U.N. mediation so that conflicts can be defused before they become costly, protracted wars. It means strengthening non-U.N. forums like the Community of Democracies and President Obama's flagship governance initiative, the Open Government Partnership. It means redoubling our efforts to end extreme poverty. And it means uniting peoples who long to live free of fear in the cause of fighting terrorism and terror of all kinds.

Mr. Chairman, Ranking Member Corker, and other distinguished Members of the Committee, let me stress before closing that this Administration will most effectively confront our current challenges if we benefit from the counsel and collaboration of this essential Committee, and if we can earn the bipartisan support of both houses of Congress. I would like to echo the words of the late Ambassador, my friend Richard Holbrooke, who told this Committee that "Congress should be in on the take-offs, not just the landings." So I appear before you not just to seek your support, but to ask to join you in a conversation about how to strengthen what is right and fix what is wrong at the U.N. If I am confirmed, I will continue this dialogue directly and personally. If the prospect of visiting the U.N. does not immediately entice you, my son Declan has resolved to become a tour guide like no other.

In closing, please know that, if I am given the privilege of sitting behind America's placard, you will be able to count on me. I will tirelessly promote and defend U.S. interests. I will be a blunt, outspoken champion of American values and of human rights. I will be a straight-shooter, always accessible to you and forthright in my dialogue with you and the American people. And above all, I will serve as a proud American, amazed that yet again this country has provided an immigrant with such opportunity—here, the ultimate privilege of representing the United States and fighting for American values at the United Nations.

Source: Power, Samantha. "Testimony of U.S. Permanent Representative-designate Samantha Power." *Hearings before the Committee on Foreign Relations, United States Senate*. 113th Cong., 1st Session, May 7–December 17. Washington, DC: U.S. Government Printing Office, 2013, 162–171.

Q

QUINDLEN, ANNA (1953–)

A prize-winning journalist and shaper of public opinion, Anna Marie Quindlen dwells on the possibilities of reclamation and reinvention of human lives that have grown off-kilter and unsatisfying. She was born on July 8, 1953, in Drexel Hill outside Philadelphia to Prudence Marguerite Pantano and Robert V. Quindlen and came of age in Kendall Park, New Jersey. In early September 1972, Robert Quindlen summoned Anna home to tend Prudence, who faced stage IV ovarian cancer and died six months later.

While Robert traveled on business, Quindlen, a newly enrolled college freshman, had to dispense morphine and mother four young siblings. The unpredictability of mortality inflamed her imagination and left her hungry for an adult mother-daughter relationship. Second wave feminism introduced her to activism.

By 1977, Quindlen began a 17-year relationship with the *New York Times*. In 1978, she married her college sweetheart, lawyer Gerald "Gerry" Krovatin, and settled in Hoboken, New Jersey. In 1983, she launched "Life in the 30s," a survey of urban yuppies, winner of Columbia University's Mike Berger Award for distinguished reportage and the impetus for a promotion to deputy editor.

Quindlen anthologized early columns in the collection *Living Out Loud* (1988). Promoted to the *New York Times* op-ed page, in 1990, she followed with "Public and Private" and the compendium *Object Lessons* (1991), source of the *Glamour* magazine selection of the 1991 woman of the year. She continued issuing collections with *Thinking Out Loud: On the Personal, the Political, the Public and the Private* (1992). In an acceptance speech for a 1992 Pulitzer Prize for social commentary, she lauded individual uniqueness, especially the human heart and soul.

After the success of the novel *One True Thing*, in 1995, Quindlen left journalism to become a novelist. Because of concern for her daughter's generation of women, the author remained at the core of debate over the place of sensitivity and gender equality in news and global leadership. She spoke on the faults of traditional standards of masculinity, which limit imagination and alienate men from their true selves.

By 1999, Quindlen returned to the media by penning "Last Word," a biweekly column for *Newsweek*, a task she fulfilled for a decade with wry comments on U.S. materialism. With the pep talk "Individuality," on May 23, 1999, she began a series of graduation addresses that started with Mount Holyoke. Her pose as a friendly adviser guided hearers to address the black hole at the center of their being and to sustain the differences that set the self apart from all other selves.

The cancellation of Quindlen's June 23, 2000, commencement speech by conservative forces at Villanova University inspired her to air the unused speech electronically. The oratory, "Get a Life," served as the impetus to a book, *A Short Guide to a Happy Life* (2000). The text fostered a passionate embrace of each day and investment of money, energy, and ideas in community outreach.

Quindlen returned to thoughts of individuality at Sarah Lawrence College on May 24, 2002, with a commencement address that reminded young graduates of their parents' involvement in character building. A speech on January 22, 2004, to the National Abortion and Reproductive Rights Action League honored passage of *Roe v. Wade* and the acknowledgement of women's reproductive rights. On May 24, 2009, at the Wesleyan University graduation, her lecture "I Won't Apologize" challenged seniors to examine national faults—a failing economy and declining job and housing markets—and to propose ways to defeat greed, racism, sexism, and animosity toward homosexuals.

At Englewood Cliffs, New Jersey, on November 3, 2013, Quindlen delivered to the Association of American Medical Colleges a keynote oration, "Health Care in an Information Age: How Doctors, Nurses, and Consumers Can Make One Another Better." To medical school professors, pupils, and residents, she tailored a humanistic message about the value of respect and compassion toward patients. Her remarks admonished the technological depersonalization that alienates the sick and robs them of touching and hands-on healing.

In a best-seller, *Lots of Candles, Plenty of Cake* (2014), Quindlen justified her separation from Catholicism, particularly the hierarchy that glossed over pedophiliac priests and obsessed over women's reproductive rights to contraception and abortion. At the San Diego Words Alive luncheon in November 2014, she lauded teachers for changing lives with praise and guidance. To a town hall gathering in Yakima, Washington, in April 2015, she denounced consumerism for thrusting the nation into debt and for the disillusionment that comes from trusting things as sources of happiness. At the heart of her speech, she pitied mothers who attempted too much responsibility and who lost touch with their children. For the 2016 Lancaster Library Luncheon, she directed thoughts to the value of home to the emerging self.

See Also: Friedan, Betty; L'Engle, Madeleine.

Reference

Sharp, Michael D., ed. *Popular Contemporary Writers*. Vol. 9. Tarrytown, NY: Marshall Cavendish, 2006.

ME AND MY EPIDURAL (EXCERPT) BY ANNA QUINDLEN ASSOCIATION OF AMERICAN MEDICAL COLLEGES UNIVERSITY OF PENNSYLVANIA, PHILADELPHIA NOVEMBER 3, 2013

Noted humanist speaker and columnist Anna Quindlen lectured an audience of medical experts on the value of one-on-one counsel to the doctor-patient relationship. She stressed compassion and respect as essentials of personalized service. In an age of technological wizardry, her message imparted faith in the oldest of medical traditions, hands-on healing. Internet sites posted the speech, giving it instant and lasting fame for its humanity.

Some years ago I had some surgery at one of the best hospitals in the country. It was a revision of a surgery I'd had six months before, but I didn't think much about that, although I had a few friends who were enraged about it, couldn't understand how something could be done and then be undone so quickly. But I'd signed the release form in which I acknowledged that medicine is not an exact science, something I'd long understood, although I'd never gotten the impression that doctors did.

Same surgeon, same hospital, different anesthesiologists. The first two had been young women and these two were slightly older men and I tried not to let that matter. They tried the epidural once and it was no go. The second time only half of me got numb, although they acted slightly skeptical of my insistence that I could still feel my right leg.

"I think we should just go to a general anesthetic," one said.

"I think you should try again," I replied.

Afterwards, as he was leaving, he patted my finally numb leg and said, "Next time you'll take the general." And at that moment I came as close as I've ever come to saying the words that, spoken by an allegedly prominent person, seem to me to reflect that they've lost their mind, or lost their way. I almost said the words I've always promised myself I would never say, not to a ticket agent, a hotel clerk, a young reporter, anyone. I almost said: "Do you know who I am?"

The answer to that question, I realize now, is a very important one as far as all of you are concerned today. Not, do you know I won a Pulitzer, or have been on the bestseller list, or give speeches like this one? But a more basic question: do you know anything about me? Do you know why I'm having an epidural rather than a general? Have you taken any time to familiarize yourself with my history in any way shape or form?

Doubtless those doctors would have contended that they didn't have the time, that there were many other cases for them to handle, that under the circumstances it didn't matter. But that flew in the face of the behavior of the pair of anesthesiologists I had during my first surgery.

The young women sat down with me before we began, to explain the general anesthetic they thought they were going to administer. I explained that I hated the idea of being unconscious, that I had chosen my surgeon in part because she was willing to operate with a local, that my doctor and I had discussed the use of an epidural extensively, and that I had brought along a CD player and an imaging CD especially designed for people undergoing surgery which I intended to use during the procedure. Which, by the way, I had heard about from my internist, who likes to play the east/west, mind/body angle a bit. Which is why she's my internist.

"That's all great!" said the more senior of the women. "You don't really need a general anesthetic for this surgery, and I prefer to use the least intrusive kind of anesthetic if the patient is willing. And can I have the name of that CD? I've never heard of it." Although she restrained my hands at the beginning of the surgery, 15 minutes in she released one so that I could scratch my nose, because it's axiomatic that your nose is going to itch when your hands are restrained. "I can tell you're not going to invade the sterile field," she said.

Only a short interchange, yet in some fashion she knew who I was. And I assume she was at least as busy as her male colleagues. . . .

Source: Quindlen, Anna. "Me and My Epidural." Association of American Medical Colleges, November 3, 2013. Used by Permission.

R

RANKIN, JEANNETTE (1880–1973)

America's first suffragist elected to the U.S. Congress, Jeannette Pickering Rankin aroused controversy in Washington, D.C., by rejecting national involvement in global combat. A Montanan born to a political clan at Grant Creek Ranch outside Missoula on June 11, 1880, she was the eldest of the seven children of teacher Olive Pickering and stockman and lumber miller John Rankin, who immigrated from Apin, Ontario, to homestead. She declined marriage and domesticity and, in 1898, entered biology courses at the University of Montana to research mountain snails.

Rankin gave up elementary school teaching and clothing and furniture design and returned to graduate work for a year at the New York School of Philanthropy. After serving Spokane as a social worker in a children's home, in 1909, she attended the University of Washington in Seattle. In 1910, her promotion of honest government through suffrage led Washington state to extend state voting rights to women, followed by Montana state suffrage in 1911. To the State Federation of Women's Clubs in Lewistown, on June 4, 1914, she upgraded stereotypes of stodgy suffragists by projecting youth and vigor in an address on scientific motherhood.

In 1916, Rankin won Montana's at-large seat in the U.S. House of Representatives by 7,600 votes. With the support of New York Congressman Fiorello LaGuardia, on March 17, 1917, at Carnegie Hall, she delivered "Democracy in Government" to alert 3,000 listeners to the growing plutocracy, which included the mining magnates of her state. During mediation of a labor strike against the Anaconda Copper Mining Company, in August 19, 1917, her speech "On the Federalization of Mines" denounced lynching by vigilantes. In straightforward declamation, she blasted both sides of the contretemps for lack of patriotism in reducing copper production during wartime.

Rankin won an office in the Women's International League for Peace and Freedom and, in Zurich, attended the 1919 Women's International Conference for Permanent Peace as a delegate. In the wake of wartime destruction, she lectured on global peace and lobbied for the National Council for the Prevention of War. As an officer of the National Consumers League, she expedited a federal welfare initiative for women's hourly wage and family health care and joined the crusade to end child labor.

Rankin moved to the South and, in 1928 established the Georgia Peace Society outside Athens. She lectured to students at Duke University and the universities of Georgia and Montana and to a Colorado Education Association conference on "Teachers and World Peace" (1929). In 1932, she addressed the U.S. congressional hearing on the exclusion of Communist immigrants. In 1940, she ran again for Congress under the slogan "Keep our men out of Europe."

On December 8, 1941, Rankin cast the lone nay vote against the 388 house ayes declaring war on Japan for bombing Pearl Harbor, Hawaii, the previous day. For her pacifism, a mob menaced her and labeled her unpatriotic. To votes on adding Germany and Italy to America's foes, she voted "present."

Rankin's speech on World War II charged that the propagandists from 1917 merely recycled their rationale in 1941. She stressed that the outcomes of the previous conflict would remain the same in World War II. Throughout the term of office, she championed veterans' rights and introduced a GI Bill extending unemployment compensation, vocational education, and living expenses to war survivors.

On retirement from politics in 1943, Rankin studied Third World economics and the passive resistance tactics of Mohandas Gandhi. She continued appealing for peace during the Korean War and Cold War. On January 15, 1968, she mobilized 5,000 protesters of the Vietnam War in Washington, D.C., to draw legislative attention to the nation's social and racial crises. With increasing difficulty eating, swallowing, and talking, she died in Carmel, California, on May 18, 1973, leaving her Georgia farm as a legacy to jobless females.

References

"Jeannette Rankin to Be Here." Canonsburg, Pennsylvania *Daily Notes*, October 27, 1917, 1.

Lopach, James J., and Jean A. Luckowski. *Jeannette Rankin: A Political Woman*. Boulder, CO: University Press of Colorado, 2005.

ON THE FEDERALIZATION OF MINES BY U.S. REPRESENTATIVE JEANNETTE RANKIN OF MONTANA U.S. HOUSE OF REPRESENTATIVES, WASHINGTON, D.C. JULY 1917

For some six decades, Congresswoman Jeannette Rankin informed and enlivened progressives with more than 6,000 speeches. Although a pacifist, she aided in winning World War I. By denouncing the Anaconda mining company's profiteering on the high price of copper in Butte, she helped to boost ore production as well as safe work conditions and fair treatment for immigrant and nonwhite miners, two issues promoted by the International Workers of the World.

Mr. Speaker, I find in studying the powers that have been granted to the President to enable him to carry on the war, he has been given power to commandeer and operate practically every industry that is engaged in supplying materials necessary for the conduct of the war. Among other things, he is given the power to take over and operate the coal mines, but nowhere has he been given the power to take over metalliferous mines.

At this time copper, a metal essential to the everyday life of people in every part of the civilized world, is a necessity in war, a basic necessity. It is a necessity that we cannot overlook at this time. You have been informed by the daily press that the copper mines in the West, in Arizona and Montana, have not been operating to their fullest capacity. This is due to the fact that the mine owners and the mineworkers have been unable to agree. The result has been an alarming decrease in the production of copper. According to the estimates of the Council of National Defense, the production in Butte in July was 12,000,000 pounds, while the normal output is 30,000,000 pounds a month. This disagreement has also meant a great lawlessness. In Bisbee hundreds of men were deported in complete contempt of law and order. In Butte a man was lynched by masked men.

MR. JOHNSON OF WASHINGTON: Mr. Speaker, will the lady yield for a question?

RANKIN: Yes.

JOHNSON: Did this man who was hanged belong to an organization which declares that it owes allegiance to no government?

RANKIN: I understand that he belonged to the organization known as the Industrial Workers of the World, if that is what the gentleman has in mind.

JOHNSON: Is the lady familiar with the preamble and the basic law of that outfit?

RANKIN: Yes; but this is a question of lawlessness. It is not a question of whom they hanged. (Applause.) As our laws read today, there is no means for handling the situation. I am advised that the President has no real power by which to act. Therefore I am introducing this resolution, which I hope the committee will have ready to report to Congress when the absent members return.

I have tried by every means that I know of to get governmental machinery in action to handle this deplorable situation in my State. I have been kept in close touch with the situation in Butte. After the deportation occurred in Bisbee I received telegrams from Butte asking for Federal protection. I reported this to the Department of Labor and was informed that the department was doing all in its power to handle the situation through its representative, Mr. Rogers. A week ago last night I received a telegram at midnight saying that Mr. Rogers had left Butte, that no satisfactory settlement had been made, and that the people feared violence, and urged me to ask Secretary Wilson for protection. I telephoned this message to the Secretary at once. He asked me to see him the next day. I tried all the next day, until late in the evening, and was still trying to see the Secretary on Wednesday morning, when I received word that a man had been lynched.

Then came more appeals for protection. I tried to see the President, the Department of Labor, the Department of Justice, and, finally, the War Department. The only satisfaction I received was in the War Department, when I convinced them that the troops guarding the mines had been federalized, and therefore were under Federal control. Then it was agreed that some investigation of the situation would be made. In a crisis of this kind, coming as it does in time of war, when all our attention should be centered upon the enemy and not on local difficulties, there should be some effective means by which the Government would be able to protect itself against a decrease in necessary productiveness, and by which the people of each State would be guaranteed the protection provided by the Constitution of the United States. (Applause.)

Some explanation of the situation in Butte may be helpful at this time. Just before the outbreak of the European war difficulties in the Butte Miners' Union resulted in the disruption of the union, so that for the past three years the men have been working in Butte mines practically unorganized. For some years the Anaconda Copper Mining Company has been using what is called in Butte the "rustling-card system." This rustling-card system is practically a blacklist on a national scale, or perhaps it had better be called a "white list." It works in this way: The Anaconda Copper Mining Company has an employment bureau to which every miner must apply if he wishes a job. Here his record is investigated, and if it is found that he has never complained of his working conditions, if he has a clean record as to unions—that is, if he is not what they call an agitator—or if he has voted the right political ticket, he is given a rustling card. This is in effect a permit, as we say in the West, "to rustle" for a job. The man who applies for work at any mine is first asked to show his rustling card. If he cannot produce one, he is not hired. This rustling card system has effectively discouraged the men from organizing. It has prevented them from demanding the enforcement of laws requiring safety devices in the mines. It has caused them to hesitate to discuss their grievances on the outside. The conditions of the mines have grown more and more unsafe. I have had heartbreaking letters from the wives of the miners saying that when their husbands went to work they never knew whether or not they would ever return, and that they lived in constant anxiety.

On June 8, 160 men were burned to death in a fire in one mine. This was the climax. The men stopped work.

The workers knew that they would never be safe as long as the rustling-card system existed. For under that system every man who complained of conditions or reported dangers or endeavored to form an organization was laid off for one reason or another, and it would be impossible for him to obtain work again in any mine in Montana or elsewhere. This rustling-card system is opposed by every legitimate labor organization in my State and it is easy to see the necessity of abolishing it.

Mr. John D. Ryan, of New York, the president of the Anaconda Copper Mining Company is the man responsible for this situation. You are probably all familiar with Mr. Ryan's name in connection with his recent affiliation with the activities of the American Red Cross. If Mr. Ryan says the rustling-card system must be abolished, it will be. I have tried in vain to draw this fact to his attention, however. My telegrams have reached Mr. Ryan, but as yet I have received no response. The question I wished to ask Mr. Ryan, whether at this time, considering the great needs of the country in war, he would agree to abolish the rustling-card system, to meet grievance committees, and to recognize a union, a bona fide union, if it was organized.

Telegrams today say that the conditions in Butte are as bad as ever. And on my own responsibility I am urging a measure which I hope may relieve the situation.

It was with regard to these same mines that the newspapers some months ago were filled with the news of large Government purchases of copper for the war. Through the patriotic efforts of some prominent men the Government was able to secure copper for 16.67 cents a pound when the market price was 32 cents. At this price the Government purchased 50,000,000 pounds of copper, and later purchased 50,000,000 more. However, the companies refused to accept this same price, and they are now waiting for the Committee on War Purchases to say what they will pay. This incident has received no publicity. But it is interesting to the American people to know that if the committee sets the price at the present market price of 28 cents, this one purchase will cost the Government $6,000,000 more than the advertised price. Added to this, the copper interests have the advantage of not being on the embargo list.

Under these circumstances I believe it is imperative that the President of the United States, the Commander-in-Chief of the Army, be given the power to take over the metalliferous mines and operate them for the benefit of the Nation.

Source: Rankin, Jeannette. "On the Federalization of Mines." *Congressional Record: Proceedings and Debates of the Congress.* 55, pt. 6. Washington, DC: U.S. Government Printing Office, 1917, 5896.

REYNOLDS, MARY (CA. 1847–CA. 1937)

A former slave in Tensas Parish, Louisiana, Mary Vaughn Reynolds filled her story with memories of bondage and life in the slave quarters. The daughter of piano tuner Tom Vaughn, a free man from the North, and Sallie Carter Vaughn, a widowed field hand, she was born at Lismore in Concordia Parish. She belonged to obstetrical surgeon Andrew Robert Kilpatrick, a graduate of Georgia Medical College and Tensas Parish planter and owner of more than 100 slaves. In retrospect of the plantation South, she described enslavement as "the worst days was ever seed in the world" (Reynolds 2014, 2).

Kilpatrick's fertile 320-acre plantation produced peas, corn, potatoes, peanuts, cotton, and cane, but he supplied thin gingham tunics and inadequate food, water, clothing, and shoes for agricultural laborers. He was known for piety and membership in the Methodist Episcopal Church, but he banned worship among his slaves. Reynolds and the other field hands cultivated their patches of peanuts and potatoes by night and slipped away from Solomon's lash to pray and sing in secret.

Andrew and Anna Kilpatrick leased Reynolds to work in Trinity on the Ouachita River for a vicious farmer named Kidd, who lashed recalcitrant slaves while the owner watched. Because she had no information about a runaway slave boy named Turner, Kidd tied her arms and legs to a tree and beat her unconscious. Kilpatrick's daughter Sara rescued Reynolds from torture. According to an examination by Dr. Kilpatrick, nothing could save her from a life of childlessness caused by Kidd's damage to her body.

With the master and mistress officiating, Mary married a slave named Reynolds. On her wedding day, the owners wreathed her head before she and her mate jumped the broom at the plantation manse front entrance. After President Abraham Lincoln emancipated slaves on January 1, 1863, she arranged an official wedding by a minister.

The next September, Dr. Kilpatrick summoned his slaves to the riverbank and fled Concordia by gunboat before General Nathaniel P. Banks's Union troops arrived. Some of the plantation slaves sought revenge by revealing to Northern raiders the family's hiding place for livestock, china, silver, and cash. Some workers followed the troops to Galveston. After the Kilpatricks departed for Texas, Reynolds chose to remain on the plantation.

Reynolds' maternal uncle, Louis Carter, wrote to his widowed sister, Sallie Vaughn, and offered to pay her way to Galveston, where she later died. After Sallie left the family, Reynolds traveled with Dr. Kilpatrick to the Tennessee Colony east of Waco. As permanent residents of Texas, she and her husband farmed while she cooked for white families and maintained a home. Sara honored Reynolds by naming a daughter after her.

In widowhood, Reynolds cooked for seven years for a household in Dallas. In 1937, a worker for the Federal Writers Project interviewed her. Blindness in her last five years forced her into a Dallas County nursing home.

References

"Mary Reynolds." *Born in Slavery: Slave Narratives from the Federal Writers' Project, 1936–1938*. WPA Slave Narrative Project, Texas Narratives. Vol. 16, pt. 3. Accessed November 26, 2014. http://memory.loc.gov/cgi-bin/query/S?ammem/mewnbib:@field(AUTHOR+@od1(Reynolds,+Mary)).

Nelson, Stanley. "Friends for Life: The Slave Girl & Master's Daughter." *Concordia Sentinel*, October 30, 2013.

A SLAVE NARRATIVE BY MARY VAUGHN REYNOLDS DALLAS COUNTY CONVALESCENT HOME DALLAS, TEXAS CA. 1938

A former slave in Tensas Parish, Louisiana, Mary Vaughn Reynolds filled her story with memories of bondage and life in the slave quarters. In 1941, the publication of the Federal Writers' Project for the Works Progress Administration featured Mary's memoir and her photo.

My paw's name was Tom Vaughn and he was from the north, born free man and lived and died free to the end of his days. He wasn't no eddicated man, but he was what he calls himself a piano man. He told me once he lived in New York and Chicago and he built the insides of pianos and knew how to make them play in tune. He said some white folks from the south told he if he'd come with them to the south he'd find a lot of work to do with pianos in them parts, and he come off with them.

He saw my maw on the Kilpatrick place and her man was dead. He told Dr. Kilpatrick, my massa, he'd buy my maw and her three chillun with all the money he had, iffen he'd sell her. But Dr. Kilpatrick was never one to sell any but the old niggers who was past workin' in the fields and past their breedin' times. So my paw marries my maw and works the fields, same as any other nigger. They had six gals: Martha and Pamela and Josephine and Ellen and Katherine and me.

I was born same time as Miss Sara Kilpatrick. Dr. Kilpatrick's first wife and my maw come to their time right together. Miss Sara's maw died and they brung Miss Sara to suck with me. It's a thing we ain't never forgot. My maw's name was Sallie and Miss Sara allus looked with kindness on my maw. We sucked till we was a fair size and played together, which wasn't no common thing. None the other li'l niggers played with the white chillun. But Miss Sara loved me so good.

I was jus' 'bout big 'nough to start playin' with a broom to go 'bout sweepin' up and not even half doin' it when Dr. Kilpatrick sold me. They was a old white man in Trinity and his wife died and he didn't have chick or child or slave or nothin'. Massa sold me cheap, 'cause he didn't want Miss Sara to play with no nigger young'un. That old man bought me a big doll and went off and left me all day, with the door open. I jus' sot on the floor and played with that doll. I used to cry. He'd come home and give me somethin' to eat and then go to bed, and I slep' on the foot of the bed with him. I was scart all the time in the dark. He never did close the door.

Miss Sara pined and sickened. Massa done what he could, but they wasn't no pertness in her. She got sicker and sicker, and massa brung 'nother doctor. He say, 'You li'l gal is grievin' the life out her body and she sho' gwine die iffen you don't do somethin' 'bout it.' Miss Sara says over and over, 'I wants Mary.' Massa say to the doctor, 'That a li'l nigger young'un I done sold.' The doctor tells him he better git me back iffen he wants to save the life of his child. Dr. Kilpatrick has to give a big plenty more to git me back than what he sold me for, but Miss Sara plumps up right off and grows into fine health.

Then massa marries a rich lady from Mississippi and they has chillun for company to Miss Sara and seem like for a time she forgits me.

Massa Kilpatrick wasn't no piddlin' man. He was a man of plenty. He had a big house with no more style to it than a crib, but it could room plenty people. He was a medicine doctor and they was rooms in the second story for sick folks what come to lay in. It would take two days to go all over the land he owned. He had cattle and stock and sheep and more'n a hundred slaves and more besides. He bought the bes' of niggers near every time the spec'lators come that way. He'd make a swap of the old ones and give money for young ones what could work.

He raised corn and cotton and cane and 'taters and goobers, 'sides the peas and other feedin' for the niggers. I 'member I helt a hoe handle mighty onsteady when they put a old woman to larn me and some other chillun to scrape the fields. That old woman would be in a frantic. She'd show me and then turn 'bout to show some other li'l nigger, and I'd have the young corn cut clean as the grass. She say, 'For the love of Gawd, you better larn it right, or Solomon will beat the breath out you body.' Old man Solomon was the nigger driver.

Slavery was the worst days was ever seed in the world. They was things past tellin', but I got the scars on my old body to show to this day. I seed worse than what happened to me. I seed them put the men and women in the stock with they hands screwed down through holes in the board and they feets tied together and they naked behinds to the world. Solomon the overseer beat them with a big whip and massa look on. The niggers better not stop in the fields when they hear them yellin'. They cut the flesh most to the bones and some they was when they taken them out of stock and put them on the beds, they never got up again.

When a nigger died they let his folks come out the fields to see him afore he died. They buried him the same day, take a big plank and bust it with a ax in the middle 'nough to bend it back, and put the dead nigger in betwixt it. They'd cart them down to the graveyard on the place and not bury them deep 'nough that buzzards wouldn't come circlin' round. Niggers mourns now, but in them days they wasn't no time for mournin'.

The conch shell blowed afore daylight and all hands better git out for roll call or Solomon bust the door down and git them out. It was work hard, git beatin's and half fed. They brung the victuals and water to the fields on a slide pulled by a old mule. Plenty times they was only a half barrel water and it stale and hot, for all us niggers on the hottes' days. Mostly we ate pickled pork and corn bread and peas and beans and 'taters. They never was as much as we needed.

The times I hated most was pickin' cotton when the frost was on the bolls. My hands git sore and crack open and bleed. We'd have a li'l fire in the fields and iffen the ones with tender hands couldn't stand it no longer, we'd run and warm our hands a li'l bit. When I could steal a 'tater, I used to slip it in the ashes and when I'd run to the fire I'd take it out and eat it on the sly.

In the cabins it was nice and warm. They was built of pine boardin' and they was one long row of them up the hill back of the big house. Near one side of the cabins was a fireplace. They'd bring in two, three big logs and put on the fire and they'd last near a week. The beds was made out of puncheons fitted in holes bored in the wall, and planks laid 'cross them poles. We had tickin' mattresses filled with corn shucks. Sometimes the men build chairs at night. We didn't know much 'bout havin' nothin', though.

Sometimes massa let niggers have a li'l patch. They'd raise 'taters or goobers. They liked to have them to help fill out on the victuals. 'Taters roasted in the ashes was the best tastin' eatin' I ever had. I could die better satisfied to have jus' one more 'tater roasted in hot ashes. The niggers had to work the patches at night and dig the 'taters and goobers at night. Then if they wanted to sell any in town they'd have to git a pass to go. They had to go at night, 'cause they couldn't ever spare a hand from the fields.

Once in a while they'd give us a li'l piece of Sat'day evenin' to wash out clothes in the branch. We hanged them on the ground in the woods to dry. They was a place to wash clothes from the well, but they was so many niggers all couldn't git round to it on Sundays. When they'd git through with the clothes on Sat'day evenin's the niggers which sold they goobers and 'taters brung fiddles and guitars and come out and play. The others clap they hands and stomp they feet and we young'uns cut a step round. I was plenty biggity and liked to cut a step.

We was scart of Solomon and his whip, though, and he didn't like frolickin'. He didn't like for us niggers to pray, either. We never heared of no church, but us have prayin' in the cabins. We'd set on the floor and pray with our heads down low and sing low, but if Solomon heared he'd come and beat on the wall with the stock of his whip. He'd say, 'I'll come in there and tear the hide off you backs.' But some the old niggers tell us we got to pray to Gawd that he don't think different of the blacks and the whites. I know that Solomon is burnin' in hell today, and it pleasures me to know it.

Once my maw and paw taken me and Katherine after night to slip to 'nother place to a prayin' and singin'. A nigger man with white beard told us a day am comin' when niggers only be slaves of Gawd. We prays for the end of Trib'lation and the end of beatin's and for shoes that fit our feet. We prayed that us niggers could have all we wanted to eat and special for fresh meat. Some the old ones say we have to bear all, 'cause that all we can do. Some say they was glad to the time they's dead, 'cause they'd rather rot in the ground than have the beatin's. What I hated most was when they'd beat me and I didn't know what they beat me for, and I hated them strippin' me naked as the day I was born.

When we's comin' back from that prayin', I thunk I heared the nigger dogs and somebody on horseback. I say, 'Maw, its them nigger hounds and they'll eat us up.' You could hear them old hounds and sluts abayin'. Maw listens and say, 'Sho 'nough, them dogs am runnin' and Gawd help us!' Then she and paw talk and they take us to a fence corner and stands us up 'gainst the rails and say don't move and if anyone comes near, don't breathe loud. They went to the woods, so the hounds chase them and not git us. Me and Katherine stand there, holdin' hands, shakin' so we can hardly stand. We hears the hounds come nearer, but we don't move. They goes after paw and maw, but they circles round to the cabins and gits in. Maw say its the power of Gawd.

In them days I weared shirts, like all the young'uns. They had collars and come below the knees and was split up the sides. That's all we weared in hot weather. The men weared jeans and the women gingham. Shoes was the worstes' trouble. We weared rough russets when it got cold, and it seem powerful strange they'd never git them to fit. Once when I was a young gal, they got me a new pair and all brass studs in the toes. They was too li'l for me, but I had to wear them. The brass trimmin's cut into my ankles and them places got mis'ble bad. I rubs tallow in them sore places and wrops rags round them and my sores got worser and worser. The scars are there to this day.

I wasn't sick much, though. Some the niggers had chills and fever a lot, but they hadn't discovered so many diseases then as now. Dr. Kilpatrick give sick niggers ipecac and asafoetida and oil and turpentine and black fever pills.

They was a cabin called the spinnin' house and two looms and two spinnin' wheels goin' all the time, and two nigger women sewing all the time. It took plenty sewin' to make all the things for a place so big. Once massa goes to Baton Rouge and brung back a yaller gal dressed in fine style. She was a seamster nigger. He builds her a house 'way from the quarters and she done fine sewin' for the whites. Us niggers knowed the doctor took a black woman quick as he did a white and took any on his place he wanted, and he took them often. But mostly the chillun born on the place looked like niggers. Aunt Cheyney allus say four of hers was massa's, but he didn't give them no mind. But this yaller gal breeds so fast and gits a mess of white young'uns. She larnt them fine manners and combs out they hair.

Onct two of them goes down the hill to the dollhouse where the Kilpatrick chillun am playin'. They wants to go in the dollhouse and one the Kilpatrick boys say, 'That's for white chillun.' They say, 'We ain't no niggers, 'cause we got the same daddy you has, and he comes to see us near every day and fetches us clothes and things from town.' They is fussin' and Missy Kilpatrick is listenin' out her chamber window. She heard them white niggers say, 'He is our daddy and we call him daddy when he comes to our house to see our mama.'

When massa come home that evenin' his wife hardly say nothin' to him, and he ask her what the matter and she tells him, 'Since you asks me, I'm studyin' in my mind 'bout them white young'uns of that yaller nigger wench from Baton Rouge.' He say, 'Now, honey, I fotches that gal jus' for you, 'cause she a fine seamster.' She say, 'It look kind of funny they got the same kind of hair and eyes as my chillun and they got a nose looks like yours.' He say, 'Honey, you jus' payin' 'tention to talk of li'l chillun that ain't got no mind to what they say.' She say, 'Over in Mississippi I got a home and plenty with my daddy and I got that in my mind.'

Well, she didn't never leave and massa bought her a fine, new span of surrey hosses. But she don't never have no more chillun and she ain't so cordial with the massa. Margaret, that yallow gal, has more white young'uns, but they don't never go down the hill no more to the big house.

Aunt Cheyney was jus' out of bed with a sucklin' baby one time, and she run away. Some say that was 'nother baby of massa's breedin'. She don't come to the house to nurse her baby, so they misses her and old Solomon gits the nigger hounds and takes her trail. They gits near her and she grabs a limb and tries to hist herself in a tree, but them dogs grab her and pull her down. The men hollers them onto her, and the dogs tore her naked and et the breasts plumb off her body. She got well and lived to be a old woman, but 'nother woman has to suck her baby and she ain't got no sign of breasts no more.

They give all the niggers fresh meat on Christmas and a plug tobacco all round. The highes' cotton picker gits a suit of clothes and all the women what had twins that year gits a outfittin' of clothes for the twins and a double, warm blanket.

Seems like after I got bigger, I 'member more'n more niggers run away. They's most allus cotched. Massa used to hire out his niggers for wage hands. One time he hired me and a nigger boy, Turner, to work for some ornery white trash name of Kidd. One day Turner goes off and don't come back. Old man Kidd say I knowed 'bout it, and he tied my wrists together and stripped me. He hanged me by the wrists from a limb on a tree and spraddled my legs round the trunk and tied my feet together. Then he beat me. He beat me worser than I ever been beat before and I faints dead away. When I come to I'm in bed, I didn't care so much iffen I died.

I didn't know 'bout the passin' of time, but Miss Sara come to me. Some white folks done git word to her. Mr. Kidd tries to talk hisself out of it, but Miss Sara fotches me home when I'm well 'nough to move. She took me in a cart and my maw takes care of me. Massa looks me over good and says I'll git well, but I'm ruint for breedin' chillun.

After while I taken a notion to marry and massa and missy marries us same as all the niggers. They stands inside the house with a broom held crosswise of the door and we stands outside. Missy puts a li'l wreath on my head they kept there and we steps over the broom into the house. Now, that's all they was to the marryin'. After freedom I gits married and has it put in the book by a preacher.

One day we was workin' in the fields and hears the conch shell blow, so we all goes to the back gate of the big house. Massa am there. He say, 'Call the roll for every nigger big 'nough to walk, and I wants them to go to the river and wait there. They's gwine be a show and I wants you to see it.' They was a big boat down there, done built up on the sides with boards and holes in the boards and a big gun barrel stickin' through every hole. We ain't never seed nothin' like that. Massa goes up the plank onto the boat and comes out on the boat porch. He say, 'This am a Yankee boat.' He goes inside and the water wheels starts movin' and that boat goes movin' up the river and they says it goes to Natches.

The boat wasn't more'n out of sight when a big drove of sojers comes into town. They say they's Fed'rals. More'n half the niggers goes off with them sojers, but I goes on back home 'cause of my old mammy.

Next day them Yankees is swarmin' the place. Some the niggers wants to show them somethin'. I follows to the woods. The niggers shows them sojers a big pit in the ground, bigger'n a big house. It is got wooden doors that lifts up, but the top am sodded and grass growin' on it, so you couldn't tell it. In that pit is stock, hosses and cows and mules and money and chinaware and silver and a mess of stuff them sojers takes.

We jus' sot on the place doin' nothin' till the white folks comes home. Miss Sara come out to the cabin and say she wants to read a letter to my mammy. It come from Louis Carter, which is brother to my mammy, and he done follow the Fed'rals to Galveston. A white man done write the letter for him. It am tored in half and massa done that. The letter say Louis am workin' in Galveston and wants mammy to come with us, and he'll pay our way. Miss Sara say massa swear, 'Damn Louis Carter. I ain't gwine tell Sallie nothin',' and he starts to tear the letter up. But she won't let him, and she reads it to mammy.

After a time massa takes all his niggers what wants to Texas with him and mammy gits to Galveston and dies there. I goes with massa to the Tennessee Colony and then to Navasota. Miss Sara marries Mr. T. Coleman and goes to El Paso. She wrote and told me to come to her and I allus meant to go.

My husband and me farmed round for times, and then I done housework and cookin' for many years. I come to Dallas and cooked seven year for one white family. My husband died years ago. I guess Miss Sara been dead these long years. I allus kep' my years by Miss Sara's years, 'count we is born so close.

I been blind and mos' helpless for five year. I'm gittin' mighty enfeeblin' and I ain't walked outside the door for a long time back. I sets and 'members the times in the world. I 'members now clear as yesterday things I forgot for a long time. I 'members 'bout the days of slavery and I don't 'lieve they ever gwine have slaves no more on this earth. I think Gawd done took that burden offen his black chillun and I'm aimin' to praise him for it to his face in the days of Glory what ain't so far off."

Source: Reynolds, Mary Vaughn. "A Slave Narrative." *Slave Narratives: A Folk History of Slavery in the United States From Interviews with Former Slaves.* The Federal Writers' Project, 1936–1938. Washington, DC: The Library of Congress, 2004.

RICH, ADRIENNE (1929–2012)

A provocative touchstone of 20th-century women's poetry and scholarship, Adrienne Cecile Rich influenced attitudes toward the lives and creativity of feminists and lesbians. Born in Baltimore, Maryland, on May 16, 1929, to Helen Elizabeth Jones, a concert pianist, and pathologist Arnold Rice Rich, she read freely in her father's library the poems of Emily Dickinson and the novels of the Brontë sisters. She entered Radcliffe and graduated Phi Beta Kappa in 1951.

On earning a Guggenheim Fellowship, Rich enrolled at Oxford University for a year and, in Florence, Italy, wrote independently from academic mentoring.

Married to Harvard economist Alfred Haskell Conrad in 1953, she lived in Cambridge among scholars. While rearing sons David, Paul "Pablo," and Jacob, she abandoned writing and absorbed the vibrancy and promise of the women's movement. The aridity of motherhood and familiarity with the philosophy of Simone de Beauvoir forced her to assess the causes of domestic frustrations and uncertainties.

A Changed Person

As a writer and translator of Persian poet Mirza Ghalib's aphoristic verse, Rich flourished in her thirties with receipt of a National Institute of Arts and Letters citation, second Guggenheim Fellowship, and Bollingen grant. She explored elements of female identity in the lyrical, yet urgent free verse collection *Snapshots of a Daughter-in-Law* (1963) and the personal essay "Split at the Root: An Essay on Jewish Identity" (1982), a reflection on anti-Semitism. In 1966, she relocated to New York City, where her husband joined the City College faculty while she taught English to at-risk students.

Increasingly assertive, Rich first identified herself as a feminist in 1970. She pursued activism for civil rights and peace and signed a writers' protest against expenditure of tax moneys for war in Southeast Asia. In an era of burgeoning women's studies, in the 1970s, she taught creative writing at Swarthmore, Columbia University, and City College and alienated her husband by raising cash for the Black Panthers and anti-Vietnam War demonstrations. Recovered from grief after Alfred's suicide on October 18, 1970, she joined the staff of Brandeis University, an outlet for her questioning mind.

The poet directed anger at conservative capitalists and compassion toward the struggles of marginalized, disaffected people. On April 18, 1974, she won a National Book Critics' Circle Award for composing skeptical, confrontational feminist verse, "Diving into the Wreck," an undersea scenario examining the status of feminism. She insisted on sharing the notoriety with poets Audre Lorde and Alice Walker and in giving one-third of the purse to the Sisterhood of Black Single Mothers. Rich's one-paragraph acceptance speech mourned the silence of women whom patriarchy muzzled. In 1975, she presented the address "Women and Honor: Some Notes on Lying," which alerted the truthful to manipulators, excuse makers, and wielders of a false sense of power.

The New Adrienne

After a teaching stint at Bryn Mawr, in 1976, Rich formed a stable relationship with Jamaican poet and teacher Michelle Cliff. Rich reassessed womanhood with the autobiographical anthology *Of Woman Born* (1976) and the 1977 commencement speech "Claiming an Education," an oft-quoted treatise on responsibility that she delivered to a female student body at Douglass College in Brunswick, New Jersey. She warned that academia tended to erase female and minority roles in history and advised graduates to take a vow of seriousness toward language, values, ideas, and method.

In a salute to egalitarianism, Rich challenged graduates of Smith College with the commencement address "What Does a Woman Need to Know?" (1979). Following positions as lecturer in English literature at City College and Rutgers, she focused on the political aspects of lesbianism, particularly the essay "Compulsory Heterosexuality and Lesbian Existence" (1980). A spate of criticism led her to clarify a feminist stance in "Reflections on Compulsory Heterosexuality" (1984), which some readers identified as a gender manifesto.

While Rich's influence mushroomed, in 1990, she surveyed the rights issues of Jewish women and established *Bridges: A Journal for Jewish Feminists and Our Friends*. More acclaim for her linguistic power and accessibility followed from honoraria issued by the *Los Angeles Times* and *The Nation*, the Frost Medal, and a Commonwealth Award preceding the 1994 Genius Grant from the MacArthur Fellowship, an acknowledgement of her verse epic *An Atlas of the Difficult World* (1991). With the apologia *What Is Found There: Notebooks on Poetry and Politics* (1993), she accounted for hero worship of Emily Dickinson, Walt Whitman, and Muriel Rukeyser.

As a citizen, Rich chose stark political topics to jolt readers out of a fear of encountering overly feminine, overly literary sensibilities. Her words impelled them toward engagement with revolutionary ideas that relieved despair and apathy. She set an example of integrity by saying no to an award. As a statement of principle, on July 3, 1997, she rejected the National Medal of Arts from the Clinton administration for its political dishonor of the growing underclass, which included women and lesbians. In an explanatory letter to Jane Alexander, president of the National Endowment for the Arts and a copy addressed to the President, she explained her position as conveyor of hope and dignity to people whom the United States was rapidly demeaning as less valuable than rich and prestigious whites.

In her seventies, the poet found satisfaction in effecting change in people's lives. In autumn 1998, she worded an interview for the *Radcliffe Quarterly* that honored the mental ferment precipitated by the public addresses of Malcolm X and Martin Luther King Jr. She delighted in bringing happiness to large assemblies—notably, the 50,000 listeners to her public readings at the 2001 International Poetry Festival in Chile.

With readings and speeches, Rich built consensus against the Iraq War and unleashed a jeremiad in *The School among the Ruins* (2004) against violence in Baghdad, Kabul, and Beirut. Additional kudos from the Academy of American

Poets, Lannan Foundation award, *Library Journal*, and the Bollingen Prize concluded in 2006 with accolades from the Jews for Racial and Economic Justice Risk Taker Award for the poet's defiant survivalism. Her acceptance speech lionized the world's risk takers and the solidarity of Jews.

On June 2, 2010, Rich received the Griffin Trust for Excellence in Poetry Lifetime Achievement Award. The honor reminded the audience that, from age 22, she had destabilized myths and stereotypes of caste, ethnicity, and gender through 19 transformative anthologies. She concluded the ceremony by reading three poems and concluding with "Ballade of the Poverties" (2011), which warned the jet-setter that the face in the mirror sinned against the homeless and hungry. Because she attacked complacency, the Equality Forum lauded her for promoting the humanity of lesbian, gay, bisexual, and transgender people. Crippled with rheumatoid arthritis, she died at home in Santa Cruz on March 27, 2012.

See Also: Lorde, Audre; Walker, Alice.

References

"Adrienne Rich." Poetry Foundation. Accessed January 2, 2015. http://www.poetryfoundation.org/bio/adrienne-rich.

Rich, Adrienne. "National Book Award Acceptance Speech." Accessed January 2, 2015. http://www.nationalbook.org/nbaacceptspeech_arich.html#.VzsgsVdh0nc

NATIONAL BOOK AWARD CEREMONY STATEMENT
NATIONAL BOOK AWARD CEREMONY
W.W. NORTON & COMPANY, NEW YORK CITY
APRIL 18, 1974

A provocative touchstone of 20th-century women's poetry and scholarship, Adrienne Cecile Rich influenced attitudes toward the lives and creativity of feminists and lesbians. At her receipt of the National Book Award, she presented an unusual address coauthored by Audre Lorde and Alice Walker on behalf of all female authors producing art in a patriarchal world.

We, Audre Lorde, Adrienne Rich, and Alice Walker, together accept this award in the name of all the women whose voices have gone and still go unheard in a patriarchal world, and in the name of those who, like us, have been tolerated as token women in this culture, often at great cost and in great pain. We believe that we can enrich ourselves more in supporting and giving to each other than by competing against each other; and that poetry—if it is poetry—exists in a realm beyond ranking and comparison. We symbolically join together here in refusing the terms of patriarchal competition and declaring that we will share this prize among us, to be used as best we can for women. We appreciate the good faith of the judges for this award, but none of us could accept this money for herself, nor could she let go unquestioned the terms on which poets are given or denied honor and livelihood in this world, especially when they are women. We dedicate this occasion to the struggle for self-determination of all women, of every color, identification, or derived class: the poet, the housewife, the lesbian, the mathematician, the mother, the dishwasher, the pregnant teenager, the teacher, the grandmother, the prostitute, the philosopher, the waitress, the women who will understand what we are doing here and those who will not understand yet; the silent women whose voices have been denied us, the articulate women who have given us strength to do our work.

Source: Rich, Adrienne, Audre Lorde, and Alice Walker. "National Book Award Ceremony Statement." April 18, 1974. Reprinted by permission from The Adrienne Rich Literary Trust.

RICHARDS, ANN (1933–2006)

A good-humored politician and governor of Texas, Dorothy Ann Willis Richards gained credibility for witty, revealing oratory. She was born to Mildred Iona "Ona" Warren and Robert Cecil Willis in Lakeview, Texas, on September 1, 1933. During the Great Depression, she played dominoes with her father and listened to Franklin Roosevelt's radio addresses on American courage, which influenced her oratorical style.

Richards's parents left rural Texas to live in Waco so she could play basketball in the eighth grade and enroll at Waco High School. Previous to a debate scholarship at Baylor University in 1950, she gained poise from winning the state debate championship and from attending Girls State and Girls Nation, during which she toured the Truman White House. While studying speech and political science, she dated David "Dave" Richards, whom she wed on May 30, 1953.

After Dave spent a year at the U.S. Civil Rights Commission in Washington, D.C., the couple settled in Dallas. While he earned a law degree and opened an Austin office specializing in civil rights cases, she added a teaching degree from the University of Texas to her training and taught history and civics at Fulmore Junior High, a job she later called her most challenging. Relocated to Red Bud Trail in Dallas in 1969, she volunteered for political campaigns and aided the careers of Judge Sarah T. Hughes and state legislators Wilhelmina Delco and Sarah Weddington, the subsequent heroine of the 1972 *Roe v. Wade* debate before the U.S. Supreme Court.

Richards promoted the Equal Rights Amendment at the November 18, 1977, National Women's Conference in Houston. In 1982, she set state records for Texas women by running successfully for state treasurer on a platform of wise banking and investments. In Atlanta, she made a national splash at the 1988 Democratic convention with a keynote speech. That evening, she warned CBS news anchor Walter Cronkite that she intended to "talk Texas," her term for native lingo. The address denounced Ronald Reagan's administration and the verbal gaffes of Vice President George H.W. Bush. Her Southern vernacular—"most proudest," "crooks," "straight talk," "Baptist pallet," "bum deal," and "that old dog won't hunt"—enriched the speech with slang and wisecracks. The mounting support for her irreverent style elevated her to Texas governor in 1990 with 57 percent of the votes.

Richards's innovations featured passing school control to districts, decriminalizing homosexual acts, updating regulatory efficiency and prison addiction treatment and anti-recidivism programs, and tightening gun laws. In the second year, she broadened the outreach to General Motors employees, secretaries, educators, and trial lawyers. To the Washington Gridiron Club on March 28, 1992, she cracked such choice Southernisms as "doesn't know diddly," "high-class crowd," and "warts and all."

In the 1994 gubernatorial campaign, Richards proposed a 1,100-agent task force to track sex offenders and violent felons. In late June 1994, she worsened her chances by delivering the "Prince Charming" warning at a Girls State assembly in Austin that romance did not necessarily precede a happy marriage. In mid-August 1994, she rallied teachers in Texarkana and defamed George W. Bush as a jerk.

Pundits declared Richards's gubernatorial loss to George W. Bush the result of her attacks on his intelligence and privileged upbringing and his ripostes about her barbed sound bites. After leaving politics, she taught political science at Brandeis University, served CNN as a commentator, and supported abortion, civil rights, and gay rights reform. Her principled speeches lauded health and exercise initiatives and women's issues, which she summarized in *I'm Not Slowing Down: Winning My Battle with Osteoporosis* (2004). By advocating calcium supplements and bone density tests and a reduction in caffeine, smoking, and alcohol, she made a mission of defeating skeletal weakness. At the University of Texas in 2005, she offered a course in female leadership.

In spring 2006, Richards sought treatment for esophageal cancer at the M.D. Anderson Cancer Center of the University of Texas. Six months later, she died at her Austin home on September 13. She left a record of achievement for Texas, the beginnings of the Ann Richards School for Young Women Leaders, chaired by daughter Ellen Richards, and received honoraria from the National Wildlife Federation, National Association for the Advancement of Colored People, and the Mexican government.

See Also: Jordan, Barbara.

References

"Ann Richards's Commencement Address." May 28, 1995. *The* (Mount Holyoke) *College Street Journal*. Accessed March 13, 2015. https://www.mtholyoke.edu/offices/comm/csj/950605/richards.html.

Kaid, Lynda Lee, and Christina Holtz-Bacha, eds. *Encyclopedia of Political Communication*. Thousand Oaks, CA: Sage, 2008.

INAUGURATION ADDRESS BY GOVERNOR ANN RICHARDS TEXAS STATE CAPITOL STEPS, AUSTIN, TEXAS JANUARY 15, 1991

A populist voice for all Texans, Ann Richards entered the office of governor with intent to reclaim the rights of all races and classes and to restore justice. Her actions affirmed her intent to restore inclusivity in business and government. Within four months, she empowered women, the handicapped, and nonwhites through appointments to state offices. Strides on behalf of women's health included advocacy for bone density tests and reductions in caffeine, smoking, and alcohol.

Welcome to the first day of the new Texas!

And welcome to the official representatives of 35 countries and the governors of the four Mexican border states who have joined us today.

I want to thank all of you for being with us. I hope we will see you often in the Capitol. We look forward to working cooperatively with your governments and to excellent relationships with your people.

Bienvenidos, mis amigos!

Eighteen months ago, I stood with many of you a few hundred yards from this platform and announced my candidacy for governor.

If you were there—in fact or in spirit—on that hot June day, if you gave your time and your energy to our campaign, if you held your ground and continued to believe when the odds seemed long and the outcome uncertain, my gratitude to you is profound.

Today is a day of celebration.

Today, we marched up Congress Avenue and said that we are reclaiming the Capitol for the people of Texas.

We say proudly that the people of Texas are back.

That statement will be given meaning by our actions during the next four years.

Today, the historians will record that a new administration, different from any in the past, began.

Twenty, fifty, one hundred years from now, school children will open their textbooks—or perhaps, switch on their video texts—and they will see a picture.

They will see us standing proudly on this bright winter noon. And looking through the eyes of a child will seem as distant and ancient as portraits of our ancestors seem to us.

Those children will read that on January 15, 1991, a woman named Ann W. Richards took the oath of office as the 45th Governor of Texas.

That much is certain.

Today, the headline has been written, but the pages that follow are blank.

Tomorrow, we begin filling in the pages, writing line by line the story that will be told long after the joy of this day is forgotten.

Like the Reverend Martin Luther King, Jr., who was born on this day, we have come this far on the strength of a dream.

Our challenge is to transform that dream into reality: to fill the pages of history with the story of Texans who came into office envisioning a new era of greatness, and breathed life into that vision.

Today, we have a vision of a Texas where opportunity knows no race or color or gender—a glimpse of the possibilities that can be when the barriers fall and the doors of government swing open.

Tomorrow, we must build that Texas.

Today, we have a vision of a Texas with clean air and land and water, a Texas where a strong economy lives in harmony with a safe environment.

Tomorrow, we must build that Texas.

Today, we have a vision of a Texas where every child receives an education that allows them to claim the full promise of their lives.

Tomorrow, we must build that Texas.

Today, we have a vision of a Texas where the government treats every citizen with respect and dignity and honesty, where consumers are protected, where business is nurtured and valued, where good jobs are plentiful, where those in need find compassion and help, where every decision is measured against a high standard of ethics and true commitment to the public trust.

Tomorrow, we must build that Texas.

The people of Texas are back, and they are waiting and watching, anxious to see if their government can rise above personal interest, rancor and division, and get on with the business of building a Texas where the people come first.

Years ago, John Kennedy said that "Life isn't fair."

Life is not fair, but government must be.

And if tomorrow, we begin with the understanding that government must stop telling people what they want, and start listening to the people and hearing what the people need, we will make government mean something good in people's lives.

Nothing is more fundamentally important to me than the understanding that this administration exists to serve the taxpayers.

Because service to the people is government's bottom line, we are creating a new position in the governor's office: a citizen's advocate who will cut red tape and bureaucratic stonewalling, who will report to me those agencies who fail to meet the test of the highest quality of service, efficiency, and financial management.

The oath I have taken today is mine, but the responsibility, the trust we have sought and been given, belongs to all of us.

And I hope that as we invoke the blessing of God on this adventure, we will all ask, in the words of the old gospel song, that the Lord lift us to higher ground, and that we will be wise enough and strong enough to do what we have set out to do.

Because when my time in office is finished, I want us to be able to look back together and say we—not he, not she, not me—but we came to this moment with a vision worthy of a great heritage, and we realized that vision in a way that was worthy of a great future.

And as we turn the corner on a new millennium, I want us to be able to look forward—to see a small child with a textbook, thumbing through the pages, coming upon a picture of a group of people standing on the Capitol steps looking out at the child across years and changes that we cannot even begin to imagine.

I want us to be able to read words beneath that picture that say that on this day in the year of our Lord nineteen hundred and ninety-one a new era began in Texas.

And I want us to know that what we started here will reach out across to that child, and do us honor.

Source: Richards, Ann. "Inaugural Address." *State Journal.* 72d Legislature, Reg. sess. Austin, TX: State Printing Office, 1991, 22–24.

RIDE, SALLY (1951–2012)

The youngest and first female U.S. astronaut, physicist Sally Kristen Ride stimulated interest in science and space travel in young girls. A Californian, she was born on May 26, 1951, in Encino to two Presbyterian elders—women's prison counselor Carol Joyce Anderson and Dale Burdell Ride, a political science teacher at Santa Monica College. She grew up in a devout Presbyterian environment and pursued her curiosity about science with a telescope and chemistry set.

Ride played pickup games of football, the reason for her initial choice of professional football as a career. In 1961, her parents homeschooled her during extensive European travels, a preparation that allowed her to skip sixth grade. For the first time, she thought of herself as a possible Nobel Prize winner. From Portola Junior High School, she entered Birmingham Community Charter High School and finished 12th grade on a tennis scholarship at Westlake School for Girls, a university preparatory academy where a science teacher encouraged academic achievement.

Another trio of schools completed Ride's education: Shakespeare courses at Swarthmore College in Pennsylvania, physics in her sophomore year at the University of California at Los Angeles, and Stanford for undergraduate degrees in English and physics. She remained at Stanford to finish an MS and doctorate in laser physics and astrophysics in 1978 with research into X-ray astronomy and free-electron lasers. During the junior year, she ran track, played softball and volleyball, and achieved a national rank in tennis, which inspired her thoughts about an athletic career.

From Earth to Orbit

After reading a 1977 newspaper advertisement for space exploration, at age 26, Ride sought one year of training by the National Aeronautics and Space Administration (NASA), which had previously recruited only military veterans. In January 1978, she entered the next class of trainees with 29 males and 5 females. The 35 potential astronauts learned jet navigation, parachute jumping, water survival, navigation, radio control, and gravity-free motion. Her contributions to NASA began as a developer of a robotic arm to release and retrieve satellites.

In August 1979, Ride received assignment as the first ground controller of communications to the orbiter *Columbia* on its flight from Kennedy Space Center on November 12, 1981. She repeated the assignment on March 22, 1982, when the orbiter completed an eight-day, 147-hour flight from Kennedy and returned to the lakebed runway at White Sands Space Harbor outside Las Cruces, New Mexico. In a Kansas wedding in July 1982, she married astronaut Steven Alan Hawley.

The media ballyhooed Mission Specialist Ride's historic role as the first U.S. female in space, an achievement the Soviets made two decades earlier with the flight of Cosmonaut Valentina Tereshkova. On June 18, 1983, Ride helped four male astronauts crew the space shuttle *Challenger*. She appeared in *People* magazine and on CBS News for an interview with Diane Sawyer. In the second row of seats on a six-day mission from Kennedy to Edwards Air Force Base in Southern California, she experienced 97 earth orbits over 2.2 million miles. On June 23, NASA honored her alma mater by playing the "Stanford Hymn" as the morning wake-up call.

On return on June 29, 1983, Ride plotted NASA's long-range strategy for space exploration and trained two years later for another space mission. On October 5, 1984, her second launch included female specialist Kathryn D. Sullivan and five male astronauts on a 197-hour flight. The mission ended at Kennedy eight days later on October 13. Because of the explosion of the *Challenger* on January 28, 1986, NASA scrubbed her third mission.

Appointed by Ronald Reagan, Ride aided a presidential commission in investigating the national catastrophe that took seven lives. She uncovered inadequate engineering of booster rocket seals that preceded the tragedy. NASA officials appointed her the first director of exploration overseeing a redesign of shuttle rockets. Following a divorce, she retired from NASA on August 15, 1987, and accepted a fellowship at Stanford's Center for International Security and Arms Control. In looking to the future, she acknowledged leadership of the Soviet Union in some areas of space exploration and proposed that NASA colonize a moon outpost as a possible business site.

Inspiration to Girls

In 1989, Ride taught physics at the University of California at San Diego and directed the campus Space Institute. She also counseled the Congressional Office of Technology Assessment, the Carnegie Institution of Washington, and the National Collegiate Athletic Association (NCAA) Foundation. From 1996 to 2000, she organized EarthKam, an innovative program that enabled preteens and teens to photograph earth with a shuttle-mounted camera and a second lens aimed from the International Space Station. She stored the image collection in a searchable archive and answered predictable questions about smearing peanut butter and jelly on bread in a weightless atmosphere and using a shuttle toilet. Through the GRAIL MoonKam, children could ask for photographs of the moon.

Catering to the interests of elementary and middle school girls, in 2001, the former astronaut formed Sally Ride Science, a motivational project for educators on careers in technology, math, and engineering. The outreach encouraged more imaginative science and math lessons for schools through clubs, summer camps, and science festivals. For texts and classroom activities, she wrote *To Space and Back*, *Voyager*, *The Third Planet*, *The Mystery of Mars*, and *Exploring Our Solar System*. With her mate, school psychologist Tam O'Shaughnessy, she issued two titles on ecology, *Mission Planet Earth* and *Mission Save the Planet*.

Ride was the only adviser to join the Columbia Accident Investigation Board to study the destruction of the *Columbia* during reentry on February 1, 2003. On C-SPAN, she queried findings about shared knowledge, abort simulations and shuttle stresses, problem solving, and oversight rules at NASA. The board completed a report on August 26, 2003. In another presentation on C-SPAN, she surveyed the solar system and remarked on the greenhouse effect from the trapping of heat by carbon dioxide vapor.

Ride's fame generated goodwill tours, public appearances, and invitations from varied locales, including a cover for *Ms.* magazine, an interview for *USA Today* in March 2006 on gendered stereotypes of scientists, a September 2007 appearance to elementary school students in Pittsburgh, and a science festival the next month in Huntsville, Alabama. She composed a special essay, "Inspired Kids Will Reach for Stars under Obama," in the October 29, 2008, issue of the *Orlando Sentinel* endorsing the Obama-Biden campaign for its grasp of space horizons. Within months, she informed the National Research Council on advances in aeronautical technology.

In 2009, Ride advised President Barack Obama's Review of U.S. Human Space Flight on costs of extending the International Space Station and the sustainability of future projects to monitor global warming, explore near-earth asteroids, and place rovers on the moon. During astronomy night on the White House lawn, she interacted with questioners on Facebook and Twitter and for a half hour replied by video. On April 25, 2009, she commented on climate change for the *Washington Journal* and stressed the fragility of the atmosphere, reduced snow paths and animal species, and rising ocean levels.

On February 11, 2011, Ride delivered the Regents' Lecture at the University of California at Berkeley on "Shoot for the Stars." Relaxed and low-key at the podium before a set of slides, she incorporated wit and personal observations into the text. She cited surveys that predicted the need for math, science, and technological skill in future jobs. An undisclosed diagnosis of pancreatic cancer in March 2011 did not hinder her enthusiasm for keeping up with future space exploration and for sharing shuttle adventures with youth.

Ride's public service earned the Beard Award for Greatest Public Service, the Werner Von Braun Award, the Lindbergh Eagle, a NASA Space Flight Medal and Lifetime Space Achievement citation, Stanford Engineering Hero commendation, the NCAA's Theodore Roosevelt Award, and a Pioneer of Women's Aviation. Following surgery and chemotherapy, she died under hospice care on July 23, 2012, at home in San Diego. In May 2013, Obama awarded her a posthumous Presidential Medal of Freedom simultaneous with a tribute to her life at the Kennedy Center. *Flying* magazine listed her among "51 Heroes of Aviation." Chicago's Legacy Walk featured her at the outdoor history museum honoring lesbian, gay, bisexual, and transgender citizens. At Anacortes, Washington, on August 10, 2014, the United States named a Scripps Institution of Oceanography research vessel the R/V *Sally Ride*. In April 2015, California congress members proposed a memorial statue to the astronaut in National Statuary Hall at the Capitol, the first gay hero in the collection.

Reference

Grady, Denise. "American Woman Who Shattered Space Ceiling." *New York Times*, July 23, 2012.

ROBINSON, HARRIET JANE (1825–1911)

A Massachusetts factory laborer in childhood, diarist and historiographer Harriet Jane Hanson Robinson exemplified the determination of females who refused second-class citizenship. Born to woodworker William Hanson and innkeeper Harriet Browne Hanson in Boston on February 8, 1825, she was the granddaughter of carpenter Seth Browne, a participant in the Boston Tea Party and a Revolutionary War minuteman. At age six, she encountered poverty and homelessness while her mother managed a boarding house after her father's death.

While attending night classes in Lowell in 1835, Robinson worked 14-hour days in the Tremont cotton factory shuttling bobbins to and from machines for a monthly wage of $8. In support of a worker's strike on October 1, 1836, her sharp-tongued speech reflected pride in Revolutionary War heroes. Apart from labor issues, she entered Lowell High School for two years to study writing, grammar, Latin, and French.

Robinson sought tutoring in German, art, and dance and joined debates of contemporary issues. Into her twenties, she labored in the textile industry and gained intellectual stimulus from book clubs and from composing letters and journal entries and submitting essays and poems to the *Lowell Offering*. Free lectures in the evenings introduced her to abolitionism, workers' rights, and the suffrage movement. On November 23, 1848, she wed antislavery, anticlerical idealist William Stevens Robinson of Concord, editor of the *Lowell Journal*.

At age 43, Robinson joined the American Woman's Suffrage Organization, which her husband supported. In widowhood in 1876, she earned enough from boarders and publication of children's works to support her children and mother. Devoting herself to feminism, with social reformer Julia Ward Howe, Robinson formed the New England Woman's Club, the first female society of its kind, and issued a speech in 1878 in the *Woman's Journal*.

At the opening of the National Woman Suffrage Association (NWSA) in Boston on May 26, 1881, Robinson called for female unity in forcing the issue of full citizenship for women. Joined by daughter Hattie, on February 6, 1882, she organized the Massachusetts state branch of NWSA and accepted the post of recording secretary. Mother and daughter addressed subsequent conventions, with Harriet delivering "The Golden Rule," a request for respect from men.

On March 27, 1888, at the International Council of Women in Washington, D.C., Robinson gained notoriety from a journalist who proclaimed her one of the nation's first strikers. She kept meticulous notes of the assembly and made significant contributions to women's history with the marching song "Hark the Song of Myriad Voices" and the speech "Political Parties and Woman Suffrage," an address on working girls. With style and shrewd logic, her oration clicked off the four parties—Democrat, Republican, Labor, Prohibition—and the faults of each. Applause erupted at her conclusion that women should desert political factions and devote efforts to a gendered all-female confederacy.

In the early 1890s, Robinson advised the newly formed General Federation of Women's Clubs and participated in the New England Historic Genealogical Society and the Daughters of the American Revolution. Her labor history, *Loom and Spindle, or Life among the Early Mill Girls* (1898), became a standard work about female involvement in the growth of the American textile industry.

Into old age, Harriet Robinson supported overburdened, underpaid female factory laborers. She lectured on mill work and alerted workers to worsening industrial conditions. Still active in reading, writing, and sewing into her eighties, she died at her Malden home on December 22, 1911.

See Also: Anthony, Susan B.; Gage; Matilda Joslyn; Howe, Julia Ward; Livermore, Mary Ashton; Stanton, Elizabeth Cady; Stone, Lucy.

Reference

Eisenmann, Linda. "'A Good Poor Man's Wife': Being a Chronicle of Harriet Hanson Robinson & Her Family in 19th-Century New England." In *Historical Journal of Massachusetts* 28, no. 2 (Summer 2000): 218–220.

POLITICAL PARTIES AND WOMAN SUFFRAGE BY HARRIET JANE HANSON ROBINSON INTERNATIONAL COUNCIL OF WOMEN ALBAUGH'S OPERA HOUSE, WASHINGTON, D.C. MARCH 27, 1888

A proponent of women's independence of male-dominated partisanship, feminist Harriet Jane Robinson joined the suffrage backlash against the rapid passage of voting rights for newly liberated bondsmen. She charged male politicians with treachery against female citizens. She characterized men's factions as stodgy and uninterested in placing gender parity on the ballot. She concluded that suffragists should abandon parties and initiate a female faction, a feat accomplished 1916 by activist Alice Paul in the establishment of the National Woman's Party.

In discussing the question of political conditions I always feel, so far as women are concerned, that we have no story to tell, so little have we gained after these forty years of struggle. I do not wish to ignore the small rights which are allowed to women in some of the States and Territories, but I propose to discuss the question in a broader sense and speak of woman's status in the parties which represent the leading thought in American politics. We see before us to-day the two dominant parties preparing for the coming political campaign, and we hear a great deal about the "sovereignty of the people," the "rights of the people," and that the "American people will not tolerate class domination." We read all this and it sounds well. We agree with it. But when we, the women, stop to think whose "rights" are discussed; who the people are whose "sovereignty must be maintained"; who "will not tolerate class domination"; we say: "This does not mean us; for, though we are of the people, we have no sovereign rights; we are women, therefore we must tolerate class domination."

These political parties, when they meet in convention, pass high-sounding resolutions on all sorts of questions—tariff reform, the fisheries, an honest and just ballot, etc.—but not one word to establish or even suggest that the political rights of one-half the citizens of the United States ought to be considered. "We, the people," these men call themselves, just as if there was not a woman in the land interested in what they say or understood what they were doing. But they go on ignoring us in their conventions and in their resolutions, just as much as they did before we had begun to vote at all, or were declared by the Supreme Court to be citizens.

There was a time when the Republican party was called, and was, the party of freedom; but since it no longer gives substantial aid to the leading reforms of the day it deserves that title no longer; for a party, no more than a person, can live on what it has done, but must depend on what it is doing. It had the chance to keep its record bright in 1872, when it advocated woman suffrage; but it failed to seize it, went back on its principles, and thus its record as the party of reform, ended. It had done a great and noble work for human freedom, and here was another opportunity given it to continue its work. The woman-suffrage cause was waiting to be recognized, prepared, from the foundation of the world, to follow in logical sequence directly upon the emancipation of the black man.

Charles Sumner, in a letter to W.S. Robinson, "Warrington," the well-known "Our Correspondent" of the *Springfield Republican* (never before published), gives his idea of the duty of Republicans in securing the rights of all classes of citizens. He writes:

> 27th April, '71.
>
> My Dear Robinson:
>
> Long before the war I insisted that our Constitution should be interpreted always for freedom, whereas it was interpreted always for slavery.

> Such interpretation would be according to reason, just rules, and the Declaration of Independence. And when slavery disappeared I insisted that the great impediment was removed, and that the new life was to begin.
>
> I was for the centralization of liberty, the upholding of human rights. Logically and constitutionally it seems to me that the nation should be able to protect and secure these everywhere with uniform power, so that they shall be the same everywhere. This is my doctrine. I mean to die by it. This interpretation is the great victory after the war.
>
> (Signed) Charles Sumner.

If the Republican party, after 1872, had continued to advocate the emancipation of the women of the country, the equal rights of all American citizens—white women as well as black men, black women as well as black men—this would have been its "victory after the war." If it had followed the teachings of its lost leader, this would have made it something more than the "G.O.P." It would be the ever new, the ever-living party of liberty. But it is as much behind the times on questions of reform, woman's suffrage, labor, prohibition, and tariff, as was the Democratic party of forty years ago on the anti-slavery question. It is hide-bound and cannot move beyond a certain point, and is no longer strong enough to take on a new issue, or carry a reform principle.

The Jeffersonian Democrats were a reform party, but the present Democratic Party has made no record for itself since the war, nor for some time before.

What claim has the Prohibition Party to the support of the suffragists? It is a well-known fact that women have helped this party, almost as much as they have the Republican party. In the years when there was no doubt as to the election of the Republican candidates, the prohibitory vote has been quite respectable. That is, those men vote for their own candidates when it is of no use; but when the time comes that they could, by voting their own ticket, show the great parties that they are a power to be both feared and respected, they make a stampede for the Republican camp.

The temperance women are learning that they can not trust a party that does not vote at all times for its own candidates, and are learning that they must demand the ballot for themselves in order to secure legislation for the temperance cause; that they need the full right of suffrage so that they can carry constitutional prohibition without the help of men, who can be frightened or persuaded into abandoning their own cause. Women will always have "leave to withdraw" as long as they trust to men to do their voting for them.

And there is no more hope for women in the Henry George, or Labor parties; so soon as the test elections come, their constituents as inevitably rush back to their old Democratic camp.

In speaking of the two dominant parties, I do not forget that there are individual members who believe in and work for the political emancipation of women, but they cannot go outside of party lines. They are Republicans, Democrats—first, last, and always—and what there is left, after doing their duty as party men, they give to the suffrage cause. They try to help us, I know, and they make every effort to get resolutions into party platforms, but as yet they have no power to change the policy or make our reform an issue within party lines. The fact is, the woman's cause is always in the way of politicians. They seem to be afraid of it; afraid to meet such a great moral issue as they know it to be. It seems to them a sort of unknown quantity—a *bête noir*—or, like Tennyson's "little speck in garnered fruit," to be quietly removed before my lord eats his apple. And these politicians act as if they did not know which way to turn when the woman question is brought to their notice. They suggest every remedy but the right one. They shrink at the idea of giving to the women of the country the same rights which they themselves enjoy. It is claimed that they hesitate, because they will not know what to do with us, or how to manage such a large "element" (as they call us) entering into politics all at once. But do not fear, gentlemen! We do not want you to do anything with us, nor yet try to manage us. Make us free—that is all we ask—and we will take care of ourselves!

Since such is the attitude of political parties, what should be the position of women themselves in regard to them? Shall they be Republican, Democrat, Prohibitionist, Labor Party? For my own part, I say belong to none of them, for, until such time as I have the right to vote there is no legitimate place for me in any party.

Old conditions of society are passing away. Nations have been scattered, but God has gathered their fragments together, and here on American soil is to be tried the experiment of self-government by and for the people. And whether it succeeds sooner or later, depends on the leaders, who hold in their hands the power to guide the people aright.

Source: Robinson, Harriet Jane Hanson. "Political Parties and Woman Suffrage." In *Report of the International Council of Women*. Washington, DC: Rufus H. Harby, 1888, 306-308.

ROOSEVELT, ELEANOR (1884–1962)

One of America's most revered humanitarians, Anna Eleanor Roosevelt served the nation as first lady, diplomat, and spokeswoman for global human rights. Born in New York City on October 11, 1884, she grieved at age 10 the deaths of her parents—philanthropist Anna Rebecca Hall from diphtheria and Elliott Bulloch Roosevelt from alcohol and suicide—and their three-year-old son, Elliott Jr., from scarlet fever. She took charge of her toddler brother, Gracie Hall Roosevelt, who in adulthood developed his father's disease of alcoholism.

In Tivoli, New York, Roosevelt reached her teens under the care of private tutors and her maternal grandmother, Mary Livingston Ludlow Hall, a compassionate Episcopalian. Roosevelt became fluent in French and Italian at Allenswood Academy, an elite London finishing school, and turned to settlement work in New York City in December 1902 to instruct tenement dwellers in gymnastics and dance. In 1904, she investigated sweatshops as a field agent of the National Consumers' League.

Wed to a cousin, attorney Franklin Delano Roosevelt (FDR), on March 17, 1905, Eleanor Roosevelt shared a residence in Hyde Park, New York, with a truculent mother-in-law, Sara Ann Delano Roosevelt. Throughout FDR's service in the New York Senate from 1911 to 1913, Sara dominated the children, Anna Eleanor, James II, Franklin (who died at eight months), Elliott, Franklin Delano Jr., and John Aspinwall. The family relocated to Washington, D.C., in 1913, when FDR served the Wilson administration as assistant secretary to the navy.

During World War I, Roosevelt learned to make artificial limbs in naval hospitals and aided the Red Cross at a military hospital in London. From 1918 to 1945, public knowledge of FDR's mistress, socialite Lucy Page Mercer Rutherfurd, dismayed Eleanor. She chose an independent career in surveying public welfare for the League of Women Voters, establishing a furniture workshop for disabled men at the Hyde Park estate, and teaching current events and American history and literature at the Todhunter School for Girls in Manhattan.

Franklin's "Legs"

FDR's paralysis from polio in August 1921 precipitated Roosevelt's speech writing for his campaign as the future governor of New York. The first address at a 1922 luncheon solicited donations from female Democrats. As the state's first lady in 1928, she traveled, raised capital for the Women's Trade Union League, and inspected industrial sites and urban tenements. On radio, she denounced prohibition of alcohol for increasing national hypocrisy and bedazzling youth with the glamour of illicit gin.

In an initial term as America's first lady from 1933 to 1937, Roosevelt attacked racism in housing and jobs and the impoverishment of West Virginia mining families. On November 2, 1933, she took to heart the emergency needs of unemployed women and the plight of the Bonus Army, World War I veterans seeking cash to feed the poor during the Great Depression. She delivered radio addresses for the National Youth Administration, held 348 media conferences with women journalists, wrote the syndicated column *My Day*, and rallied delegates at labor assemblies and national Democratic conventions. Before the American Association for Social Security, on February 8, 1934, she addressed issues of the elderly poor in "Old Age

Pensions." At the Institution of Women's Professional Relations in March 1935, she encouraged females to become more knowledgeable about citizenship.

From 1936 to 1941, Roosevelt scheduled 600 paid lectures and earned up to $1,000 per appearance for such orations as "Keepers of Democracy" in 1939 and on freedom to the Chicago Civil Liberties Committee in 1940. Her topics ventured from the Girl Scouts, libraries, and the beauty of Yellowstone National Park to neutrality in wartime and women in public office and national defense. She violated segregation protocols by sitting among black delegates at the 1938 Southern Conference for Human Welfare in Birmingham, Alabama. After the U.S. declaration of war against Japan on December 8, 1941, she joined New York Mayor Fiorello LaGuardia in directing the Office of Civilian Defense and managing blackouts, child care, and the establishment of a Civil Air Patrol.

By being the first to fly across the Atlantic and the first to fly unaccompanied by a husband, Roosevelt set two precedents for first ladies. At the height of war in Great Britain in October 1942, she visited hospitalized U.S. soldiers in London and Liverpool and followed in August–September 1943 with a Red Cross inspection of military hospitals in Guadalcanal, Australia, and New Zealand. To assure adequate supplies, in remarks to the Business and Professional Women, she endorsed the hiring of females in American industry and the federal funding of daycare for their children. To honor black pilots, she traveled to the Tuskegee flying school in Alabama for a test flight. In the last months in the White House, she advocated charity for the refugees and Jewish orphans of World War II.

An Independent Activist

In the wake of the president's sudden death from cerebral hemorrhage on April 12, 1945, in Warm Springs, Georgia, his widow recovered quickly by keeping busy. She joined the National Association for the Advancement of Colored People as a source of action for racial justice and, in December 1945, informed President Harry S. Truman of vigilantism in California against Japanese Americans. She began organizing the donation of her Hyde Park home to the federal park service as a museum and traveled to London in 1946 to appraise German refugee camps in Berlin and Frankfurt. As a champion of the United Nations, she promoted world peace with the speech "The United Nations and You" (1946) and in January 1947 by chairing the U.N. Commission on Human Rights.

Moderating meetings in French and English, Roosevelt oversaw the compilation of the Universal Declaration of Human Rights, which she based on the dignity and worth of all humankind. Ratified on December 10, 1948, the document, which she called a global Magna Carta, influenced various countries' efforts to redeem the vulnerable—children, refugees, the elderly and handicapped, displaced persons, torture victims—from the effects of war and tyranny. She remained a U.S. delegate to the U.N. General Assembly for six years.

Roosevelt applied her language acumen to national problems by radio addresses revealing the need for socialized medicine in 1950 and by defying the House Un-American Activities Commission (HUAC) in the mid-1950s for threatening rights of assembly and free speech. In September 1957, she interviewed Soviet premier Nikita Khrushchev in the Ukrainian city of Yalta and completed a memoir, *On My Own* (1958). Ill with anemia and bone marrow tuberculosis, from 1961 to her death from heart failure on November 7, 1962, she chaired the Presidential Commission on the Status of Women as a means of applying female skills to enhancing global security. In a speech to Congress on February 15, 1961, she asserted her hope for a fair and successful future for American women.

See Also: Beard, Mary Ritter.

References

Beasley, Maurine Hoffman, Holly Cowan Shulman, and Henry R. Beasley, eds. *The Eleanor Roosevelt Encyclopedia*. Westport, CT: Greenwood, 2001.

Roosevelt, Eleanor. "Pearl Harbor." December 7, 1941. *Eleanor Roosevelt Papers Project*. Accessed December 4, 2012. http://www.gwu.edu/~erpapers/teachinger/q-and-a/q21-pearl-harbor-address.cfm.

THE PRESIDENT'S COMMISSION ON THE STATUS OF WOMEN BY ELEANOR ROOSEVELT U.S. HOUSE OF REPRESENTATIVES, WASHINGTON, D.C. FEBRUARY 15, 1962

A prominent first lady and champion of democracy, Eleanor Roosevelt extended her duties to the American people into the last days of her life. After chairing the compilation of the Universal Declaration of Human Rights, she fought for socialized medicine and against the HUAC. Her brief congressional address on the social and economic gains of second wave feminism anticipated national benefits. Passage of the 1963 Equal Pay Act and 1964 Civil Rights Act made headway in destroying barriers to women's employment success.

The President's Commission was established to examine the needs and rights of American women and to make recommendations for the limitation of barriers that result in waste, injustice, and frustration.

We live in a world of rapid economic and social change. Women have much to gain from tremendous new productive possibilities. Their burdens may be further lightened, their lives enriched, and their skills utilized as homemakers or, if they wish, as workers outside the family circle.

But to translate the promises into reality we much assure rapid expansion of essential services and industries. Otherwise automation means unemployment and bitter competition for jobs.

Within a rapidly growing economy, with appropriate manpower planning, all Americans will have a better chance to develop their individual capacities, to earn a good livelihood, and to strengthen family life.

Because I anticipate success in achieving full employment and full use of America's magnificent potential, I feel confident that in the years ahead many of the remaining outmoded barriers to women's aspirations will disappear.

The President's Commission on the Status of Women can contribute notably to this accomplishment and thus bring significant long-run benefits to the entire nation and to the cause of democracy throughout the world.

Source: Roosevelt, Eleanor. "The President's Commission on the Status of Women." *Congressional Record* 108, no. 2 (February 15). Washington, DC: U.S. Government Printing Office, 1962, 2281.

ROSE, ERNESTINE L. (1810–1892)

A secular humanist dubbed "Queen of the Platform," Ernestine Louise Susmond Potowski Rose, the first Jewish feminist, devoted her life to the international advancement of human rights. A Russo-Polish radical born on January 13, 1810, southwest of Warsaw in a Piotrkow ghetto, she was the only child of a rabbi, possibly teacher and Kabbalist Aharon Pieterkowski, a conservative Jew married to a daughter of the wealthy Sigismund clan. Introduced at home to Hebrew, Torah, Talmud, and rational disputation, at age six, Ernestine began thinking independently after she suffered her mother's death and her father's remarriage to a 16-year-old bride.

To the consternation of conservative Jews, Rose championed an antireligious bias against fasting, ritual, Sabbath strictures, and sacramental marriage. At age 17, she escaped Poland to Prussia, settling in Berlin, and successfully appealed to King Frederick William III to exempt her from the law requiring Jewish immigrants to acquire a sponsor. While comparing religious dogma around the world, she determined that all dogma tyrannized women.

In 1831, Rose relocated to London, dropped her patronym in favor of her mother's name—Sigismund (or Susmond)—and earned a living as a teacher of German and Hebrew. As a disciple of Robert Dale Owen's Association of All Classes of All Nations, she wed fellow idealist William Ella Rose in 1836, and joined him in emigration from Middlesex to Skaneateles, New York, to found an Owenite colony of 36 freethinkers. They rented rooms on the Lower East Side below their watch repair shop and perfumery, which funded agitation and lobbying on behalf of slaves and disenfranchised women.

Under the mentoring of suffragist leaders such as Elizabeth Cady Stanton, Lucretia Mott, and Susan B. Anthony, Rose became the only non-Christian to climb to prominence in the women's rights movement. Her speeches covered topics ranging from the injustice of anti-Semitism, repudiating scriptural evidence for equality and the amassing of wealth by the privileged. To liberate women from androcentric religion, she rebutted theologian Antoinette Brown's assertion that scripture supported female equality and advised feminists to abandon churches.

For immigrant audiences, Rose presented egalitarian tenets in French and German. Traveling by stage and rail, she journeyed to speaking venues in 23 states and saluted the forgotten contributions of female pilgrims to the colonization of New England. In Charleston and Columbia, South Carolina, she challenged slavery advocates who threatened tar and feathers.

Although frail and sickly, in October 15, 1851, Rose attended the second annual Women's Rights Convention at Brinley Hall in Worcester, Massachusetts. At Cochituate Hall on October 19, she exhorted 1,000 delegates from 11 states with "On Woman's Rights." She examined the nature of humanity and its suppression in married women, especially widows left penniless and defenseless before unjust laws of inheritance. Her platform rhetoric, dramatic and aggressive, examined the wider sphere of global history before challenging the dismal status quo of female citizenship in the United States.

As an enthusiast of the colonial tract "Common Sense" (1776), Rose addressed the annual Thomas Paine banquet in New York, where she berated enslavers of blacks and women for violating natural law. In 1852, she extended her vilification to apathetic free people who remained silent rather than impugn the profitable slave trade. The following year, she blasted scriptural interpretations that legitimized bondage and contrasted the empty gesture of the Declaration of Independence with actual liberties granted to blacks of the British West Indies in 1834. To the *Liberator*, on August 19, 1853, she submitted the speech "Secession of the South from the North."

In 1854, Rose extended the concept of women's right to property to a state law ensuring a mother's equal access to child custody. In Philadelphia that same year, she won election to president of the National Women's Rights Convention and incurred the wrath of William Henry Milburn, the chaplain of the U.S. House of Representatives, for her atheism.

At a women's rights convention in England in early May 1856, Rose denounced the authority of the Bible in matters of women's rights and built coalitions with like-minded British, French, and German activists. She stripped matrimony of its romantic mythology and reclaimed the ballot as the central power capable of relieving women of second-class citizenship. Throughout the early 1860s, she labored for the Women's Loyal National League by supporting the Civil War as a conflict against slavery.

On May 15, 1869, Rose co-formed the National Woman Suffrage Association (NWSA). During an era of growing xenophobia and anti-Semitism, at age 59, she became a naturalized U.S. citizen. In constant pain from arthritis and neuralgia, on June 8, 1869, she repatriated to England, where she and William joined the British Atheist Association and advocated social and economic reform. Among sectarians, the couple lived more isolated than they had in New York.

In better health in 1873, Rose addressed the Universal Peace Society and an assembly of suffragists in the Edinburgh Society. On return to the United States in May for the annual assembly of the NWSA, she revived connections between U.S. and French activists. She refused publication of her works and, in 1877, chose not to compose a section of the *History of Woman Suffrage*.

After her husband's death in London in January 1882, Rose became a recluse. She resisted the urgings of Anthony and Stanton to abandon William's gravesite and return to New York. Three days after suffering a stroke at Brighton, on August 4, 1892, she died peacefully.

See Also: Anthony, Susan B.; Davis, Paulina W.; Mott, Lucretia; Stanton, Elizabeth Cady.

References

Frost-Knappman, Elizabeth, and Kathryn Cullen-DuPont. *Women's Suffrage in America*. New York: Facts on File, 2005.

Rose, Ernestine Louise. *An Address on Woman's Rights*. Boston: J.P. Mendum 1851.

Rose, Ernestine Louise. *Mistress of Herself: Speeches and Letters of Ernestine L. Rose, Early Women's Rights Leader*. New York: Feminist Press, 2008.

ON WOMAN'S RIGHTS (EXCERPT) BY ERNESTINE ROSE FIRST NATIONAL WOMEN'S RIGHTS CONVENTION BRINLEY HALL, WORCESTER, MASSACHUSETTS OCTOBER 16, 1851

One of New York's passionate orators of the mid-1800s, suffragist Ernestine Rose, a Jewish immigrant from Russo-Poland, incorporated in a plea for women's rights memories of the French Revolution and the immediacy of the rhetorical question. By dramatizing the American struggle for equality within the panorama of world history, she interwove the style and purpose of colonial pamphleteer Thomas Paine in demanding independence for women. To explain women's subservience to men, she charged society's ignorance and the traditions that pictured the female as delicate and helpless.

. . . Like man, woman comes involuntarily into existence. Like him she possesses physical and mental and moral powers on the proper cultivation of which depends her happiness. Like him she is subject to all the vicissitudes of life. Like him she has to pay the penalty for disobeying nature's laws, and far greater penalties has she to suffer from ignorance of her far more complicated nature than he. Like him she enjoys or suffers with her country.

Yet she is not recognized as his equal! In the laws of the land she has no rights, in government she has no voice. And in spite of another principle, recognized in this republic, namely, that "taxation without representation is tyranny," yet she is taxed without being represented. Her property may be consumed by taxes to defray the expenses of that unholy, unrighteous custom called war, yet she has no power to give her veto against it. From the cradle to the grave she is subject to the power and control of man. Father, guardian, or husband, one conveys her like some piece of merchandise over to the other. At marriage she loses her entire identity and her being is said to have become merged in her husband. . . .

It is high time to denounce such gross injustice, to compel man by the might of right to give to woman her political, legal, and social rights. Open to her all the avenues of emolument, distinction, and greatness. Give her an object for which to cultivate her powers, and a fair chance to do so, and there will be no need to speculate as to her proper sphere. She will find her own sphere in accordance with her capacities, powers, and tastes, and yet she will be woman still. Her rights will not change, but strengthen, develop, and elevate her nature. Away, then, with that folly and absurdity, that a possession of her rights would be detrimental to her character; that if she is recognized as the equal to man, she would cease to be woman. . . .

It is from ignorance not malice that man acts towards woman as he does. In ignorance of her nature and the interest and happiness of both sexes, he conceived ideas, laid down rules, and enacted laws concerning her destiny and rights. The same ignorance, strengthened by age, sanctified by superstition, engrafted into his being by habit, makes him carry these convictions out to the detriment of his own as well as her happiness; for is he not the loser by his injustice? Oh! How severely he suffers. Who can fathom the depth of misery and suffering to society from the subjugation and injury inflicted on woman? The race is elevated in excellence and power or kept back in progression, in accordance with the scale of woman's position in society. But so firmly has prejudice closed the eyes of man to the light of truth, that though he feels the evils, he knows not their cause. . . .

To achieve this glorious victory of right over might, woman has much to do. Man may remove her legal shackles, and recognize her as his equal, which will greatly aid in her elevation, but the law cannot compel her to cultivate her mind and take an independent stand as a free being. . . . Woman must think for herself, and use for herself that greatest of all prerogatives—judgment of right and wrong. And next she must act according to her best convictions, irrespective of any other voice than that of right and duty. The time, I trust, will come, though slowly, yet surely, when woman will occupy that high and lofty position, for which nature has so eminently fitted her, in the destinies of humanity.

Source: Rose, Ernestine Louise. *An Address on Woman's Rights.* Boston: J.P. Mendum, 1851.

S

SAMPSON, DEBORAH (1760–1827)

America's first professional female soldier, Deborah Sampson Gannett fought for colonial liberation from English tyranny in the Revolutionary War, serving in the Fourth Massachusetts Regiment. The first of the seven children of Deborah Bradford of Kingston, Massachusetts, and seaman Jonathan Sampson Jr., she was born on December 17, 1760, in Plympton, Massachusetts. Her father's disappearance on a voyage in 1765 left the mother little choice but to place her children in foster homes. Later proof indicated that Jonathan led a double life with his second family in Fayette, Maine.

While educating herself, Sampson boarded at homes owned by her aunt, Ruth Fuller, and, at age eight, with the widow Mary Thacher of Southboro. In 1770, Sampson entered a third placement at a Middleborough farm as indentured domestic to Deacon Jeremiah and Susannah Thomas. During eight years of labor in a household of six children, as the American Revolution neared, she learned to fire a musket. In summer at age 16, she taught reading, spelling, and scripture at Middleborough's one-room school.

By passing as a male and enlisting with 50 others in the Continental Army at Uxbridge on May 21, 1781, Sampson renamed herself Robert "Bob" Shurtlieff. Armed with rifle, cartridge box, bayonet, and knapsack, she served in the Fourth Massachusetts Regiment under Captain George Webb at West Point, Bellingham, and Worcester. She volunteered in early June for a scouting party to Harlem and White Plains, New York, to assess British troop strength in Manhattan.

In August 1781, Sampson's company deployed to besiege Yorktown. In the advance guard at Yorktown, she fought under the Marquis de Lafayette until the surrender of Lord Cornwallis on October 19, 1781. She gained a reputation for punctuality, riding near the British lines, and running faster than other soldiers.

Following a saber slash to the left temple and a musket shot to the front of the upper thigh, on July 3, 1782, Sampson concealed her gender from French medical aids. At the hospital, she allowed stitching of the facial wound, but fled the hospital with the musket shot still lodged in her leg. She excised the ball with a pocketknife.

Promoted to aide de camp on April 1, 1783, Corporal Sampson served the table and chambers of General John Paterson in Lenox, Massachusetts. While confined in Philadelphia during a fever epidemic that summer, she came under the treatment of Barnabas Binney, a Boston surgeon. He unbound her breasts, discovered the deception, and treated her at his home. He divulged her secret only to the general.

Sampson remained in disguise until accepting an honorable discharge from General Henry Knox on October 23, 1783. On return to Massachusetts, she encountered family disapproval of the wartime escapades and church ouster because of her gender disguise. Publication of her military service appeared in the March issue of *American Museum*. With the backing of Governor John Hancock, she received a lump sum—£34 plus interest—and a commendation for valor, but no pension.

In poverty on the family farm, Sampson dictated to writer Herman Mann her memoirs, *The Female Review; or, Memoirs of an American Young Lady* (1797). At age 42, she initiated an oratorical career in New York and New England, which she advertised with handbills. With funds from her family and Paul Revere, a visitor to the Gannett farm, over two years she delivered 20 speeches to some 2,000 listeners, becoming America's first itinerant female lecturer. Her eloquent oratory made direct comparison between the enslaved colonies and the confinement of women to a female stereotype. To the surprise of hearers, she comported herself like a refined, charming lady rather than the raucous, mannish soldier they expected.

On February 20, 1804, Revere petitioned a veteran military surgeon, U.S. Congressman William Eustis, on behalf of Sampson, who suffered postwar illness because of combat wounds. In 1816, Congress granted her an annual stipend of $76.80. The Massachusetts commonwealth awarded her an annual stipend of $48. A state act in 1818 boosted the amount to $96.

For her last nine years, Sampson managed farm finances on government pay. After a bout of yellow fever killed her on April 29, 1827, her husband filed successfully for a survivor's pension of $80, which he collected for nearly a decade until his death in January 1837. Her reputation thrived, both as a soldier in disguise and a vocal petitioner for wounded veterans' entitlements.

Reference

Young, Alfred R. *Masquerade: The Life and Times of Deborah Sampson, Continental Soldier.* New York: Vintage, 2004.

LIFE AS A FEMALE REVOLUTIONARY WAR SOLDIER BY DEBORAH SAMPSON GANNETT FEDERAL STREET THEATRE, BOSTON, MASSACHUSETTS MARCH 1802

America's first professional female soldier, 21-year-old Deborah Sampson Gannett fought for colonial liberation from English tyranny from 1781 to war's end two years later. In lieu of a pension or compensation for war wounds, she published memoirs and, in 1802, initiated a speaking career demonstrating her military training. The remarkable speeches claimed for women a history of patriotic duty in the military.

. . . Confirmed by this time in the justness of a defensive war on the one side, from the most aggravated one on the other—my mind ripened with my strength; and while our beds and our roses were sprinkled with the blood of indiscriminate youth, beauty, innocence and decrepit old age, I only seemed to want the license to become one of the severest avengers of the wrong. For several years I looked on these scenes of havoc, rapacity and devastation, as one looks on a drowning man, on the conflagration of a city—where are not only centered his coffers of gold, but with them his choicest hopes, friends, companions, his all—without being able to extend the rescuing hand to either. Wrought upon at length, you may say, by an enthusiasm and frenzy, that could brook no control—I burst the tyrant bands, which held my sex in awe, and clandestinely, or by stealth, grasped an opportunity, which custom and the world seemed to deny, as a natural privilege. And whilst poverty, hunger, nakedness, cold and disease had dwindled the American armies to a handful—whilst universal terror and dismay ran through our camps, ran through our country—while even Washington himself, at their head, though like a god, stood, as it were, on a pinnacle tottering over the abyss of destruction, the last prelude to our falling a wretched prey to the yawning jaws of the monster aiming to devour—not merely for the sake of gratifying a facetious curiosity, like that of my reputed predecessor, in her romantic excursions through the garden of bliss—did I throw off the soft habiliments of my sex and assume those of the warrior, already prepared for battle.

Thus I became an actor in that important drama, with an inflexible resolution to persevere through the last scene; when we might be permitted and, acknowledged to enjoy what we had so nobly declared we would possess, or lose with our lives—Freedom and Independence!—When the philosopher might resume his researches unmolested—the statesman be disembarrassed by his distracting theme of national politics—the divine find less occasion to invoke the indignation of heaven on the usurpers and cannibals of the inherent rights and even existence of man—when the son should again be restored to the arms of his disconsolate parent, and the lover

Sanger resolved to empower women by challenging priests and Comstock laws, which embargoed the sale of prophylactic shields and sponges and banned information on human reproduction from the U.S. mail. With the monthly issuance of *The Woman Rebel* and the pamphlet *Family Limitation*, she began campaigning in 1914 for female management of their own bodies. To identify the topic, she coined the term "birth control." Arrest in August 1914 caused her to accept help from the Free Speech League and to take a midnight train to Montreal and, under the alias "Bertha Watson," to escape to London.

Welcomed by the Fabian Society, Sanger studied ways to liberate women from fear of intimacy by encouraging coital pleasure. At Fabian Hall on July 5, 1915, her accusation of "Comstockery in America" endorsed socialism as an antidote to prudery that inhibited the free speech of workingwomen. With Dutch and French research, she replaced common anatomical language in her American orations with academic terms. In 1915 in Brownsville, an immigrant neighborhood in Brooklyn, she stocked a clinic with diaphragms imported from Germany to Rahway, New Jersey, and with tracts translated into Italian and Yiddish. On January 17, 1916, her first formal speech attacked laws inhibiting the decisions of adults.

During a four-month speaking tour in spring 1916 from New York, Pittsburgh, and St. Louis to California, Sanger composed reasoned arguments entitled "Birth Control," "Condemnation Is Misunderstanding," "This Business of Bearing Babies," "Birth Control and Society," and "Woman and Birth Control." To medical social workers at New York City's Hotel Brevoort, she charged the Catholic hierarchy and abortionists with targeting women for suppression and saddling them with misery. To social restraints on language, she declared it an honor to quash absurd expectations that women not discuss the workings of their own anatomy.

After Sanger and her sister, nurse Ethel Higgins Byrne, opened the nation's first family planning agency on October 16, 1916, they distributed cervical caps, an illegal method of blocking sperm. The founder's arrest on October 25 ended the clinic, which had served 488 clients. A second arrest of both sisters resulted in Byrne's pardon and Sanger's conviction and incarceration in the Queens County Workhouse. Because of media follow-ups, her defense of female rights aroused public consciousness and financial support for her clinic.

Crusade for Women's Rights

After a police raid delayed Sanger's appearance at the First American Birth Control Conference, on November 18, 1921, she delivered a major discourse, "A Moral Necessity for Birth Control." The text directed controversy toward medical intervention in global overpopulation, which encumbered the poor and uneducated. She contended that uncontrolled births resulted in infant exposure and murder, abandonment, disease, starvation, and war. Only through controlled reproduction did she see a future for humankind.

Through the American Birth Control League (ABCL), forerunner of Planned Parenthood, Sanger targeted black and Hispanic women for reproductive assistance. Her book *The Pivot of Civilization* (1922) advocated maternal data collection, contraceptive instruction to journalists and lawmakers, and recruitment and education of birth control counselors. In 1924, financier John David Rockefeller Jr. funded the project with a gift of $10,000.

With ready cash, Sanger backed an American distributor of diaphragms. By 1925, the 27,500 ABCL members lobbied for female civil liberties from Connecticut to British Columbia and launched the Clinical Research Bureau to train medical workers to fit diaphragms. The staff documented the first survey of female sexuality from menarche through menopause and including defloration, sex partners, conceptions, births, and venereal diseases.

A lecture tour took Sanger to churches, theaters, homes, and women's clubs. To the Sixth International Neo-Malthusian and Birth Control Conference in 1925, she delivered "The Children's Era," a whimsical dialogue in which a fetus questions parents about home stability. Her 1926 itinerary included delivery of "Racial Betterment" at Vassar College and education of the women's auxiliary of the New Jersey Ku Klux Klan. At a mass women's assembly in 1928, the "Engineer's Auditorium Speech" covered issues of immigration, epidemics, beggary, and criminality, all worsened by overbreeding.

Emerging Concerns

At age 57, Sanger retired to Tucson, Arizona, but maintained global dissemination of contraception information and devices. The radio broadcast of the lecture "Woman and the Future" to the Federation of Jewish Women's Organizations on January 25, 1937, reprised her 1931 Senate testimony and concluded that children deserved to be wanted. At a Tucson speaking engagement in early 1938, Sanger extolled Scandinavian birth control clinics in contrast to low standards of family planning in India, China, and Puerto Rico. Her presentation "Pressure of Population as a Cause of War" (1938) declared racial and religious ideals a cover for the real motivators of conflict—hunger and greed. In anticipation of the New York World's Fair, she expounded on population control and eugenics in "Creating a World of Tomorrow" (1939).

At age 73, Sanger celebrated the invention of oral contraception. In 1952, she collected funds to further the pharmaceutical formulation of Enovid, an oral ovulation suppressant. Shortly after the U.S. Supreme Court overturned Connecticut's anti-contraception law, she died in a Tucson nursing home on September 6, 1966, of congestive heart failure.

See Also: Ames, Blanche Ames; Goldman, Emma.

Reference

The Margaret Sanger Papers Project. Accessed November 5, 2014. http://www.nyu.edu/projects/sanger.

THE COMSTOCK LAWS
BY MARGARET SANGER
SUBCOMMITTEE ON THE JUDICIARY
U.S. SENATE, WASHINGTON, D.C.
FEBRUARY 13, 1931

A militant civil libertarian, Margaret Sanger of Corning, New York, championed women's rights to control the number and spacing of conceptions. She courted jailing for civil disobedience to the repressive Comstock Act of 1873. Enacted at the direction of a fanatic, the laws inhibited the dissemination of birth control information to responsible adults. As spokeswoman for the Committee on Federal Legislation for Birth Control, in 1931 and 1932, she informed congressmen on physicians' need for birth control devices and the right to teach women how to use them. In 1942, she predicted the postwar baby boom and anticipated the formulation of prescription oral contraceptives.

There is only one state in the union where the giving of advice [on birth control] would be doubtful, and that is Mississippi. All the other states give a physician the right to give such information in his private practice provided he can get [contraceptive devices] from the manufacturer. That is what our amendment provides for.

When this law was passed in 1873, there was very little known concerning the whole subject. Certainly there was no real information concerning the medical and sociological importance of the practice of contraception. The subject of birth control or contraception was wrongly classed with indecency, obscenity, and abortion. The passage of this law in 1873 really closed the avenues of proper scientific information and research by the medical profession, medical schools, and medical universities in this country.

It has done untold harm to classify contraception in that category. It is an insult to every decent married woman in the country who wants to bring up her family intelligently. It prevents her from applying the benefits of science to the cultivation of her children and the bringing up of her family; and, furthermore, to all intents and purposes, it classifies every married woman in this country as a "child-bearing conscript." Unless a woman has some means of preventing conception and spacing her children, she is forced to bear children like an animal, and in fact animals are not allowed to breed in sickness and with diseased bodies as the women of this country are made to do today.

This bill is simple. It is conservative. It is constructive, because it simply allows the physician at a hospital or licensed clinic to receive such supplies and to give such information.

The passage of this bill would be the first attempt on the part of the Congress to place the responsibility of giving contraceptive instruction into the hands of the medical profession, where it rightly belongs.

It would be the first attempt on the part of Congress to give the medical profession the control of such knowledge, which we know is very promiscuously scattered about today. It would let physicians regulate the kind of devices used and thus wipe out the present traffic in wrong and harmful devices. The poor mothers, the people who should have the information, are uninformed and are denied the proper kind of devices suitable to their own individual requirements.

Source: Sanger, Margaret. "The Comstock Laws." *Birth Control: Hearings before a Subcommittee on the Judiciary, United States Senate.* 71st Cong., 3rd sess., February 13–14. Washington, DC: U.S. Government Printing Office, 1931, 9–10.

SCHNEIDERMAN, ROSE (1882–1972)

Lobbyist and trade union organizer Rose Schneiderman surprised audiences with stinging retorts phrased from the immigrant shop girl's perspective. She absorbed the Polish Jewish work ethic of her parents, herbalist and baker Deborah Rothman and tailor Adolph Samuel Schneiderman, to whom she was born in Sawin on April 6, 1882, and originally named Rachel. While her mother made uniforms for Russian soldiers, Rose joined Polish boys at Chelm in learning Judaic principles and Hebrew at a traditional boys-only cheder.

In 1890, the family immigrated to New York City's Lower East Side, where they rented a two-room flat. She enjoyed a close relationship with her father, who read his family stories and produced stage plays at Jewish theaters. His death two years later from meningitis impoverished the family. While keeping boarders, her mother entrusted baby Jennie to a relative and the boys to the Hebrew Orphan Asylum on Amsterdam Avenue in northwest Manhattan.

Rose learned early the motivations that drove women to desperate measures. To reunite the family, her mother took in boarders and laundry, worked as a janitor, and labored for a furrier 11 hours per day. Her unemployment in 1895 ended Schneiderman's attendance at Houston Street Grammar School and increased dependence on charity food deliveries. At age 13, she found work through United Hebrew Charities as a Hearn's department store cashier for 40 cents an hour and clerked at Ridley's store. Three years later, she increased her pay by sewing lining to golf and yachting caps at the Hein & Fox factory until the building burned.

Factory Sexism

Gender unfairness impinged on Schneiderman's income after male workers struck for higher pay, which management deducted from the pay of women laborers. At age 20, she moved to Montreal to visit a maternal aunt and lived among union organizers, feminists, and radical socialists, most from Eastern Europe. From worker complaints, she learned the employees had to buy, equip, and repair their own sewing machines. A nonviolent strike and picket at five of the city's 30 garment factories raised wages $2 for shop girls. Management retaliated by hiring naïve immigrants and children for lower pay.

In 1903, Schneiderman began persuading seamstresses to form the Jewish socialist United Cloth Hat and Cap Makers' Union and represented them at the New York Central Labor Union convention. To improve wages and sweatshop conditions, halt night work, and expose firetrap conditions at factories, she allied with the Women's Trade Union League (WTUL) and, for 45 years, served as the first woman to chair a U.S. trade union.

Schneiderman published "A Cap Maker's Story" in the April 1905 edition of *The Independent.* Following election to vice president of the New York TUL in 1906, she received a scholarship from philanthropist Irene Lewisohn to improve her basic education. In 1908, she accepted salary to unionize female garment workers, whom male labor organizers ignored. When the International Ladies' Garment Workers' Union (ILGWU) fomented a strike of Jewish immigrant blouse makers on November 22, 1909, she led the Uprising of the Twenty Thousand. Her rallies caused a contingent of 15,000 factory staff to fight for themselves. By strike's end in February 1910, she enrolled 31,000 garment workers in unions.

The garment workers' strike yielded mediation of better pay and open-shop employment for all seamstresses. Influenced by the fiery rhetoric of union agitator Mother Jones, in Boston in June 1910, Schneiderman addressed an assembly of the ILGWU about the evils of white slavery. She affirmed that exploitation would not end without a pay raise, even if management counter-offered free worker lodging.

In 1911, she co-formed the Wage Earner's League for Woman Suffrage, a group that urged female shop workers to become voters through full citizenship.

The upgrade in employment preceded a Greenwich Village disaster, the Triangle Shirtwaist Factory fire of March 24, 1911, which resulted in the deaths of 23 men and 123 women from flame and smoke and from jumping out of the windows of a locked facility. Her most influential speech, "We Have Found You Wanting," appeared in the April 8, 1911, edition of *The Survey*. Delivered at the Metropolitan Opera House the previous week, the speech commemorated the martyred factory workers with grim imagery of the Spanish Inquisition.

Schneiderman's oratory reminded audiences of the martyrdom of the working poor, especially women. By choosing first-person pronouns, she counted herself among the laboring masses who risked life and health in sweatshops for barely subsistence pay. In honor of the burned seamstresses, she devoted the organization to eight-hour workdays and a minimum wage.

Women and Wages

For the National American Woman Suffrage Association (NAWSA), Schneiderman crusaded for gender equity with the leaflet "Senators vs. Working Women" (1912). In support of the textile workers' strike over pay cuts from January to March 1912 in Lawrence, Massachusetts, she coined the term "bread and roses" to encourage female immigrants to demand the benefits enjoyed by privileged American-born women. The hard-edged exhortations reminded New York legislators that the state's 800,000 female employees shared with males the grueling jobs in laundries, electric works, textile plants, canneries, and foundries.

In 1913, Schneiderman offered strategies and platform oratory for NAWSA. After campaigning for Ohio women's enfranchisement, in 1915, she began a three-year effort for the New York ballot, a liberal campaign in New York and Ohio that earned her the antilabor nickname "the Red Rose of Anarchy."

Schneiderman's socialist platform proposed federal unemployment insurance and state health care as well as public ownership of utilities and food distribution centers. For the family, she advocated nonprofit worker housing and upgrades of local schools. In 1921, she co-initiated the Bryn Mawr Summer School for Women in Industry, an opportunity to educate the working poor at a college that served mostly the daughters of the elite.

Through friendship with Eleanor and Franklin D. Roosevelt, in 1926, Schneiderman received appointment to the labor board of the National Recovery Administration, for which she compiled federal industrial codes impacting female workers. She pressed for a minimum wage and a limit of eight-hour workdays for women. For the handwork trade, she surveyed conditions in Puerto Rico in 1936 for embroiderers and returned to Washington, D.C., to lambaste industrialists for exploiting underpaid women and children. She advanced in 1937 to New York's secretary of labor and crusaded for equal pay for women and social security for domestics in beauty parlors, restaurants, and hotels.

Against the persecution of Jews by Germany's Nazi Party, Schneiderman rescued individuals from imprisonment in labor and death camps and found residences for them in the United States and Palestine. Retired in 1949, she continued addressing union assemblies and broadcasting pro-worker essays over radio. She crusaded for federal child care, maternal leave, and state regulation of offices and factories. Before her death on August 11, 1972, in New York City's Jewish Home and Hospital for the Aged, she composed an autobiography, *All for One* (1967).

See Also: Jones, Mother; Roosevelt, Eleanor.

Reference

McGuire, John Thomas. "From Socialism to Social Justice Feminism: Rose Schneiderman and the Quest for Urban Equity, 1911–1933." *Journal of Urban History* 35 (November 2009): 998–1019.

WHAT WOMEN HAVE DONE IN THE LABOR MOVEMENT BY ROSE SCHNEIDERMAN EQUALITY LEAGUE OF SELF-SUPPORTING WOMEN COOPER UNION, NEW YORK CITY JANUARY 17, 1907

An immigrant lobbyist and union organizer, Rose Schneiderman addressed audiences in the dialect of her native Sawin, Poland. While organizing the ILGWU, she goaded female laborers to reject low pay and sweatshop conditions and to join male unionists in strikes and protests. Her class-oriented speeches censured rich women in the state capital who volunteered for charity, which working-class women considered an insult to their efforts.

We went up to Albany with our poor little hushed voices. We did as we always do. We did not think it necessary to use fine sentiments to influence people. We thought that the truth would do. But we found that the rich had up there orators, very fine gentlemen. The matter was a factory bill that enabled women to work twelve hours a day and then have Saturday and Sunday off, as though they would be fit for anything but bed then.

There were rich men up there who said that God gives us fruit in time of plenty and we must prepare it in season. I wondered if that was the God of the working people. Other men said that women liked to work overtime to get a little extra money. Do the women in the workshops ever get "extra money"? Is there any such thing to the workingwomen as "extra money"?

I found out while I was in Albany something that I had not known before, that you have such things as anti-suffragists. These fine ladies stand up there and say, "Gentlemen, save us from ourselves. We don't want to vote. We have more womanly work to do. We have charity!"

Charity! I hate that word. They are the ones who live on charity—they never work. We who provide everything that they have are too nice about it. We never let them know it. These women live a tribe life. We want to be human. To be human is to think of the world as your country, not your little home alone.

Source: Schneiderman, Rose. "Teachers Scorned Idea of a Union." *New York Times*, April 5, 1907, 7.

SCHROEDER, PATRICIA (1940–)

A maverick U.S. congresswoman for 12 terms, Patricia Nell Scott "Pat" Schroeder challenged military waste and workplace injustice to women. Born in Portland, Oregon, on July 30, 1940, to first-grade teacher Bernice Lemoin and Lee Combs Scott, an aviation insurance agent, she came from a distinguished line of Nebraska pioneers, public servants, and soldiers. To overcome strabismus, she followed the regimen of patching and eye exercises, but crossed eyes made her adopt humor as recourse against student taunts.

Following the postings of her father, an Army Air Corps flight instructor, Schroeder moved often during World War II. She grew up in Des Moines, Iowa, and thrived in Congregational religious training and Girl Scouting. She graduated from Theodore Roosevelt High School in 1961 and, with a pilot's license, earned money for training at the University of Minnesota by surveying air crash sites to gauge losses for insurance companies.

While studying history, philosophy, and political science, Schroeder served in the student senate, joined a sorority, and developed a libertarian attitude toward the era's protest marches. Gender bias assailed her at Harvard School of Law, where she incurred humiliation from misogynist professors and students who considered her expertise at law a waste of time. She took refuge in a boyfriend, a naval veteran, James "Jim" Schroeder, a fellow law student. On August 18, 1962, she married Jim, who became a political adviser, attorney, and counsel to the founders of the Vail ski resort. The couple settled in Denver, Colorado.

Jim had no difficulty getting a job, but his wife labored against stereotypes that females should be secretaries, not lawyers. She produced son Scott and, following the deaths of fraternal twins in 1968, bore a healthy daughter, Jamie Schroeder. Hospitalization for postpartum hemorrhaging instilled in Schroeder the needs of women to control their reproductive lives. She served the Colorado State Personnel Board as a hearing officer to mediate employee grievances and, in 1970, cofounded the National Women's Political Caucus, a bipartisan effort to boost female participation in government.

In May 1972, Schroeder successfully ran for office, becoming the first female U.S. legislator from Colorado. To be near a Capitol Hill office, her family relocated to a house in Virginia. Amid verbal jabs at mothers in government, during the Cold War, she advised the Judiciary Committee and the Post Office and Civil Service Committee and addressed neglected issues of importance to women. She gained power as the first female on the Armed Services Committee and aimed to lower Pentagon control of more than one-third of federal spending. She aligned with the Democratic Caucus in 1975 to trim military budgets, end spending on the MX mobile missile, and lobby for a nuclear test ban.

In league with legislator Olympia Snowe, in 1976, Schroeder co-established the Congressional Women's Caucus, an advocacy for reproductive health, research on breast cancer and menopause, Social Security benefits, child care, adoption reform, and employee gender equity. On October 14, 1977, she addressed the U.S. House of Representatives on the abortion double standard by citing a satiric jab from Joseph Heller's army satire *Catch-22*. To ensure maternity and disability benefits for pregnant workers, she fostered the 1978 Pregnancy Discrimination Act.

In 1982, Schroeder impaneled the Committee on Children, Youth, and Families, which, for a decade, evaluated harmful situations affecting American children. She informed legislators on appropriate actions to aid traditional families and the 500,000 neglected and abused minors remanded to foster care. In an earnest House speech on August 2, 1983, she belittled President Ronald Reagan's Star Wars weapons system and dubbed him the Teflon president for thriving amid scandals and misdemeanors of his staff.

On October 29, 1985, Schroeder testified to the Committee on Foreign Affairs, Subcommittee on Africa, on U.S. firms exploiting natural resources in Namibia. On June 17, 1991, she introduced testimony to Congress on "The Risky Business of Adolescence: How to Help Teens Stay Safe." To the House in 1991, she exposed male officers for sexual scandals, notably, the navy and marine Tailhook debauchery of 83 female officers on September 8–12 at the Las Vegas Hilton.

Under the Clinton administration, in 1993, Schroeder accomplished citizen health initiatives by coauthoring the Family and Medical Leave Act and the National Institutes of Health Revitalization Act. She ventured into political dissent by denouncing the ban on homosexuals in the military. On November 16, 1993, she lectured to the House Judiciary on hate crimes against women under the title "Crimes of Violence Motivated by Gender." By citing rape statistics and comparing them to similar data from Germany, Great Britain, and Japan, she established that women were two times more likely to be victimized. On the issue that adjudication of abusers of females would overload federal courts, she stressed that conviction rates for robbery were six times higher than that for rape.

Schroeder reached a pinnacle of influence in 1996. On January 31, she backed an 11-month ethics inquiry into Speaker of the House Newt Gingrich for tax fraud and ethical malfeasance. In defense of same-sex couples, she declared proponents of the 1996 Defense of Marriage Act blatant fomenters of hate. In a House floor speech on September 24, 1996, she reprised the trials of feminists Margaret Sanger and Victoria Woodhull against the Comstock Act. Filled with historic details, the address alerted legislators that postal inspector Anthony Comstock's fanaticism continued to influence Internet censorship of reproductive choice, RU-486, and abortion via the Telecommunications Act.

On retirement from 24 years in Congress, Schroeder addressed the National Press Club on her pride in challenging the status quo. In June 1997, she chaired the Association of American Publishers and lobbied for stringent copyright regulation in libraries and on Google Books. She promoted availability of print works for the blind and visually impaired. In addition to issuing *24 Years of House Work . . . and the Place Is Still a Mess: My Life in Politics* (1998), she advised the Marguerite Casey Foundation, American Bar Association's Center for Human Rights Executive Committee, and the Council for a Livable World's PeacePAC. In 2006, the National Research Center for Women and Families named her a Foremother.

See Also: Sanger, Margaret; Woodhull, Victoria.

Reference

Lowy, Joan A. *Pat Schroeder: A Woman of the House.* Albuquerque: University of New Mexico Press, 2003.

THE COMSTOCK ACT (EXCERPT)
BY PATRICIA SCHROEDER
HOUSE COMMITTEE ON APPROPRIATIONS
U.S. HOUSE OF REPRESENTATIVES, WASHINGTON, D.C.
SEPTEMBER 24, 1996

Twelve-term U.S. congresswoman Pat Schroeder of Portland, Oregon, a founder of the Congressional Women's Caucus, charged the Telecommunications Act with censoring information on reproductive choice, including facts about abortion and RU-486. Similar in tone and intent to the oppressive Comstock Act of 1873, laws governing the Internet threatened First Amendment rights and public access to information about legal health procedures. The 1996 regulation of the media spawned a revolt against corporate control of information through street and community newspapers and alternative media. To revoke regulation, the House Judiciary Committee approved the Internet Freedom and Nondiscrimination Act of 2006, which never came to a vote.

. . . Comstockery has been given a new lease on life by this Congress.

The Telecommunications Act passed this year extended the Comstock Act's prohibitions to anyone who uses an interactive computer service. This Congress, therefore, revived Comstockery by making it a crime to use the Internet to provide or receive information which directly or indirectly tells where, how, of whom, or by what means an abortion may be obtained. A broader gag rule is hard to imagine. It could criminalize:

- An Internet posting of the referral directory of your local medical society, or the yellow pages of the telephone directory;
- A telemedicine consultation between two doctors who are conferring about a patient who may need an abortion to save her life; or
- Uploading or downloading medical journal articles about RU-486 or about safe abortion techniques.

I have introduced legislation to repeal the abortion-related speech provisions of the Comstock Act, but unfortunately, the leadership of the Judiciary Committee and of the Congress has refused to move this bill. So Comstockery remains alive and well, and until the Congress is motivated to renounce Comstockery once and for all, I fear that women will pay a disproportionate share of the price, with the dark shadow of Anthony Comstock hanging over our health-related speech on critical topics such as abortion.

And Comstockery seems to be enjoying a revival in other ways as well. Efforts to impose gag rules on doctors, punitive measures designed to make it harder for women to get access to information and services relating to contraception and abortion, laws that would allow the Anthony Comstocks of today to arrest and jail doctors who perform an abortion procedure that in their medical judgment is the safest to preserve the health and future fertility of their patients—all this is the Comstockery of today.

It is only President Clinton's veto of H.R. 1833 that stops us from seeing, on the evening news, the chilling image of medical doctors going in handcuffs to criminal trial for exercising their best medical judgment for women whose wanted pregnancies have gone terribly wrong.

Republican control of the Congress has brought us more than 50 votes on abortion. Every imaginable form of Comstockery is represented in this array of anti-choice measures.

Anthony Comstock's crusade against free speech and reproductive choice represents one of the worst chapters of our history. The last thing this country needs or wants is a bridge to the past represented by Comstockery. Suppression of free speech, suppression of reproductive choice, is an aberration from genuine American values.

As the Anthony Comstocks of today patrol the Halls of this Congress seeking to suppress free speech and reproductive choice in the name of morality, or family values, or whatever high-sounding purpose they may invoke, it is incumbent upon the Congress to ensure that no form of the Comstock Act is ever again enacted, and that no special agent is ever again commissioned to roam the land, persecuting Americans in the name of morality or family values.

Source: Schroeder, Patricia. "The Comstock Act." *Congressional Record* 142, no. 133. 104th Cong., 2d sess. Washington, DC: U.S. Government Printing Office, 1996, H10770.

SHALALA, DONNA (1941–)

Two-term U.S. Secretary of Health and Human Services, Donna Edna Shalala earns admiration for behind-the-scenes influence on health, education, and social reform and for being the first female chancellor of a Big Ten university. She was born in Cleveland, Ohio, on February 14, 1941, to Arab-American attorney Edna Smith and grocer and realtor James Abraham Shalala, a leader of the Syrian-Lebanese community. She and twin sister Diane attended West Tech High School and graduated in 1958.

On scholarships from the Lebanese-Syrian Women's League, Junior Achievement, and Ohio Newspaper Women, Shalala graduated from Western College for Women in Oxford, Ohio, in 1962 and joined the Peace Corps. For two years she helped build an agricultural college at the University of Ahwaz, Iran. On return to the United States, she won a Carnegie research fellowship in 1966 for an MA degree in school finance and urban education reform. While earning a doctorate from Syracuse University in 1970, she aided the New York Democratic Coalition.

On introduction to the university classroom, in 1970, Shalala lectured on social science as assistant to the dean of the Maxwell School of Citizenship and Public Affairs. She taught political science at Baruch College for two years, coauthored a textbook on American policy, and counseled the American Jewish Committee on the National Project on Ethnic America and New York State's 1973 study of public school financing. During a fiscal crisis in 1975, she advised the New York Task Force on Aid to Education, Correctional Economics Board, and the National Municipal League. Following receipt of fellowships from the Guggenheim Foundation and the National Academy of Public Administration, in 1976, she lectured at Yale Law School and gave the 1977 Phi Beta Kappa address at Miami University.

In 1980, Shalala achieved appointment from President Jimmy Carter to the Department of Housing and Urban Developing as assistant secretary of Policy Development and Research, for which she increased the availability of loans to women. In the same year, she began an eight-year stint as president of Hunter College, during which she became a governor of the American Stock Exchange and co-established EMILY's List, a feminist political action committee promoting the election of female Democrats. She lectured at Stanford on "Women and Power" and, in 1985, at the University of Texas on "The Unfinished Agenda of the Twentieth Century." As chancellor of the University of Wisconsin at Madison, in 1988, she lectured on campus about the late stages of the urban crisis.

For chairing the Children's Defense Fund, in 1993, Shalala earned appointment from President Bill Clinton to head the U.S. Department of Health and Human Services, a post that honored the first Lebanese American in a cabinet post. For two terms, she mounted a campaign against teen pregnancy, boosted child immunization and ethical organ sharing, and fostered AIDS research. She superintended allotment of a $590 billion budget, the largest of any cabinet secretary while managing Medicare, Medicaid, federal welfare, Children's Health Insurance and Head Start, and medical research. In mid-1996, she extended Medicare solvency to the next 24 years.

In 2001, Shalala accepted the presidency of the University of Miami and empowered the Momentum Campaign, an endowment drive that boosted research and academic funding by $3 billion. A year after *U.S. News & World Report* honored her as a top leader of 2004, she promoted affordable housing, women's health research, and the National Center on Addiction and Substance Abuse. With former U.S. senator Robert Dole, in March 2007, she led President George W. Bush's Commission on Care for America's Returning Wounded Warriors, an effort to aid soldiers adapting from combat to peacetime employment and family life. In September 2007 and May 2008, she testified before the Committee on Veterans' Affairs. In restrained, factual style, she simplified methods of identifying degree of disability, family needs, and long-term care and financial reimbursement.

Shalala's civic service won her the Medal of Freedom in 2008 from President Bush and listing by the Council on Excellence in Government among the most effective public servants in a quarter century. In 2015, she retired from college management. She continues to advise the American Iranian Council, National

Academy of Sciences, American Philosophical Society, and the Brookings Institution on world economics and foreign policy. For the Bipartisan Policy Center, she influences reform of nutrition and health care, energy, infrastructure, housing, and national debt control. For the Council on Foreign Relations, she joined an independent task force surveying the Emerging Global Health Crisis and noncommunicable diseases.

See Also: Edelman, Marian Wright.

Reference

Barkan, Elliott Robert. *Making It in America: A Sourcebook on Eminent Ethnic Americans*. Santa Barbara, CA: ABC-CLIO, 2001.

RETURNING WOUNDED WARRIORS BY DONNA SHALALA U.S. HOUSE OF REPRESENTATIVES, WASHINGTON, D.C. OCTOBER 17, 2007

A two-term U.S. secretary of Health and Human Services, Donna Shalala delivered a summation on the adaptation of soldiers to civilian life. For President George W. Bush's commission studying the issue, she outlined a simplified system of identifying degree of disability, family needs, and long-term care and financial reimbursement. She concluded that reducing government complexities was possible.

It was a privilege to serve on the President's Commission with Senator Dole. We never had a disagreement. He is fun to work with, but more importantly, he knows this system and cares deeply about what happens to these young men and women who come back from conflict.

Of our nine Commissioners, four were severely injured in current or past conflicts and one was the wife of a soldier from Iraq. This was not a commission of the usual suspects. It was a Commission that had a very high percentage of young people who had current information and current experiences and included people who had not been on commissions before but took a fresh look at these issues.

We presented six groundbreaking patient- and family-centered recommendations, and one of the important things about our recommendations is they were not bureaucracy-centered. They were patient-centered and family-centered. We tried to look at the issues from the point of view of the people that were directly affected, as opposed to the people that provided just the services.

Our report, which is called "Serve, Support, and Simplify," we believe is not only short, but it is a blueprint for and certainly a very clear outline for the kinds of changes we believe must take place.

Let me also emphasize, as General Scott will, that our recommendations stand on the report of others. We built upon other recommendations. We looked carefully at the Bradley Commission and all the previous commissions as well as more recent commissions.

Our six recommendations do not require massive new programs or a flurry of new legislation. We identified with the six recommendations 34 specific action steps that must be taken to implement the six recommendations. Only six of the 34 require Congressional action, and that is what I want to focus on today. I want to talk about those six that require action by Congress and then Senator Dole will discuss how the recommendations will work together to create a new system.

The first action step calls for Congress to simplify the Department of Defense and Veterans Administration disability systems. I realize in this town the word "simplify" is not often used, but I think that our point here is it ought not to take an expert to understand the system. Any injured soldier or member of their family ought to be able to understand what is going to happen to them and what benefits are available to them and how the disability system works.

Right now, DOD and VA assess each service member's disability for completely different reasons. DOD needs to determine if they can continue to do their job despite their medical condition. If they can't, then they must discharge the service member. The degree of disability, the length of time spent in service depends on the amount of military compensation and benefits.

DOD generally only rates a condition that prevents the service member from doing their job. The VA determines how disabled a veteran is based on every medical condition that occurred [or] was made worse while in the military service. The degree of disability is part of how the VA determines what benefits, services, and the amount of compensation the veteran will get.

Over the years, this evaluation system has become really convoluted as we tried to fix problems and that is the point we are making today. People of good will in this Congress and in the agencies, every time they had a problem they added a new regulation, a new requirement, a new piece of legislation, and that is why the system is so convoluted and so complex today.

We recommend simplifying the system. DOD retains their authority to determine fitness to serve. If a service member's health conditions make them unfit for duty, they would be separated from the military with a lifetime annuity payment based on their rank and years of military service. They don't have to wait 20 years.

If they get severely injured, they have been in for 11 years, they can't any longer serve in the military. They would leave the military with an annuity payment based on their rank and the 11 years of service.

This recommendation brings DOD in line with other employers of choice. That is the way the employment system works where you have an annuity system in this country, and it is a very important step in maintaining a volunteer Army, from our point of view.

We also believe that only one physical exam should be performed rather than the two required now—one by each department—and that that physical should be performed by DOD. The VA then would assume all responsibility for establishing the disability rating based on that physical and for providing all disability compensation.

So you split the two responsibilities based on their expertise and the appropriate role for each department, but it is the VA that makes the disability determination. It is a much simpler system. It supports those that are transitioning between active duty and veteran status and it puts the DOD in the right frame. They provide the necessary military strength and expertise to keep our nation safe and secure. They can determine their own fitness standard for serving.

Now, obviously, there are some soldiers that the DOD will find a job for even though they have an injury—an amputation, for example—and that is really for them to work out with those soldiers. They have an interest in doing that. They would like to keep people employed. But if the decision is that that soldier, sailor, or marine should go over to the VA system, they would leave with an annuity. They would go to the VA system and get their disability rating, the disability payment, and some other things that we recommend.

The second action step out of the six is that we recommend health coverage for service members who are found unfit because of conditions that were acquired in combat, supporting combat, or preparing for combat. We believe that Congress should authorize comprehensive lifetime health care coverage and pharmacy benefits for those service members and their families through DOD's TRICARE program, and the important phrase here is "and their families."

Many of these young people can take a job, but finding a job that has benefits that will cover their families is probably a real challenge. This will change their lives if this benefit is available. We really believe it will help them to find employment because they will have a lot more choices.

Our third action step is to ask Congress to clarify the objectives for the VA disability payment system by revising the three types of payments that are currently provided to many veterans. The primary objective should be to return the disabled veteran to normal activities insofar as possible and as quickly as possible by focusing on education, training, and employment. We recommend changing the existing disability compensation payments for injured service members to include three components: Transition support, earnings loss, and quality of life.

Transition payments are, of course, temporary payments to help with expenses as disabled veterans integrate into civilian life. Veterans should receive either three months of base pay if they are returning to their communities and not participating in further rehabilitation, or an amount to cover living expenses while they are participating in education or work training programs. We also believe that the time for participating in these training programs should be expanded to 72 months for those who may need to attend part-time. Most of the students in this country are not going to school full-time. They are going to school part-time, and our veterans, our investments in these veterans ought to reflect what is happening in the larger society.

Second, earnings loss payments. We should make up for any lower earning capacity remaining after transition and after training. That is what we mean by modernizing the system. Earnings loss payments should be credited to Social Security earnings and would end when the veteran retires and claims Social Security benefits. Now, the President has a slightly different recommendation in this area.

In addition, we believe that quality of life payments should be provided to disabled veterans, and these payments are based on a more modern concept of disability, and that is our point about the current disability system. It is very old fashioned. No one except this government is paying disability payments this way any longer. Everybody has quality of life payments as part of the payment scheme. We need to take into account an injury's impact on an individual's total quality of life, independent of the ability to work. And if you look at the private sector payments, they combine these two when someone has a disability.

We also call for the disability status of veterans to be reevaluated periodically, and we see this as a positive provision that would ensure that all disabled veterans are seen by a health professional at least every few years. What we don't want is for the payment to go out of date for an individual veteran.

By simplifying and modernizing the DOD and VA disability systems, we will make the systems less confusing, we will eliminate payment inequities, and we will provide a foundation with appropriate incentives for injured veterans.

Our fourth action step asks you to authorize the VA to provide lifetime treatment for PTSD for any veteran deployed to Iraq or Afghanistan that needs such services. This presumptive eligibility for the diagnosis and treatment of PTSD should occur regardless of the length of time that has transpired since the exposure to combat events.

One of the things that we learned from talking to young veterans is that when they get out, they want to get out, and many of them are asked but they don't answer because they want to go home. They have got to be able to come back and get evaluated. We are involved in very intense urban fighting, often against civilian combatants, and many service members witness or experience acts of terrorism. Many of these service members have deployed multiple times. We need to make sure that those services are available forever for these service members.

Next, we ask Congress to strengthen support for military families. The fact that a wife has to give up whatever she is doing, whether it is school or a job, and other family members—we met husbands, we met mothers that were giving up their positions. We have asked that they be provided benefits, as well as caregiving benefits. We have asked for more intensity in the family support systems that are made available. We have asked that the Family and Medical Leave Act, which Congress has been supportive of, goes from 12 weeks to up to 6 months for a family member of a service member who has come back with a related injury and meets the eligibility requirements.

The military does a very good job of getting family members to the bedside of an injured service member. That is not the problem. It is once they get there and the kinds of services that we provide for them and what we say to them about their lifetime responsibilities in attendant care. That is our responsibility as a nation. They will do it if they must, but it seems to us fundamentally unfair that we are not providing more support to these family members, and we have made a series of recommendations.

Mr. Chairman, I believe the government can work to improve the lives of its citizens. I also believe that when we fix problems, we often add to their complexity. I, of course, had to manage the Medicare program, which is an example of that kind of complexity. Here, we have a chance to think clearly about the system and to simplify it, make it more straightforward, make it fairer, and invest resources where they will really make a difference.

Source: Shalala, Donna. "Returning Wounded Warriors." *Hearing before the Committee on Veterans' Affairs, United States Senate.* 110th Cong., 1st sess. Washington, DC: U.S. Government Printing Office, 2007, 4–33.

SHAW, ANNA HOWARD (1847–1919)

A medical and pulpit professional, the Reverend Anna Howard Shaw rallied support for gender equity. Born in England on Valentine's Day 1847, in the northeast at Newcastle-upon-Tyne, she was the daughter of seamstress Nicolas Stott and Thomas "Tom" Shaw, a flour and grain merchant. Following the Great Famine and falling grain prices after the repeal of the Corn Law in 1850, her impractical father fled bankruptcy and moved to America with his wife and children.

The family first settled in New Bedford, Massachusetts, and moved to Lawrence in 1851 before seeking free land on the prairie. In 1859, Shaw's father staked out a 360-acre forested homestead at Mecosta, Michigan, for the family residence, but he remained in New England to assist abolitionists. While his wife despaired in a dirt-floored log cabin, her children tended the frontier farm. In the early 1860s, when Tom Shaw became a casualty of the Civil War and Eleanor Shaw died in childbirth, Shaw taught school to provide cash for household supplies.

Shaw's outlook brightened when she moved to her sister's residence in Big Rapids. With training at the town high school, at age 24, she entered the Methodist ministry in 1871 in Ashton, Michigan, with a maiden sermon. Against family and social opposition, she maintained a pulpit profession and officiated at egalitarian weddings. In 1879, she encouraged other potential preachers with the speech "Women in the Ministry."

Further training from Albion College and the Boston University School of Theology required careful budgeting and rental of an attic room. The first Methodist clergywoman, Shaw sought ordination in 1880 by reformers of the Methodist Protestant Church and pastored churches in Hingham and East Dennis, Massachusetts. She completed coursework from Boston University and, in 1886, achieved a medical degree. She treated the sick in Boston slums and built consensus on temperance with the speech "Influence versus Power" (ca. 1886).

Shaw's experience with society's preferential treatment of male clerics increased her interest in women's rights. At the International Council of Women in Washington, D.C., sponsored by Susan B. Anthony and Elizabeth Cady Stanton for the National Woman Suffrage Association in March and April 1888, she encountered European and Canadian feminists. To global leaders of temperance unions, literary clubs, trade unionists, pacifists, moral purity societies, and suffragists, she preached a pro-woman sermon, "The Heavenly Vision." The sermon blamed men for refusing women admittance to their antislavery debates and prophesied a glorious day of female vindication.

Sponsored by Susan B. Anthony, Shaw joined the American Woman Suffrage Association and shaped opinions about biblical evaluation of females. Her detailed speech "God's Women" (1891) honored the leadership of Miriam, Deborah, Vashti, Rachel, and Mary. Shaw's aggressive oratory denounced racism in "Indians versus Women" (1891). In January 1892, she testified on woman suffrage to a U.S. Senate committee.

The era produced some of Shaw's most progressive insights, which she expounded in "Woman's Right to Suffrage" (1892), "The Fate of Republics" (1892), and, at the University of Minnesota, "The New Man" (1897), a witty credo of ideals shared by both genders. Throughout the decade, she earned up to $3,700 annually in fees. Her celebration of Anthony's birthday on February 15, 1900, merged a minister's reverence with an activist's gratitude. In a few short paragraphs, the tribute summarized Shaw's gracious humility before the women's rights movement commander in chief.

With uncompromising exhortations such as the one Shaw delivered in upstate New York in June 1900, she traveled by train to Seattle and expanded suffrage volunteerism from 17,000 to 200,000, an increase of 488 percent. In 1904, she accepted the presidency of the newly formed National American Woman's Suffrage Association (NAWSA). Out of pride in group unity, in Portland, Oregon, she presented "Our Ideal" (1905), a critique of the republic's style of honoring females such as Sacajawea.

After a heavy Midwestern and Pacific Coast speaking schedule of up to 35 venues per week and eight orations per day, Shaw celebrated state suffrage in 1912 with the women of Arizona, Kansas, and Oregon. The labor movement inspired "Working Women and a Living Wage" (1913), "Under What Conditions Women Work" (1913), and "Women as Office Holders" (1915). Her international oratory for women's rights took her to Sweden, Norway, Denmark, Holland, Germany, and England and to the county tax office in Delaware, Pennsylvania, to protest taxation without female representation. In June 1914, she journeyed through Algiers and Naples to Rome to attend the International Council of Women and present "Woman Suffrage Triumphant in the Eternal City" (1914).

After testimony before New Jersey assemblymen in January 1915 and a dogged refutation of anti-suffrage leaders in Alabama in April 1915, Shaw crafted a speech, "The Fundamental Principle of a Republic," for an Ogdenburg, New York, suffrage venue on June 21, 1915. In her late sixties, she compiled a memoir, *The Story of a Pioneer* (1915), a tribute to the female pioneer spirit, and rejected partisanship in "My Position on the Different Policies of the National Association and the Congressional Union" (1916). She ended her candidacy for NAWSA offices the following December.

The modernization of feminist tactics dismayed Shaw, who preferred negotiation to a militant picket of the Woodrow Wilson White House. To urge female patriotism and unity and to coordinate volunteers and resources, from April 21, 1917, she chaired the women's division of the U.S. Council of National Defense. The committee's 71,000 local units supported army recruitment and demobilization and the work of women at canning food, stitching clothes, and knitting garments for soldiers.

From experience with great-hearted female citizens, Shaw informed the U.S. Congress on January 3, 1918, that rejecting a women's rights amendment was treasonous. She delivered commentary on "Woman in Industries" (1917) and "Women Patriots" (1918) and, on February 14, 1918, joined First Lady Edith Galt Wilson in issuing an open letter to U.S. mothers urging moral purity and sacrifice. In addition to pressing the General Federation of Women's Clubs assembly in May 1918 to lobby for suffrage and prohibition, she mobilized a peace convention to rescue children from destructive militarism.

Still pursuing female enfranchisement in her last months, Shaw published the speech "What the War Meant to Women" (1919). At the May 1919 National Conference on Lynching, she declared the slaughter of Negroes barbaric. She spoke at postwar memorial services and, in June 1919, aided the promotion of the League of Nations. Hospitalized for respiratory distress after her collapse in Springfield, Illinois, she died of pneumonia in Moylan, Pennsylvania, on July 2, 1919.

See Also: Anthony, Susan B.; Stanton, Elizabeth Cady.

Reference

Franzen, Trisha. *Anna Howard Shaw: The Work of Woman Suffrage*. Champaign: University of Illinois Press, 2014.

CELEBRATION OF SUSAN B. ANTHONY'S BIRTHDAY BY ANNA HOWARD SHAW LAFAYETTE OPERA HOUSE, WASHINGTON, D.C. FEBRUARY 15, 1900

In a stirring tribute to suffrage foremother Susan B. Anthony, Anna Howard Shaw, a pulpit minister and physician, challenged women's rights advocates to continue the task set by the past generation of leaders. Her skill at recruiting volunteers increased female canvassing worldwide by 488 percent. Ironically, her contribution to the suffrage issue ended in 1919 within months of success. On August 18, 1920, U.S. women obtained full citizenship with passage of the Nineteenth Amendment.

A little over a hundred years ago there came men who told us what freedom is and what freemen may become. Later women with the same love of it in their hearts said, "There is no sex in freedom. Whatever it makes possible for men it will make possible for women." A few of these daring souls went forth to blaze the path. Gradually the sunlight of freedom shone in their faces and they encouraged others to follow. They went slowly for the way was hard. They must make the path and it was a weary task. Sometimes darkness settled over them and they must grope their way. Mott, Stanton, Stone, Anthony—not one retraced her footsteps. The two who are left still stand on the summit, great, glorious figures. We ask, "Is the way difficult?" They answer, "Yes, but the sun shines on us and in the valley they know nothing of its glory. Their cry we hear and are calling back to those who are still in the valley."

"Leader, comrade, friend, no name can express what you are to us. You might have led us as commander, and we might have followed and obeyed, but there still might have been wanting the divine force of unchanging love. We look up to the sunlight where you stand and say, "We are coming." When we shall be fourscore we shall still be calling to you, "We are coming," for you will still be beckoning us on as you climb still loftier heights. Souls like yours can never rest in all the eternities of God.

Source: Shaw, Anna Howard. "Celebration of Susan B. Anthony's Birthday." In *The History of Woman Suffrage*. Vol. IV (403–404). Indianapolis: Hollenbeck Press, 1902.

SILKO, LESLIE MARMON (1948–)

Laguna storyteller, poet, and conservationist Leslie Marmon Silko addresses postcolonial struggles of Native Americans and mixed-blood peoples as well as the homeless and estranged. Born on March 5, 1948, in Albuquerque, New Mexico, to home economics teacher and postmaster Mary Virginia Lee and Laguna photographer and tribal council treasurer Leland "Lee" Howard Marmon, a veteran of World War II, she claims a multiracial heritage. In infancy, she lived with paternal grandparents, Lillie Stagner and Hank Marmon, at the old stucco station of the Atchison, Topeka, and Santa Fe Railroad.

Silko grew up apart from Laguna society near the San José River at the border of the Marmon ancestral home but absorbed the litany of 8,000 years of Pueblo Indian history, animal fables, trickster lore, and goddess myths of Corn Woman and Spider Woman, the creator. She learned about her Cherokee ancestry and witnessed the Navajo and Pueblo blood purification ceremony that cleansed veterans returning from World War II. She relished the outdoors, learned to shoot a rifle, and tended to feeding goats and bringing in water, coal, and firewood for 85-year-old Grandma A-mooh, who lived next door.

At age five, Silko entered the K–4 elementary school that the Bureau of Indian Affairs operated in Laguna. At faculty insistence, she stopped speaking native, but home training in Pueblo mythology filled her with reverence for history, science, and pueblo philosophy. At the post office and Laguna Trading Post run by her father, she enjoyed community anecdotes that valued each resident. From adult conversation, she monitored the Laguna class action land reclamation suit before the U.S. Court of Indian Claims.

At the Manzano Day School, a Catholic academy in Albuquerque, Silko endured isolation from non-native children but flourished at writing tales using the week's list of spelling words. At age 13, she left the reservation to attend Highland High School, a Catholic boarding academy, and read William Faulkner, Edgar

Allan Poe, John Steinbeck, and transcendental philosopher Margaret Fuller. In 1966, Silko regretted the divorce of her father from Virginia, who suffered from alcoholism.

A Beginning Writer

After marriage to Richard C. "Dick" Chapman, a graduate student in archeology at the University of New Mexico, Silko found the art department too Eurocentric and chose instead to major in creative writing. As a sophomore, she gave birth to Robert William Chapman and left her husband. On a United Daughters of the Confederacy scholarship, in 1967, she majored in English and anthropology and began composing short fiction and nonfiction. In 1969, she graduated magna cum laude from the honors program and published "Tony's Story" in the campus literary magazine and "The Man to Send Rain Clouds" in the *New Mexico Quarterly.*

While the Laguna settled a lawsuit, Leslie returned to the university to enroll in the Anglo-American legal system and sought a graduate degree in creative writing. After marriage in 1970 to Alaskan hunter and attorney John R. Silko, she resided at the ancestral Gunn house at New Laguna and raised livestock. She taught at Navajo Community College in Chinle, Arizona, for two years and submitted to the *Chicago Review* a classic husband-wife story, "Lullaby" (1974), which won a Discover Grant from the National Endowment for the Arts.

During a second pregnancy, Silko taught English and creative writing. After the birth of son Cazimir, she toned her figure through ballet, jazz, and modern kinetics. At Ketchikan Creek, Alaska, among Haida and Tlingit, she battled homesickness by refining a masterwork, *Ceremony,* a psychological novel filled with the angst of dysfunctional veterans of the Pacific half of World War II. Through summarizing the chant and expiation of kiva ritual that brings peace to Tayo, the protagonist, she exorcised her own longing for Laguna.

From publication of "A Geronimo Story," "Yellow Woman," and *Laguna Woman: Poems* (1974), Silko earned a *Chicago Review* poetry commendation, a National Endowment for the Arts fellowship, and recognition as a Pueblo wisewoman. At Bethel Middle School near the Bering Sea, she served as artist in residence among the Yupik, a native people whom she came to love and admire. For their understanding, she lectured on the holistic style of Indian oral tradition, which incorporates stories within stories. In 1975, she returned to Laguna and won more awards for short fiction and verse.

On staff at the Navajo Indian Reservation at Chinle in 1976, Silko recovered from divorce by photographing desert topography and skies. She won a 1977 Pushcart Prize for Poetry and oversaw publication of *Ceremony.* For the film *Running on the Edge of the Rainbow* (1982), shot in Tucson, she posed as a Laguna story keeper, humorist, and sage. An ectopic pregnancy in late 1977 required emergency surgery to halt bleeding.

A Renewed Outlook

While engaging in a legal custody battle for her sons, in January 1978, Silko began taking better care of herself at her desert property northwest of Tucson, Arizona. Outdoors, she communed along a sandy arroyo with birds, reptiles, and mammals and studied prophecies, constellations, and grinding stones, relics of the ancestral Hohokam, Papago, and Yaqui. On staff at the University of Arizona, she taught English. Simultaneously, she developed a literary friendship with poet James Wright in Misquamicut, Rhode Island. For an audience in Oslo, Norway, she composed the speech "Opening Up the Canon" (1979), which described the spider web style of narrative among Pueblo storytellers that survives from traditional oral lessons.

Silko spoke at Vassar College and for 10 weeks at the University of Washington in Seattle, where she taught short fiction. In September, she addressed the English Institute on Native America at Harvard and, in free moments, wrote a fool tale, "Coyote Sits with a Full House in His Hand" (1980). While supporting her mother and sons, she remained afloat financially by writing legal papers, publishing in *Mother Jones*, and scripting a mythic film, *Arrowboy and the Witches*.

For layering Acoma, Apache, Hopi, Navajo, and Sioux legend, song, genealogy, and verse in the miscellany *Storyteller* (1981), Silko earned a MacArthur Foundation Prize. In withdrawal from the literary milieu, she researched fragmentary prophecies of anticolonial retribution for *Almanac of the Dead* and filmed a video of *Running on the Edge of the Rainbow: Laguna Stories and Poems*. For the 1984 symposium of the Chinese Writers Association at the University of California at Los Angeles, she shared a platform with writers Allen Ginsberg, William Least Heat Moon, and Toni Morrison.

A promising period awarded Silko with a 1986 *Boston Globe* prize and, in 1989, identification by the New Mexico Humanities Council as a Living Cultural Treasure. She earned respect for spray-painting a satiric snake on her office exterior and for advocating conservation of the Colorado River in *A River Too Far: The Past and Future of the Arid West* (1991). She composed essays for *American Indian Quarterly* and accepted the 1992 Lila Wallace–Reader's Digest Writers' Award for merit and commitment. In a speech for a Returning the Gift festival at the University of Oklahoma in Norman, she predicted a folk renaissance moving north from Central America.

Silko elided interracial narrative in *Yellow Woman* (1993), which won her a distinguished lectureship in women's studies at the University of California at Los Angeles. From receipt of the 1994 Wordcraft Circle of Native Writers and

Storytellers Lifetime Achievement citation, she progressed in spring 1995 to a symposium at Dartmouth College with commentary on "The Writer as Activist." Publication of the feminist novel *Gardens in the Dunes* (1998) brought her a choice of public speeches and festivals, an Endowed Chair in Creative Writing at Texas State University at San Marcos, and a Lannan Literary Award for Fiction for exceptional writing.

During National Women's History Month in 2004, Silko entered the list of Women Inspiring Hope and Possibility. Over 2005–2006, she received the American Indian Festival of Words Author Award from the Tulsa Library Trust, a writing commendation from Mexico, and the Spirit of the West Award. In 2007–2008, she addressed the National Museum of the American Indian in Washington, D.C., and lectured at West Virginia University.

In 2009 at the Heard Museum in Phoenix, Silko spoke on "Indigenous Land, Culture, and Community," which preceded a reading at Arizona State University at Hoteville on October 8 from her next work, *The Turquoise Ledge: A Memoir* (2010) and a 2010 writing conference at the Colorado State University in Denver. More oratory at Macondo Nuevo Mundo anticipated the speech "On Conflict: Peace and War" at Syracuse University. From the Chicago Humanities Festival, she migrated to the Library Foundation of Los Angeles. In 2011, she issued the electronic novel *Oceanstory*, which opens on the Tohono O'Odom reverence for the Gulf of California.

See Also: Morrison, Toni.

Reference

Snodgrass, Mary Ellen. *Leslie Marmon Silko: A Literary Companion.* Jefferson, NC: McFarland, 2011.

SMITH, MARGARET CHASE (1897–1995)

A role model of the female politician, Margaret Madeline Chase Smith launched a clear, uninhibited rebuttal of the Second Red Scare of Senator Joseph McCarthy. A New Englander from Skowhegan, Maine, she was born on December 14, 1897, to Carrie Matilda Morin (or Murray), a shoemaker, Coburn Hotel waitress, and clerk at Green Brothers Five and Dime, and barber George Emery Chase. In girlhood, she shaved men at the barbershop after grade school classes at Lincoln and Garfield Elementary.

While clerking at Green Brothers Five and Dime, placing calls for the Skowhegan Telephone Company, and aiding the tax assessor, Smith completed two years of classical studies and two of clerical studies at Skowhegan High School and captained the basketball team. Following enrollment in Colby College at Waterville, Maine, her postgraduation jobs began with teaching at the one-room Pitts School, coaching basketball, selling accounts for Maine Telephone and Telegraph, and, in 1919, writing and office management for the Skowhegan weekly *Independent Reporter.*

The presidency of the Business and Professional Women's Club gave Smith a taste of women's civic organization. Employment in waste management and clerical duties at the Cummings woolen mill in 1928 preceded her marriage on May 14, 1930, to politician and newspaper owner Clyde Harold Smith. From their home overlooking the Kennebec River, she electioneered for the state Republican Party.

During Franklin D. Roosevelt's first presidency, in 1937, Clyde's successful run for the U.S. Congress introduced Smith to Washington, D.C. In October 1938, she addressed "The Experiences of a Congressman's Wife in Washington" to Kennebec County Republican women curious about her role in her husband's first term of office. In a rise from clerk to office holder, she followed Clyde's urging that she represent Maine in both the U.S. House and Senate. In spring 1940, she replaced him in the legislature after his fatal heart attack on April 8 and won four successive elections without accepting campaign contributions.

Smith introduced herself with an initial address on daycare at public nurseries but moved on to more aggressive concerns with support for the draft, increased military spending, and arming of the U.S. Merchant Marines. Among Maine isolationists, her lone voice echoed the president's enthusiasm on March 11, 1941, for passage of the Lend-Lease Act. In 1942, she championed the creation of three non-nursing female units—the WAVES (Women Accepted for Volunteer Emergency Service), Coast Guard SPARS, and Women Marines.

Because of constituent support for shipbuilding jobs in Maine, in a second legislative campaign, Smith won nearly 70 percent of the ballots. Her enthusiasm for issues of national security during World War II preceded appointment in 1943 to the House Naval Affairs Committee. In addition to studies of naval base growth and the military draft, she investigated vice and prostitution at major ports. At the height of the war in the Pacific in 1944, she surveyed congestion at naval bases, becoming the only civilian female to travel by naval ship to combat zones. In 1946, the House Armed Services Committee elected her to a branch overseeing military hospitals and medicine.

On September 13, 1948, when Smith became the first woman to have served in both chambers of the U.S. Congress, she mounted opposition to the House Un-American Activities Committee (HUAC), a congressional effort to identify subversive elements and their propaganda. Her "Declaration of Conscience," delivered to a congressional hearing on June 1, 1950, shamed male senators who protected their political careers by allowing Joseph McCarthy's "Commie" witch hunt to attack citizens in violation of First Amendment rights. Until 1954, she retained influence by issuing a syndicated column, *Washington and You*, by advocating abolition of the Electoral College, and by scolding members of congress for chronic absenteeism.

Smith's run for the U.S. presidency in 1964 called for a carefully crafted oration defending women in high public office. The failed campaign preceded her last senatorial term, during which she raised 16 questions in a September 9, 1963, address about the advisability of a nuclear test ban treaty. On May 9, 1970, she defended President Richard Nixon's escalation of the Vietnam conflict into neutral Cambodia. On June 1, 1970, her anti-hippie speech, "Second Declaration of Conscience," lambasted the anarchy of campus rioting and protests of war in Southeast Asia.

Defeat for reelection to the Senate in 1972 left Smith free to build the Margaret Chase Smith Library and to lecture at the Skowhegan junior college. In July 1989, President George H.W. Bush presented her the Medal of Freedom. Comatose from stroke, she died on May 29, 1995, in her hometown.

Reference

Crouse, Eric R. *An American Stand: Senator Margaret Chase Smith and the Communist Menace*. Lanham, MD: Lexington Books, 2010.

DECLARATION OF CONSCIENCE BY MARGARET CHASE SMITH U.S. CONGRESSIONAL HEARING, WASHINGTON, D.C. JUNE 1, 1950

A role model of the female politician, Margaret Chase Smith aimed a clear, uninhibited oration at the red baiting of demagogue Joseph McCarthy. Without naming the senator, she charged the Senate with exacerbating Cold War tensions by heightening baseless terrors of Communist infiltration. The spread of rumor, innuendo, and character assassination preceded a Senate censure of McCarthy in 1954 and his death from alcoholism in 1957. Smith's 15-minute speech retained fame for reasserting the Bill of Rights against a virulent smear campaign based on bigotry and hate. In 1964, she ran unsuccessfully for president.

Mr. President:

I would like to speak briefly and simply about a serious national condition. It is a national feeling of fear and frustration that could result in national suicide and the end of everything that we Americans hold dear. It is a condition that comes from the lack of effective leadership in either the Legislative Branch or the Executive Branch of our Government.

That leadership is so lacking that serious and responsible proposals are being made that national advisory commissions be appointed to provide such critically needed leadership.

I speak as briefly as possible because too much harm has already been done with irresponsible words of bitterness and selfish political opportunism. I speak as simply as possible because the issue is too great to be obscured by eloquence. I speak simply and briefly in the hope that my words will be taken to heart.

I speak as a Republican, I speak as a woman. I speak as a United States Senator. I speak as an American.

The United States Senate has long enjoyed worldwide respect as the greatest deliberative body in the world. But recently that deliberative character has too often been debased to the level of a forum of hate and character assassination sheltered by the shield of congressional immunity.

It is ironic that we Senators can in debate in the Senate directly or indirectly, by any form of words impute to any American, who is not a Senator, any conduct or motive unworthy or unbecoming an American—and without that non-Senator American having any legal redress against us—yet if we say the same thing in the Senate about our colleagues we can be stopped on the grounds of being out of order.

It is strange that we can verbally attack anyone else without restraint and with full protection and yet we hold ourselves above the same type of criticism here on the Senate Floor. Surely the United States Senate is big enough to take self-criticism and self-appraisal. Surely we should be able to take the same kind of character attacks that we dish out to outsiders.

I think that it is high time for the United States Senate and its members to do some soul searching—for us to weigh our consciences—on the manner in which we are performing our duty to the people of America—on the manner in which we are using or abusing our individual powers and privileges.

I think that it is high time that we remembered that we have sworn to uphold and defend the Constitution. I think that it is high time that we remembered that the Constitution, as amended, speaks not only of the freedom of speech but also of trial by jury instead of trial by accusation.

Whether it be a criminal prosecution in court or a character prosecution in the Senate, there is little practical distinction when the life of a person has been ruined.

Those of us who shout the loudest about Americanism in making character assassinations are all too frequently those who, by our own words and acts, ignore some of the basic principles of Americanism—

The right to criticize;
The right to hold unpopular beliefs;
The right to protest;
The right of independent thought.

The exercise of these rights should not cost one single American citizen his reputation or his right to a livelihood nor should he be in danger of losing his reputation or livelihood merely because he happens to know someone who holds unpopular beliefs. Who of us doesn't? Otherwise none of us could call our souls our own. Otherwise thought control would have set in.

The American people are sick and tired of being afraid to speak their minds lest they be politically smeared as "Communists" or "Fascists" by their opponents. Freedom of speech is not what it used to be in America. It has been so abused by some that it is not exercised by others. The American people are sick and tired of seeing innocent people smeared and guilty people whitewashed. But there have been enough proved cases to cause nationwide distrust and strong suspicion that there may be something to the unproved, sensational accusations.

As a Republican, I say to my colleagues on this side of the aisle that the Republican Party faces a challenge today that is not unlike the challenge that it faced back in Lincoln's day. The Republican Party so successfully met that challenge that it emerged from the Civil War as the champion of a united nation—in addition to being a party that unrelentingly fought loose spending and loose programs.

Today our country is being psychologically divided by the confusion and the suspicions that are bred in the United States Senate to spread like cancerous tentacles of "know nothing, suspect everything" attitudes. Today we have a Democratic Administration that has developed a mania for loose spending and loose programs. History is repeating itself—and the Republican Party again has the opportunity to emerge as the champion of unity and prudence.

The record of the present Democratic Administration has provided us with sufficient campaign issues without the necessity of resorting to political smears. America is rapidly losing its position as leader of the world simply because the Democratic Administration has pitifully failed to provide effective leadership.

The Democratic Administration has completely confused the American people by its daily contradictory grave warnings and optimistic assurances—that show the people that our Democratic Administration has no idea of where it is going.

The Democratic Administration has greatly lost the confidence of the American people by its complacency to the threat of Communism here at home and the leak of vital secrets to Russia through key officials of the Democratic Administration. There are enough proved cases to make this point without diluting our criticism with unproved charges.

Surely these are sufficient reasons to make it clear to the American people that it is time for a change and that a Republican victory is necessary to the security of this country. Surely it is clear that this nation will continue to suffer as long as it is governed by the present ineffective Democratic Administration.

Yet to displace it with a Republican regime embracing a philosophy that lacks political integrity or intellectual honesty would prove equally disastrous to this nation. The nation sorely needs a Republican victory. But I don't want to see the Republican Party ride to political victory on the Four Horsemen of Calumny—Fear, Ignorance, Bigotry and Smear.

I doubt if the Republican Party could—simply because I don't believe the American people will uphold any political party that puts political exploitation above national interest. Surely we Republicans aren't that desperate for victory.

I don't want to see the Republican Party win that way. While it might be a fleeting victory for the Republican Party, it would be a more lasting defeat for the American people. Surely it would ultimately be suicide for the Republican Party and the two-party system that has protected our American liberties from the dictatorship of a one-party system.

As members of the Minority Party, we do not have the primary authority to formulate the policy of our Government. But we do have the responsibility of rendering constructive criticism, of clarifying issues, of allaying fears by acting as responsible citizens.

As a woman, I wonder how the mothers, wives, sisters, and daughters feel about the way in which members of their families have been politically mangled in Senate debate—and I use the word "debate" advisedly.

As a United States Senator, I am not proud of the way in which the Senate has been made a publicity platform for irresponsible sensationalism. I am not proud of the reckless abandon in which unproved charges have been hurled from this side of the aisle. I am not proud of the obviously staged, undignified countercharges that have been attempted in retaliation from the other side of the aisle.

I don't like the way the Senate has been made a rendezvous for vilification, for selfish political gain at the sacrifice of individual reputations and national unity. I am not proud of the way we smear outsiders from the floor of the Senate and hide behind the cloak of congressional immunity and still place ourselves beyond criticism on the floor of the Senate.

As an American, I am shocked at the way Republicans and Democrats alike are playing directly into the Communist design of "confuse, divide and conquer." As an American, I don't want a Democratic Administration "whitewash" or "cover up" any more than I want a Republican smear or witch hunt.

As an American, I condemn a Republican "Fascist" just as much as I condemn a Democrat "Communist." I condemn a Democrat "Fascist" just as much as I condemn a Republican "Communist." They are equally dangerous to you and me and to our country. As an American, I want to see our nation recapture the strength and unity it once had when we fought the enemy instead of ourselves.

It is with these thoughts I have drafted what I call a "Declaration of Conscience." I am gratified that Senator [Charles W.] Tobey, Senator [George D.] Aiken, Senator [Wayne L.] Morse, Senator [Irving] Ives, Senator [Edward J.] Thye and Senator [Robert C.] Hendrickson, have concurred in that declaration and have authorized me to announce their concurrence.

Source: Smith, Margaret Chase. "A Declaration of Conscience." *Congressional Record, Senate.* 81st Cong., 2d sess. Washington, DC: U.S. Government Printing Office, 1950, 7894–7895.

SNOWE, OLYMPIA (1947–)

An accomplished unifier of thinkers and planners, first Greek-American U.S. congresswoman and centrist Republican Olympia Jean Bouchles Snowe maintains a record for advocating compromise and citizen needs over party dogma. She was born in Augusta, Maine, on February 21, 1947, to Georgia Goranites and George John Bouchles, a native of Mytilene, Greece. In 1955, Snowe lost her mother to breast cancer; the following year, her father died of cardiac disease. She lived with a maternal aunt and uncle in Auburn, Maine. In 1956, she received Greek Orthodox training at St. Basil's Academy, a home for needy children in Garrison, New York. After graduating from Edward Little High School, in 1969, she completed a political science degree from the University of Maine at Orono.

At age 22, Snowe wed state legislator Peter Trafton Snowe. She served the voter registration board and, during the Watergate investigation in 1972, staffed the office of U.S. Congressman William Cohen, a proponent of the impeachment of President Richard Nixon. Following her husband's death in 1973, Snowe won election to his seat in the Maine House of Representatives. Unlike hard-line Republicans, she maintained pro-choice tenets and supported gay rights and advanced to the State Senate in 1976.

Snowe became the first Greek-American U.S. congresswoman in 1978, and at age 31, the youngest to represent the Republican Party. In 18 years as a legislator, she influenced the House Select Committee on Aging and the Subcommittee on Human Services, two concentrations that inspired a devotion to health care. After establishing identity as an astute, empathetic politician, in February 1989, she wed Governor John McKernan Jr. As first lady, she settled across the street from the state legislative building at Blaine House, Maine's executive mansion. She achieved two aims, the Medical Leave Act and the 1991 Civil Rights Act, which banned bias against women in the workplace.

The first American female to win election to both houses of state and federal legislature, in 1994, Snowe held office in the U.S. Senate for 18 years. She gained support by rejecting partisan politics. For a graduation speech to the John F. Kennedy School of Government on June 3, 1997, she honored Harvard for inventing the American higher education system and for readying students for public service. In response to Republican dismay, she reminded the party that fiscal responsibility outweighed wrangling over abortion, homosexuality, and other social issues in importance to citizens. She promoted medical treatment for the uninsured and backed flexible, affordable health benefits, reduced regulations and taxes, and fair distribution of government contracts.

In February 1999, Snowe pressed for the impeachment of President Bill Clinton for obstruction of justice and perjury concerning his relationship with Monica Lewinsky. In 1999, Snowe voted for military action to restore order in Kosovo. Additional commitment to women's needs marked her role as co-chair of the Congressional Caucus on Women's Issues with Patricia Schroeder and the founding of the Office of Women's Health. Snowe led the drive for equal representation of women in pharmaceutical trials, an effort that balanced results from male and female patients on medicines for asthma, heart disease, and arthritis.

Snowe bucked Republican Party trends by advocating stronger gun control. She defied privatization of Social Security and halved the 2003 tax-cut initiatives of George W. Bush. She drafted a proposal to limit citizen surveillance by the National Security Administration and introduced the 2006 Internet Freedom Preservation Act. In 2006, *Time* magazine listed her among the top 10 U.S. senators. After her proposal of a Global Warming Reduction Act in February 2007, observers named her a possible presidential candidate in 2008.

Because of high-pressure Tea Party tactics and the inaction of a contentious U.S. Congress, Snowe retired from politics on February 28, 2012, earning the admiration of President Barack Obama. She continued to stump for presidential candidate Mitt Romney and voiced her approval of gay marriage. To the American Geophysical Union's fall assembly in San Francisco on December 9, 2013, she denounced the Republican failure to adopt green policies to limit carbon dioxide emission and to debate climate change.

In retirement, Snowe continues speaking, urging consensus and less polarization in Congress. She voiced despair at congressional dysfunction and the decline of the middle class in a C-SPAN panel discussion in 2014. In January 2016, Republicans floated support for Snowe during the 2016 presidential campaign.

See Also: Schroeder, Patricia; Smith, Margaret Chase.

Reference

Snowe, Olympia. *Fighting for Common Ground: How We Can Fix the Stalemate in Congress.* New York: Weinstein Books, 2013.

SPEECH TO THE JOHN F. KENNEDY SCHOOL OF GOVERNMENT (EXCERPT) BY SENATOR OLYMPIA SNOWE CAMBRIDGE, MASSACHUSETTS JUNE 3, 1997

An accomplished unifier of thinkers and planners, centrist Republican Olympia Snowe took pride in advocacy of compromise and citizen needs over party dogma. To a class of Harvard graduates, she promoted concepts of alliance and respect over partisan squabbling.

. . . There was a time in America when society accepted deadbeat dads, and child support was considered a woman's problem. There was a time in America when a husband could cancel his wife's pension without her knowledge. There was a time in America when economic equality pertained only to equality among men. There was a time in America when women's health was a missing page in America's medical textbooks, and when women were systematically excluded from clinical medical study trials that were funded by the National Institutes of Health, the nation's, if not the world's, premier research facility.

Some of you may remember the famous medical study on breast cancer that examined, you guessed it, hundreds of men. Or, what about the federally funded study involving 22,000 male physicians which examined the ability of aspirin to prevent heart attacks. Apparently, someone forgot that heart disease is the leading cause of death among women.

For years, scientists treated over half the population, women, as anomalies. These scientists complained that health research could endanger, or would be affected by women's reproductive systems. Well, it seems to me that women have been bearing children for quite some time now, and are likely to continue doing so in the future. Medical research, rather than ignoring that fact as an inconvenience, should work to accommodate it.

As I've often said, their attitude seemed to mirror Henry Higgins in "My Fair Lady" when he lamented, "Why can't a woman be more like a man?"

Outraged by these studies, and others like them, as co-chairs of the Women's Caucus, Congresswoman Pat Schroeder and I asked the General Accounting Office in 1989 to document inequities in medical research at the National Institutes of Health. The findings of these GAO studies spurred the Caucus to introduce its first Women's Health Equity Act—landmark legislation on women's health.

Under our leadership, we secured more funding and attracted more attention to breast cancer, osteoporosis, ovarian and cervical cancer research. It is now required that women be included in vital drug and medical trials where once they were excluded. And my own legislation created an Office of Women's Health Research at the National Institutes of Health, where once also there was none.

This was the Augusta model all over again. This was a case study of legislators reaching across party lines to research, consider, negotiate, and then pass legislation addressing a critical policy issue.

Those of us who led the charge for these women's issues did not agree on everything. But we shared a common vision on the needs of women. And we did not allow our differing views on abortion, or our partisan affiliations, to stand in our way.

Most of all, the political dynamic of the Caucus was governance from the center.

Today the political dynamic is different. And the question, "Can we govern?" is entirely appropriate. Indeed, it is pressing.

That's because our current system seems so often infused by a coarse partisanship, a raw ideology, a podium-thumping belligerence. The political dynamic confronting the American political system today is the ongoing erosion of bipartisanship, civility and cooperation.

In many instances, political leaders have failed to seek compromise and, instead, have approached politics as an all or nothing proposition where there are only two outcomes: a scorched earth victory for one side, or political stagnation. We've seen that the sensible center, the moderate center, the center of American politics where most Americans reside and where both political parties meet, has dissipated. Surely, our parties will not always agree on everything. That's understandable and even healthy. But, we need not always disagree.

This erosion of the center has been exacerbated, of course, by the retirement from the Senate of some of our nation's best consensus-forging leaders. . . .

Now, this may sound simplistic and obvious, but democratic (that's with a small "d") government works well only when political leaders work together. And when they don't, the dissension is palpable, painful, and it grinds down the gears of effective government.

It should not be surprising, then, that such constant friction deadens the civic impulse. Even as Americans still largely maintain faith in themselves, after years of highly partisan government and unresponsive government, they no longer trust the ability of Congress to address their concerns, or the problems of our nation, or to do the right thing.

A survey by the Roper Center revealed that 42 percent of Americans surveyed said they had "hardly any confidence" in the executive branch of government. And even a higher percentage, 43 percent, felt this way about Congress. And a full three-quarters of the American people recently surveyed by the Harris Poll reported that they believed that people in Washington are out of touch with the rest of the country.

Equally disturbing is the conclusion of a Heinz Foundation Democracy Project Study, which said, "Our youngest citizens are dropouts from the political process, with only 28 percent of the 18 to 24 year-olds bothering to vote in the 1996 election." According to this survey, half believe that politicians don't talk about the issues that are relevant to their lives.

The Pew Research Center notes that in their extensive surveys, they find that political activity is less popular than other kinds of civic activity. An interesting point, given that their own research shows that civic activity, as a whole, has increased.

These glimpses of public opinion are a tragic indictment of our system—as though like art reflecting life, society is beginning to reflect our politics.

I'm reminded of the late Edward Everett Hale, a former Senate Chaplain, who was once asked if he prayed for members of the U.S. Senate, and he responded, "No, I look at the Senators and pray for the country."

But, despite the divisions that exist, the center can hold, and even today sometimes does.

Lest we think differently, we should look at last year's passage of welfare reform, where the system very clearly did work.

When the Senate began debating the welfare reform bill in September of 1995, it was believed by many to be an exercise in futility. But, in small groups, members of Congress, sensing the exhaustion and despair of a welfare system begun with the best of intentions, focused on the first major overhaul since the Great Society. . . .

Ultimately, this became the foundation for the final reform package signed into law by the President. It was a lesson well learned, because we passed the Kassebaum-Kennedy health care reform package as well as an increase in the minimum wage soon thereafter. . . .

I can honestly say that the spirit of accomplishment lives on today—that there are plenty of us in Congress who are willing to work together across the sometimes clear and sometimes vague political party lines that separate us. What we need, however, is the leadership to bring this spirit to life.

That means leaders at both ends of Pennsylvania Avenue and on both sides of the aisle making their political points but ultimately coming together for the common good to meet our country's challenges. Simply put, it is time for our leaders to lead—and to demonstrate that their budget agreement was the beginning of a trend and not an aberration. We need to devote less energy to judging and criticizing each other, and more to forging consensus and understanding.

We live in a nation—the Great Experiment—that was born because it came together, rose up, and threw off, at the time, the largest standing army in the world. A nation where neither the Western frontier, nor the frontier of space could contain our people. Where the scourge of polio and yellow fever could not survive the onslaught of medical and scientific expertise. Where the world has turned for leadership during the torments of this century.

Every time—every single time—our people and our national leadership have responded assertively, convincingly, decisively. This is the legacy we have inherited.

The good news is that all of you here today will have the opportunity to influence how this noble mission plays out. So, as we move forward, let's promise ourselves one thing: that this new chapter in America's history will be written together with an optimism that America's greatness will not now—will not ever—be compromised.

I began by asking, "Can we govern?"

My answer is: we can—as long as we do not lose sight of the two enduring elements—indeed the two testaments—to our remarkable resolve as a people—a notion of the public good combined with the leadership to attain that public good.

And so we've come full circle. More than three decades ago, John F. Kennedy issued forth a summons: "It is a task of every generation," he said, "to build a road for the next generation."

This credo must be the yardstick by which we measure our success. We, the leaders of today, owe you—the leaders of tomorrow—nothing less.

Source: Snowe, Olympia. "Speech to the John F. Kennedy School of Government." June 3, 1997. Used by permission of Olympia J. Snowe, Former United States Senator, Senior Fellow, Bipartisan Policy Center.

SOUTHBY, JANET (1943–)

A veteran of combat nursing and proponent of public health, Janet Sue Rexrode "Jan" Southby expressed the somber thoughts of nurses who treated American casualties of the Vietnam War. A native West Virginian, she was born to Mary Simmons and Andrew Rexrode, a carpenter and farmer, in Burlington on August 13, 1943.

Southby dedicated herself to 4-H Club work and graduated from Keyser High School. During medical training at Winchester Memorial Hospital in Winchester, Virginia, she earned academic commendation. Influenced by President John F. Kennedy's call to patriotic service, she responded to a recruiter's patriotism by signing up in September 1963 for the Army Student Nurse Program. While working in pediatrics at Walter Reed Army Hospital in Bethesda, Maryland, in 1965, she entered the Army Nurse Corps at age 21 as a second lieutenant.

When American ground forces increased in number in July 1965 under the presidential command of Lyndon B. Johnson, Southby awaited deployment to Vietnam while completing four weeks of staging at Fort Bliss, Texas. In Oakland Harbor on August 13, 1965, she and her fellow nurses boarded the troop ship U.S.N.S.

Barrett as a unit for an 18-day voyage to the front. They reached Vietnam and pushed north to the fishing port of Qui Nhon to staff an orthopedic team at the 85th Evacuation Hospital, a mix of tents and Quonset huts.

The fortuitous arrival preceded the Battle of Ia Drang Valley on November 17, when the First Battalion, Seventh Cavalry engaged the North Vietnamese at an ambush. The lopsided victory that killed half of Company C introduced Southby to frontline rescue and recovery by helicopter and to clinical responsibility and pragmatism. By flashlight, beside a cot on a dirt floor, she received on-the-job training in phlebotomy. As the bed space increased 50 percent from 400 to 600, the unit's record of 96 deaths amid 7,234 surgical patients and 16 losses out of 7,589 medical admissions (largely for malaria) received compliments from General William Westmoreland.

Southby returned to Walter Reed in August 1966 as head nurse of a pediatric ward. During temporary recruiting duty in Raleigh-Durham, North Carolina, she encountered antimilitary demonstrations. One year later, she mustered out with the rank of captain.

After earning a baccalaureate at the University of Pittsburgh, Southby returned to the Army Nurse Corps and completed a master's degree at the University of Maryland. From February 1971 to August 1976, she taught pediatric and community nursing at Walter Reed and achieved the title of assistant professor. In September 1973, she volunteered for duty at the White House as the first woman senior military social aide and remained through the Nixon, Ford, and Carter administrations.

Southby's dissertation at the Catholic University of America focused on primary care nurse practitioners. She earned a doctoral degree, married Australian Richard McK. F. Southby—an Australian public health physician formerly on staff at the Royal Children's Hospital in Melbourne—and won the Federal Nursing Service Award in 1979.

As chief of nursing research at Walter Reed, from 1979 to 1982, Southby spearheaded inquiries and encouraged submission of articles to refereed journals and publication of a newsletter reporting army nursing research accomplishments. She received the DAR citation as Army Nurse of the Year 1982 and appointment as consultant for nursing research to the Surgeon General, U.S. Army.

Southby's assignments took her to the 121st Evacuation Hospital in San Francisco in 1982 and the 18th Medical Command in Yongsan, Korea, in 1983 as a medical educator. She advised the staff of Surgeon General C. Everett Koop from 1985 to 1986. She received promotion to the chief of professional development of career nurses at the support agency in Falls Church, Virginia, in 1986, when she gained membership in the Order of Military Medical Merit.

For fourteen months in 1987 and 1988, Southby advised the National Institutes of Health in Bethesda on classifying patient testing and monitoring systems. After indoctrination in 1988, at the Command and General Staff College at Fort Leavenworth, Kansas, she launched a three-year stint as head nurse at the hospital in Fort

Belvoir, Virginia. In 1992, she continued her education at the Interagency Institute for Federal Health Care and headed nursing administration at Walter Reed. The following year, she studied at the U.S. Army War College and, on September 3, addressed an Australian military conference in Sydney on health care.

Under an umbrella at the Vietnam Veterans Memorial in Washington on May 27, 1996, Southby delivered a brief but eloquent tribute to the forgotten veterans. She acclaimed the 165,000 American women who served and mourned eight who died in the effort, including two from her division. She ennobled the site of the Vietnam Women's Memorial as a sacred source of healing for veterans recovering from scars to body and spirit caused by a harrowing historical era. She closed the encomium with the refrain from the ballad, "We Were There." She retired with 31 years of active federal service at the end of that year.

Reference

Beam, T. E., and L. R. Sparacino, eds. *Military Medical Ethics*. Lounsbury, DE: Bellamy Reference Editions, 2003.

MEMORIAL DAY ADDRESS BY JANET SOUTHBY VIETNAM VETERANS MEMORIAL, WASHINGTON, D.C. MAY 27, 1996

A veteran of combat nursing and chief nurse at Walter Reed Army Medical Center, Janet Southby, Colonel, U.S. Army, expressed the somber thoughts of nurses who treated American casualties of the Vietnam War. Her brief remarks recalled that war comes at a price often borne by the younger generation.

It's my distinct honor and privilege to represent the women who served during the Vietnam Era at this Memorial Day ceremony. Ever since the Civil War, Americans have paused in remembrance each year to pay respect to lost lives, especially to honor those members of the armed forces who have given their lives to their country.

This ceremony pays special tribute to more than 58,000 men and women whose names are etched on the Wall and others who gave their lives in service to the United States in Vietnam. We also honor those who served and lived to return to their homeland, many bearing the physical and psychological scars of war.

Thirty years ago this day, I was serving in Vietnam, caring for the injured at the 85th Evacuation Hospital. Our unit was among those sent early in support of the 44 combat battalions committed in July 1965 to the war effort. We had the good fortune to arrive together as a unit, a cohesive group aboard the U.S.N.S. *Barrett.* The ship's first officer recently wrote that one of his most enduring and vivid memories stemmed from the morning that we debarked in Quin Nhon.

He recalled: "The sudden grim reality that you were going to war started settling over you, and the effect was almost palpable." However, we were determined to be functional and soon readied ourselves to look after those first casualties in need of our lifesaving and comforting skills. I sometimes felt that I was too young or too inexperienced to bear the responsibility. Yet I soon realized that most of those injured were younger than I.

In conversation, they often asked, "Why are you here?" It was easy to tell them the truth, "If you were my brother, father, husband or son, I would want to know that qualified, compassionate, and skilled American nurses were here caring for you to the very best of their ability." This answer satisfied them and gave me purpose as we cared for more and more of their colleagues.

During the 12 years of the Vietnam conflict, 265,000 American women, both civilian and military, volunteered to serve in many capacities. Each brought special talents or skills to support the efforts of their fellow man. The names of eight of these women who lost their lives while on military service in Vietnam are etched on the wall. It is in their memory and to recognize and honor all women who served that the Vietnam Women's Memorial was placed here on the grounds of the Vietnam Veterans' Memorial.

For me personally, for all of us Vietnam veterans, and for all Americans, this wall, the statue of the three servicemen, and the women's sculpture have become significant symbols of a challenging period in our history. Many come here and return here often for comfort and solace and to reflect on the meaning of patriotism, sacrifice, and courage.

The refrain of the ballad *We Were There* speaks for our veterans:

When we were needed, we were there.
We were there when we were needed, we were there.
No, it wasn't always easy, it wasn't always fair.
But when freedom called, we answered, we were there.

Source: Reprinted by permission of Janet Southby.

STANTON, ELIZABETH CADY (1815–1902)

By coordinating correspondence and print research with the efforts of orator Susan B. Anthony and chronicler Matilda Joslyn Gage, Elizabeth Smith Cady Stanton served the women's movement as theoretician and ethics clearinghouse. The eighth child of Margaret Livingston and district attorney and New York assemblyman

Daniel Cady, she was born to a family of eleven in Johnstown, New York, on November 12, 1815. From elementary skills learned at home, she advanced to math, science, composition, French, classics, and composition at the Johnstown Academy, where she won the Greek language prize.

Stanton learned about abolitionism from her first cousin, Gerrit Smith, a proponent of universal suffrage, and from Peter Teabout, the family slave and bodyguard for the youngest Stanton girls. She knew from experience the fury of a woman locked out of her chosen profession because of gender-based bias. She began mining facts and opinions from the popular press and European feminist texts.

Three weeks after the union of Elizabeth with journalist and lawyer Henry Brewster Stanton on May 21, 1840, the couple attended the World Anti-Slavery Convention in London. She and Lucretia Mott incurred rejection from the program and relegation to the women's gallery. The insults raised her fury at the men who dominated females.

The physical ailments of Stanton's husband in 1847 caused the family to move to Seneca Falls, the birthplace of feminism. At age 33, she petitioned the state legislature for married women's rights to property. In lieu of intellectual stimulus, she found ways of escaping housewifery and involved herself in consciousness-raising on women's issues.

At an historic meeting in Waterloo, New York, in 1848, Stanton seconded Mott's proposal of a suffrage summit. After strategy sessions in Seneca Falls and Rochester, Stanton read aloud the raw text of "Declaration of Sentiments," a feminist manifesto rewording the Declaration of Independence and attacking the double standard. The text, presented at the 1848 Women's Rights Convention on July 19, emulated the parallelism and scriptural tone of Thomas Jefferson. In 1850, she composed an exposition for the first National Women's Rights Convention in Worcester, Massachusetts.

Stanton's oral rebuke of the New York legislature in 1854 charged men with taxation without representation. She began crusading across her home state for black rights. With "The Case for Universal Suffrage," articulated to the American Equal Rights Association assembly in New York on May 9, 1867, she lauded the dedication of suffragists.

At the 1868 Women's Suffrage Convention in Washington, D.C., Stanton delivered a scathing denunciation in "The Destructive Male." The carefully organized lecture belittled male behavior as violent and corrupt and blamed them for repressing the natural tendencies of females toward charity and peace. As the first president of the National Women's Suffrage Association in 1869, she initiated two decades of toil for women's issues, including a symbolic candidacy for the U.S. House of Representatives in 1868.

Into the 1870s, Stanton lectured at lyceums for fair marriage laws, sensible divorce negotiation, coeducation, and humane imprisonment. She pressed for suffrage in Michigan in 1874 and targeted next California, Utah, and Wyoming. As a jolt to Americans, at the national centennial celebration in Philadelphia, she coauthored the "Women's Declaration of Rights," a speech that mourned a flag that flew over devalued females. In 1878, she composed her most famous sentence, the proposed constitutional amendment that dogged every U.S. congressman for the next 42 years: "The right of citizens of the United States to vote shall not be denied or abridged by the United States or by any State on account of sex."

Stanton's outreach grew with the opening address of the first International Council of Women in 1888, the healing of a suffragist breach in 1890 over the Fourteenth and Fifteenth Amendments, and her presidency of the National Woman's Suffrage Association in May 1890, an office that prevented fundamentalist Christians from seizing control. To the U.S. House Committee on the Judiciary, she addressed the existential speech "Self-Sovereignty," the kernel of *The Solitude of Self* (1892) that reduced the question of female worth to an evaluation of the human soul. She chose the term "self-sovereignty" as the acme of human dignity, responsibility, and merit.

In Stanton's last decade, she published *The Woman's Bible* (1895–1898) and a memoir, *Eight Years and More: Reminiscences 1815–1897.* Still enthusiastic for a self-governing republic, she began lobbying President Theodore Roosevelt. Leaving her letter unsent, she died at home of heart failure on October 26, 1902.

See Also: Anthony, Susan B.; Blatch, Harriot Eaton Stanton; Davis, Paulina W.; Dickinson, Anna; Gage, Matilda Joslyn; Hazlett, Adelle; Mott, Lucretia; Robinson, Harriet Jane; Rose, Ernestine L.; Stone, Lucy.

Reference

Ginzberg, Lori D. *Elizabeth Cady Stanton: An American Life.* New York: Hill and Wang, 2009.

DECLARATION OF SENTIMENTS
BY ELIZABETH CADY STANTON
FIRST WOMEN'S RIGHTS CONVENTION
WESLEYAN METHODIST CHURCH, SENECA FALLS, NEW YORK
JULY 19, 1848

The researcher and speechwriter for suffrage leader Susan B. Anthony, Elizabeth Cady Stanton of Seneca Falls, New York, rewrote the Declaration of Independence from a female perspective into a women's manifesto. By comparing the two documents and the charges of American colonists against England's King George III, composed 72 years earlier, she opposed a double standard that denied female humanity and reduced women to partial citizenship. For style, she emulated the parallelism and scriptural tone of Thomas Jefferson.

When, in the course of human events, it becomes necessary for one portion of the family of man to assume among the people of the earth a position different from that which they have hitherto occupied, but one to which the laws of nature and of nature's God entitle them, a decent respect to the opinions of mankind requires that they should declare the causes that impel them to such a course.

We hold these truths to be self-evident: that all men and women are created equal; that they are endowed by their Creator with certain inalienable rights; that among these are life, liberty, and the pursuit of happiness; that to secure these rights governments are instituted, deriving their just powers from the consent of the governed. Whenever any form of government becomes destructive of these ends, it is the right of those who suffer from it to refuse allegiance to it, and to insist upon the institution of a new government, laying its foundation on such principles, and organizing its powers in such form, as to them shall seem most likely to effect their safety and happiness.

Prudence, indeed, will dictate that governments long established should not be changed for light and transient causes; and, accordingly, all experience has shown that mankind are more disposed to suffer, while evils are sufferable, than to right themselves by abolishing the forms to which they were accustomed. But when a long train of abuses and usurpations, pursuing invariably the same object, evinces a design to reduce them under absolute despotism, it is their duty to throw off such government and to provide new guards for their future security. Such has been the patient sufferance of the women under this government, and such is now the necessity which constrains them to demand the equal station to which they are entitled.

The history of mankind is a history of repeated injuries and usurpations on the part of man toward woman, having in direct object the establishment of an absolute tyranny over her. To prove this, let facts be submitted to a candid world.

He has never permitted her to exercise her inalienable right to the elective franchise. He has compelled her to submit to law in the formation of which she had no voice.

He has withheld from her rights which are given to the most ignorant and degraded men, both natives and foreigners. Having deprived her of this first right as a citizen, the elective franchise, thereby leaving her without representation in the halls of legislation, he has oppressed her on all sides.

He has made her, if married, in the eye of the law, civilly dead.

He has taken from her all right in property, even to the wages she earns.

He has made her morally, an irresponsible being, as she can commit many crimes with impunity, provided they be done in the presence of her husband.

In the covenant of marriage, she is compelled to promise obedience to her husband, he becoming, to all intents and purposes, her master—the law giving him power to deprive her of her liberty and to administer chastisement.

He has so framed the laws of divorce, as to what shall be the proper causes and, in case of separation, to whom the guardianship of the children shall be given, as to be wholly regardless of the happiness of the women—the law, in all cases, going upon a false supposition of the supremacy of man and giving all power into his hands.

After depriving her of all rights as a married woman, if single and the owner of property, he has taxed her to support a government which recognizes her only when her property can be made profitable to it.

He has monopolized nearly all the profitable employments, and from those she is permitted to follow, she receives but a scanty remuneration. He closes against her all the avenues to wealth and distinction which he considers most honorable to himself. As a teacher of theology, medicine, or law, she is not known.

He has denied her the facilities for obtaining a thorough education, all colleges being closed against her.

He allows her in church, as well as state, but a subordinate position, claiming apostolic authority for her exclusion from the ministry, and, with some exceptions, from any public participation in the affairs of the church.

He has created a false public sentiment by giving to the world a different code of morals for men and women, by which moral delinquencies which exclude women from society are not only tolerated but deemed of little account in man.

He has usurped the prerogative of Jehovah himself, claiming it as his right to assign for her a sphere of action, when that belongs to her conscience and to her God.

He has endeavored, in every way that he could, to destroy her confidence in her own powers, to lessen her self-respect, and to make her willing to lead a dependent and abject life. Now, in view of this entire disfranchisement of one-half the people of this country, their social and religious degradation, in view of the unjust laws above mentioned, and because women do feel themselves aggrieved, oppressed, and fraudulently deprived of their most sacred rights, we insist that they have immediate admission to all the rights and privileges which belong to them as citizens of the United States.

In entering upon the great work before us, we anticipate no small amount of misconception, misrepresentation, and ridicule; but we shall use every instrumentality within our power to effect our object. We shall employ agents, circulate tracts, petition the state and national legislatures, and endeavor to enlist the pulpit and the press in our behalf. We hope this Convention will be followed by a series of conventions embracing every part of the country.

Resolutions

Whereas, the great precept of nature is conceded to be that "man shall pursue his own true and substantial happiness." Blackstone in his Commentaries remarks that this law of nature, being coeval with mankind and dictated by God himself, is, of course, superior in obligation to any other. It is binding over all the globe, in all countries and at all times; no human laws are of any validity if contrary to this, and such of them as are valid derive all their force, and all their validity, and all their authority, mediately and immediately, from this original; therefore,

Resolved, that such laws as conflict, in any way, with the true and substantial happiness of woman, are contrary to the great precept of nature and of no validity, for this is "superior in obligation to any other."

Resolved, that all laws which prevent woman from occupying such a station in society as her conscience shall dictate, or which place her in a position inferior to that of man, are contrary to the great precept of nature and therefore of no force or authority.

Resolved, that woman is man's equal, was intended to be so by the Creator, and the highest good of the race demands that she should be recognized as such.

Resolved, that the women of this country ought to be enlightened in regard to the laws under which they live, that they may no longer publish their degradation by declaring themselves satisfied with their present position, nor their ignorance, by asserting that they have all the rights they want.

Resolved, that inasmuch as man, while claiming for himself intellectual superiority, does accord to woman moral superiority, it is preeminently his duty to encourage her to speak and teach, as she has an opportunity, in all religious assemblies.

Resolved, that the same amount of virtue, delicacy, and refinement of behavior that is required of woman in the social state also be required of man, and the same transgressions should be visited with equal severity on both man and woman.

Resolved, that the objection of indelicacy and impropriety, which is so often brought against woman when she addresses a public audience, comes with a very ill grace from those who encourage, by their attendance, her appearance on the stage, in the concert, or in feats of the circus.

Resolved, that woman has too long rested satisfied in the circumscribed limits which corrupt customs and a perverted application of the Scriptures have marked out for her, and that it is time she should move in the enlarged sphere which her great Creator has assigned her.

Resolved, that it is the duty of the women of this country to secure to themselves their sacred right to the elective franchise.

Resolved, that the equality of human rights results necessarily from the fact of the identity of the race in capabilities and responsibilities.

Resolved, that the speedy success of our cause depends upon the zealous and untiring efforts of both men and women for the overthrow of the monopoly of the pulpit, and for the securing to woman an equal participation with men in the various trades, professions, and commerce.

Resolved, therefore, that, being invested by the Creator with the same capabilities and same consciousness of responsibility for their exercise, it is demonstrably the right and duty of woman, equally with man, to promote every righteous cause by every righteous means; and especially in regard to the great subjects of morals and religion, it is self-evidently her right to participate with her brother in teaching them, both in private and in public, by writing and by speaking, by any instrumentalities proper to be used, and in any assemblies proper to be held; and this being a self-evident truth growing out of the divinely implanted principles of human nature, any custom or authority adverse to it, whether modern or wearing the hoary sanction of antiquity, is to be regarded as a self-evident falsehood, and at war with mankind.

Source: Stanton, Elizabeth Cady, Susan Brownell Anthony, and Matilda Joslyn Gage, eds. *History of Woman Suffrage: 1861–1876.* Vol. II (70–73). New York: Fowler & Wells, 1882.

STARHAWK (1951–)

An ecofeminist, pacifist, and neo-pagan philosopher, Miriam "Starhawk" Simos lectures worldwide on indigenous folk culture, global justice, earth stewardship, and woman-centered faith. A Minnesotan born on June 17, 1951, in St. Paul, she is the daughter of sociology professor and psychotherapist Bertha Claire Goldfarb and communist drama therapist Jack Simon, a first-generation Russian-American Jew who died in 1956. Homeschooled from age five, she pondered rabbinical training at a Hebrew high school.

Following rebellion in her teens against the Vietnam War, Starhawk studied fine arts and psychology at the University of California at Los Angeles and, at age 22, began an advanced degree in film. She joined hippie communes along the Pacific Coast and furthered antinuclear protests at Diablo Canyon, Livermore Weapons Lab, Vandenberg Air Force Base, and the Nevada Test Site. In 1977, she entered a five-year marriage to Edwin Walter Rahsman.

Starhawk professed pacifism during her travels to Nicaragua, El Salvador, the Gaza Strip, and Palestine's West Bank. She became a celebrant of earth's holiness and a proponent of sustainable life on earth through feminist collegiality. In 1979, her novel *The Spiral Dance: A Rebirth of the Ancient Religion of the Great Goddess*, told the story of victims of European witch hunts, which persecuted primarily preliterate women, many of them mentally and/or physically handicapped.

She gave up pursuing a writing career in New York and joined a California-based neo-pagan sect, which reclaimed mysticism and witchcraft from its 19th-century aesthetics.

With reverence for goddess worship, Starhawk based her pantheistic ministry on the Dianic traditions of Wicca. Gynocentric activities commemorated the female cycle of life. Through the Reclaiming Collective, disciples in North America, Europe, and Australia advocated ecological, socioeconomic, and political advances via a return to tribalism and matriarchal worship based on seasonal cycles and rites of passage. In San Francisco in 1982, she completed an advanced degree from Antioch University West in feminist psychological therapy.

In 1985, Starhawk's devotion to nature influenced Unitarian Universalists to incorporate geocentric liturgy and training materials into their congregational training and to promote planetary cleansing and healing. Practitioners collaborated with England's Unitarian Earth Spirit Network, a sect formed in 1990 to espouse New Age philosophy and tenets.

In support of women's self-liberation from patriarchal governments and institutions, Starhawk's feminism took new direction in *Truth or Dare: Encounters with Power, Authority and Mystery* (1998), a defiance of male conquest. At the Bodhi Tree lecture in West Hollywood in 1999, she asserted the living continuity of the cosmos and, with soothing phrases, envisioned a utopia free of pollution, hunger, and violence. She nurtured women's history programs by speaking at the 2000 National Women's Studies Association assembly, denounced the Free Trade Area of the Americas in Quebec in April 2001, and supported safe havens of the Earth and Animal Liberation Fronts.

Listed among the world's 100 most spiritually influential people, Starhawk personalized the approach of "How Real Is the Earth to You?" (2009) and "Spirituality" (2009), of the documentary *Permaculture: The Growing Edge* (2010), and of the televised lecture at Harvard Divinity School on "Permaculture and the Sacred" (2013). In Los Angeles in December 2013, she led an annual winter solstice ritual and workshop encouraging mutual caretaking of others and the planet. At the heart of the text, she rooted climate change and nature crises in the greed of capitalism. She continues lecturing at universities and maintains archives at the Graduate Theological Union library at Berkeley.

References

Mirriam-Goldberg, Caryn. "Visionary Activist." *Women's Review of Books* 20, no. 3 (December 2002): 11–12.

Starhawk. "The Bodhi Tree Lecture." Bodhi Tree House. Accessed June 2, 2015. http://www.bodhitree.com/lectures/starhawk.html.

OUR CHILDREN, CLIMATE, FAITH (EXCERPT)
BY STARHAWK
OUR CHILDREN, CLIMATE, FAITH SYMPOSIUM
TOWN HOUSE, STRAFFORD, VERMONT
AUGUST 24, 2014

Miriam "Starhawk" Simos, an ecofeminist, pacifist, and neo-pagan philosopher, addresses ethical concerns of life on a polluted planet among powers that coerce and repress the underclass. In a keynote address to an annual symposium of thinkers and reformers, she stressed the unity of earth and its residents in a struggle to survive and to shape a cleaner, less depressing life. Her proposal for change anticipated mounting small and large group action on a number of issues, notably, the Intergovernmental Panel on Climate Change, demands for action against genocide, and the U.S. reclamation of diplomacy with Cuba.

I fortunately do not feel it is my task to convince you that climate change is a problem. I assume we are all here because we already know that. It is one of two great problems and huge crises that we are facing right now: the first being the erosion of the life support systems and the stability of the living system that is the earth and the planet; and the second being this tremendous injustice, this tremendous concentration of wealth and power in fewer and fewer hands that we see going on right now all over the world under many different guises. And along with that the increase in military power, police power, repression that supports it.

The main issues of climate change are not separate from what's going on at Ferguson or what's going on in Gaza or what's going on in the Middle East or what's going on in the Ukraine or what's going on in Europe with their austerity programs. In fact, I think these two great crises are not actually two great crises. I think they are one great crisis.

In some ways that's good news because the things that we actually need to do to address climate change are the same things we need to do to address the problems of injustice. They can't really be separated. That is because centralized power likes centralized power. Those centralized economic and political powers depend on the need of those centralized energy powers, that of oil and gas and fossil fuels and nuclear so far as they can get it in order to sustain this system of centralized and top-down control.

I think that the more radical analysis that is emerging out of the climate-justice movement is recognizing that dealing with climate change is not just a matter of changing our light bulbs and not just a matter of putting solar panels on our homes. It's really a matter of looking at these huge systems and recognizing that climate change itself is a symptom of a dysfunctional, overarching system that we live in.

Because I like to be optimistic, I like to think that's good news. It gives us a challenge of really addressing it, and it gives us the opportunity to create a world that is better balanced in terms of the energy and technology but better balanced in terms of its human energies and the human connections and the way of life we can live.

This is one place where faith comes in. I am really glad to see people addressing it through that lens because our great traditions that talk to us about deep value, that talk to us not just about what is expedient, but about what is important. Not just about what is comfortable or profitable, but what is sacred. And sacred not in the sense of the image we bow down to and what is the name we call it. What is it we care about so deeply that we are willing to take a stand for it. . . .

What is it we care so deeply about that we value it beyond the value of profitability and comfort and convenience that it sets the other standards for our lives. I think that has already been the role of religion and faith. Whether it is pagan or Christian or Jewish or Muslim or Buddhist or Hindu, people come to religion because they are asking important and deep questions like how do I live my life in a good way? How do I act with integrity, what does that mean? How do I become a good and a moral person?

I think it's vital that we are able to give people some of those answers and to address that in the contest of the politics and the climate change. If we don't, we leave that whole terrain of faith and deep value and morality to people who have no hesitation in coming in and telling people exactly how they should live their lives in great detail, people who usually are far more restrictive and repressive. I think it is really, really important that we do address these issues, not just through the heavy lens of policy but through the emotional lens of value and morality and faith.

I also think that we actually need faith right now. Faith in the sense that it is very easy to look at what's happening and give up. We have many, many voices telling us, "Give up. You are already doomed." We have the voices in the media. We have the voices of those vested interests who would love to see us give up. And sometimes we also have the voices of our allies. Any of you know those environmentalists who seem to believe human beings are a blight on the planet and we'd be better off if we just opened ourselves up and caught the ebola fever and went out. . . .

I actually think that in this part of our faith whatever, however you define it. For me, my faith is earthist. As the earth is alive, it is a living being; it's something we are all a part of. Nature is alive, and it's always communicating to us and always speaking to us. We are part of nature. We are not separate from nature. And out of that faith, I have faith in the resilience of that earth, and I have faith that we as human beings are not some kind of mistake in the evolutionary program.

We actually are something that the earth is trying to evolve for a reason. We have a purpose that reason is to be the earth's reflective eyes, appreciative eyes. To be the voices to sing her praises, to be the great communicators back to nature. To open our ears and listen to the lessons that the leaves and the trees and the frogs and the birds are speaking and telling us. We need to get good at that. We have had a lot to work out in our childhood and adolescence. But I have hopes for us that we have the ability to work that out. We do have a reason and a purpose and a responsibility to be here. . . .

Source: Starhawk. "Our Children, Climate, Faith." August 24, 2014. Reprinted by permission from Starhawk.

STEINEM, GLORIA (1934–)

The most prominent figure in feminism and pro-woman humanitarianism, Gloria Marie Steinem brought polish and intelligence to oratorical venues. She was born on March 25, 1934, in Toledo, Ohio, to Ruth Nuneviller, a journalist for *The Blade*, and Leo Steinem, an itinerant antiques dealer. Her life altered dramatically at age 10, when her father left the family.

Steinem supplied sustenance and nursing care for her mentally unstable mother. She perceived asylum stays as abasing to women, who lacked the social value of males. After enrollment at Monroe Elementary School, Waite High School, and Western High School in Washington, D.C., she displayed brilliance in government courses at Smith College, where she graduated magna cum laude in 1956. On a Bowles Asian Fellowship, she conducted research on Gandhian activism among peasants for two years in India for the treatise *The Thousand Indias* (1957).

At age 26, Steinem relocated to New York City to write for *Help!*, a short-lived underground satiric magazine. As a freelancer, she surveyed the availability and reliability of contraception for *Esquire* and used the birth control angle to depict the dilemma of homebound women who longed for a career. For the article "A Bunny's Tale" (1963) in *Show* magazine, she posed as a bunny at the New York Playboy Club for three weeks to survey working conditions and sexual exploitation of provocatively dressed cocktail waitresses.

After lengthy unemployment, in 1968, Steinem wrote for *Cosmopolitan* and the television show *That Was the Week That Was*. In awe of abortion survivors at the three-hour First Abortion Speakout at the Washington Square Methodist Church in March 1969, she embraced feminism for valorizing women. To mobilize activists supporting female independence and reproductive freedom, she co-founded the Feminist Majority Foundation.

In one of Steinem's first attention-getting efforts, she debated *Playboy* publisher Hugh Hefner on women's rights and gender equality. She delivered strength and direction to a coalition of women by testifying before the Senate Judiciary

Committee on May 6, 1970, for the Equal Rights Amendment. She supported Stewardesses for Women's Rights, a visibly abused profession subject to smarmy womanizers and workplace discrimination based on the beauty myth. Her speeches, interviews, and essays pummeled long-lived myths reviling the emotional female, the run-around mother, the slovenly housewife, and the whiny drudge.

On July 10, 1971, Steinem empowered the National Women's Political Caucus by allying with feminist pacesetters Bella Abzug, Betty Friedan, and Shirley Chisholm. Steinem's opening salvo, "Address to the Women of America," one of the landmarks of U.S. female oratory, called for a humanistic revolution against racism and sexism, two controls of society that yielded cheap labor for capitalists. The speech showcased "choice," a term that directed subsequent liberating upheaval into the 21st century.

On donated money, in January 1972, Steinem joined Letty Cottin Pogrebin and a feminist staff in disseminating the maiden issue of *Ms.* By July 1972, her female-controlled magazine appeared monthly and remained a formative source for women for 15 years on such topics as domestic violence and the return of former homemakers to the workforce. On July 10, 1972, she rallied opposition to white male delegations at the National Democratic Convention in Miami and demanded that the party recognize the importance of abortion to women.

Steinem founded Take Our Daughters to Work Day, and in 1972, became the first female to address the National Press Club and proposed restoring the comic figure Wonder Woman to her original costume and power. She opposed the nomination to the Supreme Court of Clarence Thomas for his sexual harassment of attorney Anita Hill. To ready feminists for the demands of the media on surprise heroes like Hill, Steinem compiled a test on assertiveness, *Revolution from Within: A Book of Self-Esteem* (1992).

In Massachusetts at Salem State College in March 1993, Steinem lectured on "Scholars, Witches and Other Freedom Fighters," a speech commemorating the 300th anniversary of the Salem Witch Trials. With generous remarks, she energized the rebellious spirits of female scholars against ethnocentrism and sexism, the philosophies that place white males at the acme of civilization. She itemized gaps in world history that omitted women's accomplishments and the torment of victims of the Inquisition, 80 percent of whom were female. She linked anti-witch hysteria to the illogic of Pat Robertson, the Mormon Church, the Ayatollah, and the Moral Majority, all of whom disempowered the independent thinker.

With Voters for Choice and Planned Parenthood, Steinem led feminist reproach against the George W. Bush administration for replacing sex education with abstinence-only programs and for failure to support AIDS drugs, stem cell research, the environment, and reproductive autonomy. Her speaking engagements introduced new audiences to her views on equality, including interviews over the *Stephen*

Colbert Report, NY1, Northeast Public Radio, PBS *Need to Know, HBO, ABC News, CNN*, and *CBS News*. Additional oratory on the Occupy Wall Street movement, at the annual Canadian Women's Foundation luncheon, and, in April 2012 at McNally Jackson Booksellers ranged from female health to threats to libraries, student loans, and feminist venues worldwide.

In support of human rights, Steinem's rebuttal of the presidential campaign speeches of Mitt Romney exposed his intent to destroy reproductive rights by granting personhood to fertilized ova. In November 2013, she addressed listeners in Beverly Hills on "Make Equality Reality." Strong stands against extremism earned her the Humanist of 2012 citation, 2013 Presidential Medal of Freedom, 2014 New York Women's Foundation Century Award, and Furstenberg Lifetime Leadership commendation. At the University of Southern California in February 2016, she stressed the inclusion of women of color in feminist discourse.

See Also: Abzug, Bella; Bird, Caroline; Chisholm, Shirley; Friedan, Betty; Hill, Anita.

Reference

Marcello, Patricia Cronin. *Gloria Steinem: A Biography*. Westport, CT: Greenwood, 2004.

TESTIMONY BEFORE SENATE HEARINGS ON THE EQUAL RIGHTS AMENDMENT BY GLORIA STEINEM SENATE HEARINGS ON THE EQUAL RIGHTS AMENDMENT U.S. SENATE, WASHINGTON, D.C. MAY 6, 1970

A deliberate, reasoned philosopher, Gloria Steinem applied scholarship and restraint in lecturing the U.S. Senate on the changes of gendered relationships during second wave feminism. By stressing comparisons with the civil rights movement, she established a basis for women's rights to equality as citizens, parents, and workers. Over the following decades, her predictions proved accurate.

My name is Gloria Steinem. I am a writer and editor, and I am currently a member of the Policy Council of the Democratic National Committee. And, I work regularly with the lowest-paid workers in the country, the migrant workers, men, women, and children both in California and in my own State of New York.

I am here in support of the equal rights amendment. . . . Some protective legislation is gradually proving to be unenforceable or contrary to title VII. It gives poor women jobs but serves to keep them poor. Restrictions on working hours, for instance, may keep women in the assembly line from becoming foremen. No one is trying to say that there is no difference between men and women, only as I will discuss more in my statement that the differences between, the differences within the groups, male and female, are much, much greater than the differences between the two groups. Therefore, requirements can only be sensibly suited to the requirements of the job itself.

During twelve years of working for a living, I have experienced much of the legal and social discrimination reserved for women in this country. I have been refused service in public restaurants, ordered out of public gathering places, and turned away from apartment rentals; all for the clearly stated, sole reason that I am a woman. And all without the legal remedies available to blacks and other minorities. I have been excluded from professional groups, writing assignments on so-called "unfeminine" subjects such as politics, full participation in the Democratic Party, jury duty, and even from such small male privileges as discounts on airline fares. Most important to me, I have been denied a society in which women are encouraged, or even allowed to think of themselves as first-class citizens and responsible human beings.

However, after two years of researching the status of American women, I have discovered that in reality, I am very, very lucky. Most women, both wage earners and housewives, routinely suffer more humiliation and injustice than I do.

As a freelance writer, I don't work in the male-dominated hierarchy of an office. (Women, like blacks and other visibly different minorities, do better in individual professions such as the arts, sports, or domestic work; anything in which they don't have authority over white males.) I am not one of the millions of women who must support a family. Therefore, I haven't had to go on welfare because there are no day-care centers for my children while I work, and I haven't had to submit to the humiliating welfare inquiries about my private and sexual life, inquiries from which men are exempt. I haven't had to brave the sex bias of labor unions and employers, only to see my family subsist on a median salary 40 percent less than the male median salary.

I hope this committee will hear the personal, daily injustices suffered by many women—professionals and day laborers, women housebound by welfare as well as suburbia. We have all been silent for too long. But we won't be silent anymore.

The truth is that all our problems stem from the same sex based myths. We may appear before you as white radicals or the middle-aged middleclass or black soul sisters, but we are all sisters in fighting against these outdated myths. Like racial myths, they have been reflected in our laws. Let me list a few.

That women are biologically inferior to men. In fact, an equally good case can be made for the reverse. Women live longer than men, even when the men are not subject to business pressures. Women survived Nazi concentration camps better, keep cooler heads in emergencies currently studied by disaster-researchers, are protected against heart attacks by their female sex hormones, and are so much more durable at every stage of life that nature must conceive 20 to 50 percent more males in order to keep some balance going.

Man's hunting activities are forever being pointed to as tribal proof of superiority. But while he was hunting, women built houses, tilled the fields, developed animal husbandry, and perfected language. Man, being all alone in the bush, often developed into a creature as strong as women, fleeter of foot, but not very bright.

However, I don't want to prove the superiority of one sex to another. That would only be repeating a male mistake. English scientists once definitively proved, after all, that the English were descended from the angels, while the Irish were descended from the apes: it was the rationale for England's domination of Ireland for more than a century. The point is that science is used to support current myth and economics almost as much as the church was.

What we do know is that the difference between two races or two sexes is much smaller than the differences to be found within each group. Therefore, in spite of the slide show on female inferiorities that I understand was shown to you yesterday, the law makes much more sense when it treats individuals, not groups bundled together by some condition of birth.

A word should be said about Dr. Freud, the great 19th century perpetuator of female inferiority. Many of the differences he assumed to be biological, and therefore changeless, have turned out to be societal, and have already changed. Penis envy, for instance, is clinically disappearing. Just as black people envied white skins, 19th century women envied penises. A second-class group envies whatever it is that makes the first-class group first class.

Another myth, that women are already treated equally in this society. I am sure there has been ample testimony to prove that equal pay for equal work, equal chance for advancement, and equal training or encouragement is obscenely scarce in every field, even those—like food and fashion industries—that are supposedly "feminine."

A deeper result of social and legal injustice, however, is what sociologists refer to as "Internalized Aggression." Victims of aggression absorb the myth of their own inferiority, and come to believe that their group is in fact second-class. Even when they themselves realize they are not second-class, they may still think their group is, thus the tendency to be the only Jew in the club, the only black woman on the block, the only woman in the office.

Women suffer this second-class treatment from the moment they are born. They are expected to be, rather than achieve, to function biologically rather than learn. A brother, whatever his intellect, is more likely to get the family's encouragement and education money, while girls are often pressured to conceal ambition and intelligence, to "Uncle Tom."

I interviewed a New York public school teacher who told me about a black teenager's desire to be a doctor. With all the barriers in mind, she suggested kindly that he be a veterinarian instead.

The same day, a high school teacher mentioned a girl who wanted to be a doctor. The teacher said, "How about a nurse?"

Teachers, parents, and the Supreme Court may exude a protective, well-meaning rationale, but limiting the individual's ambition is doing no one a favor. Certainly not this country; it needs all the talent it can get.

Another myth, that American women hold great economic power. Fifty-one percent of all shareholders in this country are women. That is a favorite male-chauvinist statistic. However, the number of shares they hold is so small that the total is only 18 percent of all shares. Even those holdings are often controlled by men.

Similarly, only 5 percent of all the people in the country who receive $10,000 a year or more, earned or otherwise, are women. And that includes the famous rich widows.

The constantly repeated myth of our economic power seems less testimony to our real power than to the resentment of what little power we do have.

Another myth, that children must have full-time mothers. American mothers spend more time with their homes and children than those of any other society we know about. In the past, joint families, servants, a prevalent system in which grandparents raised the children, or family field work in the agrarian systems—all these factors contributed more to child care than the laborsaving devices of which we are so proud.

The truth is that most American children seem to be suffering from too much mother, and too little father. Part of the program of Women's Liberation is a return of fathers to their children. If laws permit women equal work and pay opportunities, men will then be relieved of their role as sole breadwinner. Fewer ulcers, fewer hours of meaningless work, equal responsibility for his own children: these are a few of the reasons that Women's Liberation is Men's Liberation, too.

As for the psychic health of the children, studies show that the quality of time spent by parents is more important than the quantity. The most damaged children were not those whose mothers worked, but those whose mothers preferred to work but stayed home out of role-playing desire to be a "good mother."

Another myth, that the women's movement is not political, won't last, or is somehow not "serious."

When black people leave their 19th century roles, they are feared. When women dare to leave theirs, they are ridiculed. We understand this: we accept the burden of ridicule. It won't keep us quiet anymore.

Similarly, it shouldn't deceive male observers into thinking that this is somehow a joke. We are 51 percent of the population; we are essentially united on these issues across boundaries of class or race or age; and we may well end by changing this society more than the civil rights movement. That is an apt parallel. We, too, have our right wing and left wing, our separatists, gradualists, and Uncle Toms. But we are changing our own consciousness, and that of the country. Engels noted the relationship of the authoritarian, nuclear family to capitalism: the father as capitalist, the mother as means of production, and the children as labor. He said the family would change as the economic system did, and that seems to have happened, whether we want to admit it or not. Women's bodies will no longer be owned by the state for the production of workers and soldiers; birth control and abortion are facts of everyday life. The new family is an egalitarian family.

Gunnar Myrdal noted 30 years ago the parallel between women and Negroes in this country. Both suffered from such restricting social myths as: smaller brains, passive natures, inability to govern themselves (and certainly not white men), sex objects only, childlike natures, special skills, and the like. When evaluating a general statement about women, it might be valuable to substitute "black people" for "women"—just to test the prejudice at work.

And it might be valuable to do this constitutionally as well. Neither group is going to be content as a cheap labor pool anymore. And neither is going to be content without full constitutional rights.

Finally, I would like to say one thing about this time in which I am testifying.

I had deep misgivings about discussing this topic when National Guardsmen are occupying our campuses, the country is being turned against itself in a terrible polarization, and America is enlarging an already inhuman and unjustifiable war. But it seems to me that much of the trouble in this country has to do with the "masculine mystique"; with the myth that masculinity somehow depends on the subjugation of other people. It is a bipartisan problem; both our past and current presidents seem to be victims of this myth, and to behave accordingly.

Women are not more moral than men. We are only uncorrupted by power. But we do not want to imitate men, to join this country as it is, and I think our very participation will change it. Perhaps women elected leaders—and there will be many more of them—will not be so likely to dominate black people or yellow people or men; anybody who looks different from us.

After all, we won't have our masculinity to prove.

Source: Steinem, Gloria. "Testimony before Senate Hearings on Equal Rights Amendment, May 6, 1970." *U.S. Congress, Senate Committee on the Judiciary, Subcommittee on*

Constitutional Amendments. Hearings to Amend the Constitution So As to Provide Equal Rights For Men and Women. 91st Cong., 2d sess., May 5–7, 1970. Washington, DC: U.S. Government Printing Office, 1971, 335–337.

STONE, LUCY (1818–1893)

A spirited advocate of gender equality and historic organizer of volunteers, Lucy Stone retained leadership and vigor throughout the first wave of suffrage advocacy. She was born in West Brookfield on August 13, 1818, to Hannah Matthews and Francis Stone Jr., a farmer and firm Congregationalist head of household. In defiance of her father's tyranny, at age 16, she taught classes at North Brookfield and Paxton and protested the reduced salary of female staff.

At age 18, Stone followed media accounts of the abolitionist discourse of Angelina and Sarah Grimké and the uproar among conservative Protestant pastors over the impropriety of female public oratory. Her coursework in manners during one conventional semester at Mount Holyoke Female Seminary preceded more scholarly training at Wesleyan Academy in Wilbraham. Inspired by the rebellion of Connecticut antislavery agent Abby Kelley, Stone denounced female silencing.

Having completed two semesters at the congregational academy at Monson, in fall 1841, Stone enrolled in classical studies at Quaboag Seminary in Warren before saving enough money to enter Oberlin College in northern Ohio. To better interpret scripture, she added Hebrew to her language classes. Through a literary society and *The Plain Speaker*, she agitated for women's place in public discussions.

Stone began an oratorical career on August 1, 1846, with "Why Do We Rejoice Today?" in praise of the British West Indies for freeing slaves in 1833. To gain experience in public speaking, she partnered with Antoinette Brown in forming the first women's debate society and in discussions in rhetoric class, previously limited to male public speakers. On graduation in 1847, Stone refused to write a valedictory for a man to read aloud in her place.

Stone accepted an office in the National Women's Rights movement and directed the 1850 rights assembly of 1,000 suffragists in Worcester, Massachusetts. In October 1847, she asserted her mastery of oratory with the address "The Province of Women" to the Evangelical Congregation Church in Gardner, Massachusetts, and by joining the Boston speaker's bureau of the Massachusetts Anti-Slavery Society. Earning $16 per month, she spoke extemporaneously, leaving no written record of her words. Detractors opposed her advocacy for slaves by hissing and hurling ice water, pepper, eggs, and Bibles.

When Stone addressed the women's rights convention in Syracuse, New York, in 1852, her persuasive spark drew praise from the *New York Tribune* and won to the cause Susan B. Anthony. At the 1853 National Women's Rights Convention in Cleveland, Ohio, Stone appealed to young women to face change with courage and self-reliance. With "Disappointment Is the Lot of Women" (1855), delivered to the Woman's Rights Convention in Saratoga, New York, Stone outlined the obstacles that society and institutions placed in the way of females. She minimized the value of courtesies to women and declared, "We want rights" (Stone 1887, 165). Her fostering of divorce to end wife beating by drunken husbands defied orthodox ritual and raised antipathies among less liberal suffragists, including her sister-in-law, Antoinette Brown Blackwell.

Stone's crusades for black voting rights preceded a voters' campaign in Kansas and her lengthy, detailed tirade "Woman Suffrage in New Jersey" (1867) to state legislators protesting unfair elections, inheritances, and jury trials of females who had proved themselves loyal, patriotic citizens. She held an executive office with the American Woman Suffrage Association in 1869 and, with her husband, co-founded the *Woman's Journal.* With Julia Ward Howe, Stone incited the 1873 New England Women's Tea Party, held by 300 suffragists on December 15 at Boston's historical Faneuil Hall and satirized by cartoonist Thomas Nast in *Harper's Weekly.*

In 1887, Stone accepted an office in the newly established National American Woman Suffrage Association, a suffrage society led by the triumvirate of Stone, Susan B. Anthony, and Elizabeth Cady Stanton. In March 1888 at the International Council of Women, activist Julia Ward Howe proclaimed Stone a pioneer motivator and recruiter of leaders. A roll call of admirers confirmed Stone's status in the vanguard of suffrage and lauded her sobriquets—the "morning star" and "heart and soul of the movement."

As Stone's health worsened from lung and heart disease, she educated Carrie Chapman Catt as her replacement in the gender equity movement. After Stone died of stomach cancer on October 18, 1893, her wish for cremation established an additional first for Massachusetts.

See Also: Anthony, Susan B.; Blackwell, Antoinette Brown; Catt, Carrie Chapman; Howe, Julia Ward; Stanton, Elizabeth Cady.

References

McMillen, Sally G. *Seneca Falls and the Origins of the Women's Rights Movement.* New York: Oxford University Press, 2008.

Proceedings of the Seventh National Woman's Rights Convention. New York: Edward O. Jenkins, 1856.

Stone, Lucy. "Disappointment Is the Lot of Women." In *History of Woman Suffrage*, Vol. I (165–166). Rochester, NY: Charles Mann, 1887.

DISAPPOINTMENT IS THE LOT OF WOMEN
BY LUCY STONE
SEVENTH NATIONAL WOMEN'S RIGHTS CONVENTION
SMITH & NIXON'S HALL, CINCINNATI, OHIO
OCTOBER 17, 1855

A champion of female autonomy, National Women's Rights leader Lucy Stone of West Brookfield, Massachusetts, addressed the seventh suffrage assembly on the many barriers to the fulfillment of women's promise. She personalized the harangue by citing discouragement of girls by men in her own family, who denied her an education equal to that of her brother. In rejection of the standard employ of women as teachers, maids, and seamstresses, she demanded that females achieve the spheres that God intended for them.

From the first years to which my memory stretches, I have been a disappointed woman. When, with my brothers, I reached forth after the sources of knowledge, I was reproved with "It isn't fit for you; it doesn't belong to women." Then there was but one college in the world where women were admitted, and that was in Brazil. I would have found my way there, but by the time I was prepared to go, one was opened in the young state of Ohio—the first in the United States where women and Negroes could enjoy opportunities with white men. I was disappointed when I came to seek a profession worthy an immortal being—every employment was closed to me, except those of the teacher, the seamstress, and the housekeeper. In education, in marriage, in religion, in everything, disappointment is the lot of woman. It shall be the business of my life to deepen this disappointment in every woman's heart until she bows down to it no longer. I wish that women, instead of being walking showcases, instead of begging of their fathers and brothers the latest and gayest new bonnet, would ask of them their rights. The question of woman's rights is a practical one. The notion has prevailed that it was only an ephemeral idea; that it was but women claiming the right to smoke cigars in the streets, and to frequent bar rooms. Others have supposed it a question of comparative intellect; others still, of sphere. Too much has already been said and written about woman's sphere. Trace all the doctrines to their source and they will be found to have no basis except in the usages and prejudices of the age. This is seen in the fact that what is tolerated in woman in one country is not tolerated in another. In this country, women may hold prayer meetings, et cetera, but in Mohammedan countries it is written upon their mosques, "Women and dogs and other impure animals are not permitted to enter."

Wendell Phillips says, "The best and greatest thing one is capable of doing, that is his sphere." I have confidence in the Father to believe that when He gives us the capacity to do anything He does not make a blunder. Leave women, then, to find their sphere. And do not tell us before we are born even, that our province is to cook dinners, darn stockings, and sew on buttons. We are told woman has all the rights she wants; and even women, I am ashamed to say, tell us so. They mistake the politeness of men for rights—seats while men stand in this hall tonight, and their adulations; but these are mere courtesies. We want rights. The flour merchant, the house builder, and the postman charge us no less on account of our sex; but when we endeavor to earn money to pay all these, then, indeed, we find the difference. Man, if he have energy, may hew out for himself a path where no mortal has ever trod, held back by nothing but what is in himself; the world is all before him, where to choose; and we are glad for you, brothers, men, that is so. But the same society that drives forth the young man keeps woman at home—a dependent—working little cats on worsted and little dogs on punctured paper; but if she goes heartily and bravely to give herself to some worthy purpose, she is out of her sphere and she loses caste. Women working in tailor shops are paid one-third as much as men. Someone in Philadelphia has stated that women make fine shirts for twelve and a half cents apiece; that no woman can make more than nine a week, and the sum thus earned, after deducting rent, fuel, et cetera, leaves her just three and a half cents a day for bread. Is it a wonder that women are driven to prostitution? Female teachers in New York are paid fifty dollars a year, and for every such situation there are five hundred applications. I know not what you believe of God, but I believe He gave yearnings and longings to be filled, and that He did not mean all our time should be devoted to feeding and clothing the body. The present condition of woman causes a horrible perversion of the marriage relation. It is asked of a lady, "Has she married well?" "Oh, yes, her husband is rich." Woman must marry for a home, and you men are the sufferers by this; for a woman who loathes you may marry you because you have the means to get money which she cannot have. But when woman can enter the lists with you and make money for herself, she will marry you only for deep and earnest affection.

I am detaining you too long, many of you standing, that I ought to apologize, but women have been wronged so long that I may wrong you a little. A woman undertook in Lowell to sell shoes to ladies. Men laughed at her, but in six years she has run them all out and has a monopoly of the trade. Sarah Tyndale, whose husband was an importer of china, and died bankrupt, continued his business, paid off his debts, and has made a fortune and built the largest china warehouse in the world. Mrs. Tyndale herself drew the plan of her warehouse and it is the best plan ever drawn. A laborer to whom the architect showed it said: "Don't she know e'en as much as some men?" I have seen a woman at manual labor turning out chair-legs in a cabinet shop with a dress short enough not to drag in the shavings. I wish other women would imitate her in this. It made her hands harder and broader, it is true, but I think a hand with a dollar and a quarter a day in it, better than one with a crossed ninepence. The men in the shop didn't use tobacco, nor swear—they can't do those things where there are women, and we owe it to our brothers to go wherever they work to keep them decent. The widening of woman's sphere is to improve her lot. Let us do it, and if the world scoff, let it scoff—if it sneer, let it sneer—but we will go on emulating the example of the sisters Grimké and Abby Kelley. When they first lectured against slavery they were not listened to as respectfully as you listen to us. So the first female physician meets many difficulties, but to the next the path will be made easy.

Lucretia Mott has been a preacher for years; her right to do so is not questioned among Friends. But when Antoinette Brown felt that she was commanded to preach and to arrest the progress of thousands that were on the road to hell, why, when she applied for ordination, they acted as they had rather the whole world should go to hell than that Antoinette Brown should be allowed to tell them how to keep out of it. She is now ordained over a parish in the state of New York, but when she meets on the temperance platform the Reverend John Chambers or your own General Carey, they greet her with hisses. Theodore Parker said: "The acorn that the schoolboy carries in his pocket and the squirrel stows in his cheek has in it the possibility of an oak, able to withstand, for ages, the cold winter and the driving blast." I have seen the acorn men and women, but never the perfect oak; all are but abortions. The young mother, when first the newborn babe nestles in her bosom and a heretofore unknown love springs up in her heart finds herself unprepared for this new relation in life, and she sends forth the child scarred and dwarfed by her own weakness and imbecility, as no stream can rise higher than its fountain.

Source: Stone, Lucy. "Disappointment Is the Lot of Women." In *History of Woman Suffrage* Vol. I (165–166). Rochester, NY: Charles Mann, 1887.

STREISAND, BARBRA (1942–)

An iconic actor, singer, and humanitarian, Barbara Joan Streisand epitomizes the brave, assertive self-starter in song and film. Born of Polish-Russian-Jewish lineage in Brooklyn on April 24, 1942, to secretary and singer Ida Rosen and Emanuel Streisand, a teacher of English at Elmira Reformatory, she grew up in genteel poverty. While she lived in Williamsburg, her maternal grandmother proclaimed her "on fire."

In 1947, Streisand began schooling at the Jewish Orthodox Yeshiva for girls and attended Shul with her grandfather. After she progressed to P.S. 89, in 1949, her mother wed realtor Louis Kind, adding to the family a stepsister. Streisand escaped her verbally abusive stepfather by gorging on movies and fantasizing a film career. She sang in the high school chorus and at neighborhood celebrations and thrived at history, Spanish, and English. At age 13, she auditioned for professional recordings with "You'll Never Know."

Streisand educated herself by reading the lives of actors Sarah Bernhardt and Eleanora Duse; studying the dramas of William Shakespeare, Anton Chekhov, and Henrik Ibsen; and analyzing Susan Strasberg's stage role in *The Diary of Anne Frank* (1956). In 1959, she graduated from Erasmus High School and pursued stardom in Manhattan. On rejection from the Actors Studio, she studied stagecraft with Alan Miller, took voice lessons, and competed for jobs at the Lion Club gay bar and the Bon Soir nightclub. To develop nuance, she mimicked the recordings of Edith Piaf, Ethel Waters, Lena Horne, and Billie Holiday.

The Rise to Stardom

After succeeding at a string of cabarets in the Midwest, at age 19, Streisand appeared on Jack Paar's television show in April 1961 and performed at the Blue Angel and on *The Garry Moore Show* and *PMEast/PMWest* with Mike Wallace. With her first Broadway audition in late November 1961, she snagged a singing role in the Jerome Weidman–Harold Rome musical *I Can Get It for You Wholesale.* In Boston, Philadelphia, and New York, she played the garment district secretary Miss Marmelstein, an idiosyncratic graceless spinster whose self-deprecating lyrics won applause from Leonard Bernstein. In late 1962, she thrived on the *Ed Sullivan Show,* Bob Hope reviews, and Harrah's in Lake Tahoe.

After Streisand married actor Elliott Gould in Carson City, Nevada, she signed a first record contract with Columbia for *The Barbra Streisand Album* (1963), winner of three Grammys, and toured in California, Indiana, and Illinois. Within a year, her photo appeared on the covers of *Life* and *Time.* In 1966, she bore son Jason Emmanuel Gould and starred in the romantic comedy *Funny Girl* (1968), a stage biography of comedian Fanny Brice featuring elegant costumes that became Streisand's screen trademark. The first of two cinemas on Brice, it won Streisand an Oscar and Golden Globe for setting a unique style of poise and beauty and for the songs "Don't Rain on My Parade" and "People."

In the role of an ebullient Jewish widow, Streisand coordinated a spectacular production number to round out *Hello, Dolly!* (1969), a reprise of Thornton Wilder's romantic comedy *The Matchmaker.* During a difficult two years, she failed at the next films, *On a Clear Day You Can See Forever* (1970) and *The Owl and the Pussycat* (1970). The Streisand-Gould union ended in divorce in 1971.

In 1972, Streisand established Barwood Films and starred in *Up the Sandbox,* the first of two films that featured her son. Costarring with Ryan O'Neal in *What's Up, Doc?* (1972) preceded her breakthrough as a McCarthy era activist opposite Robert Redford in *The Way We Were* (1973), source of a hit title song composed by her friend Marvin Hamlisch. Her rapid rise to fame incorporated acting with Omar Sharif in *Funny Lady* (1975) and alongside Kris Kristofferson in *A Star Is Born* (1976), source of the romantic ballad "Evergreen," winner of an Oscar for musical composition.

Art and Charity

Streisand's versatility reached new heights with *Classical Barbra* (1976), a collection of 10 art songs rendered in English, French, German, Italian, Latin, and Provençal. The singles "What Kind of Fool" and "Woman in Love" energized the pop album *Guilty* (1980), produced by Barry Gibb. With "You Don't Bring Me Flowers" (1978), a duet with Neil Diamond, and the ballad "Memory" from *Cats* in 1981, she set records for female balladeers.

Venturing deeper into female emotions, Streisand played a troubled court defendant in *Nuts* (1987). She expanded her psychological range by directing and featuring in *Yentl* (1983), a cross-gender drama set in Jewish Poland and adapted from a story by Isaac Bashevis Singer. The tour de force established her as a pioneer female writer, producer, director, and star of major feature films.

In memory of her father, Streisand financed a center for Jewish Studies at Hebrew University in Jerusalem. She achieved two Grammys for *The Broadway Album* (1986). Her double role as director and star of *The Prince of Tides* (1991), a cinema version of Pat Conroy's autobiographical novel, earned money and acclaim but few awards for her role as an unhappily married Jewish psychiatrist.

At the American Academy of Achievement in 1992, Streisand's "Women in Film" speech stated outrage that women and minorities had far to go toward grasping fairness. She joined the campaign staff of presidential candidate Bill Clinton and enlarged her political involvement by launching a boycott of Colorado resorts for enacting antigay laws. Following a 1994 tour, she garnered $10 million for environmental, antinuclear, and civil rights funding. For her acceptance of a second Peabody Award from HBO in 1995, she expressed gratitude for opportunities to give back to the people who built her greatness.

On February 3, 1995, Streisand delivered at Harvard's school of government the address "The Artist as Citizen," which exonerated celebrities for their patriotism and political activism. She defended countercultural involvement that sided with poor mothers and the homeless and valorized liberalism for challenging slavery, child labor, fascism, segregation, and apartheid. Dismayed by reactionaries brought to power by the 1994 election, she inveighed against intolerance and efforts to silence artists. She warned, "To deny artists, or any of us, for that matter, free expression and free thought—or worse, to force us to conform to some rigid notion of 'mainstream American values'—is to weaken the very foundation of our democracy" (Streisand 1995).

Streisand resumed her film career in November 1996 with *The Mirror Has Two Faces*, a psychological study of the ugly duckling syndrome. On July 1, 1998, she wed actor James Brolin and settled at a luxurious estate in Malibu. In an interview for *The Advocate* on August 17, 1999, she defended her homosexual son and praised his talents and kindness. She embedded in the statement the names of President George W. Bush, Pat Buchanan, and Newt Gingrich for denying the rights of gay people to marry and predicted a difficult fight for gay rights.

The singer performed two concerts in Australia in 2000 and launched a 2006 tour, the source of the album *Life in Concert* and a gift of $1 million to environmental efforts of the William J. Clinton Foundation. Backed by a traveling orchestra, she spent summer 2007 singing in Switzerland, Austria, France, Germany, Sweden, England, and Ireland and raised funds to defeat an antigay measure in California. Her gift of $5 million in 2009 for cardiovascular research aided a women's center at Cedars-Sinai Hospital.

Streisand's charity performance of "We Are the World" (2010) sent funds to survivors of an earthquake in Haiti. In 2011, she performed to raise funds for the Israel Defense Forces. Her body of work has earned a Golden Globe for the only female best director as well as 10 more Golden Globes, a Cable ACE, New York Drama Critic's Prize, 5 Emmys, 8 Grammys, 2 Oscars, Kennedy Center Honor, a Peabody commendation, and a Tony, a record unexcelled by any other performer. For altruism, she won the Israel Freedom Medal, Woman of Courage Award from the National Organization for Women, and MusiCares Person of 2011 award.

On receipt of a PhD from Hebrew University of Jerusalem, on June 20, 2013, Streisand celebrated a campus where differing ethnic groups, both native and immigrant, shared classes. Against strong orthodox tradition, she claimed the rights of Jewish women to pray at the Wailing Wall and sing in public ritual. She compared the sacred nature of ritual to the everyday respect for compassion, generosity, and dignity.

Five months later, Streisand addressed the *Glamour* magazine Women of 2013 Awards at Carnegie Hall. In a four-minute speech, she seized on the issue of women's health, especially dangers of cardiovascular disease. Her text championed women's rights and urged females to follow Malala Yousafzai's example by denouncing injustice and gendered inequalities.

References

Santopietro, Tom. *The Importance of Being Barbra*. New York: Macmillan, 2006.

Streisand, Barbara. "The Artist as Citizen." February 3, 1995. Harvard IOP at The Kennedy School. Accessed May 15, 2015. http://forum.iop.harvard.edu/content/artist-citizen-barbra-Streisand.

SUTER, SUE (1950–)

An advocate for disabled females, Susan E. Sowle "Sue" Suter breaks the boundaries of entrapment, isolation, and labeling that segregate the handicapped from normal fulfillment and prosperity. Born in Rockford, Illinois, on April 16, 1950, she is the daughter of teacher Shirley Mae Flanagan and endodontist John Thompson Sowle Sr. She learned in toddlerhood the meaning of devaluation for the handicapped. At age two, she contracted polio that required her to wear braces. A doctor advised the family that she would be bedfast the rest of her years.

Because of an inaccessible stairway, Suter missed first grade and entered special education school in second grade. At age seven, she gained from her father a glimpse of her future as an unwed professional who took care of herself. She accepted his direction to study clinical psychology and ventured into regular middle school classes, a dare she later defined as cliff jumping. She entered the University of Illinois in the late 1960s and superintended orientation for incoming freshmen. She completed a BA in psychology in 1972.

Against the direction of a college career adviser, Suter sought an advanced degree in psychology from Eastern Illinois University and graduated in 1974. After marriage to Carl Alexander Suter, a fellow victim of polio and assistant director of the Illinois Department of Rehabilitation Services, in 1972, she interviewed for a first job as a secretary and found her employer wedded to the view of female staff as servants. Because of stairs, she failed at a position with a mental health center.

Independence

To increase the range of employment possibilities, Suter moved into administration. In 1975, she joined the Illinois Department of Mental Health and Developmental Disabilities as a psychologist. On leaving the maternity ward with her infant son Josh in 1980, she heard the doubts of a social worker who feared that a cripple was not capable of tending a newborn. Such double distinctions in disabled females required twice the initiative and affirmation to live beyond a wheelchair.

Paraplegia News extolled Suter's selection in August 1981 as Illinois state coordinator of the U.N. International Year of Disabled Persons. In March 1982, she assembled a conference of the handicapped in Chicago to list recommendations for legislative action and to promote a trade and information fair. Chief among needs, the handicapped and elderly sought improved transportation and mainstream classes and school activities to include the impaired.

In 1984, Suter accepted appointment from Governor James Thompson as director of the Illinois Department of Rehabilitation Services. Her office superintended 2,200 employees in 50 offices and a budget of $150 million intended for vocational rehabilitation. In addition to providing educational options, work placement, transportation, and training, she boosted the number of centers for independent living from 2 to 100 and managed a yearly handicapped rights conference. She won a Harold Scharper Achievement Award and appeared on *Hour Magazine* as a model of ability. In the February 1987 issue, *Glamour* magazine listed her among 10 outstanding young workingwomen.

Mainstream and *Worklife* magazines honored Suter on March 14, 1988, when President Ronald Reagan appointed her director of the U.S. Rehabilitation Services Administration, part of the U.S. Department of Education in Washington, D.C. The commute to the nation's capital rid her of the need to cling to home. Her office managed a budget of $1.5 billion and, after October 1988, shaped Title II of the Family Support Act.

At the end of Suter's federal work, on October 1, 1988, Illinois governor James R. Thompson recruited her to lead the Department of Public Aid in Springfield. In the same year, she received the honor of 1988 Illinois Citizen of the Year, which preceded additional acclaim in 1989 for advancing the Chicago AIDS Advisory Council. While directing the Department of Children and Family Services in Peoria, in fall 1991, she assembled state attorneys, public defenders, judges, and child social workers to a conference on juvenile justice.

To Suter's surprise, she encountered two children who assumed a bullet reduced her to braces and crutches. More than violence, she fought a budget cut of $18.9 million and looming reductions in a staff of 3,200 to achieve reforms in aiding some 29,000 abused, neglected, and abandoned children. Rather than fire 300 workers, in early August 1992, she resigned the job.

On September 3, 1990, when Suter went on job hiatus to run as the Republican candidate for Illinois state comptroller, she became the first handicapped person to seek a state office. In September and October, she pioneered televised ads closed-captioned for the deaf and, on October 7, debated the opposition in a matchup sponsored by the League of Women Voters. On October 16, she received verbal endorsement by candidate George W. Bush at a presidential rally.

During the campaign, Suter overcame difficulties boarding small planes, riding in parades, and addressing supporters from haystacks. Because of the Democratic challenger's charges of fiscal mismanagement in state accounting systems, she pledged to increase efficiency, monitor debt collection, and refuse contracts to businesses in arrears to the state. She lost the election on November 6 but won an award from the Illinois Easter Seal Society.

Advocacy

As president of the World Institute on Disabilities Services, on August 16, 1993, Suter addressed the Ethics in Rehabilitation Conference in Dunedin, New Zealand, on "Women with Disabilities: How to Become a Boat Rocker," a tribute to members of the disability community who fight the fights that other dissidents avoid. She depicted the negative image of handicapped women as weak and sexless and rallied support for females in rich and poor countries who live at the lowest levels of poverty and hopelessness. The text lauded disabled nurturers of children and professional employers who rejected the idea that the handicapped deserved no role in society.

Suter inveighed against the concept of human perfection by blaming advertising for equating normality with consumerism. She legitimized useful and dignified places for the handicapped in ordinary families, among feminists, and on planning and finance committees. In a summary of deaf education, she recited the cycles that replaced handicapped teachers and American Sign Language with nondisabled teachers who guided students toward speech. The lack of role models among the staff dismayed deaf pupils, who saw no examples of the hearing-impaired as adults.

Suter's lecture cited areas of achievement denied to the handicapped female because of poverty, illiteracy, unemployment, inadequate gynecological services, unreliable support services, and alienation from normal society. She recognized a need for vocational education and for empowerment of disabled citizens through civil rights initiatives, such as the Women's Center at the Rehabilitation Institute of Chicago.

Podiums defined Suter's working world. At the Robert Morris College commencement in December 1996, she emphasized changes in careers, missteps, and failures. Above other resources, she reminded graduating seniors that family and friends stood ready to support and encourage.

On September 22, 1999, Suter presented a keynote address to the Association for the Severely Handicapped stressing the dreams, values, and contributions of the disabled. In a recap of the infanticide of less than perfect babies throughout history, she declared human defects normal. To combat stereotypes and bias against the blind, deaf, and crippled, she charged counselors with suppressing client ambition by reducing risk factors in their careers.

Suter endeared her audience by claiming them as family. The text named the Americans with Disabilities Act and the Individuals with Disabilities Education Act as victories under challenge. She warned that clients on waiting lists stymied the Bureaucratic Quality Assurance systems and proposed vouchers giving choices in negotiating services. The detailed speech accused higher education of catering to football stars and lab researchers rather than supplying the basic needs of the disabled.

In lectures and panel discussions, such as the Disability Research Institute Symposium on April 26, 2001, Suter accentuated the centrality of inclusion in business and the value of a paycheck to the disabled. She joined the Social Security

Administration as associate commission of the Office of Employment Support in 2004. On June 21, 2007, before the U.S. Senate Finance Committee, she proposed detailed changes to the Ticket to Work program reflecting the value of employment to the blind and handicapped, who preferred self-support rather than Social Security benefits.

Suter continued to advocate for the disabled as a member of the Post-Polio Health International board in 2009 and, on May 19, 2009, in testimony before the U.S. House Ways and Means Subcommittee on Social Security. In 2013, in Urbana, Illinois, she acquired a three-year membership on the board for the Care & Treatment of Persons with a Developmental Disability. Her honors include a Rubloff Memorial Award from the United Cerebral Palsy Association, an achievement commendation from the Illinois Coalition of Citizens with Disabilities, and a citation for distinguished service from the National Governor's Association.

Source: Bowman, Cynthia Grant. *Dawn Clark Netsch: A Political Life*. Evanston, IL: Northwestern University Press, 2010.

T

TAN, AMY (1952–)

A popular author and speaker, Amy Tan introduces readers to Chinese-American perspectives on womanhood and blended cultures. Born in Oakland, California, on February 19, 1952, to nurse Daisy Tu Ching, a Shanghai native, and electrical engineer John Tan, a Baptist preacher at the Chinese Baptist Church in Fresno, she and brothers Peter and John Tan Jr. experienced the expectations of old and new countries common to first-generation Americans. After four moves about central California, the family located to Santa Clara, where Tan was the only Asian child in school.

Tan tried to fit in with whites by squeezing her Chinese nose with a clothespin and avoiding Chinese foods. She eavesdropped on gossip sessions of her mother and aunt, who conversed in Mandarin and Shanghainese. She won a transistor radio in an essay contest in 1960 for "What the Library Means to Me," her tribute to the Santa Rosa Library, where she read Grimms' fairy tales, the Bible, World Book Encyclopedia, and a forbidden copy of *The Catcher in the Rye.* From the single achievement, she decided on becoming a writer.

To satisfy a love of words, Tan had to elude her parents' choice of neurosurgery and classical piano as her future. In 1967, the deaths of her father and brother Peter six months apart from brain tumors catapulted Daisy into suicidal thoughts and attempts to slit her daughter's throat with a meat cleaver. To flee memories of loss and fear that a curse clouded their destiny, Daisy moved the family through Rotterdam, The Hague, Utrecht, Werkhoven, and Amsterdam to Switzerland.

At the resort town of Montreux, Daisy enrolled her "Amy-ah" at the Institut Monte Rosa, an international academy. Among rich pupils, Tan identified with hippies and lax morals but managed to graduate a year early. Daisy lectured her on shallow, transitory values and longings to be popular rather than a strong individual.

Deracination unbalanced Tan and influenced her to enter an affair and plot an elopement to Austria with a 24-year-old German army deserter and dealer in marijuana and hashish. Rescued by her mother from jail for possessing hashish cigarettes, Tan returned to California. In 1969, she began majoring in medicine on scholarship at Linfield College in McMinnville, Oregon, while working at a pizzeria. She spent her sophomore year at San Jose City College to be near Italian-American law student Louis DeMattei. By majoring in English and linguistics and earning graduate degrees in both, she angered Daisy and cut off communication with home.

A Writing Career

After marrying DeMattei, a tax attorney, in 1974, Tan pursued a PhD in linguistics at the University of California at Berkeley and relaxed by improvising jazz for the piano. In 1976, she worked as language adviser to the Alameda County program for the mentally handicapped and developed programs to increase verbal communication with retarded children. By age 30, she freelanced technical writing for Bank of America, Pacific Bell, IBM, AT&T, and *Emergency Room Reports.* Her commercial career instilled an appreciation of deadlines but left her drained of spirit.

The workaholic schedule coincided with the rise of Asian and feminist fiction in the global market, which intrigued Tan to experiment with short fiction in 1983 at the Squaw Valley Community of Writers workshop. In 1985, she assuaged her ailing mother by interviewing her for topics to apply to fiction. In 1987, Tan and her husband accompanied Daisy on a trip to China to meet three half-sisters—Jindo, Yuhang, and June "Liljun" Wang—whom their mother abandoned during the Communist takeover of 1949. The visit placed Tan in an evocative setting and filled in gaps in her genealogy after her mother emigrated to San Francisco.

Beginning with tentative short fiction marked by distinctive voice and style, Tan wrote "Waiting between the Trees." With the aid of editor Faith Sale at G. P. Putnam's Sons, Tan developed the story "Endgame" into a confessional novel, *The Joy Luck Club* (1989), an international bestseller and the subject of a 1993 film adaptation. The plot disclosed the secrets and longings of female mahjong players through episodic talk-story. The story earned acclaim from the Bay Area Book Reviewers, a Commonwealth Club Gold Award, and nominations from the National Book Critics Circle and a National Book Award.

At Daisy's insistence, Tan fictionalized her mother's life in *The Kitchen God's Wife* (1991), a harrowing tale of an abused drudge who survived the bombing of Nanking in World War II. From jail, she escaped on the last boat from Shanghai to the United States to unite with her lover. The second novel won a *Booklist* editor's choice, commendation from Bay Area Book Reviewers, and selection for college courses in Asian-American literature and ethnic and women's studies.

To stem a mental disease that had harmed her mother and maternal grandmother, Tan began taking antidepressants. Success encouraged her variance of modes—to historical fiction for *The Year of No Flood*, to collections in *State of the Language* and *Best American Short Stories 1999*, and to magazine stories for *Seventeen*, *Atlantic Monthly*, and *McCall's*. Still inspired by annual trips to China, she turned to children's picture books for *The Moon Lady*, the tale of a harvest festival, and *Sagwa, the Chinese Siamese Cat*, source of a PBS-TV children's series.

Global Recognition

As a recognized leader of feminist fiction, Tan won subsequent audiences with *The Hundred Secret Senses* (1995), a story of bicultural sisterhood. A ban on foreign travelers in 1996 kept her from returning to China. Shortly after her mother's death from heart disease and dementia in 1999, the novelist composed *The Bonesetter's Daughter* (2000), a taut framework mystery alternately set during the Taiping Rebellion of 1850 and in the early 20th century during analysis of the fossilized skeleton known as Peking Man. On a book tour, she addressed readers in 50 cities and advised filmmakers of a PBS documentary *Journey of the Bonesetter's Daughter*. Her honors increased with a 1996 Golden Plate Award, Parents' Choice Award, and an Audie from the Audio Publishers Association.

Tan traveled with authors Barbara Kingsolver, Dave Barry, and Stephen King, members of the singing group the Rock Bottom Remainders. She compiled *The Opposite of Fate: A Book of Musings* (2003), recapping a medical nightmare from July 1999 to 2002 with late-stage Lyme disease. She and her husband built an open-plan house in Sausalito in 2006 to accommodate her infirmities. To advocate for victims suffering the joint pain, nausea, exhaustion, hallucination, and epileptic seizures brought on by tick bite, she co-formed LymeAid 4 Kids, a foundation that underwrites diagnosis and a lifetime of treatment with intravenous antibiotics for uninsured children.

Continuing a motif of the outsider in Asia, Tan published *Saving Fish from Drowning* (2005), a model of storytelling set in Yunnan and on the Burma Road. The novel won honors from the Asian Pacific American Librarians Association. For TED Talks, she delivered an address, "Where Does Creativity Hide?" (2008), punctuated by rigorous gestures at slides.

Tan's speaking career bifurcated with interviews and discussions of her publications and health crisis with Lyme disease. At the Chautauqua Institution on July 10, 2008, she presented "Finding Meaning through Writing," a witty, relaxed reflection on her immersion in reading and letter writing in childhood under the fictional name Effie May Hoodwinkle. On a personal note, with "A Genius Mind Goes Missing" for *Candid* in summer 2012, she described to a television audience the exotic symptoms of Lyme disease that she identified on the Internet. The spread of bacteria through her nervous system left her mentally muddled, unable to drive, and dependent on a cane and her Yorkshire terrier, Tux.

Tan's reprise of mother-daughter hostility in the saga *The Valley of Amazement* (2013) extends the milieu to the urban Chinese entertainment world of courtesans skilled at the illusion of romance. She based the story of family estrangement on a snapshot taken in Shanghai around 1910 of nine prostitutes and her grandmother, Jing-mei, who may have died of suicide or poisoning. She investigated details at Dimen, a village in Guizhou province, and studied an ethnic group that spoke a lilting language never captured in print. She summarized the trek in an essay for *National Geographic.*

Following a two-book tour of Iceland, Italy, Belgium, Germany, and Holland, at Baylor University in Waco, Texas, on September 29, 2014, Tan endorsed the humanities for their value to the individual encountering the intergenerational tensions that assailed her in girlhood. In October 2014, she promoted humanitarianism by delivering a keynote speech at the first Philippine Literary Festival in Manila and supporting an ingathering of books for Filipino libraries destroyed by Typhoon Yolanda. In a televised interview for *CBS This Morning*, she explained her need for extensive research into aphrodisiacs, the sale of girls to brothels, and sexual bondage that sometimes ended in the deaths of teenaged concubines.

Reference

McLoughlin, Kate. "Reading in Reverse." *Oxonian Review* 3, no. 2 (March 1, 2004): 1.

TERRELL, MARY CHURCH (1863–1954)

A first-generation free black educator and language scholar, Mary "Mollie" Eliza Church Terrell compounded racial aspirations with an appeal for suffrage. A Tennessean, she was born on September 23, 1863, during the Union army's occupation of Memphis some nine months after the Emancipation Proclamation of January 1, 1863. She internalized the work ethic of her freed parents, hairdresser Louisa Ayers, owner of Lou Church's Store, and Robert Reed "Bob" Church, a mulatto cabin boy and mess hall dishwasher and steward on steamboat trips from New Orleans along the Mississippi as far north as Cairo, Illinois.

At age three, Terrell saw the results of the Memphis race riots from May 1 to 3, 1866, when her father was attacked and his business vandalized. After martial law restored calm to the city, she entered kindergarten held in a church basement. Eviction from a whites-only first-class train car in 1868 impressed on her the second-class citizenship of blacks and the prominence of her father, who pulled a pistol and faced down a racist railroad conductor.

After Robert Church's divorce from Louisa in 1869, Terrell and her brother Thomas passed to their mother's custody. Terrell sought an advanced degree at Oberlin College, the only institution that accepted female and nonwhite students. Before graduation in 1884 with a degree in classics, she edited the *Oberlin Review* and earned membership in literary societies and the title of class poet. During a sojourn in New York City, she realized that life in Memphis and at Oberlin had lulled her into false assumptions about the Jim Crow era.

Terrell completed an MA in language arts and, in 1890, returned to the Washington school system. In Memphis on October 18, 1891, she wed future federal judge Robert Heberton Terrell, an attorney from Virginia who taught law courses at Howard University. Because of his income, she could pursue an oratorical career.

Already the only woman to preside over the Bethel Literary and Historical Society in Washington, D.C., in 1895, Terrell did volunteer work and became the nation's first black female school board member. A friend, orator Frederick Douglass, convinced her to push for female participation in the electorate, which she did through professional oratory on behalf of the National American Woman Suffrage Association and the Federation of Afro-American Women. In 1896, she chaired the National Association of Colored Women (NACW), a merger of small women's clubs that devoted energies to the welfare of infants, preschoolers, orphans, and the aged and poor. Her first keynote address to the NACW in Nashville on September 15, 1897, called for ethnic pride, activism, and solidarity and self-respect for children.

In 1897, *New England Magazine* printed Terrell's oration "How Shall the Colored Youth of the South Be Educated?" Her immersion in education preceded her formation of the National Association of College Women, for which she delivered the address "The Progress of Colored Women" (1898). A measured evaluation, the speech detailed the numerous methods by which educated black females benefited society.

To the United Women's Club in Washington, D.C., on October 10, 1906, Terrell's lecture "What It Means to Be Colored in the Capital of the U.S." focused on personal observations and experiences. She cited hotel accommodations for Asian and Amerindian guests, but none for blacks. She deplored the humiliation of her people while they tried to access streetcars, restaurants, theaters, colleges, trade unions, hospitals, and monuments, especially George Washington's tomb. The few well-paid jobs for black women she identified as dressmaker, nurse, and teacher.

At the establishment of the National Association for the Advancement of Colored People in 1909, Terrell joined founder W. E. B. Du Bois, a black critic and historian, in establishing goals and in protesting the court martial of black Buffalo Soldiers arrested at the Brownsville riot on August 13, 1906, in southeastern Texas. Reviving the suffrage push, she celebrated the Nineteenth Amendment to the U.S. Constitution, which Congress ratified on August 18, 1920. She advised the Republican National Committee on encouraging the vote of women and blacks.

Following Robert's death on December 20, 1924, at home in Annapolis, Maryland, Terrell began composing a memoir, *A Colored Woman in a White World* (1940). In 1949, a year after Oberlin College conferred on her an honorary doctorate, she integrated the American Association of University Women. Eight weeks after the Supreme Court's *Brown v. Board of Education* integrated public schools nationally, she died on July 24, 1954.

References

Fradin, Dennis B., and Judith Bloom Fradin. *Fight On!: Mary Church Terrell's Battle for Integration*. New York: Houghton Mifflin, 2003.

Terrell, Mary Church. "Lynching from a Negro's Point of View." In *Witnessing Lynching: American Writers Respond*. Piscataway, NJ: Rutgers University Press, 2003, 98–105.

THE PROGRESS OF COLORED WOMEN (EXCERPT) BY MARY CHURCH TERRELL NATIONAL AMERICAN WOMEN'S SUFFRAGE ASSOCIATION COLUMBIA THEATER, WASHINGTON, D.C. FEBRUARY 18, 1898

A model achiever of first-generation freeborn blacks, Mary Church Terrell of Memphis, Tennessee, rallied audiences to support women's and civil rights. As president of NACW, she focused on the needs of orphans, infants, and preschoolers as a means of preventing juvenile delinquency. On the 50th anniversary of the Seneca Falls Convention and the beginning of the women's suffrage movement, her push for civility and cultivation of the youngest citizens through early childhood education anticipated the success of the K–12 system and Head Start, initiated in 1965.

. . . As an organization of women, nothing lies nearer the heart of the National Association than the children, many of whose lives, so sad and dark, we might brighten and bless. It is the kindergarten we need. Free kindergartens in every city and hamlet of this broad land we must have, if the children are to receive from us what it is our duty to give. Already during the past year kindergartens have been established and successfully maintained by several organizations, from which most encouraging reports have come. May their worthy example be emulated, till in no branch of the Association shall the children of the poor, at least, be deprived of the blessings which flow from the kindergarten alone.

The more unfavorable the environments of children, the more necessary is it that steps be taken to counteract baleful influences on innocent victims. How imperative is it then that as colored women, we inculcate correct principles and set good examples for our own youth, whose little feet will have so many thorny paths of prejudice temptation, and injustice to tread. The colored youth is vicious we are told, and statistics showing the multitudes of our boys and girls who crowd the penitentiaries and fill the jails appall and dishearten us. But side by side with these facts and figures of crime I would have presented and pictured the miserable hovels from which these youth criminals come.

Make a tour of the settlements of colored people, who in many cities are relegated to the most noisome sections permitted by the municipal government, and behold the mites of humanity who infest them. Here are our little ones, the future representatives of the race, fairly drinking in the pernicious example of their elders, coming in contact with nothing but ignorance and vice, till at the age of six, evil habits are formed which no amount of civilizing or Christianizing can ever completely break.

Listen to the cry of our children. In imitation of the example set by the Great Teacher of men, who could not offer himself as a sacrifice, until he had made an eternal plea for the innocence and helplessness of childhood, colored women are everywhere reaching out after the waifs and strays, who without their aid may be doomed to lives of evil and shame. As an organization, the National Association of Colored Women feels that the establishment of kindergartens is the special mission which we are called to fulfill. So keenly alive are we to the necessity of rescuing our little ones, whose noble qualities are deadened and dwarfed by the very atmosphere which they breathe, that the officers of the Association are now trying to secure means by which to send out a kindergarten organizer, whose duty it shall be both to arouse the conscience of our women, and to establish kindergartens, wherever the means therefore can be secured.

And so, lifting as we climb, onward and upward we go, struggling and striving and hoping that the buds and blossoms of our desires will burst into glorious fruition ere long. With courage born of success achieved in the past, with a keen sense of the responsibility which we shall continue to assume, we look forward to a future large with promise and hope. Seeking no favors because of our color, nor patronage because of our needs, we knock at the bar of justice, asking an equal chance.

Source: Terrell, Mary Church. *The Progress of Colored Women*. Washington, DC: Smith Brothers, 1898.

THOMPSON, DOROTHY (1893–1961)

Journalist and broadcaster Dorothy Celene Thompson Lewis delivered prophetic radio addresses preceding World War II and peace initiatives during the Cold War. Born in Lancaster, New York, on July 9, 1893, to Margaret Grierson of Staffordshire,

England, and emigrant Peter Thompson, a Methodist Episcopal minister from Northumberland, she was motherless by age seven after Margaret died from a bungled home abortion. After two years at the Lewis Institute, she completed a BA degree in economics and political science from Syracuse University.

In Buffalo from 1914 to 1917, Thompson joined the final push for suffrage in New York and crusaded throughout the state for social equity. With a year of writing for the Jewish Correspondent Bureau and the American Red Cross in Paris, in 1920, she achieved a posting in Vienna for the *Chicago Daily News*. She investigated Irish political party Sinn Féin in Cork in August and advocated resettlement of European Jews in Israel. For the Philadelphia *Public Ledger* and *New York Evening News*, in 1925, she managed Berlin press corps news from Germany, Czechoslovakia, Austria, Hungary, Romania, Yugoslavia, Turkey, and Greece.

Thompson moved on in 1927 to an international assignment for the *New York Post*, for which she covered the 10th anniversary of the Russian Revolution and the careers of Turkey's modernizer, Kemal Atatürk, musician Richard Strauss, and neurologist Sigmund Freud. At age 35, she divorced Hungarian-Jewish novelist Joseph Bard and, in London on May 14, 1928, wed Nobel laureate Harry Sinclair Lewis, father of their son, Michael Lewis. Under her patronym, she began lecturing in Canada on prohibition and rescuing European refugees.

In Munich in 1931, Thompson became the first Western reporter to interview Adolf Hitler, whose appearance and political significance she demeaned in an article for *Cosmopolitan*. She incorporated antifascist opinions in the eyewitness history *I Saw Hitler!* (1932) and commented on foreign affairs for *Saturday Evening Post* and *Pictorial Review*. For criticizing the rise of Nazism in the Third Reich, on August 25, 1934, Hitler himself ordered National Socialist officials to oust her from Germany.

To the Women's Conference on Current Problems in September 1934, Thompson presented a talk on changing gender standards, an introit to her two decades as an internationally renowned political analyst. For eight million readers of the *New York Herald Tribune*, in 1936, she began writing on power mongering, propaganda, neutrality, and hunger in France in the syndicated column *On the Record*, which ran thrice weekly in 170 newspapers. In addition to producing monthly domestic commentary in *Ladies' Home Journal*, she published *Refugees: Anarchy or Organization?* (1938), broadcast from Pall Mall in crisp and objective prose, and lectured on a span of topics ranging from conditions in Poland, Russia, and the Middle East to the Jewish question and the changing world order.

With radio addresses, Thompson advanced her career from reporter and author to media celebrity. For NBC and the Mutual Network, she aired editorials challenging U.S. isolationism and raised cash to provide legal defense for Herschel Grynszpan, a 17-year-old Polish-Jewish assassin and martyr. Beginning on September 1,

1939, she remained at the microphone for 15 days reporting in English and German on the Nazi invasion of Poland.

Because Thompson endorsed Franklin D. Roosevelt's last presidential campaign, in 1941, she lost her post at the *Herald Tribune*, a Republican newspaper that supported Wendell Willkie. To the International Affiliation of Sales and Advertising Clubs in Toronto, she delivered a commanding oratory, "Hitler's Plans for Canada and the United States," which she broadcast over the CBC on May 2, 1941. She warned, "What happened to the Jews, and then happened to the Czechs and the Poles, is proposed for the English, the greatest Diaspora in human history" (Thompson 1941, 3).

After Thompson wed Czechoslovakian painter Maximilian Kopf, a refugee from a German concentration camp, in 1943, she visited Jerusalem to witness the status of Jews. Although she suffered hearing loss, her only departure from a regular radio address occurred on November 13, 1944, when she received news of the combat death of her stepson, Wells Lewis. Her sympathy for the 700,000 Arab refugees in Palestine and support for global disarmament indicated a political shift toward conservatism and away from the mainstream direction of previous topics.

Thompson renewed the compelling analyses of World War II by warning Americans of the dangers of Communism, the nuclear arms race, and the Cold War. In a return to feminism in September 1947, she formed World Organization of Mothers of All Nations (Woman, Inc.). She intended her "Woman's Manifesto" in the November issue of *Ladies' Home Journal* to denounce war as a global cancer, bolster peace among families, and impress on the United Nations Security Council that females nurture nonviolence in the home.

Thompson continued probing global politics in the 1950s with speeches on Stalinism, the Arab world, and globalism. Because of attacks on her integrity for embracing unpopular opinions, her long dominance of newspaper, radio, and lecture events ended abruptly. After she ceased writing *On the Record* in 1958, her health declined from cardiac disease. On January 30, 1961, during a visit to her son and two grandsons in Lisbon, Portugal, she died of heart attack.

References

Laville, Helen. *Cold War Women: The International Activities of American Women's Organisations*. Manchester, UK: University of Manchester Press, 2002.

"Noted German Correspondent Deplores Banishment of Women to Kitchen." *Vassar Miscellany News* 19, no. 10 (November 3, 1934): 1, 4.

Thompson, Dorothy. "Hitler's Plans for Canada and the United States." Accessed May 12, 2014. http://podcast.klsh.kl.edu.tw/.

THE MODERN COUP D'ETAT (EXCERPT)
BY DOROTHY THOMPSON
U.S. SENATE JUDICIAL HEARINGS, WASHINGTON, D.C.
MARCH 31, 1937

A member of the bipartisan National Committee to Uphold Constitutional Government, Dorothy Thompson, a print and radio journalist from Lancaster, New York, applied her experience with failed democracies in Germany and Italy to a proposed infringement on constitutional law by the Roosevelt administration. With courtesy, but concern for the nation, she concluded that the Judiciary Bill gave the executive branch too much power to stymie constitutional checks and balances. To ensure input from varied professions, the committee involved businessmen, attorneys, clergymen, and physicians through leaflets and media addresses. As a result of concerted effort, the judiciary reform lost steam via a rewriting by the Senate and passed into law on August 26 in a revised and weakened form.

I am not an expert on constitutional law. . . . I have been for some years, as a foreign correspondent, an observer at the collapse of constitutional democracies. You might say I have been a researcher into the mortality of republics. The outstanding fact of our times is the decline and fall of constitutional democracy. A great need of our time is for more accurate analysis of the pathology of constitutional government. . . .

I have never suggested President Roosevelt is trying to establish a dictatorship. But I have said that if any president wanted to establish a dictatorship and do so with all the appearance of legality, this is the way he would take. The President's plan may be legally constitutional, but it is not politically constitutional. It strikes at the Supreme Court and Constitution in the most radical and drastic fashion imaginable, because it proposes to switch the Supreme Bench into line with the current political majority. What it proposes to create is a court whose eyes are fixed, not upon the Constitution and upon the whole body of existing law, but upon the White House and the ruling majority in Congress. It proposes to make the Supreme Court the instrument of that majority. . . .

The modern coup d'etat, by which so many democratic systems have fallen, does not destroy the legal apparatus of the state. The modern revolution is not made by violence. It keeps it, for the coup d'etat wishes to appear legal. It only alters its spirit and its aim. Mr. Hitler took an oath to the constitution of Weimar, and he has never offered another constitution. He has just obliterated it by a series of decrees backed by a supine parliament. The courts are all there but they are packed. He calls his system democracy, but we call it dictatorship. . . .

The failure of the German republic was not a failure to respond to the demands of the masses. It perished, not because it failed to meet human needs, but rather because it guaranteed to meet them and there came a time when it could not possibly meet them on the scale to which the people had become accustomed. And eventually the German people followed a leader who promised them neither shorter hours nor higher wages, but who demanded sacrifice, and in return promised only one thing: order and the establishment of a unifying principle of a unified Germany. . . .

The prevention against today's majority mortgaging tomorrow's majority lay in a written constitution and an independent Supreme Court to interpret that Constitution. It is true that the Supreme Court is conservative. It is conservative by its very nature. And that, gentlemen, is its function—to conserve.

These bills . . . add up to a consistent picture. The picture is of a tremendously centralized government with a power and authority vested in the president not far from equal to the power and authority vested in Mussolini or in Stalin. . . .

Source: Thompson, Dorothy. "Reorganization of the Federal Judiciary." *Hearings on S. 1392.* 75th Cong., 1st sess. Washington, DC: U.S. Government Printing Office, 1937, 858–873.

TRECKEL, PAULA (1953–)

Academic and book reviewer Paula Ann Treckel channels her love of female history into the mentoring of college students in studies of the women's movement. A native of Kent, Ohio, she was born on March 15, 1953, to Eleanore Lucille Ciufo, a school nurse at the Kent State University clinic, and economics professor Karl Frederick Treckel, an employee of Eastman Kodak and trainer of officers during World War II.

With the intent of following her father's career teaching labor law, collective bargaining, and trade unions, Treckel attended Kent State University. While majoring in history, she served on the student activities board. During pursuit of advanced degrees at Syracuse University in 1976 and 1978, she focused scholarship on American women's history. As outcomes of research, she published "An Historiographical Essay: Women on the American Frontier" (1975) and completed the dissertation "English Women on Seventeenth Century American Frontiers" (1978). Her treatise "Jane Grey Swisshelm and Feminism in Early Minnesota" appeared in the spring 1980 issue of *Midwest Review.*

In 1980, Treckel wed Herbert A. "Herb" Page, a golf pro and coach at Kent State, and retained her patronym. She earned student respect as a deliverer of comprehensive lectures on such topics as contemporary wedding customs and the education and marriage of white women in the antebellum South. From 1981, she commuted daily from Ohio to teach American history at Allegheny College in

Meadville, Pennsylvania, and filled women's studies courses with biographies of such figures as colonial gentlewomen Maria Taylor Byrd and Lucy Parke Byrd, a rebel against the dominance of her husband, William Byrd II, a stalwart of the Southern patriarchal ideal.

Treckel's 1989 publication, "Breastfeeding and Maternal Sexuality in Colonial America" for the *Journal of Interdisciplinary History*, examined the extension of lactation to regulate the frequency of conception and childbearing. She accounted for the medical assumptions that breast milk diverted menstrual flow and that breasts became conduits of infection, sexual impurity, and the physical and emotional traits and values of the mother. She disclosed the discussions of slave owners on setting the minimal nutritional standards required to yield viable black children. Her treatise also described the gradual acceptance of black breast milk as suitable for wet nurses to feed white babies. On the Allegheny campus on March 10, 1994, she extended her interest in gender history with the humanities lecture "Lucy Parke Byrd: The Dynamics of Gender and Race in Early Virginia."

In celebration of 75 years of female enfranchisement, to the Chautauqua Institution in New York on July 28, 1995, Treckel presented to 5,500 listeners "Forging the Thunderbolts: Elizabeth Cady Stanton and American Feminism." Recapping the Seneca Falls assembly of suffragists in New York on July 19, 1848, Treckel pictured Stanton as a diminutive mother of three who developed a case of nerves at the thought that her Declaration of Sentiments would appear in U.S. newspapers.

Treckel stressed the poignant fact that neither Elizabeth nor her colleague, Susan B. Anthony, survived to the end of the campaign in August 1920. The addition of feminists Lucretia Mott, Sojourner Truth, Antoinette Brown Blackwell, Lucy Stone, and Sarah and Angelina Grimké to the historic coterie increased a sisterhood that burgeoned into a national feminist drive to secure the vote for women. Her Chautauqua topic explored the synergy of Stanton and Anthony. Stanton stayed home and combed letters and news clippings for usable material for the suffrage campaign and forwarded finished speeches to Anthony. While Anthony epitomized the voice of feminism, Stanton symbolized the advocacy and dissent of the middle-class, married woman.

In 1996, Treckel compiled *To Comfort the Heart: Women in Seventeenth-Century America*, a summation of interaction among female slaves, Indians, housewives, and gentlewomen on the North American mainland from 1600 to 1900. For the course "Life in Colonial America," she followed English pilgrims and Puritans on their voyages to the New World and surveyed warfare and the developing tobacco and rice economies in New England, on Chesapeake Bay, and in the plantations of Carolina and Roanoke, Virginia. The text noted the criminalization of wife beating by the Plymouth and Massachusetts Bay legislatures.

Treckel's probing analyses of female intellect included the ingenuity of Eliza Lucas Pinckney, the plantation mistress who, in 1739, introduced commercial indigo to the Southern economy. In a treatise for *Southern Women* and the text *Developing Dixie: Modernization in a Traditional Society* (1985), the author described Pinckney as dutiful, affectionate, and obedient. Treckel's lectures won her the 1996 Julian Ross Award for Excellence in Teaching. She issued her conclusions about the clash between patriarchal and companionate wedlock with the treatise "The Empire of My Heart" in the 1997 issue of *Virginia Magazine of History & Biography.*

In the 2000s, Treckel turned her scrutiny of women's lives to the 21st century with comments on the focus on the modern bride at weddings and the need of working-class women to remain employed rather than rear children at home. On October 7, 2000, she appeared at the National Women's Hall of Fame in Seneca Falls to accept a posthumous honor to Ida Tarbell, whom she lionized in the 2001 *American History* article "Lady Muckraker." After completing the course "Problems in the History of American Women" and a spring seminar on the colonial witchcraft trials and Satanism, in April 2014, Treckel retired from 35 years in the classrooms at St. Benedict and St. John's and Allegheny College.

See Also: Anthony, Susan B.; Blackwell, Antoinette Brown; Mott, Lucretia; Stanton, Elizabeth Cady; Stone, Lucy; Truth, Sojourner.

Reference

Holmes, Alex. "Retiring Professor Profile: Paula Treckel." *The Campus*, April 25, 2014.

FORGING THE THUNDERBOLTS: ELIZABETH CADY STANTON AND AMERICAN FEMINISM (EXCERPT) BY PAULA TRECKEL CHAUTAUQUA INSTITUTION, CHAUTAUQUA, NEW YORK JULY 28, 1995

Women's history scholar Paula Treckel vivified the Seneca Falls assembly of suffragists in New York on July 19, 1848. By channeling her love of female history into the minds of listeners, she cultivated appreciation of the women's movement. Two decades later, the message of "sovereignty of self" continued to inspire women to declare their individuality and equality and to demand full citizenship devoid of gendered obstacles.

As we gather today to commemorate the 75th anniversary of the passage of the 19th Amendment to the Constitution granting women the right to vote, I would like to pay tribute to the work of the woman who began it all. A woman who dared to dream, who asked "why not?" A woman who started a revolution: Elizabeth Cady Stanton. . . . Together with friends and sister-reformers, [she] had called the meeting that would inaugurate the women's rights movement in America.

. . . Stanton asserted, "It is the duty of women of this country to secure to themselves their sacred right to the elective franchise." . . . The vote was an emblem of women's equality, a symbol of their citizenship. It was also a necessary political tool enabling women to secure their rights and free themselves from their dependence upon men.

. . . For Elizabeth Cady Stanton, the women's rights movement was intensely personal, it was also highly political. . . . She shared her husband's belief that reformers must use the political process to bring about change. Deprived of the vote, their voices muted, women would forever be dependent upon men to achieve their equality. To be free, women must become politically involved. And to do that they must demand the right to vote.

. . . The 15th Amendment (adopted in 1870) was the great betrayal: "The Right of citizens of the United States to vote shall not be denied or abridged on account of race, color, or previous condition of servitude." No mention of sex was made. The battle lines were drawn. . . . How could the nation grant the right to vote to ignorant, uneducated black men and immigrant men, yet deny the right to vote to educated, native born white women?

Elizabeth Cady Stanton and Susan B. Anthony . . . advocated women's right to divorce, and to voluntary motherhood (or what we would call birth control today). They supported the expansion of women's property rights, equal education opportunities, access to the professions, and equal pay for equal work—ideas that are goals of the feminist movement even to today. . . . It was Stanton's attacks on marriage, the very bedrock of nineteenth century gender roles, that upset her audience the most, and her words were calculated to provoke: "A man marrying gives up no right, she argued, but a woman, every right, even the most sacred of all, the right to her own person." . . . This was the very basis of Stanton's feminism—women's "Sovereignty of Self." . . . In many ways, Stanton was too radical for this new generation of women; her ideas too outrageous for the vast majority of women who became involved in suffrage by the end of the century. She spoke less and less on the suffrage trail. Instead, she retired to her study and wrote. . . .

For Elizabeth Cady Stanton, while the vote was important—she was its first supporter, after all—it was just a tool. A means to a larger end—the Sovereignty of Self. . . . [She] systematically attacked the institutions she believed impeded women's freedom and progress—education, the law, government, the economy, marriage, . . . the church. . . .

Stanton's writings, her speeches, her enthusiasm and her life provide inspiration for generations of American feminists, even to the present day.

Source: Treckel, Paula. "Forging the Thunderbolts: Elizabeth Cady Stanton and American Feminism." Chautauqua Institution, July 28, 1995. Reprinted by permission from Paula Treckel.

TRUTH, SOJOURNER (CA. 1797–1883)

A commanding figure on the abolitionist speaker's circuit, Sojourner Truth shaped a pseudonym as well as a shrewd persona based on black dialect, song, and experience with human bondage. An illiterate black native of Hurley, New York, she was born Isabella Hardenbergh Baumfree around 1797 to James Baumfree (or Bomefree) and his third wife, Elizabeth Betsey Baumfree, an abductee from Guinea. The slave family belonged to merchant Johannis and Catherine Rutsen Hardenbergh, rich Dutch landowners in Ulster, Sullivan, and Delaware counties, where the patent originally extended over two million acres of the Catskill Mountains.

Sold to numerous owners, Truth labored in corn, flax, and tobacco fields as a child. While working as a domestic, she endured lashings for not speaking English and sexual abuse at the hands of enslaver Isaac Dumont in New Paltz, New York. In 1815, she wed an older slave, Thomas Dumont, and in 1820, lost value from an injury to the fingers on her right hand. When New York abolished slavery in 1826, Sojourner was freed and adopted the name Isabella "Belle" Van Wagener (or Wagenen).

Living with her baby, Sophia, in New York, in 1829, the freedwoman experienced a divine vision and involved herself in Methodist evangelism. On June 1, 1843, she experienced hallucinations and voices ordering her to adopt her pseudonym and to sing gospel songs and preach love and universal brotherhood based on scriptural examples. For seven years, she meandered New England addressing churches, camp meetings, and street audiences in her mannish voice.

Sojourner made an initial abolitionist oratory in autumn 1844, followed by an address to the American Anti-Slavery Society in New York City in May 1845. After another oration to the Rhode Island Anti-Slavery Society in Providence in 1850, she altered her mission field to Indiana, Kansas, Missouri, and Ohio. She financed her efforts by publishing a feminist memoir, *The Narrative of Sojourner Truth: A Bondswoman of Olden Time*, ghostwritten by Massachusetts abolitionist Olive Gilbert.

A rigorous schedule in late 1850–1857 directed Truth to an abolition society in Plymouth, Massachusetts, and a formal platform presentation in Rochester, New York. On October 23, 1850, at Brinley Hall in Worcester, Massachusetts, she integrated the first Women's Rights Convention. At a pinnacle of female oratory in the United States, she delivered an extempore address, "Ain't I a Woman?" and disclosed the sale of most of her children.

The earnest testimony silenced preachers who heckled and debased her. Worded as a first-person challenge to attendees of the Ohio Women's Rights Convention in Akron on May 29, 1851, the speech entered history in three versions issued by the *New York Tribune*, by William Lloyd Garrison's *The Liberator*, and by Marius Robinson's paper, the *Anti-Slavery Bugle*. The standard text resulted in 1863 from another recollection by Frances Dana Barker Gage in the *National Anti-Slavery Standard*. In the final text, Truth pondered a conundrum through a series of self-revelatory questions and answers—that she lacked the courtesies accorded to white women and that she worked as hard as a man for no pay. Her oration anticipated that the liberation of all women would correct both problems.

As the Civil War approached, Truth canvassed for financial support and clothing for a black volunteer regiment in Detroit and for the whole Union army, including the Fifty-fourth Massachusetts, in which her 17-year-old grandson, James Caldwell, served. With 14-year-old grandson Sammy Banks, on October 29, 1864, she traveled to the office of Abraham Lincoln to receive the president's thanks for integrating streetcars.

Truth counseled freed slaves for the National Freedmen's Relief Association in Arlington, Virginia, and campaigned for free public land on the Kansas-Missouri frontier to be farmed by former bondsmen. At Providence, Rhode Island, in February 1870, she insisted that freedmen were more likely to evolve a work ethic from providing for themselves rather than expecting handouts.

The orator's folksy message appealed to suffragists, temperance workers, and freedmen's aid volunteers. She retired to Battle Creek in 1875 and continued to rail against racial bias and capital punishment, which fell disproportionately on blacks. A cause célèbre, she received well-wishers during two months of treatment for leg ulcers. Tended by daughters Diana and Sophia, after treatment at Dr. John Harvey Kellogg's sanitarium, she died at home on November 26, 1883.

See Also: Mott, Lucretia.

Reference

Washington, Margaret. *Sojourner Truth's America*. Champaign: University of Illinois Press, 2009.

WHAT TIME OF NIGHT IT IS
BY SOJOURNER TRUTH
BROADWAY TEMPLE, NEW YORK CITY
SEPTEMBER 6, 1853

An illiterate former slave from Hurley, New York, Sojourner Truth adopted evangelism as a method of ending slavery and women's bondage to patriarchy. Heeding a divine revelation, at age 56, she delivered a scathing platform denunciation of male discourtesy toward elderly women. By comparing suffragists to the victorious Queen Esther in the Bible, Sojourner Truth forecast the rise of American females and the inevitable punishment of rude, disrespectful men such as the ones misbehaving in the audience during her speech.

Is it not good for me to come and draw forth a spirit, to see what kind of spirit people are of? I see that some of you have got the spirit of a goose, and some have got the spirit of a snake. I feel at home here. I come to you, citizens of New York, as I suppose you ought to be. I am a citizen of the state of New York; I was born in it, and I was a slave in the state of New York; and now I am a good citizen of this State. I was born here, and I can tell you I feel at home here. I've been lookin' round and watchin' things, and I know a little mite 'bout woman's rights, too. I come forth to speak 'bout woman's rights, and want to throw in my little mite, to keep the scales a-movin'. I know that it feels a kind o' hissin' and ticklin' like to see a colored woman get up and tell you about things, and woman's rights. We have all been thrown down so low that nobody thought we'd ever get up again; but we have been long enough trodden now; we will come up again, and now I am here.

I was a-thinkin', when I see women contendin' for their rights, I was a-thinkin' what a difference there is now, and what there was in old times. I have only a few minutes to speak; but in the old times the kings of the earth would hear a woman. There was a king in the Scriptures; and then it was the kings of the earth would kill a woman if she come into their presence; but Queen Esther come forth, for she was oppressed, and felt there was a great wrong, and she said I will die or I will bring my complaint before the king. Should the king of the United States be greater, or more crueler, or more harder? But the king, he raised up his sceptre and said: "Thy request shall be granted unto thee—to the half of my kingdom will I grant it to thee!" Then he said he would hang Haman on the gallows he had made up high. But that is not what women come forward to contend. The women want their rights as Esther. She only wanted to explain her rights. And he was so liberal that he said, "the half of my kingdom shall be granted to thee," and he did not wait for her to ask, he was so liberal with her.

Now, women do not ask half of a kingdom, but their rights, and they don't get 'em. When she comes to demand 'em, don't you hear how sons hiss their mothers like snakes, because they ask for their rights; and can they ask for anything less? The king ordered Haman to be hung on the gallows which he prepared to hang others; but I do not want any man to be killed, but I am sorry to see them so short-minded. But we'll have our rights; see if we don't; and you can't stop us from them; see if you can. You may hiss as much as you like, but it is comin'. Women don't get half as much rights as they ought to; we want more, and we will have it. Jesus says: "What I say to one, I say to all—watch!" I'm a-watchin'. God says: "Honor your father and your mother." Sons and daughters ought to behave themselves before their mothers, but they do not. I can see them a-laughin' and pointin' at their mothers up here on the stage. They hiss when an aged woman comes forth. If they'd been brought up proper they'd have known better than hissing like snakes and geese. I'm 'round watchin' these things, and I wanted to come up and say these few things to you, and I'm glad of the hearin' you give me. I wanted to tell you a mite about woman's rights, and so I came out and said so. I am sittin' among you to watch; and every once and awhile I will come out and tell you what time of night it is.

Source: Truth, Sojourner. "What Time of Night It Is?" In *History of Woman Suffrage: 1861–1876.* Vol. I (567–568). Rochester, NY: Charles Mann, 1887.

V

VAID, URVASHI (1958–)

A passionate, witty Indian American civil rights visionary and attorney, Urvashi "Urv" Vaid sets the direction of 20th-century gay rights protests toward inclusion in families, social institutions, and the feminist movement. Born in New Delhi on October 8, 1958, to teacher, abstract painter, and Hindi poet Champa R. Vaid and Indo-Pakistani novelist, playwright, and Harvard professor Krishna Baldev Vaid, she immigrated to Potsdam, New York, with her family in 1966. Her father taught English literature and composition at the State University of New York at Potsdam and supported the opinions of his daughters, Rachna, Jyotsna, and Urvashi.

Urvashi Vaid grew up in a creative household and read academic works in her parents' library. She immersed herself in the Watergate hearings and, in 1966, posted a picture of her hero, Martin Luther King Jr. in her bedroom. As a preteen in 1969, she wrote a letter to Richard Nixon advocating U.S. agreement to the ABM missile treaty. She demonstrated in marches against apartheid and the Vietnam War and, in 1970, delivered a middle school valedictory supporting the presidential candidacy of George McGovern.

After graduating early from high school, Vaid continued promoting socioeconomic justice during her years on scholarship to study English and political science at Vassar College. During her college experience, she was often the only nonwhite woman in classrooms, but a comrade of feminists and supporter of radical orator Shulamith Firestone. After making friends at the Michigan Womyn's Music Festival, she acknowledged a vital lesbian orientation that she had felt from childhood. She listed as personal aims pay equity for the poor, research into cancer among lesbians, care for the environment, and lower college debt for students.

On October 14, 1979, Vaid joined the National March on Washington for Lesbian and Gay Rights. On graduating in 1979, she co-formed the Allston-Brighton Greenlight Safehouse Network, a neighborhood antiviolence cooperative, and worked as secretary and administrative assistant at a Boston law firm specializing in business and criminal cases. On her own time, she volunteered to publish the *Gay Community News* and, in 1980, revealed her sexual orientation to her parents, whom she educated on the looks and behaviors of lesbians. At a protest action at the Seabrook nuclear facility in New Hampshire, she joined the Lesbians United in Non-Nuclear Action in civil disobedience. During the AIDS epidemic in 1983, she influenced urban candidate selection and elections by guiding the Boston Lesbian/Gay Political Alliance at Northeastern University School of Law in Boston, where she completed an LLD.

In Washington, D.C., at age 25, Vaid represented the American Civil Liberties Union as legal adviser of the National Women's Prison Project, for which she had interned in 1970. Central to her involvement were civil suits improving the lives and medical treatment of incarcerated victims of HIV/AIDS. After meeting Kate Clinton, a former English teacher, feminist news commentator, and political satirist, in February 1988 at a war conference, Vaid shared residence in Manhattan with her mate. In 1992, they moved to Provincetown, Massachusetts.

Forcing Issues

As public information coordinator, Vaid began rallying support for the National Gay and Lesbian Task Force (NGLTF), the nation's oldest lobby for equal rights based on gender and sexuality. She advanced to executive director in 1989, a post she held for four years, and coordinated conferences of the NGLTF Policy Institute think tank. She protested the Persian Gulf War and antichoice, antiwoman legislation and, in September 1990, opposed the confirmation of David Souter to the U.S. Supreme Court.

In May 1991, Vaid debated the antigay intent of traditional values supporters. Key to her success was the denunciation of George W. Bush's antigay policies at the "Committing to the Future" Feminist Conference of the National Organization for Women in January 1992. In addition to advocating reproductive choice at the Abortion Rights Rally on April 5, 1992, and the "Save Our Cities and Save Our Children" initiative of mayors on May 16, 1992, she supported Bill Clinton's presidential campaign.

As keynote speaker at the April 25, 1993, March on Washington for Lesbian, Gay, and Bisexual Equal Rights and Liberation, Vaid presented "Gay Rights." Her text marked the end of exile and despair for marginalized people and invisibility for gay schoolchildren. She accused Christian supremacists with seeking to declare gay people freaks and untouchables and to exterminate them. In celebration of the Boycott Colorado movement, she depicted the far right as evil power wielders against pluralism and democracy and urged defiers of theistic tyranny and intolerance to volunteer to aid hotlines and youth groups.

Often dressed in kurta pajamas or saris, Vaid enlarged the crusade by promoting human diversity, alternative families, and universal inclusion of all classes, genders, and ethnicities. She voiced her opinions in a column for *The Advocate*. On C-SPAN on October 21, 1995, she joined homosexual journalists in addressing inequities for gay people. For a summation of civil rights advances into fair employment, housing, transportation, and education in the treatise *Virtual Equality: The Mainstreaming of Gay and Lesbian Liberation* (1995), she won the 1996 Stonewall Book Award for advocating normalization of gay and lesbian lives.

While working as a senior fellow at the City University of New York graduate school, Vaid appeared on the Charlie Rose television series. In July 1998, she refuted the legitimacy of Christian Coalition media ads claiming to represent homosexuals who renounced their sexual orientation. She remained focused on effecting change by speaking in August 1999 in Washington, D.C., on the future of justice for the gay minority and in April 2000 on gains by the religious right in demonizing non-normative sexual orientation.

During the rise in concern about physical and electronic gay bashing, Vaid copublished an essay compendium, *Creating Change: Sexuality, Public Policy, and Civil Rights* (2000). In 2002, she delivered "Sexuality and Its Discontents: What's Race, Class, and War Got To Do With It?" at the Center for Justice, Tolerance, and Community at the University of California in Santa Cruz. After directing the Governance and Civil Society Unit of the Ford Foundation for four years, in 2005, she began a five-year stint championing advocacy for simians and non-normative sexual rights for the Michigan-based Arcus Foundation. Under her leadership, the agency opened offices in New York City and Cambridge, England. For her commitment to cultural and ideological freedom for gay Americans, she received an *Out* magazine 2009 listing among the 50 most influential gay Americans.

Supporting an Intergenerational Group

To support youth facing bias, suicidal urges, and threats, Vaid spoke on October 11, 2009, at the National Equality Rally against the Defense of Marriage Act, hate crimes, workplace discrimination, and the military "don't ask, don't tell" policy. At the Center for LGBTQ Studies at City University of New York, the only LGBT research center at a U.S. institute of higher learning, she delivered the 2010 Kessler Lecture, "What Can Brown Do for You? Race, Sexuality, and the Future of LGBT Politics." Her exuberant text traced a maze of political ups and down in an era of cultural progress and stagnation for immigrants, gays, and nonwhite people in a nation committed to white privilege and superiority.

In an optimistic essay to a bestseller, *It Gets Better: Coming Out, Overcoming Bullying, and Creating a Life Worth Living* (2011), Vaid encouraged involvement in activist idealism to foster change and liberation. In July 2012, she launched the Lesbian Political Action Committee, a lobbying effort to develop strategies to extend civil rights to homosexual women. The group celebrated the coalition of poor, homosexual, immigrant, nonwhite, and feminist forces that achieved the 2012 vote for marriage equality.

As a source of innovation in sexual orientation and gender identity, Vaid established the Vaid Group, a consulting office helping nonprofits and individuals attain social justice. To scrutinize the aspects of gender and sexuality that influenced past and current legislation, from 2011 to 2015, she directed the Engaging Tradition Project at the Center for Gender and Sexuality Law at Columbia Law School. During this period, she completed *Irresistible Revolution: Confronting Race, Class and the Assumptions of LGBT Politics* (2012) by detailing areas of concern—health insurance, police abuse, courtroom bias, single-parent homes, prison violence, reproductive injustice, and unemployment—not covered by the mounting acceptance of gay marriage nationwide.

In a 2013 interview, Vaid backed socially responsible capitalism, a mainstream position at odds with socialism. She also advised directors of the Planned Parenthood Action Fund and the Gill Foundation, a philanthropic agency that grants funds to promote equal opportunity and unrestrained gender expression for lesbian, gay, bisexual, and transgender citizens. At a ceremony in Boston on October 24, 2014, she added to her honors the Gay & Lesbian Advocates & Defenders (GLAD) Spirit of Justice award. In February 2015, she continued championing gay rights with a lecture on gender, health, and well-being at the Resurrection Metropolitan Community Church in Houston, Texas.

See Also: Firestone, Shulamith.

Reference

Killian, Chris. "New Leadership Announced for Arcus Foundation." *Kalamazoo Gazette*, May 29, 2010.

W

WALD, LILLIAN (1867–1940)

A champion of immigrants, nurse Lillian Wald advocated improvements to health, sanitation, fire protection, work safety, and recreation in urban slums. An Ohioan from Cincinnati, she was born on March 10, 1867, to Minnie Schwarz and Max D. Wald and grew up in Rochester, New York. During a lifetime of service, she administered fund-raising projects and publicized needs among the poor in speeches to Rotary Clubs, college assemblies, and letters to the *New York Times* and *Crisis* and *Survey* magazines.

Wald began medical studies in 1885 at New York Hospital Training School and, in autumn 1892, entered the Woman's Medical College. As a visiting nurse living in a Lower East Side tenement, in 1893, she and Mary M. Brewster surveyed the conditions of 125 families. They found unsanitary outhouses, inadequate hydrants and fire escapes, septic home births, and children playing in streets. The first cadre of visiting nurses preceded formation in 1893 of the National Organization of Public Health Nurses, over which Wald presided. Wald's speech "The Nurse's Settlement in New York" (1901), delivered to the International Congress of Nurses in Buffalo, promoted healing as an act of community service toward well-being.

In 1903, Wald co-founded the Women's Trade Union League to improve industrial conditions and crusaded for women's enfranchisement at the New York State Suffrage Convention. She investigated exploitive conditions at labor camps and canal and highway projects. League picketers urged inquiry by the Joint Board of Sanitary Control into safety, cleanliness, ventilation, and lighting. Her campaign for hands-on community nursing at the New York School of Philanthropy in 1910 and at Cornell University in 1911 resulted in the opening of Columbia University's School of Nursing.

Because of Wald's earnest oratory, in 1913, Metropolitan Life offered laborer health insurance and the New York Board of Health established the world's first system of public health nurses. At the Hotel Astor, she addressed the city's Equal

Suffrage League on the need for full citizenship for women. At the beginning of World War I, she joined a 1,000-woman march against militarism and advocated industrial training at the 1914 National Society for the Promotion of Education. At Vassar's 50th anniversary in October 1915, she delivered "The New Aspects of Social Responsibilities," an address enlightening young women on volunteerism.

After the armistice, Wald delivered a 1918 encomium on public health nursing at the Pan-American Congress on Child Welfare in Montevideo, Uruguay, and recruited volunteers at Spanish influenza clinics, which she compared to a war zone. In a five-minute summary of the epidemic on February 1, 1919, she briefed the Nurses' Emergency Council on the need of 90 percent of the sick for hospitalization. Because city facilities could accommodate only 10 percent, the remaining patients in Bronx, Manhattan, and Staten Island depended on visiting nurses.

Wald's speech cited large families dependent on youngsters for food and care and the household left "undressed and unwashed" while the mother slipped toward death ("Lillian D. Wald Papers, 1919," 4). Because nurses managed 10-hour days to fill in for ailing and deceased parents, she described a dilemma—her need to call nurses back from days off, but her realization that teams could collapse and die from overwork. With oratorical grace, she quoted one dying staff member as apologizing for being ill during the emergency.

Throughout Wald's speaking tours of the 1920s and 1930s, she recruited multiethnic health workers and promoted the Red Cross, the National Association for the Advancement of Colored People, credit unions, school lunch programs, prohibition, the Federal Children's Bureau, and a moratorium on the death penalty. To aid Russian Jews, she advanced grassroots defiance of Adolf Hitler's fascism, a pro-international stance that earned her spurious accusations of Bolshevism. Before her death from a second stroke on September 1, 1940, at a retirement home in Westport, Connecticut, she received the Lincoln Medallion and a radio commendation for philanthropy from President Franklin D. Roosevelt.

See Also: Goldman, Emma; Sanger, Margaret.

References

Feld, Marjorie N. *Lillian Wald: A Biography.* Chapel Hill: University of North Carolina Press, 2008.

"Lillian D. Wald Papers, 1919." Influenza Encyclopedia, University of Michigan. Accessed October 9, 2014. http://quod.lib.umich.edu/f/flu/2510flu.0016.152/1/--lillian-wald-writings-speeches-1919?page=root;size=125;view=image.

Wald, Lillian D. "Organization Amongst Working Women." *Annals of the American Academy of Political and Social Science* 27 (May 1906): 638–645.

CROWDED DISTRICTS OF LARGE CITIES (EXCERPT) BY LILLIAN D. WALD NATIONAL COUNCIL OF JEWISH WOMEN TUXEDO HALL, NEW YORK CITY NOVEMBER 17, 1896

To engage wealthy Jewish women in philanthropic work for the poor, public health nurse Lillian Wald delivered a detailed, at times lyrical description of decaying New York City neighborhoods and the difficulties of immigrant newcomers in rearing healthy families amid high rents and low wages. Because Wald and her cadre of visiting nurses lived in the district, they gave eyewitness accounts of vermin, fires, and children playing in narrow alleys and traffic as well as of factory girls dying of tuberculosis in sweatshops. For an even-handed report, Wald complimented the poor for doing their best to stay clean and comfortable amid the filth and odor of the slums.

The houses are dilapidated, filth-infected, and dark: old houses, once the homes of the wealthy and fastidious, converted to present uses by a process of decay, and maintained at the smallest expense possible to bring the largest returns possible; rear tenements, built upon what was left of the city lots of front houses; houses facing the street, utilizing the space that was once a garden; tall new tenements built upon single city lots 25 × 100 feet, with four families to a floor, each single lot tenanted by twenty to twenty-four different families; with saloon and one store generally in the basement. This variety of tenement-house, the familiar "double-decker," occupying 86 to 90 percent of the lot's depth, is in many ways worse than the old remodeled residence, its airshafts and basement furnishing contaminated air and frequent fires to its 100 to 150 inhabitants. The houses are not fireproof, though provided with fire escapes; and the almost constant use of kerosene, the darkness, the many children, the occupations in the houses, are causes of frequent fires. The fire department records show that in this third of the population of New York, the fires are more than one-half the whole number, and deaths and accidents are very frequent.

There are two so-called "model tenements" in the region we are describing, and in one part of this area, several houses occupied by single families, and at least two streets wide and favorably situated; but there are blocks almost entirely covered by buildings, one (brought up before the Tenement-Houses Commission of 1894) covering 93 percent of the total area, and a total area of thirty-four blocks showing 78 percent built upon.

The very small space between the houses, sometimes only 18 inches, is utilized for the drying of clothes and as a receptacle for refuse of all kinds. The narrow street space is a jostling, shoving, pushcart market for the selling of over-ripe fruit, fish, vegetables, etc. The halls of the houses are so dark that groping is the method of movement in them, and the little girl described hers when she lost something and said: "Oh! I'll find it at night when the gas is lighted."

The nurses never overcome the fear of trampling on the children in the hall or on the street, a sound warning them when to tread carefully, or sometimes out of the darkness a tiny hand on the railing shocking suddenly with the sense of accident averted. It is not uncommon to go in daytime into the closet-room with candle in hand, in order to be able to see the patient at all. Nor is it uncommon to go at night and see ten or eleven people occupying two small rooms—people who have been working all day, freed for the night's rest, stretched on the floor, one next to the other, dividing the pillows, different sexes, not always the same family, for there are "boarders," who pay a small sum for shelter, among their own, the family glad of the help toward paying the rent.

The price of rooms in the most wretched basement in the rear tenements is so high in comparison with the wage earned that it is for those who have employment based on something like regular income about one-fourth of the whole. But it must be remembered that few trades give employment all the year round. We hear more often than any other plaint that of the uncertainty of having a roof: the failure comes so often, and with it the "dispossess paper," that the sight of the household effects on the sidewalk following its presentment is too common to collect a crowd, where crowds collect quickly.

During the hot months of July and August is the time to observe a crowded district at its worst. The vermin and the heat drive the people to the streets, which are crowded with these unfortunates the greater part of the night. Mothers sit on the curbstone with nursing babies, and the cool of the door stone is coveted for a pillow, or the refreshment of sleep on the roof or in the courts between the houses is sought unless, indeed, the odors of the closets there are worse than the vermin or the heat within.

On the other hand, within these tenements are sometimes found the most scrupulously kept rooms; plants by the windows, happiness, and a real home; courtesy, devotion, and charity, such as one may seek for among the elect of the earth, and reverence; sufficient evidence of the original nobility of character, which can remain high despite all discouragements.

Source: Wald, Lillian D. "Crowded Districts of Large Cities." *Proceedings of the National Council of Jewish Women*. Philadelphia: Jewish Publication Society of America, 1897, 95–103.

WALKER, ALICE (1944–)

A great-granddaughter of slaves and an American literary icon, Alice Malsenior Walker advocated for a greater appreciation for the roles of African Americans and women in history, formulated the concept of womanism, and informed the Western world of the primitive Islamic practice of female circumcision. The last of eight children, she was born in the Jim Crow era at Eatonton in Putnam County, Georgia, on February 9, 1944, to Minnie Lou Tallulah Grant, a gardener and storyteller, and Willie Lee Walker, an unsuccessful sharecropper. At her mother's insistence, she entered primary grades in 1948 and learned the cadences of storytelling from her grandfather. From her older sister Annie Ruth, she memorized the South African national anthem, "Nkosi Sikeleli'Afrika," and, at age six, delivered an Easter sermon.

A wound to Walker's eye from her brother's BB gun in 1952 blinded her on the right side. In secret from the family, she began writing at age eight and evolved a wary personality that shielded her from the curious. Surgical excision of unsightly scar tissue in 1958 ended her withdrawal and encouraged her compilation of an unpublished verse chapbook, *Poems of a Childhood Poetess.* She graduated most popular, senior class queen, and valedictorian.

A scholarship and contributions from her mother's earnings of $1.55 an hour as a domestic enabled Walker to major in literature at Spelman College in Atlanta, where she extended her love for Africa through friendship with a Ugandan woman. Out of enthusiasm for the 18,000 attendees from 137 countries at the Eighth Youth World Peace Festival in Helsinki, Finland, on August 6, 1962, she visited the home of Martin Luther King Jr. He persuaded her to support civil rights at the August 27, 1963, March on Washington.

Walker transferred to Sarah Lawrence College in New York, where she majored in sociology and education and wrote her first adult poems. After marrying Melvyn Roseman Leventhal, a Jewish civil rights attorney, on March 17, 1967, she made their home in Jackson, Mississippi, where they became the state's first interracial married couple. For her work, she won an Ingram Merrill Foundation Fellowship and Rosenthal award and accepted a poetry residency at Jackson State College, Mississippi.

Activism and Writing

After giving birth to daughter Rebecca Grant, Walker accepted another poet-in-residency in 1970, at Tougaloo College, Mississippi. She also advised the Friends of the Children of Mississippi Head Start on black history. She edited for *Ms.*, published the novel *The Third Life of Grange Copeland* (1970), and revived readership for the works of ethnographer Zora Neale Hurston.

Walker made her first aggressive speech in the early 1970s. To the faculty of Sarah Lawrence College, she crusaded for a larger presence of black and women's history in the curriculum. In 1972, she voiced the country's loss in "Choice: A Tribute to Dr. Martin Luther King, Jr." Her writing—essays for *Ms.*, a verse collection *Revolutionary Petunias and Other Poems* (1973), the multigenerational anthology

In Love and Trouble: Stories of Black Women (1973), and the young adult biography *Langston Hughes: American Poet*—garnered national honoraria, including the American Academy and Institute of Arts and Letters Award.

Walker's introduction to Deep South volunteerism registering black voters in Liberty County, Georgia, produced material for a semi-fictional memoir, *Meridian* (1976). In 1973, she located the unmarked burial site of Hurston in Fort Pierce, Florida, and honored it with a gravestone. She composed "Saving the Life That Is Your Own," a lecture delivered at Barnard College on November 11, 1975, and issued the article "In Search of Zora Neale Hurston" (1975), the beginning of a Hurston renaissance.

Following a divorce in 1977, Walker relocated north of San Francisco, California, to raise chickens, meditate, and study Eastern religions and yoga. She made oral tributes to poet Langston Hughes, author Tillie Olsen, and civil rights heroes Jesse Jackson, Ella Baker, and Rosa Parks and received a 1978 National Endowment for the Arts honorarium. She compiled a masterwork on sisterhood and endurance, *The Color Purple* (1982), and became the first black female to achieve a 1983 National Book Award and a Pulitzer Prize. The novel elicited both popular acclaim and outrage by black males who accused her of demeaning them through the main character, whom she debases as "Mr. _____."

A Feminist Voice

Walker delved more intimately into women's history with *In Search of Our Mothers' Gardens: Womanist Prose* (1983). In Anderson Valley, California, in 1984, she joined author Robert L. Allen in publishing through Wild Tree Press, a feminist venue, and traveled to Uganda and Kenya. A Stephen Spielberg film version of *The Color Purple* featured major black actors—Whoopi Goldberg, Danny Glover, and Oprah Winfrey—and preceded a Tony-winning Broadway musical version about the American South and the animism derived from colonial Africa.

In addition to teaching women's studies at Wellesley, the University of Massachusetts at Boston, Yale, and the University of California at Berkeley, Walker initiated instruction on black American female writers at Brandeis and formulated the concept of womanism, an oppression based on classism and racism. She addressed the Bay Area Critics Circle, honored the U.S. Constitution for USA-TV, and accepted the 1986 Matrix Award. With public appearances, she continued to promote antinuclear demonstrations and lauded ecological feminism with "Testimony for the Ocean" (1988). In 1989, her speeches enlightened the Institute for Practice of Non-Violence, the Keep Abortion Legal Rally, and supporters of Leonard Peltier, whom the Federal Bureau of Investigation charged with a shooting on the Pine Ridge Reservation.

Shortly after achieving an O. Henry award for *Kindred Spirits*, Walker was less successful with the matriarchal novel *The Temple of My Familiar* (1989) and a children's allegory, *Finding the Green Stone* (1991). Her 1991 address to the American Booksellers extolled "The Satisfaction of Finding My Books on the Shelf." At the Peace for Cuba rally on February 1, 1992, she delivered "The Story of Why I Am Here: Or, A Woman Connects Oppressions."

Walker generated international discussion of clitoral excision and vulvar and labial mutilation with *Possessing the Secret of Joy* (1992), which extends characterization from *The Color Purple* with her perspective on female circumcision, which she discovered in Kenya. On the same topic, she compiled a documentary, *Warrior Marks: Female Genital Mutilation and the Sexual Blinding of Women* (1993). Later in the 1990s, she accepted a Humanist of the Year 1997 citation, spoke at Radcliffe and to the National Black Women's Health Project, and addressed the American Humanist Association Conference in Denver. Her schedule included lectures at Oakland, Auburn Theological Seminary, and Agnes Scott College. She issued a postmodern Persephone myth, *By the Light of My Father's Smile* (1998).

Walker's varied topics included a post-9/11 talk, "Sent by Earth," to the Midwives Alliance of North America, "Of Gifts and Hands" (2002), and "My Friends the Chinese and Tibetan People" (2002). On International Women's Day, March 8, 2003, Capitol police arrested her with author Maxine Hong Kingston for rallying at the White House against the Iraq War, a protest Walker described in *We Are the Ones We Have Been Waiting For: Inner Light in a Time of Darkness* (2006). In a speech at Barnard College on October 3, 2003, she intrigued more scholars and publishers to reverence Zora Neale Hurston as a literary foremother. Her quest novel *Now Is the Time to Open Your Heart* (2004) dramatized a spiritual river journey through the Amazon Basin.

Walker protested the ethnic divide in Israel and celebrated the rise of Barack Obama to the U.S. presidency. Her honors increased in Reykjavik, Iceland, with a 2007 Domestic Human Rights Award and a 2010 Lennon-Ono Grant for Peace, the impetus to her Steve Biko lecture, "Coming to See You Since I was Five Years Old: A Poet's Connection to the South African Soul," on September 9 at the University of Cape Town, South Africa. The text, interweaving prose with verse, defied lies about savage Africans and murderous Palestinians, two untruths she compared to the diminution of all women as underlings and whores. At the crux of her speech, she declared, "No lie will live forever" and anticipated that truth would revive humankind (Walker 2010). She concluded by extolling the sacred circle that joined people into an organic whole with Mother Earth.

Walker's pro-Palestinian rhetoric severed some of her warm relationships with free speech movements, the media, and campuses, beginning in August 2013 with rejection by the University of Michigan. In 2010 and 2012, she served as jurist on a people's court, addressed the Russell Tribunal on Palestine, and celebrated the 50th anniversary of the University of California at Berkeley with oratory to the history department. At the University of Michigan on November 5, 2014, she delivered an oration on social justice that defined parameters of feminist scholarship and activism.

See Also: Hurston, Zora Neale; Olsen Tillie.

References

Snodgrass, Mary Ellen. *Encyclopedia of Feminist Literature.* New York: Facts on File, 2006.

Walker, Alice. "Coming to See You Since I Was Five Years Old: A Poet's Connection to the South African Soul." 2010. Accessed July 2, 2015. http://alicewalkersgarden.com/2010/09/coming-to-see-you-since-i-was-five-years-old-an-american-poets-connection-to-the-south-african-soul/#more-9.

WALLERSTEIN, JUDITH (1921–2012)

The coauthor of a contentious cultural discourse on divorce, psychologist and teacher Judith Hannah Saretsky "Judy" Wallerstein researched the effects of dysfunctional families on children. A native New Yorker born on December 27, 1921, she was the only daughter of teacher Augusta "Gussie" Tucker and Samuel Seretsky, a director of Jewish community centers. The parents kept Shabbat and Jewish holidays and taught Hebrew to Judith and her brother David.

At the beginning of the Great Depression, Wallerstein suffered a shock when Samuel died of a cancer that no one explained to her. During her troubled teens, for five years, she lived in Tel Aviv in British Palestine, where Gussie taught English. Wallerstein served the paramilitary Haganah as a courier and developed a lasting Zionist zeal. On return to New York in 1935, she enrolled at Hunter College.

In the midst of World War II, Wallerstein pursued an advanced degree in social work at Columbia University and graduated in 1946. She met her future husband, Robert Solomon Wallerstein of Berlin, Germany, during their training in psychoanalysis at the Topeka Institute for Psychoanalysis, part of the Menninger Clinic in Topeka, Kansas. She married Robert in 1947 and reared their daughters Amy and Nina and son Michael Wallerstein while teaching Hebrew at a synagogue.

After settling on Belvedere Island off San Francisco, California, while her husband chaired the psychiatry department at Mount Zion Hospital and the University of California at San Francisco, Wallerstein began a quarter century of lecturing in

1966 at the School of Social Welfare at the University of California at Berkeley, from which she earned a Distinguished Teaching Award. In her fourth year as the Marin County psychologist at a therapy center in Corte Madera, she incurred questions from kindergarten teachers about troubled preschoolers of separated parents, the fallout of California's institution of no-fault divorce under the Family Law Act of 1969. The youths shared difficulties with insomnia and displayed uncontrolled crying and rough play with their contemporaries.

Longitudinal Research

To solve quandaries about the children of disrupted homes, in 1971, Wallerstein launched the California Children of Divorce Study, a 25-year survey of the adaptation of 131 homogeneous subjects. The children derived from 60 educated middle-class families referred by attorneys and judges in Marin County. The adults dissolved high-conflict marriages because of betrayal or apathy. Some sought to avoid child support. Judith's hundreds of hours of post-divorce interviews with parents and children from toddlers to teens to adults followed five-year cycles. The research yielded "The Effects of Parental Divorce: Experiences of the Preschool Child," published in the *Journal of the American Academy of Child & Adolescent*, and "The Effects of Parental Divorce: Experiences of the Child in Later Latency."

Wallerstein's anecdotal results disclosed that failed nuclear unions created cumulative, long-lasting crises in the social and psychological experience of older offspring, who were also prone to divorce. Unlike adults, who anticipated a second chance at love and an intimate marital bond, their children lost security during the formative years. They reported loneliness, domestic violence, and fear of abandonment. As a group, single divorced mothers complained of backaches, constipation, respiratory ills, colitis, hypertension, migraines, and mandibular pain.

In revelations about sleeper effects, Wallerstein's data established that the children lost financial support for college because of the high cost of counseling and litigation and investments in parental remarriage and second families. Throughout childhood, the offspring resented forced residency with the noncustodial parent because shifting households deprived them of friends and familiar settings. Some 60 percent experimented with sex in their early teens and remained unwed out of fear of replicating their parents' inability to sustain wedlock in a traditional setting. Half of the participants never recovered from low achievement and self-esteem, worry, anger, depression, alcohol and drug abuse, physical abuse, silent hostility, and the inability to commit to a loving intimate relationship.

At age 57, Wallerstein completed a PhD in psychology in Sweden at Lund University, a world-class training center in medicine, social sciences, and the humanities.

In 1980, she personalized clinical counseling for parents and their young by establishing the Judith Wallerstein Center for the Family in Transition in Madera, California. She reported to *Newsday* the moral dilemma of unfulfilled couples who faced the uprooting of children and loss of parenting time and opportunity because of separation and/or divorce.

In addition to writing *Second Chances: Men, Women and Children a Decade After Divorce* (1989) in collaboration with science writer Sandra Blakeslee and psychologist Julia Lewis, Wallerstein advised editors of law and psychology journals as an amicus curiae. She also campaigned for the right of mothers to relocate. For her influence on a cultural shift in the nuclear family and the erosion of traditional long-term monogamy, *Time* magazine dubbed her the godmother of the backlash against divorce.

An Influential Career

Wallerstein's prominence in social work increased with articles in popular magazines and scientific journals on inconsistent parenting and an insidious residue of rancor that could remain virulent for decades. In 1992, she received a Rockefeller Foundation fellowship for study in Bellagio, Italy. Demand for her oratory took her to radio talk shows in the United States and Canada and on *Oprah*, *The Today Show*, and *Good Morning America*.

An acknowledged expert on family dynamics, Wallerstein lectured at the Hebrew University of Jerusalem, Harvard, Cornell, Stanford, Yale, and Pahlavi University Medical School in Shiraz, Iran. She held advisory posts for the Commission on Family Law to the California Senate Subcommittee on Administrative Justice, Commission on Law and Mental Health, State Bar of California, and California Senate Task Force on Family Equity. In addition, she joined seminars and panel discussions and counseled domestic judges on the relocation of children from separated caregivers and on periodic reevaluations and adjustments to custody situations to meet the needs of maturing children. In 1992, she informed the Council on Families in America, an advocacy group on U.S. values founded by Dan Quayle, and influenced publication of the 1995 report "Marriage in America: A Report to the Nation."

On a more optimistic note, Wallerstein compiled *The Good Marriage: How and Why Love Lasts* (1995), an upbeat guide to home solidarity. Applying holistic reasoning, she issued *Surviving the Breakup: How Children and Parents Cope with Divorce* (1996) and delivered the speech "Marriage Reform" (1996), an effort to restore society's confidence in monogamy and replenish the family after the debilitation of work strain and social breakdown. In 1998, the *Journal of the American Academy of Psychiatry and the Law* published her commentary on more permissive court stipulations about the relocation of primary custodial parents. The essay emphasized emotional bonding between parent and child.

Wallerstein summarized a quarter century of family interviews in *The Unexpected Legacy of Divorce: A 25-year Landmark Study* (2000), a compilation of five life stories that alerted adults to the needs of their children long after a breakup. In July 2000, she shared a podium with Justice Sandra Day O'Connor at the annual assembly of U.S. chief justices from 50 states and informed the gathering on child development and attachment theory. Her speech exploded myths that minors are more content after their parents' divorce, especially the youngest children, and that parental affection counterbalances pre-separation antagonisms.

Critics challenged the subjectivity and unsubstantiated pessimism of Wallerstein's conclusions. They alleged that her narrow field reduced verisimilitude because it concentrated on predominantly white families seeking psychoanalysis for emotional problems that preceded marriage. Some charged her with defending toxic relationships and with rejecting divorce as a solution to hostile environments for child rearing that tormented children into troubled teens and an insecure young adulthood.

Throughout Wallerstein's writing and speaking career, she continued refining her critique of family issues and injecting updated statistics. On September 21, 2000, she spoke on PBS about the growth of the U.S. divorce rate to 45 percent. She scripted a new introduction to the 2001 edition of *The Unexpected Legacy of Divorce* and dedicated the work to the individuals she revered as the vanguard of a generation marked by family dissolution. With critical support from her husband, she published *What About the Kids? Raising Children Before, During, and After Divorce* (2003), a handbook for parents during the breakup of a nuclear household.

In her late eighties, Wallerstein contributed to a third edition of the textbook *Why Marriage Matters: 30 Conclusions from the Social Sciences* (2005) and posted Internet commentary on wedlock, grandpa renting, schooling, divorce, and second marriages. For her expertise, she earned commendations that included a Koshland Award in Social Welfare from the San Francisco Foundation, a citation from the State of California Senate Rules Subcommittee, the Rene Spitz Lectureship from the Denver Psychoanalytic Society, and the Dale Richmond Award from the American Academy of Pediatrics. Six years after the death of son Michael, on June 18, 2012, in Piedmont, California, she died following complications from surgery for a gastrointestinal obstruction.

Reference

Woo, Elaine. "Judith Wallerstein Dies at 90." *Los Angeles Times*, July 4, 2012.

WEDDINGTON, SARAH (1945–)

A law professor and Texas legislator, Sarah Ragle Weddington became the youngest attorney to win a case before the U.S. Supreme Court by fighting for *Roe v. Wade*. Born in Abilene, Texas, on February 5, 1945, to Lena Catherine Morrison and Herbert Doyle Ragle, an officer of the Northwest Texas Conference of the United Methodist Church, she grew up in a Protestant environment in a series of parsonages in Munday, Canyon, Vernon, and Lubbock. At age 16, she took a post in the Austin statehouse as legislative clerk and typist.

Weddington studied English, speech, and secondary education at McMurry University in Abilene and graduated magna cum laude at age 19. During three years at the University of Texas Law School, she ended an unplanned pregnancy in fall 1967 by opting for an illegal abortion at a clinic in Piedras Negras, Mexico. In 1968, she married her lover, army veteran and attorney James Ronald Weddington.

While sharing a practice with her husband, in early March 1970, Weddington spearheaded a federal challenge to the constitutionality of a 19th-century state anti-abortion statute by filing suit against Dallas district attorney Henry Menasco Wade. On June 17, 1970, three judges on the federal court overturned the state's anti-abortion law. The following day, Wade remained adamant that he would prosecute violators of the Texas anti-abortion law.

By defending civil and privacy rights pro bono, on December 13, 1971, Weddington successfully argued a class action demand for due process rights. The case advanced from a Texas district court to a U.S. Supreme Court hearing and threatened the constitutionality of criminal abortion laws. She backed the plaintiff, Norma Leah McCorvey, an unwed mother of Cajun-Cherokee descent, rendered anonymous as Jane Roe in the October 11, 1972, re-argument of *Roe v. Wade*.

After threading through angry groups, in the allotted half hour, Weddington stated her case before a court packed with reporters and witnesses. She prevailed on January 22, 1973. The nine judges, led by justice Harry Blackmun, supported Roe's suit against a Texas law that denied her the right to make private decisions about a pregnancy. The decision favoring abortion in the first trimester passed on a vote of 7 against 2 dissents, written by justices William H. Rehnquist and Byron R. White. Although abortion became instantly available through the state of Texas, Roe received exoneration too late for an abortion and surrendered the child for adoption.

Weddington gained a reputation for courage that earned her election three times as a Republican to the Texas House of Representatives, beginning in November 1972. During four years in the state house, she continued to represent women's needs for pregnancy leave for teachers, equal custody rights, and individual financial credit and collaborated with Kay Bailey Hutchison on suppressing a victim's sexual history from rape trials.

In 1988, Weddington joined the faculty at the University of Texas at Austin as an adjunct professor of government and pre-law and staff member of the Center for Women's and Gender Studies. For the *Time* magazine special issue "80 Days That Changed the World," she wrote on pro-choice advocacy with the March 31, 2003, article "Getting the Right to Choose," a reprint of a 1973 announcement of the *Roe v. Wade* decision.

On January 22, 2013, Weddington celebrated the 40th anniversary of *Roe* in Seattle, Washington, and Portland, Oregon, with members of Planned Parenthood Northwest. To an audience of 1,000 in Columbia Willamette, she discussed efforts by the Tea Party, evangelicals, and the National Conference of Catholic Bishops to curtail Planned Parenthood programs offering mammograms, pap smears, mandatory sonograms, and well-woman and well-baby care.

Still dogged by antichoice opinions, Weddington made another 40th anniversary presentation on April 14, 2013, at Colorado University at Boulder and encountered ongoing discussion of the Blackmun opinion. To the American Bar Foundation Awards Reception in Houston on February 8, 2015, she recounted the *Roe* victory. In good humor, she joked about the lack of a women's lavatory in the Supreme Court building. She remains a council representative for the American Bar Association's Section of Individual Rights and Responsibilities.

See Also: Hill, Anita; Richards, Ann.

Reference

Reaves, Jessica. "Interview with Sarah Weddington." *Time*, January 16, 2003.

DUE PROCESS RIGHTS (EXCERPT)
BY SARAH WEDDINGTON
ROE V. WADE
U.S. SUPREME COURT, WASHINGTON, D.C.
DECEMBER 13, 1971

By defending civil and privacy rights, attorney Sarah Weddington successfully argued for due process rights that overturned Texas anti-abortion law. Ensuing decades of debate continue to query the same premises she postulated in her pro-choice argument, including the rights to "life, liberty, and the pursuit of happiness." Nominations for seats on the U.S. Supreme Court gravitate toward the nominee's past judgments concerning women's right to choose.

Abortion now, for a woman, is safer than childbirth. In the absence of abortions—or legal medically safe abortions—women often resort to the illegal abortions, which certainly carry risks of death, all the side effects such as severe infections, permanent sterility, all the complications that result. And, in fact, if the woman is unable to get either a legal abortion or an illegal abortion in our state, she can do a self-abortion, which is certainly, perhaps, by far the most dangerous. And that is no crime.

Texas, for example, it appears to us, would not allow any relief at all, even in situations where the mother would suffer perhaps serious physical or mental harm. There is certainly a great question about it. If the pregnancy would result in the birth of a deformed or defective child, she has no relief. Regardless of the circumstances of conception, whether it was because of rape, incest, whether she is extremely immature, she has no relief.

I think it's without question that pregnancy to a woman can completely disrupt her life. Whether she's unmarried; whether she's pursuing an education; whether she's pursuing a career; whether she has family problems; all of the problems of personal and family life, for a woman, are bound up in the problem of abortion.

For example, in our State there are many schools where a woman is forced to quit if she becomes pregnant. In the City of Austin that is true. A woman, if she becomes pregnant, and is in high school, must resign or drop out of regular education process. And that's true of some colleges in our State.

In the matter of employment, she often is forced to quit at an early point in her pregnancy. She has no provision for maternity leave. She has—she cannot get unemployment compensation under our laws, because the laws hold that she is not eligible for employment, being pregnant, and therefore is eligible for no unemployment compensation.

At the same time, she can get no welfare to help her at a time when she has no unemployment compensation and she's not eligible for any help in getting a job to provide for herself. There is no duty for employers to rehire women if they must drop out to carry a pregnancy to term.

And, of course, this is especially hard on the many women in Texas who are heads of their own households and must provide for their already existing children.

And, obviously, the responsibility of raising a child is a most serious one, and at times an emotional investment that must be made, cannot be denied. So, a pregnancy to a woman is perhaps one of the most determinative aspects of her life.

It disrupts her body. It disrupts her education. It disrupts her employment. And it often disrupts her entire family life.

And we feel that, because of the impact on the woman, this certainly—in as far as there are any rights which are fundamental—is a matter which is of such fundamental and basic concern to the woman involved that she should be allowed to make the choice as to whether to continue or to terminate her pregnancy.

I think the question is equally serious for the physicians of our state. They are seeking to practice medicine in what they consider the highest method of practice.

We have affidavits in the back of our brief from each of the heads of public—of heads of obstetrics and gynecology departments from each of our public medical schools in Texas.

And each of them points out that they were willing and interested to immediately begin to formulate methods of providing care and services for women who are pregnant and do not desire to continue the pregnancy.

They were stopped cold in their efforts, even with the declaratory judgment, because of the DA's position that they would continue to prosecute.

. . . In the lower court, as I'm sure you're aware, the court held that the right to determine whether or not to continue a pregnancy rested upon the Ninth Amendment which, of course, reserves those rights not specifically enumerated to the government, to the people.

I think it is important to note, in a law review article recently submitted to the Court and distributed among counsel by Professor Cyril Means, Jr., entitled "The Phoenix of Abortional Freedom," that at the time the Constitution was adopted there was no common law prohibition against abortions; that they were available to the women of this country.

Certainly, under the Griswold decision, it appears that the members of the Court in that case were obviously divided as to the specific constitutional framework of the right which they held to exist in the Griswold decision.

I'm a little reluctant to . . . aspire to a wisdom that the Court did not . . . was not in agreement on. I do feel that it is—that the Ninth Amendment is an appropriate place for the freedom to rest. I think the Fourteenth Amendment is equally an appropriate place, under the rights of persons to life, liberty, and the pursuit of happiness. I think that in as far as "liberty" is meaningful, that liberty to these women would mean liberty from being forced to continue the unwanted pregnancy. . . .

Source: Weddington, Sarah. "Roe v. Wade." *Transcript of First Oral Argument in Roe v. Wade 410 U.S. 113 (1973).* U.S. Supreme Court, December 13, 1971.

WELD, ANGELINA GRIMKÉ (1805–1879)

A human rights advocate and conductor for the Underground Railroad, Angelina Emily Grimké "Nina" Weld joined her older sister, Sarah Moore Grimké, in becoming the most prominent Southern white female fighters of slavery. The last of 14 siblings, Angelina was born in Charleston, South Carolina, on February 5, 1805, to Mary "Polly" Smith and John Faucheraud Grimké. Under an aristocratic Episcopalian father, Angelina grew up in Union at Belmont Plantation among black laborers who cultivated and harvested rice and cotton.

While Sarah read law and Presbyterian theology, crusaded for women's rights, and, in 1821, relocated to Philadelphia following the judge's death, Angelina remained in the South with her mother and violated state laws by teaching scripture and literacy to Belmont bondsmen. In October 1827, Sarah returned to Charleston to influence Angelina, who began attending Quaker meetings. In May 1829, Angelina sold her personal servants and, in November, moved to Philadelphia. She first lived with Sarah and, in 1832, with their widowed sister, Anna Rutledge Grimké Frost, and taught at a nursery school.

Historic Activism

Angelina and Sarah embraced Quaker beliefs and activism but earned disapproval for sitting among black church attendees on the back row. A participating member of the interracial Philadelphia Female Anti-Slavery Society after May 1835, Angelina became the first female abolitionist orator to exhort a mixed gender, mixed race audience. While Sarah upbraided pro-slavery clergy in print, Angelina submitted a letter to William Lloyd Garrison, editor of the abolitionist weekly *The Liberator*, on August 20, 1835, declaring immediate abolition a cause worthy of martyrdom. She issued a radical monograph, *An Appeal to the Christian Women of the South* (1836), to mobilize Southern female Christians into a force to crush human bondage.

The silencing of Sarah in a Quaker meeting forced the Grimké sisters to move to Providence, Rhode Island. For personal enlightenment, Angelina began perusing thousands of back issues of abolitionist newspapers and espousing nontraditional views on civil rights. From New York City on May 9, 1837, her outreach extended to Boston, Lynn, and Philadelphia the first Anti-Slavery Convention of American Women, where she challenged delegates to uplift national morals. She declared both the Northern and Southern states bastions of ethnic bias. For pointed lectures and defense of female abolitionist oratory, she earned the spiteful nickname "Devilina."

Angelina published *An Appeal to the Women of the Nominally Free States* (1837), an emotional pamphlet spotlighting female morality as a bulwark against antiwoman politics. With *Letters to Catharine Beecher in Reply to an Essay on Slavery and Abolitionism Addressed to A.E. Grimké* (1837), Angelina hoped to radicalize Beecher to champion civil rights. Angelina's speech to members of a Massachusetts legislative committee on February 21, 1838, compared female abolitionists to Old Testament heroine Esther, the bold opponent of courtly custom. In a series of lectures in Boston in March 1838, she promoted an abolitionist petition to Congress signed by 2,000 women. The campaign set a precedent for the first female to appeal to a lawmaking body.

An Abolitionist Trio

Angelina disproved a widespread belief that she rebelled too eagerly and debated too heatedly to settle into domesticity. After a Presbyterian wedding to the Reverend Theodore Dwight Weld of Hampton, Connecticut, on May 14, 1838, she incurred expulsion from the Society of Friends. In defiance of standards suppressing female orators at the Second Anti-Slavery Convention of American Women, on May 16, 1838, Weld entreated listeners in Philadelphia's Pennsylvania Hall of Freedom while slavery advocates hurled rocks at the windows. Her exhortatory style sprinkled calls to action with biblical phrases, a style that caught the attention of future orator Mary Ashton Rice. For a model, Angelina extolled disenfranchised Englishwomen who refused to stand impotent while the colonial flesh trade limited human liberty.

Residing together in Fort Lee, New Jersey, in July 1838, Theodore Weld and the sister pamphleteers compiled *American Slavery As It Is: Testimony of a Thousand Witnesses* (1839). Angelina and Sarah weathered ouster by Quakers, who censured marriage outside the faith, and continued circulating abolitionist petitions. Following the birth of Charles Stuart Faucheraud "Charley" Weld on December 14, 1839, Angelina suffered an infection that limited breast-feeding. She retired from the speaking platform, leaving to Abby Kelley the task of abolishing bondage in Washington, D.C.

Angelina's activism revived in 1850 with the stirrings of temperance and suffrage and a vigorous suffrage rally by Lucretia Mott and Elizabeth Cady Stanton. On October 15, 1851, Angelina traveled to Worcester, Massachusetts, to support the Woman's Rights Convention. The next year, the sisters sent a letter backing an assembly in Syracuse. On Raritan Bay, the duo opened the Eagleswood School in October 1854 and taught coeducational, interracial classes in history and French for the next eight years. As an Underground Railroad conductor, Angelina dispatched runaways to Canada via barge traffic on the Raritan River and prayed that abolitionism would not end in war.

Post-Abolition Feminism

In the wake of the Emancipation Proclamation of January 1, 1863, on May 14, Weld addressed a national women's convention in New York City on "The Rights of Women and Negroes." The alliance of blacks and females against tyranny prefaced the era's drive for women's suffrage for black and white and for social and civil equality and education for all. In 1864, the Welds relocated to Hyde Park, Massachusetts, where Angelina and Sarah promoted the agenda of the Massachusetts Woman Suffrage Association and taught in West Newton at Diocletian Lewis's

Young Ladies Boarding School. In February 1868, Angelina learned of the existence of nephews Francis James Grimké and Archibald Henry Grimké, two of the three biracial sons of their deceased brother, Henry W. Grimké, and Nancy Weston, a slave.

Sarah's death on December 23, 1873, precipitated paralytic strokes in Angelina, immobilizing her right side and garbling her speech. In 1878, she disclosed a heart free of racism by supporting Francis Grimké in marrying a black diarist and scholar, Charlotte Lottie Forten, a fellow egalitarian. At Angelina's death in Boston on October 26, 1879, orators Wendell Phillips, Garrison, and Lucy Stone delivered eulogies, which Theodore Weld compiled as *In Memory: Angelina Grimké Weld* (1880).

See Also: Beecher, Catharine Esther; Foster, Abby Kelley; Livermore, Mary Ashton; Mott, Lucretia; Stanton, Elizabeth Cady; Stone, Lucy.

References

Berkin, Carol. *Civil War Wives: The Lives and Times of Angelina Grimké Weld, Varina Howell Davis, & Julia Dent Grant.* New York: Knopf, 2009.

Stanton, Elizabeth Cady, Susan Brownell Anthony, and Matilda Joslyn Gage, eds. *History of Woman Suffrage: 1861–1876.* Vol. II. New York: Fowler & Wells, 1882.

WHAT CAME YE OUT FOR TO SEE? (EXCERPT) BY ANGELINA GRIMKÉ WELD SECOND ANTI-SLAVERY CONVENTION OF AMERICAN WOMEN PENNSYLVANIA HALL OF FREEDOM, PHILADELPHIA MAY 17, 1838

The rare Southern female orator opposing slavery, Angelina Grimké Weld of Charleston, South Carolina, lectured women in Boston and Philadelphia on the breeding of black children for sale, a vicious system of press gang labor, and the lashing and torture of runaways. At the Pennsylvania Hall of Freedom in a last public address, she risked the vengeance of anti-black rioters and the burning of her publications to impart a biblical exhortation on human rights.

Women of Philadelphia! Allow me as a Southern woman, with much attachment to the land of my birth, to entreat you to come up to this work. Especially let me urge you to petition. *Men* may settle this and other questions at the ballot box, but you have no such right; it is only through petitions that you can reach the

Legislature. It is therefore peculiarly *your* duty to petition. Do you say, "It does no good?" The South already turns pale at the number sent. They have read the reports of the proceedings of Congress, and there have seen that among other petitions were very many from the women of the North on the subject of slavery. This fact has called the attention of the South to the subject. How could we expect to have done more as yet? Men who hold the rod over slaves, rule in the councils of the nation: and they deny our right to petition and to remonstrate against abuses of our sex and of our kind. We have these rights, however, from our God. Only let us exercise them: and though often turned away unanswered, let us remember the influence of importunity upon the unjust judge, and act accordingly. The fact that the South looks with jealousy upon our measures shows that they are effectual. There is, therefore, no cause for doubting or despair, but rather for rejoicing.

It was remarked in England that women did much to abolish slavery in her colonies. Nor are they now idle. Numerous petitions from them have recently been presented to the Queen, to abolish the apprenticeship with its cruelties nearly equal to those of the system whose place it supplies. One petition two miles and a quarter long has been presented. And do you think these labors will be in vain? Let the history of the past answer. When the women of these states send up to Congress such a petition, our legislators will arise as did those of England, and say, "When all the maids and matrons of the land are knocking at our doors we must legislate." Let the zeal and love, the faith and works of our English sisters quicken ours—that while the slaves continue to suffer, and when they shout deliverance, we may feel the satisfaction of *having done what we could.*

Source: Pennsylvania Hall Association. *History of Pennsylvania Hall, Which Was Destroyed by a Mob.* Philadelphia: Merrihew and Gunn, 1838.

WELLS, IDA B. (1862–1931)

Journalist and political commentator Ida Bell Wells-Barnett analyzed the racist hatred that resulted in lynching of blacks. One of the seven children of an enslaved cook, Elizabeth "Lizzie" Bell Warrenton, and woodworker and equal rights advocate James Wells, Ida was born in Holly Springs, Mississippi, southeast of Memphis on July 16, 1862. She was five months old at the passage of the Emancipation Proclamation.

From 1870 to 1877, Wells studied at Shaw University in Raleigh, North Carolina. After her parents died in the 1878 yellow fever outbreak, she supported her grandmother and younger siblings by teaching elementary school classes. At 21, Ida and her sisters moved to Memphis, where she continued teaching first grade in Woodstock.

Speaking for Herself

While teaching, Wells wrote articles on black welfare for a weekly, *The Living Way*, and for the Washington, D.C., *Daily Evening Star*, which spread her documented columns nationwide. In 1891, the Memphis school board fired her for exposing in print staff inefficiencies and the inadequacy of black schools. She revealed the growing menace of Ku Klux Klan members, who murdered prosperous and vocal blacks. Because of mob bloodshed, media sensationalism, and the shooting of three black men, she denounced the execution of black males without a criminal charge or adjudication. After she urged blacks to boycott white businesses and to abandon a town that disrespected their race, 6,000 black Tennesseans relocated to Oklahoma.

Wells's crusade against lynching began with investigation of race riots, post-Reconstruction retribution, and white emasculations and executions of blacks. She discovered that causes ranged from rude retorts, quarreling, sharing sidewalks with whites, and public drunkenness to rustling livestock, indebtedness to whites, and operating competitive businesses. To defeat the myth that lynching avenged the rape of white women by black men, she collected proof that most sexual relations of white females with black males were consensual. In retaliation, on May 27, 1892, angry whites demolished the *Free Speech* office and threatened anyone reviving it.

Spreading Truth

Speaking tours took Wells from men's clubs in Memphis to New York City to encourage freedmen to help themselves through determination, education, and capitalism. A militant tone built her reputation for combativeness and concern for minorities. As death threats increased, she carried a gun and moved to Chicago to pursue the antilynching campaign for *The New York Age*, *Detroit Plaindealer*, *Indianapolis World*, *Gate City Press*, and *Little Rock Sun*.

Wells enlightened listeners in New York City on October 5, 1892, with the speech "Lynch Law in All Its Phases." She repeated the oration in Boston on February 13, 1893, and throughout New England. The first-person style detailed the slaughter of three successful black grocers and mobs' trampling of citizen rights, an outrage she termed "the doctrine of white supremacy" (Wells 1893, 338). With the collaboration of Frederick Douglass, she led a boycott of the 1893 Columbian Exposition in Chicago for omitting blacks from American history exhibits and disseminated 20,000 tracts on the erasure.

For three months in 1893, Wells toured England, Wales, and Scotland and published the column Ida B. Wells Abroad protesting American apathy toward lynching and shaming the U.S. legal system for taking no action against blatant lawlessness. With English Quaker Catherine Impey, she initiated the Society for the Recognition of the Universal Brotherhood of Man and the London Anti-Lynching Committee. During litigation against two Tennessee lawyers for libel, she engaged assistant state attorney Ferdinand Lee Barnett, former editor of the *Chicago Conservator*, the city's first black newspaper.

Wells campaigned in Great Britain in 1894, becoming the first black foreign correspondent for a white newspaper by writing for the Chicago *Daily Inter-Ocean*. During the six-month tour, she confronted Frances Willard for whites-only membership of the Women's Christian Temperance Union. An attack on Wells's integrity by the *New York Times* increased British outrage at lynching and recruited support from parliament, the staff of the *Manchester Guardian*, and the Archbishop of Canterbury. On her return to New York in summer 1894, thugs attacked her on the Fulton Ferry.

In June 1895, Wells married widower Ferdinand L. Barnett and hyphenated their surnames. In a model of egalitarianism, the couple resided in a white Chicago district and befriended their neighbors. To aid black women in Boston and Chicago, in 1896, she established the National Association of Colored Women, Women's Era Club, Negro Fellowship League, and National Afro-American Council.

With the essays "Mob Rule in New Orleans: Robert Charles and His Fight to the Death" (1900) and "Lynch Law in America" (1900), Wells cited the states involved in the 241 lynchings of 1892, with Louisiana, Tennessee, Arkansas, and Alabama leading the carnage and Georgia, Mississippi, and Texas not far behind. Two of the dead, she noted, were children. She elicited compassion by describing the burning of live victims and the riddling of corpses with bullets.

Subsequent National Association for the Advancement of Colored People (NAACP) essays retained Wells's crusade against assaults on blacks, beginning in April 1910 with "The Northern Negro Woman's Social and Moral Condition." Her June 1910 oration in New York City, "How Enfranchisement Stops Lynching," found a wide audience in *Original Rights Magazine*, the NAACP journal. In 1913, she launched the Alpha Suffrage Club, the first of its kind for black females. At the end of World War I, she presented to the Fulton Street Methodist Episcopal Church a feminist text, "Negro Women in the Wars of Our Country" (1917). The Fourth of July speech evidenced her alliance with suffragists and zeal for black history.

During the Great Migration of blacks from the agrarian South to Northern industry, Wells promoted suffrage and equity in employment and housing. She addressed the U.S. legislature and demanded that President Woodrow Wilson desegregate the civil service and declare lynching a federal crime. She interviewed 50 eyewitnesses of race riots on July 2, 1917, in East St. Louis and researched clashes in Chicago and Elaine, Arkansas.

Wells suffered a gallstone attack in 1920 after the closure of Chicago's Negro Fellowship League, a reversal of her social settlement. In retirement, she published an apologia, *Crusade for Justice* (1928), questioning racism of the National Baptist Convention. A year after running for the Illinois legislature, she died suddenly on March 25, 1931, in a Chicago hospital of kidney failure.

References

Schechter, Patricia Ann. *Ida B. Wells-Barnett and American Reform, 1880–1930.* Chapel Hill: University of North Carolina Press, 2001.

Wells, Ida B. "Lynching: Our National Crime." *Proceedings of the National Negro Conference, 1909.* New York: Arno Press, 1909, 174–179.

Wells, Ida B. "Lynch Law in All Its Phases." *Our Day* (May 1893): 333–347.

LYNCH LAW IN ALL ITS PHASES (EXCERPT) BY IDA BELL WELLS LYRIC HALL, NEW YORK CITY OCTOBER 5, 1892

At a fund-raising event, Ida B. Wells, the acclaimed "Princess of the Press," dramatized Southern lynching with graphic details of stripping, peeling, immolating, shooting, and hanging of innocent blacks by vengeful whites. She cited statistics disproving myths about black men's sexual assaults on white women as the cause of racist retaliation. The New York audience response plus $500 in donations fueled her northeastern tour of Providence, Rhode Island, Wilmington, Delaware, Washington, D.C., and Boston and carried her message to news reporters and government investigators. Revered as the first phase of the civil rights movement, Wells's crusade took her twice to Great Britain in an effort to publicize hate crimes and embarrass the United States before its European allies.

I am before the American people today through no inclination of my own, but because of a deep seated conviction that the country at large does not know the extent to which lynch law prevails in parts of the republic nor the conditions which force into exile those who speak the truth. I cannot believe that the apathy and indifference which so largely obtains regarding mob rule is other than the result of ignorance of the true situation. And yet the observing and thoughtful must know that in one section, at least, of our common country, a government of the people, by the people, and for the people, means a government by the mob.

Where the land of the free and home of the brave means a land of lawlessness, murder, and outrage, and where liberty of speech means the license of might to destroy the business and drive from home those who exercise this privilege contrary to the will of the mob. Repeated attacks on the life, liberty and happiness of any citizen or class of citizens are attacks on distinctive American institutions. Such attacks imperiling as they do the foundation of government, law, and order merit the thoughtful consideration of far-sighted Americans, not from a standpoint of sentiment, not even so much from a standpoint of justice to a weak race, as from a desire to preserve our institutions.

The race problem or Negro question, as it has been called, has been omnipresent and all pervading since long before the Afro-American was raised from the degradation of the slave to the dignity of the citizen. It has never been settled because the right methods have not been employed in the solution. It is the Banquo's ghost of politics, religion, and sociology which will not lie down at the bidding of those who are tormented with its ubiquitous appearance on every occasion.

Times without number, since invested with citizenship, the race has been indicted for ignorance, immorality and general worthlessness and declared guilty and executed by its self-constituted judges. The operations of law do not dispose of Negroes fast enough, and lynching bees have become the favorite pastime of the South. As excuse for the same, a new cry, as false as it is foul, is raised in an effort to blast race character, a cry which has proclaimed to the world that virtue and innocence are violated by Afro-Americans who must be killed like wild beasts to protect womanhood and childhood.

Source: Wells, Ida B. "Lynch Law in All Its Phases." *Our Day* (May 1893): 333–347.

WINNEMUCCA, SARAH (1844–1891)

A multilingual crusader for Indian rights, Sarah Winnemucca became the United States' first native orator and reformer of government policies. The daughter of Tuboitony and the war chief and antelope charmer Winnemucca the Younger and granddaughter of Old Truckee Winnemucca, a Shoshone healer and headman of some 150 Northern Paiute, she received the name Thocmetony (Shellflower) in 1844 at her birth at Humboldt Lake in the desert of west-central Nevada. Reared with two sisters and a brother, she was 10 years old in 1854 when her grandfather guided explorer John Charles Frémont to California.

Winnemucca excelled at native languages, English and Spanish, and tribal debate as well as translation for adult councils. In her teens, she adopted Methodism and took the name of the biblical Abraham's wife, a scriptural matriarch and grandmother of the twelve tribes of Israel. Her mother and other females wielded equal influence with males on Paiute affairs and vetoed a move from the Great Basin Desert nearer pioneer villages for fear of white men targeting Indian girls and women. At the request of her dying grandfather, Winnemucca and her sister, Elma, relocated to San Jose, California, to the Convent of Notre Dame de Namur. Winnemucca obeyed his hopes for her by mastering academics and the nuns' lessons in needlework until whites insisted that the institution not desegregate for the sake of two Indians.

When cold and malnutrition stalked Paiutes following the loss of game and pine nuts, their natural foods, in 1864, Winnemucca and her father walked 435 miles to Virginia City and stopped before the International Hotel to beg for money, food, and blankets. The decimation of her people increased through racist violence. In March 1865, a raid of the Mud Lake camp by the Nevada Volunteers killed 29 noncombatants that included Sarah's two paternal grandmothers, mother, sister, and infant half-brother.

A Resilient Life

At age 21, Winnemucca lived with her brother Natchez at the Pyramid Lake Reservation in western Nevada. She gained employment in 1868 as a U.S. Cavalry scout, courier, and an interpreter for General Oliver Otis Howard at Fort McDonald for the lump sum of $500. As cavalry negotiator, she bore authority and an insider's knowledge of epidemics of European diseases that killed 50 percent of desert Indians. General Howard awarded her a medal for courage and reported her assistance to the national press. To boost a just perspective in Washington, D.C., she advocated women's suffrage, temperance, and passive resistance.

Following marriage to Lieutenant Edward C. Bartlett in 1872, Winnemucca experienced the adversities of battered wives of alcoholics. She supported the family by proceeds from oratory and tracts on Indian sufferings under racist agents, some posing as Christian missionaries. In April 1875, she followed her father, brother Natchez, and 700 Paiutes to Malheur Reservation on the Nevada-Oregon border, where she served as mediator and language instructor.

Becoming an Orator

Winnemucca reported to President Rutherford B. Hayes on the status of families at Yakima Reservation in south central Washington. Carl Schurz, Secretary of the Interior, arranged a reassignment of Paiutes to Malheur. To accommodate white ranchers, he broke his promise, leaving the tribe in limbo at Pyramid Lake. At Russ House in San Francisco on December 5, 1881, she married Lieutenant Lewis

H. Hopkins, a spendthrift and gambler who had worked five years for the Indian department.

In commentary to the *Californian*, Winnemucca declared, "I know something about sermons myself and can preach a better sermon than any [Methodist] ministers" (Winnemucca 1882, 256). According to "On the Treatment of the Indians," a media version in *The Peacemaker and Court* of a speech made in Boston on May 2, 1883, the orator chose a direct, factual approach for disclosing wrongs against the Paiute. To illustrate the hardships of forced residence on reservations, she charged whites with snatching native children and despoiling Indian females. She described Indians in cold weather sharing piteously few blankets, even though the U.S. government had promised enough for all. She concluded that such dereliction of covenants resulted from greed that violated the kinship of races.

Activist sisters Mary Peabody Mann and Elizabeth Palmer Peabody funded Winnemucca's speaking tour from April 1883 to August 1884 throughout New England. At a height of influence on the East and West coasts, she compiled history and personal experience in *Life among the Piutes: Their Wrongs and Claims* (1883). She became the nation's first native female to publish a memoir and earned the media nickname "Princess Sarah." Her orations included testimony to the U.S. House Subcommittee on Indian Affairs on April 22, 1884, followed by newspaper interviews, a collection of signatures in New York supporting First Peoples, and some 300 verbal exposés of the corrupt agents superintending the reservation network.

Applying the Quaker method at the biracial Peabody Institute, the first English-language school taught by an Indian, Winnemucca formed a curriculum of songs, hymns, math, geography, and literacy as well as cultivation of vegetables, barley, and wheat. By the 1885–1886 school year, when parents of 400 children sought enrollment, she petitioned the federal government and missionaries to provide dormitories for boarding. A lack of missionary donors and congressional aid doomed the academy to failure.

Before varied audiences, Winnemucca crusaded for Indian welfare and citizenship. Two years after Lt. Hopkins's death from tuberculosis on October 18, 1887, she relocated to Henry's Lake, Idaho, with her sister Elma, also a widow. On October 17, 1891, Winnemucca died of tuberculosis.

References

Hopkins, Sarah Winnemucca. *Reproduction of Life among the Piutes: Their Wrongs and Claims*. Bishop, CA: Chalfant Press, 1883.

Winnemucca, Sarah. "The Pah-Utes." *The Californian* 6 (September 1882): 252–256.

ON THE TREATMENT OF THE INDIANS BY SARAH WINNEMUCCA HOTEL WINTHROP PARLOR, BOSTON, MASSACHUSETTS MAY 2, 1883

A translator and mediator for the Northern Paiute in government negotiations, Sarah Winnemucca of Humboldt Lake, Nevada, gave 300 talks in major cities to explain the tenuous survival of First Peoples. She began the campaign in 1879 in San Francisco and Sacramento and progressed to Washington, D.C. At the invitation of the Massachusetts Indian Association, she audaciously informed Bostonians of the plunder by dishonest Indian agents of government goods. With the profits, the agents financed bribes to treasury officials. To add authenticity to the appeal, she dressed in buckskin and answered to the title of "princess." She continued the crusade for a permanent home for her people by distributing a circular and speaking in Providence, Rhode Island; Hartford, Connecticut; Pittsfield and Salem, Massachusetts; Philadelphia; Baltimore; and New York City.

We are told to love one another. It is no new thing for Indians to love one another. They are taught to do that when little children in their wigwams. They don't kill for pleasure. They only kill when forced to do so in self-defense when they have been outraged. Had slaughtering white people been a pleasure, how easily they might have massacred the white people when they first landed on these shores or how easily the Paiutes might have killed the white settlers when they first came among them in the long ago.

You know not what Indian agents and white men do in the far West. How they steal the Indian land; how they deprive them of the government supplies: how they ruthlessly tear the babe from the mother's breast; how they insult the virtue of the Indian girls, and virtue is as precious a jewel among the Paiutes as here in Boston. For these outrages the Indians take up arms and never an Indian raid was made but what was brought about by such causes as these.

I can tell you the sad truth about the Indian agents. I can tell you how few of the government supplies reach the Indians: how one little blanket was provided to shelter a family of six from the cold; how three blankets were supposed to be enough for fifteen Indians, when each of them should by right have had one; how indeed they often have to buy the very supplies that the government has promised to give them in exchange for their lands.

I have asked the agents why they did these wrong things. They have told me it was necessary for them to do so in order to get money enough to send the Great Father at Washington to keep their position. I assure you that there is an Indian ring; that it is a corrupt ring and that it has its head and shoulders in the treasury of Washington. But yet we know there are good men and women among the white people. We call you brothers despite all the wrong that is done, for you are our brothers according to our tradition.

The first parent of us all, says the legend, had both white and red children. They did not agree together so the father separated them and placed a great ocean between. He said that some day they should be united. And this is why we believe you are our brothers. We hope our true friends will aid us and stand by us in our trouble.

Source: Winnemucca, Sarah. "On the Treatment of the Indians." *The Peacemaker and Court of Arbitration* 1, no. 1 (July 1882): 188.

WOLF, NAOMI (1962–)

Polemicist and social critic Naomi Rebekah Wolf informed third wave feminists of the beauty trap, an element of tyranny and diminution of women. She was born on November 12, 1962, in San Francisco to anthropologist and psychotherapist Deborah Ruth Goleman, a specialist in women's studies, and Leonard L. Wolf, a theorist on Gothic literature and professor of English at San Francisco State University. She and brother Aaron grew up in the raffish Haight-Ashbury district, where she read feminist literature and identified with the second wave revolution. In the mid-1960s, the family toured Europe by van.

While Wolf attended an urban Hebrew school, she rebutted her father's respect for Western literature and humanism. In 1984, a rude remark from a male peer about the size of her abdomen caused her to develop anorexia and drop 20 percent of her weight, from 105 pounds to 84. A doctor warned her of the danger of self-starvation. As a member of the Lowell High School forensic society, she excelled at speech and debate.

At Yale, Wolf majored in English literature and graduated magna cum laude. Two decades later, she failed to recruit the university hierarchy in backing her claim that scholar Harold Bloom groped her thigh during her junior year. Following a complaint filed by 16 Yale students with the U.S. Department of Education Office for Civil Rights, she issued statements in the April 2011 *Daily Mail* and over CBS-TV on *The Early Show* charging that the university concealed serious sexual crimes as a means of shielding the institution's reputation. Government investigators concurred with the grievances in 2012.

Feminist Theory

In 1985, Wolf entered New College at Oxford on a Rhodes scholarship. Of the female scholars she met in England, five had suffered eating disorders. During a three-year sojourn in Edinburgh, she began compiling facts on patriarchy and its effects on women's self-image.

In 1988, Wolf set aside her thesis on female beauty in literature of the 1800s and 1900s. She married newspaperman David Julian Shipley, editor of the *New York Times* op-ed page, and produced two children, Rosa and Joseph. Still occupied in 1991 with a doctoral dissertation reflecting Victorian and Edwardian ideals and exposing the shallow values of contemporary culture, she separated from Shipley and dated movie producer Avram Ludwig.

Wolf's zeal for reform preceded publication of *The Beauty Myth: How Images of Beauty Are Used Against Women* (1991), a best-selling social critique of the feminist canon in the United States and Great Britain. The text alerted career women of the late 1900s that society demanded beauty treatments and a chic wardrobe of females who rose to economic, political, and social eminence. She warned of the prevalence of anorexia nervosa, bulimia, drastic dieting, and cosmetic surgery as antidotes to low self-esteem and insecurity.

Wolf's treatise denounced the beauty and fashion merchandisers as exploiters of the pop cultural veneration of youth, sexuality, and thinness. She reported that the American Society of Plastic and Reconstructive Surgeons characterized a gender breakdown of clients as 87 percent women. Her scrutiny of women's magazines, film, billboards, television, and the Internet disclosed a constant assault of images and photos reflecting an artificial standard of looks. Women viewed too many elegant models addicted to beauty maintenance and too many articles on how to prolong a titillating appearance through dieting, anti-wrinkle oils, and extreme exercise. The resulting generation of self-deprecating girls and passive women fed an artificial ideal of beauty as the measure of womanly worth in society and the workplace.

For stressing the self-improvement of the individual, Wolf's feminist theory gained the attention of leaders Germaine Greer, Betty Friedan, and Gloria Steinem and popularized the term "beauty myth" as a critique of antifemale discrimination in the late 1900s. Wolf compared social adherence to superficial criteria as a religious rite feeding the multibillion-dollar cosmetic industry. Instead of building character and accepting evidence of mortality, women put their faith in products and regimens that purified hair and skin to emit radiance.

To Congress on July 10, 1997, Wolf presented the address "Dying to Be Thin." While reporting her own experience with anorexia, she explained how food subsumes the victim's consciousness. She declared the obsession a political issue because of the dependence of girls on smoking, narcotics, and weight-loss drugs to keep them thin.

Opinions and Views

By advising President Bill Clinton on methods of appealing to female voters during his reelection campaign, Wolf took on new responsibilities in 1996. She extended her influence on Democratic presidential hopefuls by counseling Al Gore on women's needs for Social Security and flex-time in the workplace. In classes at the Woodhull Institute for Ethical Leadership, which she co-founded in September 1997, her assertiveness retreats introduced women to platform speaking requiring focus and energy.

Wolf's controversial *Promiscuities: The Secret Struggle for Womanhood (or a Secret History of Female Desire)* (1998) narrowed her inquiry to cultural icons of teens. She emphasized the male maturity cycles in the novels of Ernest Hemingway, D.H. Lawrence, and J.D. Salinger and the antiwoman cant in fiction by Norman Mailer, Henry Miller, and Philip Roth. Left without literary role models, girls had fewer guidelines on forming intimate relationships. Even worse for normal development, contemporary literature assailed girl readers with skewed stereotypes of female arousal and carnality.

Wolf's next nonfiction work, *Misconceptions: Truth, Lies, and the Unexpected on the Journey to Motherhood* (2001), applied subjective analysis to pregnancy and childbirth, especially the high rate of surgical deliveries via caesarian section. She valorized the slower, woman-to-woman birthing methods of midwives. The remainder of the book contrasted a father's involvement in tending babies and toddlers as opposed to the mother's role. With "The Porn Myth," an article for the October 20, 2003, issue of *New York*, she denounced Internet pornography for deadening male desire for real female attributes.

In 2005, Wolf settled in a one-bedroom apartment in Manhattan and divorced. In Washington, D.C., before the Institute for Progressive Christianity on November 18, 2006, she stigmatized the rise of religious fundamentalism as a tool of politicians and theocrats. Her speech excoriated the fanaticism, torture, and intolerance of conservative religions for suppressing the progressive ideals and traditions of American Christianity and Judaism.

Wolf turned to political defiance of the George W. Bush administration with *The End of America: Letter of Warning to a Young Patriot* (2007), a summation of the sabotage of democracy by fascism. The following year, the text appeared as a documentary that denounced the 2001 Patriot Act as an assault on the Bill of Rights. She listed as components of suppression the creation of paramilitary policing, surveillance, arbitrary arrests, and jailing at secret prisons. She alerted readers to the suspension of constitutional law and the vilification of the media, dissident individuals and groups, and emblematic citizens and heroes, all despotic tactics she repeated on C-SPAN in September 2007. By comparing post-9/11 America to the rise of tyrannical Nazis and Mussolini's brown shirts, she warned of ominous political trends in U.S. government.

As a sequel to *The End of America*, Wolf issued *Give Me Liberty: A Handbook for American Revolutionaries* (2008), a salute to citizens who resisted threats to the U.S. Constitution. She reprised the commonalities of ordinary colonists who backed the framers of liberty. Looking to the future, she queried readers on apathy toward torture and illegal wiretapping revealed during the Iraq War and the secret machinations of the National Security Administration (NSA).

Wolf stirred audiences with print and verbal conjecture. On August 30, 2008, she published in the *Sydney Morning Herald* "Behind the Veil Lives a Thriving Muslim Sexuality," a defense of Islamic family values that reverenced female allure as a private realm of the husband sanctioned by God. In January 2009, she addressed Brooklyn Law School with a persuasive lecture on dishonest female values. On October 18, 2011, she incurred arrest for joining the Occupy Wall Street protest and postulated a theory implicating mayors and agents of the Department of Homeland Security in a conspiracy to quell a legal civil demonstration. Evidence obtained from emails in early 2012 substantiated her charge that bank officials colluded with the Federal Bureau of Investigation to station counterterrorism agents among protesters.

After the poor reception of *Vagina: A New Biography* (2012), Wolf defended her interpretation of gender differences according to anatomical facts ascertained by sex experts and endorsed by the International Society for the Study of Women's Sexual Health. She linked her conclusions about pleasure to release of women's creative energy. While living in Millerton, New York, she maintained a following for columns in *The Guardian* and *Project Syndicate* and spoke on issues concerning eating disorders, female sexuality, and repressive governments. In October 2013 at the National Mall, she energized a rally against NSA surveillance.

See Also: Friedan, Betty; Steinem, Gloria.

Reference

Beasley, Chris. *Gender and Sexuality: Critical Theories, Critical Thinkers.* Thousand Oaks, CA: Sage, 2005.

WOODHULL, VICTORIA (1838–1927)

Tractarian and social agitator Victoria California Claflin Woodhull lobbed concepts of sexual autonomy into the suffrage fray and became the first American female to run for the U.S. presidency. The seventh of ten children, she was born in Homer, Ohio, on September 24, 1838, to Roxanna "Roxy" Hummel and Reuben Buckman Claflin, a bartender, counterfeiter, and mail thief. In 1846, she entered elementary school but left in 1849 following her father's fraudulent burning of the family flour mill.

After divorcing her first husband in 1866, Woodhull wed James Harvey Blood, a Union army veteran and city auditor of St. Louis, and established a fashionable salon in New York City. In public lectures in 1868, she commended women for maintaining their own standards of bodybuilding, homeopathy, comfortable dress, and carnal pleasure. She proposed less stringent divorce laws and acceptance of children born of true love.

Wooodhull and her sister, Tennessee Celeste Claflin, introduced women to high finance by opening a Wall Street business. With the backing of financier Cornelius Vanderbilt, the duo succeeded from investment in stocks, earning the media nickname "the Lady Brokers of Broad Street." In February 1870, they opened the first female-owned Wall Street stock brokerage, Woodhull, Claflin & Company. With $700,000 in earnings, they published *Woodhull & Claflin's Weekly*, a propaganda tool for suffrage and birth control issued under the motto "Upward & Onward."

To further stir Reconstruction era controversies, Woodhull challenged anti-woman sentiment by declaring that the Fourteenth and Fifteenth Amendments guaranteed enfranchisement to both black males and women. She initiated public oratory claiming that society owed women personal liberty. On December 19, 1870, she and Isabella Beecher Hooker became the first and second women to petition Congress for gender equality. On January 11, 1871, Woodhull testified before the House Judiciary Committee that women suffered the crime of taxation without representation, the crime that had launched the American Revolution.

Woodhull turned notoriety into opportunities for lectures. Her speeches generated sympathy in New York, New Jersey, Indiana, Illinois, and Washington, D.C. At the 10th annual assembly of the American Association of Spiritualists in Chicago on September 18, 1873, she returned to her denunciation of abusive marriage and nonconsensual intercourse with "The Elixir of Life; or, Why Do We Die?" Through complex leaps of logic, her text defined health as mental, physical, and social balance, a source of wholesome infants and relief from thwarted libido and social disease.

In 1877, Woodhull and Claflin accepted bribes to depart for England on an oratorical tour. Woodhull accepted the support of the National Woman Suffragists' Nomination Convention alongside running mate Mary L. Stowe in 1892. Woodhull announced the two-woman candidacy in the October issue of her journal *The Humanitarian*. A lengthy editorial summarized a platform calling for suffrage, financial reform, health care, crime and labor initiatives, and the analysis of impure food, all topics that dominated women's politics into the next century. Still an expatriate, she died at Norton Park, Tewkesbury, her daughter Zula's estate, on June 9, 1927.

See Also: Anthony, Susan B.; Davis, Paulina W.; Hooker, Isabella Beecher; Mott, Lucretia; Stanton, Elizabeth Cady.

Reference

Frisken, Amanda. *Victoria Woodhull's Sexual Revolution: Political Theater and the Popular Press in Nineteenth-Century America.* Philadelphia: University of Pennsylvania Press, 2004.

THE ELIXIR OF LIFE; OR, WHY DO WE DIE? BY VICTORIA WOODHULL AMERICAN ASSOCIATION OF SPIRITUALISTS GROW'S OPERA HOUSE, CHICAGO, ILLINOIS SEPTEMBER 18, 1873

In a manifesto denouncing marital rape, lecturer Victoria Woodhull defied the abusive wedlock and coercive coitus that demeaned and harmed married women, forcing them to bear children out of pain and fear. Her crusade against wifely bondage outlined a central tenet of women's rights, female autonomy. She promoted a balance of desire and satisfaction as the source of healthy, loved infants and a wholesome home life. Her focus anticipated the efforts of second wave feminism in the 1960s to end violence against women.

I appear before you to-night to speak of a subject which, more than any other, ought to command the attention of the enlightened world; but which, more than any other, receives the anathemas of its professed representatives—the so-called Christians—because, forsooth, to discuss it, is to attack necessarily one of the chiefest pillars of the Christian edifice. . . . If health depend upon proper sexuality, it follows that disease depends upon improper sexuality. To this general proposition I make another and a specific one: That all disease not directly to be attributed to so-called accidental causes, is the result of improper, or the want of proper, sexual conditions. And this applies to persons of all ages and both sexes. Show me the man or woman, married or single, old or young, who is suffering from any chronic complaint, and I will show you a person who has either improper or no sexual relations.

Now, just here arises the great and grave question: What are and what are not proper sexual relations. In endeavoring to answer this, I must be permitted to speak so as to be properly understood. And why should I not? Are we not endowed by nature with the sexual passion; and is it not given us for a purpose—one that should be a blessing, instead of a curse as it mostly is, to humanity? Nobody will pretend to answer, No! Then why should we not discuss it as freely as we do any other subject? Is it because our thoughts and desires about it have become so abominable, so perverted and so impure, obscene and vulgar, that any, even needed reference to the subject, brings the blush of shame to the face and a sense of degradation to the soul? Are we indeed so impure that to us all sexual things are impure? I lay it down as an axiom that he or she who blushes and is ashamed at any mention of sexual intercourse, has, at some time or other, done something sexually of which to be ashamed. I hold that everything connected with the manner and method in which human life has its fountain, is a proper and a modest subject for either public or private discussion, and I simply pit all who say Nay! to this.

Sexual intercourse that is in accordance with nature, and therefore proper, is that which is based upon mutual love and desire, and that ultimates in reciprocal benefit. Sexual intercourse that is improper is that which is not based upon mutual love and desire, and that does not ultimate in reciprocal benefit. Of the former there is but one class of cases, since in this class, all the conditions of perfectness are present. First, love; second, desire based upon love; and, third, mutual happiness as the result. Who is there that shall dare to interfere with such sexual relations? Let it be whoever it may, he is an impious wretch, and an enemy to human happiness, and consequently to humanity.

Of the latter there are several classes, which deserve to be enumerated, so that they may be understood wherever any of them may be met. First, that class where it is claimed by legal right; second, that class where the female, to please the male, submits without the proper self desire; third, that class where, for money, or any motive other than love, the female sells the use of her body to the male for his gratification; fourth, that class where mutual love and desire exist, but where there is such want of adaptation as to make mutual consummation impossible.

Now, under either of these conditions, if sexual intercourse be maintained for any considerable length of time, disease and sexual demoralization will surely follow; but the most destructive to health as well as the most numerous, are the first and the last classes, which occur almost against her wishes or desires, virtually commits suicide; while the husband who compels it commits murder and ought just as much to be punished for it, as though he strangled her to death for refusing him.

But this even is not so destructive to health as is that intercourse carried on habitually without regard to perfect and reciprocal consummation. And when it is known that three-fourths of all married women, who otherwise might be happily mated, suffer from this cause, the terrible and widespread results may be readily understood. I need not explain to any woman the effects of unconsummated intercourse though she may attempt to deceive herself about it; but every man needs to have it thundered in his ears until he wakes to the fact that he is not the only party to the act, and that the other party demands a return for all that he receives; demands that he shall not be enriched at her expense; demands that he shall not, either from ignorance or selfish desire, carry her impulse forward on its mission only to cast it backward with the mission unfulfilled, to prostrate the impelling power and to breed nervous debility or irritability and sexual demoralization, and to sow the seeds of disease broadcast among humanity. What is merely hinted at here involves a whole science and a fine art, incomparably the most important of all the sciences and of all the arts, hardly yet broached to the human thought, and now criminally repressed and defeated in their effort at birth by the prejudices of mankind—by your prejudices, and even, perhaps, by mine.

It is a fact terrible to contemplate, yet it is nevertheless true and ought to be pressed upon the world for its recognition: that fully one-half of all women seldom or never experience any pleasure whatever in the sexual act. Now this is an impeachment of nature, a disgrace to our civilization—an eternal blotch upon the otherwise chivalrous conduct of men toward women. It is a standing reproach upon physiological science that this ignorance has existed so long; and upon medical science, that its dire effects have been so long concealed. I have recently had repeated interviews with a member, in high standing, of the New York College of Physicians; and he does not hesitate to acknowledge that, more than all I have yet said is true about the sexual demoralization of the race; but the age of hypocrisy reigns as supremely in this as in the clerical profession. Its members are waiting for the world to get ready to hear the truth and have thus made it necessary that an authority, competent to enforce her statements, is almost crucified, because she feels it her duty to do what they should have done, whose business it is to guard the health of humanity. . . .

Source: Woodhull, Victoria Claflin. *The Elixir of Life; or, Why Do We Die?* New York: Woodhull & Claflin, 1873.

Y

YARD, MOLLY (1912–2005)

A vigorous feminist reformer and campaigner, Mary Alexander "Molly" Yard gained momentum as a behind-the-scenes radical operative and strategist for labor, affirmative action, and civil rights. The daughter of Methodist missionaries Mabel Merriman Hickcox and James Maxson Yard, she was born on July 6, 1912, in Shanghai during the Chinese Revolution and grew up during a cholera epidemic in Chengdu, the capital of Sichuan Province. After relocating to Shanghai in 1922, she arrived in the United States in 1925.

While her father directed religious activities at Northwestern University in Evanston, Illinois, Yard observed his fervor for civil rights and labor unions. During the Great Depression, her mother sold imported Chinese merchandise through the mail to pay for higher education for her daughters. On scholarship, from 1929 to 1933, Yard majored in political science at Swarthmore College.

Yard joined the staff of First Lady Eleanor Roosevelt as an assistant and served the National Youth Administration with educator Mary McLeod Bethune. In 1938, Yard married a classmate, Sylvester Garrett, a labor mediator for the United Steelworkers Union, and insisted on retaining her birth name. While he taught labor law at Stanford and chaired the Regional War Labor Board for the Roosevelt administration, she reared their children, Joan, James, and John Garrett.

While living in Philadelphia in 1953, Yard settled in the Squirrel Hill district of Pittsburgh while her husband taught at the university. She applied her political acumen to the 1960 presidential candidacy of John F. Kennedy and gained sponsorship from the Young Women's Christian Association for the August 18, 1963, March on Washington for Jobs and Freedom. After she failed in 1964 in a run for the Pennsylvania House of Representatives, she used her notoriety to organize the Democratic Club and to advance President Lyndon B. Johnson's War on Poverty.

In the 1970s, Yard pushed for women's rights through local involvement in the National Organization for Women (NOW). On the national level, she raised funds, organized forums, and pondered organizing a third party that would pull women away from both Democrats and Republicans and concentrate power on equalizing military promotions, pensions, insurance, property rights, and Social Security. With funding of $1 million amassed in six months, she lobbied for ratification of the Equal Rights Amendment.

Yard's NOW staff masterminded female opposition to the 1987 nomination of Robert H. Bork for the U.S. Supreme Court, where his conservatism threatened abortion rights and justice to minorities and the elderly and disabled. She gained media credibility for second wave feminism by launching a bus tour rallying support for abortion rights, more than tripling membership from 80,000 to 250,000, and increasing the budget to $10 million. In retaliation against her strident harangues, adversaries made up the jingle "Here Comes Molly Yard" to the tune of "Here Comes Santa Claus."

Sharing a platform with feminist icon Gloria Steinem, on February 1, 1991, Yard addressed the First National Young Feminist Conference in Akron, Ohio, on issues of women's health, women's sports, media sexism, and violence against women. Following a debate on C-SPAN with Phyllis Schlafly on the status of American women, Molly suffered a stroke in mid-May 1991 that ended her advocacy. In January 1992, she received commendation from the Feminist Majority Foundation for personal sacrifice for women's rights.

In widowhood and advanced age, Yard lived in Arlington, Virginia, and continued agitating for gender equality. On February 2, 1996, she addressed legislators and activists at the Feminist Expo, which censured the 104th Congress for failing to back civil rights. After 75 years of commitment to women's rights, she died in Dormont, Pennsylvania, at the Fair Oaks Nursing Home on September 20, 2005.

See Also: Bethune, Mary McLeod; Douglas, Helen Gahagan; Ireland, Patricia; Roosevelt, Eleanor; Schroeder, Patricia; Steinem, Gloria.

References

Nelson, Valerie J. "Molly Yard, 93; Led Fight for Women's Rights." *Los Angeles Times*, September 22, 2005.

Yard, Molly. "Testimony." *Hearings on the Nomination of Anthony M. Kennedy to Be Associate Justice of the Supreme Court, Senate Committee on the Judiciary.* 100th Cong., 1st sess. Washington, DC: U.S. Government Printing Office, 1989.

NOMINATION OF DAVID SOUTER BY MOLLY YARD SENATE COMMITTEE ON THE JUDICIARY U.S. SENATE, WASHINGTON, D.C. DECEMBER 16, 1987

A radical agent and strategist for labor, affirmative action, and civil rights, Molly Yard predicted that, should females lose their reproductive rights, hospitals would again see "Saturday night massacres" of self-aborted women ravaged by fever, infection, and hemorrhaging. In the fervid style of Elizabeth Cady Stanton and Alice Paul, Yard continued crusading for women's health and safety and for gender equality for another two decades and chastised legislators for failing to back civil rights.

These hearings are taking place on David Souter, because you must replace Justice Brennan. For women and all minorities, all women, no matter our color, no matter our economic circumstances, no matter our age, all lesbians and gays, for all minorities of every race, Justice Brennan stood for the highest standards on individual rights, and it is painful for us to see him go.

I appreciate the fact that on the floor of the Senate last week, you spoke of Justice Brennan and his contribution to this country. I think I have never felt that I was speaking at a more solemn occasion, because we are here literally on behalf of the lives of the women of this country. It is no little matter. We have been struggling for years to eradicate discrimination and to be free in this society.

When this Constitution was written, African-Americans were slaves and women were the property of their husbands. We had no rights. We did not vote, we could not serve on juries, we could not own property, we could not be much of anything. And we had hoped that, through the democratic process of this country, we could step by step win our freedoms, and we have made progress. We did finally win the right to vote. We celebrate this year the 70th anniversary of the right to vote for women in this country.

But we have a long ways to go, and when the Supreme Court in 1973 gave us the *Roe* v. *Wade* decision edict, that court declared freedom for the women of this country. You have no freedom if you can't control your life, and none of you will ever face that problem. Not one of you. If your birth control fails, which is why most women get abortions in this country, and you can't get an abortion and you are forced to carry a pregnancy to term, you haven't any freedom to plan your life, to carry out your life, to do with your life what you dream it to become.

You know, Justice Brennan said that the way women are treated in this society, we think we treat them well, but he said, "The real treatment is ending up not putting women on a pedestal but putting them in a cage." And we have been in that cage, and the door was opened in 1973. How can you contemplate letting that door close on us again? Because we are absolutely convinced that David Souter—and we listened very carefully. We hoped we were wrong, but we are not wrong. He will be the fifth vote to overturn *Roe* v. *Wade*. And I tell you, we are not going to obey the law in this country. Women will not. There will be lawlessness everywhere. The jails won't be big enough to hold those who break the law and the people who help women break the law.

We are literally—I don't know how to say it to you so that you understand that women's lives are on the line. And if they can't control them because abortion is illegal, they will either break the law and/or they will die. Never, please, forget that illegal abortion was the leading cause of death in this country, maternal death. And it will be again. It will be again.

I would just like to say that, you know, I sit at a desk of the largest feminist organization in this country—250,000 of us—but we speak for many more than that. Last April 1989, we brought 650,000 people here, women, men, and children, to petition this Government, Congress, the Supreme Court, and the White House, asking that *Roe* v. *Wade* not be overturned. And we understand so well why our forebears came to this country and why people keep coming to this country from all over the world. They come for freedom, for freedom from interference by government on what they believe in, what religion they practice, with whom they associate, what they speak out on, and, above all, to run their lives as they see fit.

Would you deny women that right by allowing *Roe* v. *Wade* to be overturned? Would you allow the discrimination against women to go on and on in education, in employment? In every area I get these letters day after day after day after day about what women suffer and the pain they go through, and yet we have a nominee and we have no idea how he is going to treat sex discrimination.

I wish there was some way to make every one of you understand what is at stake here.

Source: Yard, Molly. "Nomination of David Souter." *Hearings on the Nomination of David H. Souter to be Associate Justice of the Supreme Court of the United States.* 101st Cong., 2d sess. Washington, DC: U.S. Government Printing Office, 1990, 666–667.

Selected Bibliography

Primary Sources

Abzug, Bella. "The Conduct of the President." *Congressional Record, House* 119, no. 15. 93rd Cong., 1st sess. Washington, DC: U.S. Government Printing Office, 1973, 19264–19266.

Addams, Jane. "The Objective Value of a Social Settlement." In *Philanthropy and Social Progress*, 27–56. New York: Thomas Y. Crowell, 1893.

Addams, Jane. "The Subjective Necessity for Social Settlements." In *Philanthropy and Social Progress*, 113–128. New York: Thomas Y. Crowell, 1893.

Anderson, Mary. "Equal Pay for Men and Women." *Hearings before the Special Subcommittee of the Committee on Education and Labor*, May 17, 18, 19. Washington, DC: U.S. Government Printing Office, 1950, 81–82.

Anderson, Mary. *Women's Place in Industry in Ten Southern States*. Washington, DC: U.S. Government Printing Office, 1931.

Anthony, Susan B. "Organization among Women as an Instrument in Promoting the Interests of Political Liberty." In *World's Congress of Representative Women*, 463–466. Chicago and New York: Rand, McNally, 1894.

Balch, Emily Greene. *Toward Human Unity or Beyond Nationalism*. Stockholm, Sweden: P.A. Norstedt & Söner, 1949.

Balch, Emily Greene. *Women at The Hague: The International Congress of Woman and Its Results*. New York: Macmillan, 1915.

Beard, Mary Ritter. "The State Rights Shibboleth." *Congressional Record: Proceedings and Debates of the Congress* 51, pt. 5. 63rd Cong., 2d sess. Washington, DC: U.S. Government Printing Office, 1914, 4957–4958.

Beecher, Catharine Esther. *An Essay on the Education of Female Teachers*. New York: Van Nostrand & Dwight, 1835.

Beecher, Catharine Esther. *The Evils Suffered by American Women and American Children: The Causes and the Remedy*. New York: Harper & Brothers, 1846.

Bird, Caroline. *The Case against College*. New York: David McKay, 1975.

Blackwell, Alice Stone. *Why Women Should Vote*. Philadelphia: Pennsylvania Woman Suffrage Association, 1915.

Blackwell, Antoinette Brown. "Where Is the Work of Women Equal, Where Superior, Where Inferior to That of Men." In *Report of the International Council of Women*. Washington, DC: Rufus H. Harby, 1888.

Blake, Lille Devereux. "Our Forgotten Foremothers." In *The Congress of Women: Held in the Woman's Building, World's Columbian Exposition, Chicago, U.S.A., 1893*. Chicago: Monarch Book Company, 1894, 841–842.

Blake, Lille Devereux. "The Unknown Quantity in Politics." In *National Woman Suffrage Association Report of the Sixteenth Annual Washington Convention*. Rochester, NY: Press of Charles Mann, 1884, 27–33.

Blatch, Harriot Stanton. "Woman as an Economic Factor." In *The History of Woman Suffrage*. Vol. IV. Indianapolis: Hollenbeck Press, 1902, 310–311.

Brady, Sarah. *A Good Fight*. Cambridge, MA: PublicAffairs, 2002.

Breckinridge, Sophonisba P. "Home Administration." *Proceedings of the Sixth Annual Conference*. Lake Placid, NY: n.p., 1906, 62–63.

Buck, Pearl. "Universal Military Training." *Hearings before the Committee on Armed Services, United States Senate*. 80th Cong., 2d sess. Washington, DC: U.S. Government Printing Office, 1948, 451–456.

Carson, Rachel. "Interagency Coordination in Environmental Hazards (Pesticides)." *Hearings before the Subcommittee on Reorganization and International Organizations of the Committee on Government Operations, United States Senate*. 88th Cong., 1st sess., June 4, 1963. Washington, DC: U.S. Government Printing Office, 1964, 215–216.

Carter, Rosalynn. "Caregiving." *Hearing before the Special Committee on Aging, U.S. Senate*. 105th Cong., 2d sess. Washington, DC: U.S. Government Printing Office, 1998, 8–13.

Catt, Carrie Chapman. "Why We Ask for the Submission of an Amendment." In *The History of Woman Suffrage*. Vol. IV (369–372). Indianapolis: Hollenbeck Press, 1902.

Chicago, Judy. *Institutional Time: A Critique of Studio Art Education*. New York: Monacelli Press, 2014.

Chisholm, Shirley. "The Conflict in Vietnam." *Congressional Record, House* 115. 91st Cong., 1st sess. Washington, DC: U.S. Government Printing Office, 1969, H7765.

Clinton, Hillary. "Nomination Speech." *Hearing before the Committee on Foreign Relations, United States Senate*. 111th Cong., 1st sess. Washington, DC: U.S. Government Printing Office, 2010, 15–24.

Cooper, Anna Julia. "The Needs and the Status of Black Women." In *The World's Congress of Representative Women*, 711–715. Chicago and New York: Rand, McNally, 1894.

Cooper, Anna Julia. *A Voice from the South by a Black Woman of the South*. Xenia, OH: Aldine Printing House, 1892.

Davis, Angela Y. *The Meaning of Freedom: And Other Difficult Dialogues*. San Francisco: City Lights Books, 2012.

Davis, Paulina W. *A History of the National Woman's Rights Movement*. New York: Journeymen Printers' Co-operative Association, 1871, 7.

Davis, Paulina W. *Proceedings of the Woman's Convention, Held at Worcester, 1850*. Boston: Prentiss Sawyer, 1851.

Day, Dorothy. "Against Military Conscription." In *Compulsory Military Training and Service*, 159–160. Washington, DC: U.S. Government Printing Office, 1940.

De Cleyre, Voltairine. *Exquisite Rebel: The Essays of Voltairine de Cleyre—Anarchist, Feminist, Genius*. Albany: State University of New York Press, 2005.

DeLauro, Rosa. "Honoring the *Amistad* and Connecticut's Role in the Underground Railroad." *Congressional Record* 143, no. 10. 105th Cong., 1st sess. Washington, DC: U.S. Government Printing Office, 1997, E962.

Dock, Lavinia Lloyd. "The Relation of Training Schools to Hospitals." *Papers and Discussions in the International Congress of Charities, Correction and Philanthropy*. Baltimore: Johns Hopkins Press, 1894.

Douglas, Helen Gahagan. "My Democratic Credo." *Congressional Record*. 79th Cong., 2d sess. Washington, DC: U.S. Government Printing Office, 1946, 92.

Eastman, Crystal. "The Michigan Campaign." In *Handbook of the Annual Conference of the National American Woman Suffrage Association*, 78–79. Philadelphia: O. Warren, 1912.

Eddy, Mary Baker. *Miscellaneous Writings: 1883–1896*. Boston: privately published, 1896.

Ehrenreich, Barbara. *Living with a Wild God: A Nonbeliever's Search for the Truth about Everything*. New York: Hachette, 2014.

Elders, Joycelyn. "Confirmation Statement." *Hearing of the Committee on Labor and Human Resources, United State Senate*. 103rd Cong., 1st sess. Washington, DC: U.S. Government Printing Office, 1993, 10–12.

Eshoo, Anna. "Progress Report on Women's Health." *Congressional Record* 143, no. 56, May 5. 105th Cong., 1st sess. Washington, DC: U.S. Government Printing Office, 1997.

Feinstein, Dianne. "Reform of Legal Immigration." *Hearing before the Subcommittee on Immigration of the Committee on the Judiciary, United States Senate*. 104th Cong., 1st sess., 1995. Washington, DC: U.S. Government Printing Office, 1997, 6–8.

Ferraro, Geraldine. "Blood Cancers." *Subcommittee of the Committee on Appropriations, United States Senate*. 107th Cong., 1st sess. Washington, DC: U.S. Government Printing Office, 2002.

Firestone, Shulamith. *The Dialectic of Sex: The Case for Feminist Revolution.* New York: William Morrow, 1970.

Fisher, Mary. "If Not Now . . ." *Congressional Record* 143, no. 59. 105th Cong., 1st. sess. Washington, DC: U.S. Government Printing Office, 1997, E879–E880.

Fonda, Jane. "After Visiting Dikes and Dams at Nam Sach Hit by U.S. Aircraft." *Hearings Regarding Restraints on Travel to Hostile Areas.* 92d Cong., 2d sess., September 19, 25. Washington, DC: U.S. Government Printing Office, 1972, 7654.

Friedan, Betty. "Judge Carswell and the 'Sex Plus' Doctrine." *Hearings before the Committee on the Judiciary, U.S. Senate.* 91st Cong., 2d sess. Washington, DC: U.S. Government Printing Office, 1970, 88–97.

Fuller, Kathryn. "Rhino and Tiger Conservation." *Hearing before the Subcommittee on Fisheries Conservation, Wildlife and Oceans of the Committee on Resources.* 105th Cong., 2d sess. Washington, DC: U.S. Government Printing Office, 1998.

Furness, Betty. "Bank Credit-Card and Check-Credit Plans." *Senate Subcommittee on Financial Institutions.* Washington, DC: U.S. Government Printing Office, 1968, 63–66.

Gage, Matilda Joslyn. "Speech." In *The Trial of Susan B. Anthony.* Rochester, NY: Daily Democrat and Chronicle Book Print, 1874, 179–205.

Gannett, Deborah Sampson. "An Address Delivered in 1802 in Various Towns in Massachusetts, Rhode Island, and New York." Boston: H.M. Hight, 1905.

Gertner, Nancy. "Cameras and Electronic Media in the Courtroom." *Hearing before the Subcommittee on Administrative Oversight and the Courts, of the Committee on the Judiciary.* 106th Cong., 2d sess. Washington, DC: U.S. Government Printing Office, 2001, 19–38.

Gertner, Nancy. *In Defense of Women: Memoirs of an Unrepentant Advocate.* Boston: Beacon Press, 2011.

Goldman, Emma. *Anarchism and Other Essays.* New York: Mother Earth Publishing, 1910.

Goldman, Emma. *The International Anarchist Congress: Held at the Plancius Hall, Amsterdam, on August 26th–31st, 1907.* London: "Freedom" Office, 1907.

Gore, Al, and Tipper Gore. *Joined at the Heart: The Transformation of the American Family.* New York: Macmillan, 2002.

Gore, Tipper. "Contents of Music and the Lyrics of Records." *Senate Hearing before the Commerce, Science, and Transportation Committee.* 99th Cong., 1st sess. Washington, DC: U.S. Government Printing Office, 12–13.

Graham, Katharine. "The Activism of the Press." *Nieman Report* (Spring–Summer 1974): 21–25.

Griffiths, Martha Wright. "The Equal Rights Amendment." *Congressional Record* 118, pt. 5. Washington, DC: U.S. Government Printing Office, 1972, 6143.

Hamer, Fannie Lou. "Hearing before a Select Panel on Mississippi and Civil Rights at the National Theater." *Congressional Record, June 16, 1964*. Washington, DC: U.S. Government Printing Office, 1968, 503–504.

Harper, Frances. "We Are All Bound Up Together." *Proceedings of the Eleventh Women's Rights Convention*. New York: Robert J. Johnston, 1866.

Haskett, William J. *Shakerism Unmasked, or the History of the Shakers*. Pittsfield, MA: self-published, 1828.

Hazlett, Adelle. "Endorsing Women's Enfranchisement." In *A History of the National Women's Rights Movement*, 52–57. New York: Journeymen Printers' Co-operative Association, 1871.

Herman, Alexis. "Children Who Toil." *Congressional Record* 144, no. 128 (September 23, 1998). Washington, DC: U.S. Government Printing Office, 1999, E1786–E1787.

Hernandez, Aileen. "Beyond Sexism: Educating Women for the Future." Mills College Conference. Oakland, CA: Mills College, 1973.

Hernandez, Aileen. "The Equal Rights Amendment." *Hearings before the Subcommittee on Constitutional Amendments*. 91st Cong., 2d sess. Washington, DC: U.S. Government Printing Office, 1970, 54–56.

Hill, Anita. "Testimony on the Clarence Thomas Confirmation." *Hearings before the Committee on the Judiciary, United States Senate*. 102d Cong., 1st sess. Washington, DC: U.S. Government Printing Office, 1993, 36–40.

Hobby, Oveta Culp. "A Debt to Democracy, a Date with Destiny." *United States Army in World War II*. Washington, DC: U.S. Government Printing Office, 1991.

Hooker, Isabella Beecher. *The Constitutional Rights of the Women of the United States*. Hartford, CT: Hartford Press, 1900.

Hopkins, Sarah Winnemucca. *Reproduction of Life among the Piutes: Their Wrongs and Claims*. Bishop, CA: Chalfant Press, 1883.

Howe, Julia Ward. "Morality Equality Between the Sexes." *The National Purity Congress, Its Papers, Addresses, Portraits*. New York: American Purity Alliance, 1896.

Hutchinson, Thomas. *History of the Colony and Province of Massachusetts Bay*. Vol. 1 (366–391). Boston: Thomas and John Fleet, 1767.

Iman, David Bowie, and Peter Hill Beard. *I Am Iman*. New York: Universe, 2001.

Johnson, Lady Bird. "Beauty for America." *Proceedings of the White House Conference on Natural Beauty, May 24–25, 1965*. Washington, DC: U.S. Government Printing Office, 1965, 17–18.

Jones, Mother. *The Autobiography of Mother Jones*. Chicago: Charles H. Kerr, 1925.

Jordan, Barbara. *Debate on Articles of Impeachment Hearings of the Committee on the Judiciary House of Representatives*. 93rd Cong., 2d sess. Washington, DC: U.S. Government Printing Office, 1974, 110–113.

Jordan, Barbara. "1976 Democratic National Convention Keynote Address." *Congressional Record* 122 (July 27). Washington, DC: U.S. Government Printing Office, 1976, 24127–24128.

Kelley, Florence. "Working Woman's Need of the Ballot." In *The History of Woman Suffrage*. Vol. IV. Indianapolis: Hollenbeck Press, 1902, 305–307.

Koedt, Anne. "The Myth of the Vaginal Orgasm." In *Notes from the Second Year*, 37–41. New York: New York Radical Feminists, 1970.

Koontz, Elizabeth Duncan. "Toward a Full Share in Abundance." *Hearings before the Special Committee on Aging*. 91st Cong., 2d sess. Washington, DC: U.S. Government Printing Office, 1970, 1803–1806.

Lee, Barbara Coombs. "Death with Dignity." *Hearing before the Subcommittee on the Constitution of the Committee on the Judiciary*. 104th Cong., 2d sess. Washington, DC: U.S. Government Printing Office, 1996, 163–166.

Leopold, Alice K. *The Effective Use of Womanpower*. Washington, DC: U.S. Government Printing Office, 1955.

Livermore, Mary A. "Industrial Gains of Women during the Last Half-Century." In *Report of the International Council of Women*. Washington, DC: Rufus H. Harby, 1888, 131–136.

Luce, Clare Boothe. "America's Destiny in the Air." *Congressional Record, House*. 78th Cong., 1st sess., February 9. Washington, DC: U.S. Government Printing Office, 1943, 759–764.

Mankiller, Wilma. "Oklahoma Tribal Concerns." *Oversight Hearing before the Subcommittee on Native American Affairs of the Committee on Natural Resources, House of Representatives*. 103rd Cong., 2d sess. Washington, DC: U.S. Government Printing Office, 1995, 8–10.

McPherson, Aimee Semple. "Lost and Restored." In *This Is That: Personal Experiences, Sermons and Writings*, 380–382. Los Angeles: Bridal Call Publishing, 1919.

Michelman, Kate. "Partial Birth Abortion." *Hearing before the Senate Committee on the Judiciary and the Subcommittee on the Constitution of the House Committee on the Judiciary*. 105th Cong., 1st sess. Washington, DC: U.S. Government Printing Office, 1997, 19–20.

Mink, Patsy. "English Language Empowerment Act of 1996." *Hearings before the Committee on Governmental Affairs, United States Senate*. 104th Cong., 1st and 2d sess., December 6, 1995 and March 7, 1996. Washington D.C., U.S. Government Printing Office, 1996, 56–57.

Mott, Lucretia. *Lucretia Mott's Discourse, at the Friend's Quarterly Meeting, in the Hester Street House*. New York: Ross & Tousey, 1850.

Nation, Carry Amelia. *The Use and Need of the Life of Carry A. Nation*. Topeka, KS: F.M. Steves & Sons, 1905.

Noor, Queen. *Leap of Faith: Memoirs of an Unexpected Life*. Waterville, ME: Wheeler, 2003.

Pennsylvania Hall Association. *History of Pennsylvania Hall, Which Was Destroyed by a Mob*. Philadelphia: Merrihew and Gunn, 1838.

Power, Samantha. "Rwanda's Genocide: Looking Back." *Hearing before the Subcommittee on Africa of the Committee on International Relations, House of Representatives*. 108th Cong., 2d sess. Washington, DC: U.S. Government Printing Office, 2004, 25–30.

Proceedings of the Seventh National Woman's Rights Convention. New York: Edward O. Jenkins, 1856.

Rankin, Jeannette. "On the Federalization of Mines." *Congressional Record: Proceedings and Debates of the Congress* 55, pt 6. Washington, DC: U.S. Government Printing Office, 1917, 5896.

Richards, Ann. "Inaugural Address." *State Journal*. 72d Legislature, Reg. sess. Austin, TX: State Printing Office, 1991, 22–24.

Robinson, Harriet Jane Hanson. "Political Parties and Woman Suffrage." In *Report of the International Council of Women*. Washington, DC: Rupus H. Harby, 1888, 306–308.

Roosevelt, Eleanor. "The President's Commission on the Status of Women." *Congressional Record* 108, no. 2 (February 15). Washington, DC: U.S. Government Printing Office, 1962, 2281.

Rose, Ernestine Louise. *An Address on Woman's Rights*. Boston: J.P. Mendum, 1851.

Rose, Ernestine Louise. *Mistress of Herself: Speeches and Letters of Ernestine L. Rose, Early Women's Rights Leader*. New York: Feminist Press, 2008.

Sanger, Margaret. "The Comstock Laws." *Birth Control: Hearings before a Subcommittee on the Judiciary, United States Senate*. 71st Cong., 3rd sess., February 13–14. Washington, DC: U.S. Government Printing Office, 1931, 9–10.

Schroeder, Patricia. "The Comstock Act." *Congressional Record* 142, no. 133. 104th Cong., 2d sess. Washington, DC: U.S. Government Printing Office, 1996, H10770.

Shalala, Donna. "Returning Wounded Warriors." *Hearing before the Committee on Veterans' Affairs, United States Senate*. 110th Cong., 1st sess. Washington, DC: U.S. Government Printing Office, 2007, 4–33.

Shaw, Anna Howard. "Celebration of Susan B. Anthony's Birthday." In *The History of Woman Suffrage*. Vol. IV (403–404). Indianapolis: Hollenbeck Press, 1902.

Smith, Margaret Chase. "A Declaration of Conscience." *Congressional Record, Senate*. 81st Cong., 2d sess. Washington, DC: U.S. Government Printing Office, 1950, 7894–7895.

Snowe, Olympia. *Fighting for Common Ground: How We Can Fix the Stalemate in Congress*. New York: Weinstein Books, 2013.
Stanton, Elizabeth Cady. "Declaration of Sentiments." In *Report of the Woman's Rights Convention*. Rochester, NY: 1848.
Stanton, Elizabeth Cady, Susan Brownell Anthony, and Matilda Joslyn Gage, eds. *History of Woman Suffrage: 1861–1876*. Vol. I. Rochester, NY: Charles Mann, 1887.
Stanton, Elizabeth Cady, Susan Brownell Anthony, and Matilda Joslyn Gage, eds. *History of Woman Suffrage: 1861–1876*. Vol. II. New York: Fowler & Wells, 1882.
Stone, Lucy. "Disappointment Is the Lot of Women." In *History of Woman Suffrage*. Vol. 1 (165–166). Rochester, NY: Charles Mann, 1887.
Terrell, Mary Church. "Lynching from a Negro's Point of View." In *Witnessing Lynching: American Writers Respond*. Piscataway, NJ: Rutgers University Press, 2003, 98–105.
Terrell, Mary Church. *The Progress of Colored Women*. Washington, DC: Smith Brothers, 1898.
Thirtieth Anniversary of the American Anti-Slavery Society. New York: American Anti-Slavery Society, 1863, 70–73.
Truth, Sojourner. "What Time of Night It Is?" In *History of Woman Suffrage: 1861–1876*. Vol. I (567–568). Rochester, NY: Charles Mann, 1887.
Wald, Lillian D. "Crowded Districts of Large Cities." *Proceedings of the National Council of Jewish Women*. Philadelphia: Jewish Publication Society of America, 1897, 95–103.
Wells, Ida B. "Lynching: Our National Crime." *Proceedings of the National Negro Conference, 1909*. New York: Arno Press, 1909, 174–179.
Woodhull, Victoria Claflin. *The Elixir of Life; or, Why Do We Die?* New York: Woodhull & Claflin, 1873.
Yard, Molly. "Testimony." *Hearings on the Nomination of Anthony M. Kennedy to Be Associate Justice of the Supreme Court, Senate Committee on the Judiciary*. 100th Cong., 1st sess. Washington, DC: U.S. Government Printing Office, 1989.

Periodicals and Collections

Alexander, Jane. "Interview." C-SPAN, *Booknotes*, June 15, 2000.
"At Home and Abroad." *The Deseret Weekly* 49 (August 25, 1894): 812.
Buck, Pearl. "Women's Place in a Democracy." *Appendix to the Congressional Record*. Washington, DC: U.S. Government Printing Office, 1941, A221–A225.
Day, Dorothy. "Address to the Liberal-Socialist Alliance." *Dorothy Day-Catholic Worker Collection*. Milwaukee, WI: Marquette University Library, 1941.

Dickinson, Anna Elizabeth. "Address to Congress." New York *Independent*, January 21, 1864.

Dickinson, Anna Elizabeth. "Whited Sepulchres." *Titusville* (Pennsylvania) *Morning Herald*, March 24, 1870.

Faludi, Susan. "Hers: Speak for Yourself." *New York Times Magazine*, January 26, 1992, 10, 29.

Firestone, Shulamith. "On Abortion." *Notes from the First Year: Woman's Liberation* (June 1968): 26–27.

Flanders, Laura. "Can 'Caring across Generations' Change the World?" *The Nation*, April 30, 2012.

Forbes, Esther. "The Newbery Acceptance Speech." *Horn Book* 20 (May–June 1944): 260–291.

Gilman, Charlotte Perkins. "A New Light on the Woman Question." *The Woman's Journal* (April 25, 1904): 76–77.

Harper, Frances. "Liberty for Slaves." *National Anti-Slavery Standard* (May 23, 1857): 3.

Harriman, Florence. "For, By, and About Women." *Atlanta Constitution*, March 9, 1908, 6.

Holmes, Alex. "Retiring Professor Profile: Paula Treckel." *The Campus*, April 25, 2014.

Hunt, Irene. "Books and the Learning Process." *Horn Book* 43 (August 1967): 424–429.

Jackson, Bonnie. "We Don't Mess Around." *Sweet Briar Alumnae Magazine* (1978): 4–5.

"Jeannette Rankin to Be Here." Canonsburg, Pennsylvania *Daily Notes*, October 27, 1917, 1.

Killian, Chris. "New Leadership Announced for Arcus Foundation." *Kalamazoo Gazette*, May 29, 2010.

Koontz, Elizabeth Duncan. "Complete Integration Must Be the Goal." *Ebony* 25, no. 10 (August 1970): 138–141.

"'Mother' Jones Speaks." *Reading* (Pennsylvania) *Times*, March 18, 1901, 1.

Mott, Lucretia. "Cherry Street Friends Meeting, Philadelphia." *Inter Ocean*, January 24, 1881, 3.

"Noted German Correspondent Deplores Banishment of Women to Kitchen." *Vassar Miscellany News* 19, no. 10 (November 3, 1934): 1, 4.

Pollitt, Katha. "Hers: The Smurfette Principle." *New York Times Magazine*, April 7, 1991.

Schneiderman, Rose. "Teachers Scorned Idea of a Union." *New York Times*, April 5, 1907, 7.

"Virginia Hemley Obituary." *El Paso Times*, April 3, 2014.

Wald, Lillian D. "Organization Amongst Working Women." *Annals of the American Academy of Political and Social Science* 27 (May 1906): 638–645.

Wasniewski, Matthew Andrew. *Women in Congress, 1917–2006*. H. Con. Res. 66, 107th Cong., 1st sess. Washington, DC: U.S. Government Printing Office, 2006.

Wells, Ida B. "Lynch Law in All Its Phases." *Our Day* (May 1893): 333–347.

Winnemucca, Sarah. "On the Treatment of the Indians." *The Peacemaker and Court of Arbitration* 1, no. 1 (July 1882): 188.

Winnemucca, Sarah. "The Pah-Utes." *The Californian* 6 (September 1882): 252–256.

"Women's Bureau Director Likes Woes of Others." *Corpus Christi* (Texas) *Caller-Times*, January 10, 1954, 10.

"The Workingman's Heroine." *The Tammany Times* 17, no. 15 (August 12, 1901): 10.

Electronic Sources

Anderson, Mary. "Equal Pay for Men and Women." Women and Social Movements in the United States, 1600–2000. Accessed December 9, 2014. http://womhist.alexanderstreet.com/lwvi/doc12.htm.

"Ann Richards's Commencement Address." May 28, 1995. *The* (Mount Holyoke) *College Street Journal*. Accessed March 13, 2015. https://www.mtholyoke.edu/offices/comm/csj/950605/richards.html.

"Anna Julia (Haywood) Cooper." Voices from the Gaps. University of Minnesota Digital Conservancy. Accessed October 23, 2014. http://hdl.handle.net/11299/166130.

Barton, Clara. "Testimony before Congress." In *The Reports of the Committees of the House of Representatives*. 39th Cong., 1st sess., 1865–1866. Accessed October 15, 2014. http://www.nps.gov/clba/historyculture/cbcongress.htm.

"Bella Abzug Convenes National Women's Conference in Houston." Jewish Women's Archive. Accessed March 11, 2015. http://jwa.org/thisweek/nov/18/1977/national-womens-conference.

Brady, Sarah. "Handguns." Accessed March 26, 2015. http://ptexans.com/sarah.htm.

Buck, Pearl S. "Nobel Lecture: The Chinese Novel." December 12, 1938. Accessed December 5, 2014. http://www.nobelprize.org/nobel_prizes/literature/laureates/1938/buck-lecture.html.

Dworkin, Andrea. "Pornography Is a Civil Rights Issue." *Attorney General's Commission on Pornography: Final Report, July 1986*. Accessed April 1, 2015. http://www.porn-report.com.

Elders, M. Joycelyn. "Interview." *National Visionary Leadership Project*. Accessed April 2, 2015. http://www.visionaryproject.org/eldersjoycelyn/.

Faludi, Susan. "The Disneyfication of the Media." *Democracy Now!*, March 1, 1996. Accessed April 8, 2015. http://www.democracynow.org/1996/3/1/susan_faludis_speech_from_the_opening.

Flynn, Elizabeth Gurley. "Statement at the Smith Act Trial." April 24, 1952. American Rhetoric. Accessed January 6, 2015. http://www.americanrhetoric.com/speeches/elizabethgurleyflynn.htm.

Fonda, Jane. "Life's Third Act." TEDxWomen 2011. Accessed January 6, 2015. http://www.ted.com/talks/jane_fonda_life_s_third_act/transcript?language=en.

"Forbidden Discourse: The Silencing of Feminist Criticism of 'Gender.'" Accessed December 30, 2014. http://meetinggroundonline.org/wp-content/uploads/2013/10/GENDER-Statement-InterActive-930.pdf.

Fuller, Kathryn. "A Few Thoughts on Bees, Fungi, and the Importance of Perspective in a Code Orange World." Brown University News Service, May 31, 2004. Accessed April 13, 2015. http://www.brown.edu/Administration/News_Bureau/2003-04/03-135f.html.

Gilbreth, Lillian Moller. "Widening Horizons." Ben Graham Corp. Accessed November 25, 2014. http://www.worksimp.com/articlesWidening%20horizong%20-%10gilbreth.htm.

Glaser, Elizabeth. "1991 Democratic National Convention Address." July 14, 1992. American Rhetoric. Accessed April 15, 2015. http://www.americanrhetoric.com/speeches/elizabethglaser1992dnc.htm.

Graham, Katharine. "Speech on Court Records and Privacy Concerns." Reporters Committee for Freedom of the Press. May 22, 2001. Accessed January 9, 2015. http://www.rcfp.org/browse-media-law-resources/news/katharine-graham-speech-court-records-and-privacy-concerns.

Griffin, Ada Gay, and Michelle Parkerson. *A Litany for Survival: The Life and Work of Audre Lorde* (film). New York: Third World Newsreel, 1995.

Herman, Alexis. "Remarks by Secretary of Labor Alexis Herman." Howard University Law School Commencement, May 13, 2000. United States Department of Labor. Accessed April 20, 2015. http://www.dol.gov/dol/aboutdol/history/herman/speeches/howard2.htm.

Hoey, Jane M. "Understanding the Delinquent: Society in Relation to the Child." *National Conference on Social Welfare Proceedings, 1931*. University of Michigan Digital Library Text Collections. Accessed November 25, 2014. http://quod.lib.umich. edu/n/ncosw/ACH8650.1931.001?rgn=main;view=fulltext.

Holmes, Freedwoman. "Interview." *Federal Writers' Project, 1936–1938*. Accessed November 23, 2014. http://memory.loc.gov/cgi-/mesnbib:@field(bin/query/S?ammemAUTHOR+@od1(Davis,+Lucinda)).

Hurston, Zora Neale. "Turpentine Camp—Cross City." *Florida Memory* (August 1939): 15–18. Accessed December 2, 2014. https://www.floridamemory.com/onlineclassroom/zora_hurston/documents/.

The Jane Addams Papers Project. Accessed November 4, 2014. http://www.janeaddamsproject.org.

Keller, Helen, "I Want to Be Adopted." June 30, 1925. Lions Clubs International. Accessed November 12, 2014. http://www.lionsclubs.org/EN/about-lions/mission-and-history/our-history/lions-history-hkspeech.php. With permission of media director Dana LaJoye.

Lee, Barbara Coombs. "Review of Book about the Death-with-Dignity Movement." September 5, 2012. Accessed April 27, 2015. http://zoefitzgeraldcarter.com/blog/tag/barbara-coombs-lee/.

Le Guin, Ursula K. "Bryn Mawr Commencement Address (1986)." Serendip Studio. Accessed March 20, 2015. http://serendip.brynmawr.edu/sci_cult/leguin/.

Levertov, Denise. Statement for a Television Program." May 1972. Gifts of Speech: Women's Speeches from Around the World. Accessed December 31, 2014. http://gos.sbc.edu/l/levertov2.html.

"Lillian D. Wald Papers, 1919." Influenza Encyclopedia, University of Michigan. Accessed October 9, 2015. http://quod.lib.umich.edu/f/flu/2510flu.0016.152/1/--lillian-wald-writings-speeches-1919?page=root;size=125;view=image.

Lorde, Audre. "The Transformation of Silence into Language and Action." December 28, 1977. The Incredible Shrinking Phallus. Accessed March 24, 2015. https://shrinkingphallus.wordpress.com/the-transformation-of-silence-into-language-and-action-by-audre-lorde/.

Luce, Clare Boothe. "A Greater and Freer America: G.I. Joe's Future." June 27, 1944. Accessed December 4, 2014. http://www.ibiblio.org/pha/policy/1944/1944-06-27a.html.

"Lucinda Davis." *Born in Slavery: Slave Narratives from the Federal Writers' Project, 1936–1938.* WPA Slave Narrative Project, Oklahoma Narratives. Vol. 13 (53–64). Accessed November 23, 2014. http://memory.loc.gov/cgi-bin/query/S?ammem/mesnbib:@field(AUTHOR+@od1(Davis,+Lucinda)).

The Margaret Sanger Papers Project. Accessed November 5, 2014. http://www.nyu.edu/projects/sanger.

"Mary McLeod Bethune: Renowned Educator, Political Activist, Presidential Advisor." Accessed November 20, 2014. http://www.nps.gov/mamc/photosmultimedia/multimedia.htm.

"Mary Reynolds." *Born in Slavery: Slave Narratives from the Federal Writers' Project, 1936–1938.* WPA Slave Narrative Project, Texas Narratives. Vol. 16, pt. 3. Accessed November 26, 2014. http://memory.loc.gov/cgi-bin/query/S?ammem/mewnbib:@field(AUTHOR+@od1(Reynolds,+Mary)).

Meir, Golda. "The Speech That Made Possible a Jewish State." January 2, 1948. Tamilnation.org. Accessed December 15, 2014. http://tamilnation.co/ideology/golda.htm.

Monk, Meredith. "Some Thoughts about Art, America and Jumping Off the Cliff." April 1990. Gifts of Speech: Women's Speeches from Around the World. Accessed May 5, 2015. http://gos.sbc.edu/m/monk1.html.

"A Portrait of Queer America." January 2011. Accessed April 22, 2015. http://lgbtqamerica.blogspot.com/2011/01/70s-assassination.html.

Power, Samantha. "Testimony of U.S. Permanent Representative-designate Samantha Power." Accessed June 8, 2015. http://www.foreign.senate.gov/imo/media/doc/Power_Testimony.pdf.

Provizer, Norman. "Golda Meir: An Outline of a Unique Life." Metropolitan State University of Denver. Accessed December 15, 2014. https://www.msudenver.edu/golda/goldameir/chronologyofgoldameir.

Rich, Adrienne. "National Book Award Acceptance Speech." Accessed January 2, 2015. http://www.nationalbook.org/nbaacceptspeech_arich.html#.VwZpbTEUVPY.

Roosevelt, Eleanor. "On the Universal Declaration of Human Rights." *Eleanor Roosevelt Papers Project*. Accessed December 15, 2014. https://www.gwu.edu/~erpapers/teachinger/glossary/udhr.cfm.

Roosevelt, Eleanor. "Pearl Harbor." December 7, 1941. *Eleanor Roosevelt Papers Project*. Accessed December 4, 2012. http://www.gwu.edu/~erpapers/teachinger/q-and-a/q21-pearl-harbor-address.cfm.

Sealander, Judith. "'Tigers and Oranges': The Interactions of the Federal Women's Bureau with Management." 1979. Accessed December 10, 2014. http://www.thebhc.org/siges/default/files/beh/BEH print/v008/p0067-p0075.pdf.

Starhawk. "The Bodhi Tree Lecture." Bodhi Tree House. Accessed June 2, 2015. http://www.bodhitree.com/lectures/starhawk.html.

Streisand, Barbara. "The Artist as Citizen." February 3, 1995. Harvard IOP at The Kennedy School. Accessed May 15, 2015. http://forum.iop.harvard.edu/content/artist-citizen-barbra-Streisand.

Thompson, Dorothy. "Hitler's Plans for Canada and the United States." Accessed May 12, 2014. http://podcast.klsh.kl.edu.tw/.

Walker, Alice. "Coming to See You Since I Was Five Years Old: A Poet's Connection to the South African Soul." 2010. Accessed July 2, 2015. http://alicewalkersgarden.com/2010/09/coming-to-see-you-since-i-was-five-years-old-an-american-poets-connection-to-the-south-african-soul/#more-9.

Secondary Sources

Adams, Nicole, Tashina Etter, and Sarah Hernandez. *Relationships, Respect and Revitalization: Grantmaking Strategies*. Portland, OR: Grantmakers for Education, 2006.

Allen, Judith A. *The Feminism of Charlotte Perkins Gilman: Sexualities, Histories, Progressivism*. Chicago: University of Chicago Press, 2009.

Austenfeld, Thomas. *Critical Insights: Barbara Kingsolver*. Pasadena, CA: Salem, 2010.

Axelrod-Contrada, Joan. *Isabel Allende*. New York: Marshall Cavendish Benchmark, 2011.

Baer, Ellen Davidson, Patricia D'Antonio, Sylvia Rinker, and Joan E. Lynaugh, eds. *Enduring Issues in American Nursing*. New York: Springer, 2002.

Baker, Jean H., ed. *Votes for Women: The Struggle for Suffrage Revisited*. New York: Oxford University Press, 2002.

Barkan, Elliott Robert. *Making It in America: A Sourcebook on Eminent Ethnic Americans*. Santa Barbara, CA: ABC-CLIO, 2001.

Beam, T. E., and L. R. Sparacino, eds. *Military Medical Ethics*. Lounsbury, DE: Bellamy Reference Editions, 2003.

Beasley, Chris. *Gender and Sexuality: Critical Theories, Critical Thinkers*. Thousand Oaks, CA: Sage, 2005.

Beasley, Maurine Hoffman, Holly Cowan Shulman, and Henry R. Beasley, eds. *The Eleanor Roosevelt Encyclopedia*. Westport, CT: Greenwood, 2001.

Benbow-Pfalzgraf, Taryn. *American Women Writers: A Critical Reference Guide*. New York: St. James Press, 2000.

Berkin, Carol. *Civil War Wives: The Lives and Times of Angelina Grimké Weld, Varina Howell Davis, & Julia Dent Grant*. New York: Knopf, 2009.

Berne, Emma Carlson, and Marie Hodge. *Helen Keller: Courage in Darkness*. New York: Sterling, 2009.

Bostrom, Kathleen Long. *Winning Authors: Profiles of the Newbery Medalists*. Westport, CT: Libraries Unlimited, 2003.

Bosworth, Patricia. *Jane Fonda: The Private Life of a Public Woman*. New York: Houghton Mifflin, 2011.

Bouson, J. Brooks. *Jamaica Kincaid: Writing Memory, Writing Back to the Mother*. Albany: State University of New York Press, 2005.

Bowman, Cynthia Grant. *Dawn Clark Netsch: A Political Life*. Evanston, IL: Northwestern University Press, 2010.

Boyd, Valerie. *Wrapped in Rainbows: The Life of Zora Neale Hurston*. New York: Simon & Schuster, 2003.

Calvert-Koyzis, Nancy, and Heather E. Veir, eds. *Strangely Familiar: Protofeminist Interpretations of Patriarchal Biblical Texts*. Boston: Society of Biblical Literature, 2009.

Campbell, Susan. *Tempest-Tossed: The Spirit of Isabella Beecher Hooker*. Middletown, CT: Wesleyan University Press, 2014.

Champion, Laurie. *American Women Writers, 1900–1945*. Westport, CT: Greenwood, 2000.

Cordery, Simon. *Mother Jones: Raising Cain and Consciousness*. Albuquerque: University of New Mexico Press, 2010.

Crouse, Eric R. *An American Stand: Senator Margaret Chase Smith and the Communist Menace*. Lanham, MD: Lexington Books, 2010.

Curtis, Edward E. IV, and Danielle Brune Sigler, eds. *The New Black Gods: Arthur Huff Fauset and the Study of African American Religions*. Bloomington: Indiana University Press, 2009.

Davis, Rocío G. *Begin Here: Reading Asian North American Autobiographies of Childhood*. Honolulu: University of Hawaii Press, 2007.

Denton, Sally. *The Pink Lady: The Many Lives of Helen Gahagan Douglas*. New York: Bloomsbury, 2009.

Duffy, Bernard K., and Richard W. Leeman. *American Voices: An Encyclopedia of Contemporary Orators*. Westport, CT: Greenwood, 2005.

Feld, Marjorie N. *Lillian Wald: A Biography*. Chapel Hill: University of North Carolina Press, 2008.

Ford, Lynne E. *Encyclopedia of Women and American Politics*. New York: Facts on File, 2008.

Fradin, Dennis B., and Judith Bloom Fradin. *Fight On!: Mary Church Terrell's Battle for Integration*. New York: Houghton Mifflin, 2003.

Franzen, Trisha. *Anna Howard Shaw: The Work of Woman Suffrage*. Champaign: University of Illinois Press, 2014.

Frisken, Amanda. *Victoria Woodhull's Sexual Revolution: Political Theater and the Popular Press in Nineteenth-Century America*. Philadelphia: University of Pennsylvania Press, 2004.

Frost-Knappman, Elizabeth, and Kathryn Cullen-DuPont. *Women's Suffrage in America*. New York: Facts on File, 2005.

Gallman, J. Matthew. *America's Joan of Arc: The Life of Anna Elizabeth Dickinson*. New York: Oxford University Press, 2006.

Gillespie, Marcia, Rosa Johnson Butler, and Richard A. Long. *Maya Angelou: A Glorious Celebration*. New York: Knopf Doubleday, 2008.

Ginzberg, Lori D. *Elizabeth Cady Stanton: An American Life*. New York: Hill and Wang, 2009.

Godbold, E. Stanley Jr. *Jimmy and Rosalynn Carter: The Georgia Years, 1924–1974*. New York: Oxford University Press, 2010.
Gornick, Vivian. *Emma Goldman: Revolution as a Way of Life*. New Haven, CT: Yale University Press, 2011.
Grace, Fran. *Carry A. Nation: Retelling the Life*. Bloomington: Indiana University Press, 2001.
Green, James. *The Devil Is Here in These Hills: West Virginia's Coal Miners and Their Battle for Freedom*. New York: Grove Press, 2015.
Greene, Elaine. *If These Walls Could Talk: Thoughts of Home*. New York: Sterling, 2004.
Gwinn, Kristen E. *Emily Greene Balch: The Long Road to Internationalism*. Urbana: University of Illinois, 2010.
Hall, Timothy D., and Mark C. Carnes. *Anne Hutchinson: Puritan Prophet*. Upper Saddle River, NJ: Pearson, 2010.
Johnson, Joan Marie. *Southern Women at the Seven Sister Colleges: Feminist Values and Social Activism, 1875–1915*. Athens: University of Georgia Press, 2008.
Kaid, Lynda Lee, and Christina Holtz-Bacha, eds. *Encyclopedia of Political Communication*. Thousand Oaks, CA: Sage, 2008.
Keller, Rosemary Skinner, and Marie Cantlon, eds. *Encyclopedia of Women and Religion in North America*. Bloomington: Indiana University Press, 2006.
Kort, Carol. *A to Z of American Women Writers*. New York: Facts on File, 2007.
Kouadio, Germain N'Guessan. *The Dynamics of Politics and Didacticism in Frances E. W. Harper's Writing*. Paris: Editions Publibook, 2011.
Lancaster, Jane. *Making Time: Lillian Moller Gilbreth*. Boston: Northeastern University Press, 2004.
Lane, Ann J., ed. *Making Women's History: The Essential Mary Ritter Beard*. New York: Feminist Press at CUNY, 2001.
Laville, Helen. *Cold War Women: The International Activities of American Women's Organisations*. Manchester, UK: University of Manchester Press, 2002.
Levine, Suzanne Braun, and Mary Thom, eds. *Bella Abzug: How One Tough Broad from the Bronx Fought Jim Crow and Joe McCarthy*. New York: Macmillan, 2007.
Li, Stephanie. *Toni Morrison: A Biography*. Westport, CT: Greenwood, 2010.
Liebovich, L. W. *Richard Nixon, Watergate, and the Press: A Historical Perspective*. Westport, CT: Praeger, 2003.
Lockhart, Michele, and Kathleen Mollick, eds. *Global Women Leaders: Studies in Feminist Political Rhetoric*. Lanham, MD: Lexington Books, 2014.
Lopach, James J., and Jean A. Luckowski. *Jeannette Rankin: A Political Woman*. Boulder, CO: University Press of Colorado, 2005.

Love, Barbara J., ed. *Feminists Who Changed America, 1963–1975*. Chicago: University of Illinois Press, 2006.
Lowy, Joan A. *Pat Schroeder: A Woman of the House*. Albuquerque: University of New Mexico Press, 2003.
Marcello, Patricia Cronin. *Gloria Steinem: A Biography*. Westport, CT: Greenwood, 2004.
Marcus, Leonard S. *Listening for Madeleine: A Portrait of Madeleine L'Engle in Many Voices*. New York: Macmillan, 2012.
Marshall, Brenda DeVore, and Molly A. Mayhead, eds. *Telling Political Lives: The Rhetorical Autobiographies of Women Leaders in the United States*. Lanham, MD: Lexington Books, 2008.
McMillen, Sally G. *Seneca Falls and the Origins of the Women's Rights Movement*. New York: Oxford University Press, 2008.
Mertha, Andrew C. *The Politics of Piracy: Intellectual Property in Contemporary China*. Ithaca, NY: Cornell University Press, 2005.
Morris, Sylvia Jukes. *Price of Fame: The Honorable Clare Boothe Luce*. New York: Random House, 2014.
Myers, JoAnne. *The A to Z of the Lesbian Liberation Movement: Still the Rage*. Lanham, MD: Scarecrow Press, 2003.
Nüesch, Hanspeter. *Ruth and Billy Graham: The Legacy of a Couple*. Grand Rapids, MI: Baker Books, 2014.
Patterson, David S. *The Search for Negotiated Peace: Women's Activism and Citizen Diplomacy in World War I*. New York: Routledge, 2008.
Payne, Erica. *Practical Progressive: How to Build a 21st Century Political Movement*. New York: PublicAffairs, 2008.
Pernicone, Nunzio. *Carlo Tresca: Portrait of a Rebel*. New York: Palgrave Macmillan, 2005.
Recchiuti, John Louis. *Civic Engagement: Social Science and Progressive-Era Reform in New York City*. Philadelphia: University of Pennsylvania Press, 2007.
Reid, Panthea. *Tillie Olsen: One Woman, Many Riddles*. New Brunswick, NJ: Rutgers University Press, 2010.
Risjord, Norman K. *The Civil War Generation*. Lanham, MD: Rowman & Littlefield, 2002.
Rosen, Robyn L. *Reproductive Health, Reproductive Rights: Reformers and the Politics of Maternal Welfare, 1917–1940*. Columbus: Ohio State University Press, 2003.
Rosensaft, Jean Bloch, ed. *Judy Chicago: Jewish Identity*. New York: Hebrew Union College–Jewish Institute of Religion Museum, 2007.
Ruíz, Vicki, and Virginia Sánchez Korrol. *Latinas in the United States: A Historical Encyclopedia*. Bloomington: Indiana University Press, 2006.

Santopietro, Tom. *The Importance of Being Barbra.* New York: Macmillan, 2006.

Schechter, Patricia Ann. *Ida B. Wells-Barnett and American Reform, 1880–1930.* Chapel Hill: University of North Carolina Press, 2001.

Sharp, Michael D., ed. *Popular Contemporary Writers.* Vol. 9. Tarrytown, NY: Marshall Cavendish, 2006.

Sherman, Janann, ed. *Interviews with Betty Friedan.* Jackson: University Press of Mississippi, 2002.

Silverstone, Michael. *Winona LaDuke: Restoring Land and Culture in North America.* New York: Feminist Press at CUNY, 2001.

Slevin, Peter. *Michelle Obama: A Life.* New York: Knopf Doubleday, 2014.

Snodgrass, Mary Ellen. *Encyclopedia of Feminist Literature.* New York: Facts on File, 2006.

Snodgrass, Mary Ellen. *Leslie Marmon Silko: A Literary Companion.* Jefferson, NC: McFarland, 2011.

Sutton, M. A. *Aimee Semple McPherson and the Resurrection of Christian America.* Cambridge, MA: Harvard University Press, 2007.

Tetrault, Lisa. *The Myth of Seneca Falls: Memory and the Women's Suffrage Movement, 1848–1898.* Chapel Hill: University of North Carolina Press, 2014.

Tichi, Cecelia. *Civic Passions: Seven Who Launched Progressive America (and What They Teach Us).* Chapel Hill: University of North Carolina Press, 2009.

Trotman, C. James, ed. *Multiculturalism: Roots and Realities.* Bloomington: Indiana University Press, 2002.

Venet, Wendy Hamand. *A Strong-Minded Woman: The Life of Mary Livermore.* Amherst: University of Massachusetts Press, 2005.

Waisman, Charlotte S., and Jill S. Tietjen. *Her Story: A Timeline of the Women Who Changed America.* New York: Harper Collins, 2013.

Wallace, Mike, ed. *The Way We Will Be 50 Years from Today: 60 of the World's Greatest Minds.* Nashville, TN: Thomas Nelson, 2008.

Warner, Laceye C. *Saving Women: Retrieving Evangelistic Theology and Practice.* Waco, TX: Baylor University Press, 2007.

Washington, Margaret. *Sojourner Truth's America.* Champaign: University of Illinois Press, 2009.

Wasniewski, Matthew A. *Women in Congress, 1917–2006.* H. Con. Res. 66, 107th Cong., 1st sess. Washington, DC: U.S. Government Printing Office, 2006.

Wayne, Tiffany K. *Woman Thinking: Feminism and Transcendentalism in Nineteenth-Century America.* Oxford, UK: Lexington Books, 2005.

Weatherford, Doris. *American Women during World War II: An Encyclopedia.* New York: Routledge, 2009.

Weller, Sheila. *The News Sorority: Diane Sawyer, Katie Couric, Christiane Amanpour.* New York: Penguin, 2014.

Wilson, Mildred. *A Passionate Crusader for Women's Education: The Story of Catharine Beecher*. Victoria, BC: Friesen Press, 2012.

Winegarten, Debra L. *Oveta Culp Hobby: Colonel, Cabinet Member, Philanthropist*. Austin: University of Texas Press, 2014.

Winslow, Barbara. *Shirley Chisholm: Catalyst for Change, 1926–2005*. Boston: Credo Reference, 2014.

Wood, Jamie Martinez. *Latino Writers and Journalists*. New York: Facts on File, 2007.

Young, Alfred R. *Masquerade: The Life and Times of Deborah Sampson, Continental Soldier*. New York: Vintage, 2004.

Yount, Lisa. *A to Z of Women in Science and Math*. New York: Facts on File, 2008.

Zink-Sawyer, Beverly. *From Preachers to Suffragists: Woman's Rights and Religious Conviction in the Lives of Three Nineteenth-Century American Clergywomen*. Louisville, KY: Westminster John Knox Press, 2003.

Periodicals

Arvide, Cynthia. "Author Isabel Allende Proves Strategic Funding Changes Lives for the Better." *Women News Network*, April 16, 2012, 1–2.

Bernstein, Adam. "Elizabeth Janeway Dies; Feminist Author." *Washington Post*, January 13, 2005, B5.

Brody, Jane E. "Mary S. Calderone, Advocate of Sexual Education, Dies at 94." *New York Times*, October 25, 1998.

Eisenmann, Linda. "'A Good Poor Man's Wife': Being a Chronicle of Harriet Hanson Robinson & Her Family in 19th-Century New England." *Historical Journal of Massachusetts* 28, no. 2 (Summer 2000): 218–220.

Faludi, Susan. "Death of a Revolutionary." *New Yorker* 89, no. 9 (April 15, 2013): 52–61.

Gootman, Elissa. "Patsy Mink, Veteran Hawaii Congresswoman, Dies at 74." *New York Times*, September 30, 2002.

Grady, Denise. "American Woman Who Shattered Space Ceiling." *New York Times*, July 23, 2012.

Hill, Anita. "Interview." *Brandeis Now*, April 21, 2015.

Holley, Joe. "Champion of Conservation, Loyal Force behind LBJ." *Washington Post*, July 12, 2007.

Keeling, Arlene Wynbeek. "'Carrying Ointments and Even Pills!' Medicines in the Work of Henry Street Settlement Visiting Nurses, 1893–1944." *Nursing History Review* 14 (2006): 7–30.

Lee, Catherine. "Calderone & the Women's Movement." *The* (Vassar) *Miscellany News*, February 18, 1983, 5.

Lyons, Courtney. "'Dont DONT D-O-N-T' to 'I Do': Antoinette Brown Blackwell's Relationship with Marriage." *Ohio History* 117 (2010): 108–128.

McFadden, Robert D. "Juanita M. Kreps, Commerce Secretary, Dies at 89." *New York Times*, July 7, 2010.

McGuire, John Thomas. "From Socialism to Social Justice Feminism: Rose Schneiderman and the Quest for Urban Equity, 1911–1933." *Journal of Urban History* 35 (November 2009): 998–1019.

McLoughlin, Kate. "Reading in Reverse." *Oxonian Review* 3, no. 2 (March 1, 2004): 1.

Mirriam-Goldberg, Caryn. "Visionary Activist." *Women's Review of Books* 20, no. 3 (December 2002): 11–12.

Nelson, Stanley. "Friends for Life: The Slave Girl & Master's Daughter." *Concordia Sentinel*, October 30, 2013.

Nelson, Valerie J. "Molly Yard, 93; Led Fight for Women's Rights." *Los Angeles Times*, September 22, 2005.

Paull, John. "The Rachel Carson Letters and the Making of *Silent Spring*." *SAGE Open* (July–September 2013): 1–12.

Reaves, Jessica. "Interview with Sarah Weddington. *Time*, January 16, 2003.

Rubin, Joan Shelley. "Silver Linings: Print and Gentility in the World of Johnny Tremain." *Proceedings of the American Antiquarian Society* 113, no. 1 (2005): 37–52.

Schwartz, John. "To Revive Shuttle, NASA Called on a Cool Leader." *New York Times*, April 18, 2005.

Shaw, Dan. "Defined by Words, Not by a Disease." *New York Times*, August 22, 2012.

Stearns, David Patrick. "Arts Abounding." *Philadelphia Enquirer WKND*, February 4, 2011, 16, 18.

Stoltenburg, John. "Living with Andrea Dworkin." *Lambda Book Report* (May–June 1994).

Weeks, Linton. "Kate Michelman, the Public Face of a Woman's Right to Privacy." *Washington Post*, January 12, 2006.

Woo, Elaine. "Judith Wallerstein Dies at 90." *Los Angeles Times*, July 2012.

Wray, John. "Ursula Le Guin, the Art of Fiction." *Paris Review* 206 (Fall 2013): 48–78.

Electronic Sources

"Adrienne Rich." Poetry Foundation. Accessed January 2, 2015. http://www.poetryfoundation.org/bio/adrienne-rich.

"Aileen Clarke Hernandez." The History Makers. Accessed January 12, 2015. http://www.thehistorymakers.com/biography/aileen-clark-hernandez-41.

Barnwell, Carol E. "Bishop Calls Church to Reconciliation, Service, and Evangelism." The Episcopal Diocese of Texas. Accessed March 31, 2015. http://www.epicenter.org/article/bishop-calls-church-to-reconciliation-service-and-evangelism/.

Bowman, David. "The 'Sex Woman.'" Salon, June 14, 2003. Accessed April 24, 2015. http://www.salon.com/2003/06/14/jong_2/.

Crass, Chris. "Organizing for Radical Social Change: Voltairine de Cleyre and Anarcha-feminism." Spunk Library. Accessed October 29, 2014. http://www.spunk.org/texts/writers/decleyre/sp001860.html.

"Final Portfolio: Post 3—Sweet Briar Coach Encourages Holistic Wellness in Self, Students." May 8, 2010. Accessed April 24, 2015. http://sbcmmc.blogspot.com.

Hamilton, Neil A. "Fuller, Kathryn." *American Social Leaders and Activists*, American Biographies. New York: Facts On File, Inc., 2002. *American History Online*. Facts On File, Inc. April 13, 2015. http://www.fofweb.com/activelink2.asp?ItemID=WE52&iPin=ASL098&SingleRecord=True.

Hinson-Hasty, Elizabeth. "Timeline of Significant Events in Dorothy Day's Life." Accessed November 28, 2014. http://dorothyday.catholicworker.org/timeline.pdf.

"Mrs. Blatch's Talk to Suffragists." Miller NASWA Suffrage Scrapbooks, 1897–1911. Scrapbook 3, 146–147. Accessed January 19, 2015. http://memory.loc.gov/cgi-bin/query/h?ammem/rbcmillerbib:@field (DOCID+@lit(rbcmiller001720)).

"She Made It: Betty Furness, Television Journalist, Radio Host." *Paley Center for Media*. Accessed January 7, 2015. http://www.shemadeit.org/meet/biography.aspx?m=127.

Thomas, Henry, and Dana Lee Thomas. "Mary Baker Eddy: A Biographical Sketch." Accessed January 23, 2015. http://marybakereddy.wwwhubs.com/mbe1.html.

Wagner, Sally Roesch. "Matilda Joslyn Gage: Forgotten Feminist." *New York History Net*. Accessed October 8, 2014. www.nyhistory.com/gagepage.htm.

Index

Page numbers in **bold** indicate main entries in the encyclopedia.

About the Author

MARY ELLEN SNODGRASS is the author of some 135 textbooks and general reference works, including *Encyclopedia of the Literature of Empire*, *Shakespeare on the Double* (8 vols.), *Greek & Roman Classics* (2 vols.), *Isabel Allende: A Literary Companion*, *The Encyclopedia of World Ballet*, *Civil Disobedience* (2 vols.), *Pioneers: Settlers of the American West*, *World Food* (2 vols.), *Chronology of World Epidemics*, *Coins and Currency in History*, and *The Underground Railroad* (2 vols.). Her honoraria include two Star Teacher citations, two New York Public Library awards, two *Choice* magazine reference books of the year, three *Library Journal* reference books of the year, a *Booklist* Editor's Choice award, and an American Library Association reference book of the year.

Snodgrass has been a vocal feminist for 53 years. She holds degrees in British literature, classics, and gifted education from the University of North Carolina at Greensboro, Appalachian State University, and Lenoir-Rhyne University. In addition to teaching English and Latin at the high school and university levels for 23 years, she has served her home state as a library commissioner, a traveling humanities lecturer, and guest lecturer at the University of North Carolina at Greensboro Honors College. A foster mother of six teens, she lives in Hickory, North Carolina, with her husband, Hugh, and five rescued dogs—McIver, Duncan, Jasper, Augusta, and Cassidy.